2024KX © Westermann

Hoddesdon

Harlow

Cheshunt

Waltham
Abbey

Epping

Chipping
Ongar

Chelmsford

Enfield

Loughton

Billericay

Chigwell

Brentwood

Wickford

ingey

Waltham
Forest

Redbridge

Basildon

don

Havering

South
Benfleet

Hackney

Barking and
Dagenham

Newham

London City
Airport

South
Ockendon

Stanford-
le-Hope

Canvey
Island

y of
don

Greenwich

Southwark

Bexley

Brixton

Lewisham

Dartford

Gravesend

Bromley

Swanley

Gillingham

Croydon

erham

Oxted

Edenbridge

D171789·3

City of London

St Pancras
International

King's
Cross

Pentonville Road

City Road

Euston

Euston Rd

Old Street

Commercial St.

British
Museum

Clerkenwell   Road

Museum
of London

Liverpool
Street

City
Thameslink

St Paul's
Cathedral

Oxford St.

Chinatown

Blackfriars

Millennium
Bridge

Cannon
Street

London
Bridge

The Tower
of London

Charing
Cross

Waterloo
Bridge

Tower
Bridge

The Mall

Waterloo

London
Bridge

Buckingham
Palace

St James's
Park

London Eye

Westminster
Bridge

River Thames

Westminster
Abbey

Houses of
Parliament

Victoria

1 mile

0   1 km

westermann

NOTTING HILL GATE

Textbook 7
Allgemeine Ausgabe

Erarbeitet von:
Hanna Hoof (Schacht-Audorf), Gabriele Linke (Marburg),
Sascha Mohr (Wiesbaden), Penelope Pedder (Köln),
Maike Pegler (Sarstedt/Gödringen)

sowie Denise Arrandale (Neumünster), Michael Biermann (Hamburg),
Hannelore Debus (Mörfelden-Walldorf), Phil Mothershaw-Rogalla
(Volkmarsen-Külte), Susanne Quandt (Bremen)

Fachliche Beratung:
Angela Berkenkamp (Wetzlar), Imke del Federico (Kerpen),
Dr. Matthias Munsch (Frankfurt am Main), Anke Riemer (Hamburg),
Kathleen Unterspann (Halstenbek)

Story „Jamie and Lucy" von Lisa Fast

Notting Hill Gate 7
Allgemeine Ausgabe
Textbook

Zusatzmaterialien zu Notting Hill Gate 7

Für Lehrkräfte:
- Textbook für Lehrkräfte 7 (ISBN 978-3-14-128286-3)
- Materialien für Lehrkräfte 7 (ISBN 978-3-14-128296-2)
- Lernerfolgskontrollen 7 (ISBN 978-3-14-128322-8)
- CD für Lehrkräfte 7 (ISBN 978-3-14-128306-8)
- DVD für Lehrkräfte 7 (ISBN 978-3-14-128316-7)
- Online-Diagnose zu Notting Hill Gate 7
  www.onlinediagnose.de

Für Schülerinnen und Schüler:
- Workbook 7 (inkl. Audios) (ISBN 978-3-14-128212-2)
- Interaktive Übungen 7 (WEB-14-128222)
- Arbeitsbuch Inklusion 7 (inkl. Audios)
  (ISBN 978-3-14-128232-0)
- Klassenarbeitstrainer 7 (ISBN 978-3-14-128248-1)
- Grammatiktrainer 7 (ISBN 978-3-14-128388-4)
- Wortschatztrainer 7 (ISBN 978-3-14-128242-9)

Das digitale Schulbuch und digitale Unterrichtsmaterialien für Schülerinnen und Schüler und für Lehrkräfte finden Sie in der BiBox – dem digitalen Unterrichtssystem passend zum Lehrwerk. Mehr Informationen über aktuelle Lizenzen finden Sie auf www.bibox.schule.

www.westermann.de/nhg

 DIGITAL+

Alle digitalen Ergänzungen zum Buch erkennen Sie an dem Symbol ▦ DIGITAL+.
Dazu zählen Audiotracks, Videoclips, Arbeitsblätter zur Medienbildung, zusätzliche Übungen zu den Practise-Seiten und Zusatzmaterialien zum Buch. Gehen Sie auf www.westermann.de/webcode und geben Sie den Webcode WES-128202-001 ein. Sie können auch den QR-Code scannen.

© 2024 Westermann Bildungsmedien Verlag GmbH, Georg-Westermann-Allee 66, 38104 Braunschweig
www.westermann.de

Druck A[1] / Jahr 2024
Alle Drucke der Serie A sind im Unterricht parallel verwendbar.

Redaktion: Lisa Fast und Dr. Katja Nandorf sowie Doris Bos
Vokabelanhang: Doris Bos
Illustrationen: Mario Ellert, Bremen
Umschlaggestaltung: LIO Design GmbH, Braunschweig
Layout: LIO Design GmbH, Braunschweig
Druck und Bindung: Westermann Druck GmbH, Georg-Westermann-Allee 66, 38104 Braunschweig

ISBN 978-3-14-**128202**-3

So arbeitest du mit dem Buch

Im Buch findest du folgende Verweise:

1 audio — Hier gibt es einen Audiotrack, den du auch online abrufen kannst.

2 video — Hier gibt es einen Videoclip, den du auch online abrufen kannst.

3 workbook — Hier siehst du, auf welcher Seite im Workbook es weitere Übungen gibt.

4 wordbank — In den Wordbanks findest du Wörter nach Wortfeldern geordnet.

5 skill — Auf den Skills-Seiten findest du Tipps und Strategien fürs Lernen.

6 grammar — Zu dieser Aufgabe gibt es Erklärungen und Beispiele im Grammatik-Teil.

7 media worksheet — Dieser Hinweis kennzeichnet Aufgaben, in denen du Medienkompetenz aufbaust und trainierst. Zu diesen Aufgaben gibt es Arbeitsblätter, die du über den Webcode oder den QR-Code auf Seite 2 abrufen kannst.

DIGITAL+ practise more — Dieser Hinweis zeigt, dass es zusätzliches Material auf der Webseite gibt.

In den Units gibt es verschiedene Arten von Aufgaben:

8 CHOOSE YOUR LEVEL — Bei diesen Aufgaben gibt es drei unterschiedliche Schwierigkeitsgrade:
I leicht II mittel III schwierig

9 GET TOGETHER — Hier arbeitest du mit einem Partner oder einer Partnerin zusammen. Entscheidet, wer Partner A und wer Partner B ist und wählt jeweils einen Schwierigkeitsgrad. Geht dann zur entsprechenden Seite und bearbeitet die Aufgabe.

Partner A
I Go to page 128.
II Go to page 131.
III Go to page 134.

Partner B
I Go to page 137.
II Go to page 140.
III Go to page 143.

10 CHOOSE YOUR TASK — Hier gibt es drei Aufgaben, von denen du dir eine aussuchen kannst. Du kannst mit einem Partner oder einer Partnerin oder in einer Gruppe arbeiten.

TARGET TASK — In der Target Task (Zielaufgabe) wendest du an, was du gelernt hast. Du erarbeitest ein kleines Produkt, das du in der Klasse vorstellen und in deinem Portfolio aufbewahren kannst.

Unit 1 – Food 7

Part A: Delicious dishes 8
Part B: At a restaurant 18
Story: Delicious disaster 28
Challenge: Curious about curry? 30

Unit 2 – Healthy living 31

Part A: Keeping fit 32
Part B: At the doctor's 42
Story: Sports day 52
Challenge: Paralympics 54

Unit 3 – What's on? 55

Part A: At the car boot sale 56
Part B: Festivals 66
Story: Medieval mischief 76
Challenge: Glastonbury and the legend of King Arthur ... 78

Unit 4 – You are not alone 79

Part A: Exploring roots 80
Part B: Giving a helping hand 90
Story: Wrong impressions 100
Challenge: On the Move Again 102

Unit 5 – Everyday science 103

Part A: Inventions 104
Part B: Communication 114
Story: A field trip 124
Challenge: Inventions inspired by nature 127

Get together 128

Projects 146

Project 1: A country profile: India 146
Project 2: Music 148

Skills 150

1. Wortschatzarbeit 150
2. Hören 151
3. Mit anderen sprechen 152
4. Schreiben 153
5. Lesen 154
6. Sprachmittlung 155
7. Videoclips verstehen 156
8. Im Internet recherchieren 157
9. Präsentationen halten 158
10. Eine Szene vorspielen 159

Wordbanks — 160

Eating and eating out	160
Keeping fit	162
Health	163
What's on?	164
Buying and selling	164
Events	165
Expressing opinions	165
Family history	166
Talking about pictures	166
Feelings	167
Seeking and giving advice	167
Inventions	168
Presenting something	168
Communication	169
Going online	169

Classroom phrases — 170

Grammar — 172

1. Das Perfekt: Aussagen *(revision)*	172
2. Das Perfekt: Fragen *(revision)*	173
3. Mengenangaben *(revision)*	174
4. Die Steigerung von Adjektiven *(revision)*	175
5. Die Verlaufsform der Gegenwart *(revision)*	176
6. Das Gerundium	177
7. Bedingungssätze 1	178
8. Modalverben *(revision)*	179
9. Relativsätze	180
10. Die Stützwörter *one* und *ones*	181
11. Die Verlaufsform der Vergangenheit: Aussagen	182
12. Die Verlaufsform der Vergangenheit: Fragen	183
13. Die einfache Vergangenheit: Aussagen *(revision)*	184
14. Die einfache Vergangenheit: Fragen *(revision)*	185
15. Indirekte Rede 1	186
16. Das Passiv	187
17. Das Futur mit *going to:* Aussagen *(revision)*	188
18. Das Futur mit *going to:* Fragen *(revision)*	189

Words — 190

Einleitung	190
Wortlisten nach Units	193
Dictionary	219
Names	252
Numbers	254
Irregular verbs	255

Ausführliches Inhaltsverzeichnis — 258

Bild- und Textquellen — 264

Ein ausführliches Inhaltsverzeichnis befindet sich auf den Seiten 258 bis 263.

Lily and Harry Norris

- 13 years old (twins)
- live with their mums, Olivia and Sarah
- used to live in Brighton
- their grandparents live in Bristol
- have got two rabbits, Double and Trouble
- like playing board games
- Lily's hobby is upcycling
- Harry plays the guitar in the school band

Ava Kogan

- 13 years old
- lives with her mum, her dad and her two brothers: Joshua (8) and Noah (14)
- has got a dog, Ollie
- likes skateboarding
- wants to be an engineer when she grows up
- her grandma Edyta lives in Poland

Tarek Adil

- 14 years old
- lives with his dad
- has got an uncle, Sami
- his family is originally from Egypt
- plays hockey in a team
- likes science fiction books and cooking

1. What can you see in the pictures?
2. Which of the foods in the pictures do you like?
3. Have you ever cooked a meal? What was it?

Food

Part A Delicious dishes

- You will talk about food from all around the world.
- You will listen to a podcast.
- Together with your classmates you will create an international cookbook.

Part B At a restaurant

- You will read about eating out at a restaurant.
- You will talk about restaurant menus.
- You will present a scene at a restaurant in a role play.

Favourite food

1   workbook p. 4 / 1-2

What do you like to eat? Collect the names of your favourite dishes in class and talk about them.

Different dishes

2a

Look at the pictures on this double page and talk about them.

2b

Read the text messages and blog posts on this double page. Where are the dishes from?

1

🔲 BFF

Emily Greetings from our family holiday in Greece. Look what the fishermen have just caught ... Octopus! 8:15 am

Emily Now look what Dad has ordered! Salad with cucumber, olives, tomato and grilled octopus! He loves it, but I don't think it tastes good. Have you ever tried anything like this? 2:05 pm

2

🔲 Foodlover   ♡ ◯ ✉ 🔖

Foodlover I've just eaten the best Sunday roast ever at my aunt's house. I am so full now. There was so much I couldn't finish it. Have you had your roast dinner today?

Isabel3589 This looks absolutely delicious! Are those mashed potatoes?
Foodlover Yes, and a lot of gravy!

AyazLondon I've just moved to London from Istanbul, I have never eaten a Sunday roast! Can you explain what it is, please?
Foodlover It's a traditional British dish, you usually have it for lunch on Sundays. It's roast chicken, lamb, beef or pork with vegetables, Yorkshire pudding and potatoes. You should try it! You can also get really good vegetarian versions in restaurants here in London.
AyazLondon Yorkshire pudding? Is it sweet?
Foodlover No, it's savoury.

3   https://www.katie.co.uk/berlinstreetfood   × –

KATIE'S BLOG

Berlin street food

I spent a week in Berlin in the summer – since then my comfort food has been Lahmacun. I first tried it in Berlin and it was so good! It's a thin rolled flatbread filled with minced meat, onions and tomato. It's a spicy dish from Turkey, but there are similar dishes in many other countries, like Lebanon or Egypt. And I've found some places in London where you get good Lahmacun, too!
There's also a German speciality you must try when you are in Berlin: currywurst. You sometimes get currywurst in London, too – but it's not as good as it is in Berlin!

4   https://www.worldfoodfestival/.streetfood   × −

Fantastic street food at the World Food Festival -- *by Jason and Laura* --

Read about the World Food Festival and find out about amazing street food from around the world!

Poutine
We really loved this dish from Canada! Double fried chips with any topping you can imagine: from the traditional brown sauce, pork and cheese to a vegetarian version with mushrooms, red pepper, chilli and cream cheese.

Shakshuka
Our number one street food is very popular in Israel and North Africa: Shakshuka. It's a savoury, healthy and vegetarian dish served with flatbread. The tomatoes were perfectly cooked, the eggs were fresh and super soft – and the dish contains just a little bit of garlic. All in all: perfect.

Dim Sum
One of our favourites was Dim Sum, a delicious selection of traditional Chinese food served in small portions. You could choose from dishes with or without meat. There were also lots of vegan options! We liked the vegetarian spring rolls best. They were filled with carrots and cabbage and came with a fantastic, but really hot, chilli-and-garlic sauce.

2c CHOOSE YOUR LEVEL skill: reading p. 154

I Match the sentence parts. Write down the sentences.

1 In Greece
2 The Sunday roast
3 Yorkshire pudding
4 Lahmacun

A is not sweet.
B is a dish from Turkey.
C you can eat grilled octopus.
D is a traditional British dish.

II True or false? Correct the false statements and write down all the sentences.

1 In the holiday, Emily's dad had a salad with grilled octopus.
2 You can't get a vegetarian Sunday roast in London.
3 Lahmacun is filled with minced meat, cheese and olives.
4 In Lebanon or Egypt you can find dishes that are similar to Lahmacun.
5 Katie thinks that the currywurst in London is better than the currywurst in Berlin.

III Make up five or more true or false statements for a partner. Take turns.

2d skill: talking with people p. 152, workbook p. 5/3

Walk around the classroom. Talk to your classmates.

You can ask:
Have you ever tried …?
Have you ever eaten …?
Did you like it?
What was it like?
…

You can answer:
No, I haven't.
Yes, I have. I …
Yes, I did.
…

ACTIVATE PRACTISE DEVELOP PRACTISE APPLY

GRAMMAR HELP   the present perfect (R) p. 172-173

Schau dir die Beispielsätze an. Kannst du erklären, wann man das *present perfect* benutzt?

I have never tried a vegetarian Sunday roast. Dad has just eaten lots of octopus. Now he is full. We have already made lunch. It's ready now.	I haven't tried Lahmacun yet. Mum hasn't finished her salad yet. She is still eating. She hasn't eaten lunch yet. She is still hungry.

Auf den Seiten 172 und 173 findest du ausführliche Erklärungen und weitere Beispiele zum *present perfect*. Eine Liste mit unregelmäßigen Verben gibt es auf den Seiten 255-257.

What have they done?

3   grammar: present perfect (R) p. 172, workbook p. 5/4

Write about Ollie and the children. Use the present perfect.

1. Ava (not finish) her breakfast yet.
2. Tarek (not tidy) the kitchen yet.
3. Ollie (already eat) all his food.
4. Harry and Lily (not do) their homework yet.
5. Joshua (already brush) his teeth.

You can write:

Ava hasn't finished her breakfast yet.
...

Have you tried Lahmacun?

4   grammar: present perfect (R) p. 172, wordbank: eating and eating out p. 160, workbook p. 5/5

Write about five or more dishes that you have tried.

You can write:

I have tried ... and I liked it. It was delicious.
It's a savoury / sweet / ...

Food words

5a   wordbank: eating and eating out p. 160, skill: working with words p. 150

Make a list of English food words that are similar to food words in German or in other languages you know.

You can write:

English	German	???
tomato	Tomate	...
...	...	...

5b

Work with a partner. Compare your lists and add words from your partner's list.

DIGITAL+ practise more 1-3

International week

6a

Look at the web page. What is it about?

https://www.worldfoodfestival/streetfood   x –

Holland Park School Cafeteria
International week
**Next week it's international week at the school cafeteria.
Come and enjoy dishes from around the world!**

MONDAY	TUESDAY	WEDNESDAY	THURSDAY	FRIDAY
Currywurst	Fried noodles	Chicken tikka masala	Vegetarian sushi	Spaghetti bolognese
Germany	China	India	Japan	Italy

6b 🔊 audio 1/1

**Listen to Lily, Harry, Ava and Tarek. What is the problem?
What do they decide to do? Take notes.**

6c CHOOSE YOUR LEVEL skill: listening p. 151

I Listen again and answer the questions.

1 What did Harry have for lunch?
2 What did Harry eat for breakfast?
3 What did Lily have for lunch?
4 What is Harry looking forward to?

II Listen again and answer the questions.

1 Why is Harry annoyed?
2 Why didn't Harry eat in the cafeteria?
3 Why is Harry looking forward to next week?
4 What does Tarek miss on the menu?

III Listen again and answer the questions.

1 Why didn't Harry eat in the cafeteria?
2 What does Lily say about today's food in the cafeteria?
3 Why is Harry looking forward to next week?
4 What does Lily say about sushi?
5 Why is Tarek disappointed?
6 Where do the children want to go?

6d workbook p. 6/6-7

Do you have a cafeteria at your school? What are your three favourite dishes there?

Home cooking

7a   🔊 audio 1/4

Listen and read along. What are the children talking about?

The children are in the kitchen at Tarek's house.

Harry: What could we cook? Have you got any ideas?

Ava: We could make one-pot pasta!

Tarek: What's that?

Ava: You cook everything together in one pot – it's quick and easy and you only have to wash one pot afterwards! Noah and I sometimes make it for dinner.

Harry: Quick and easy sounds good – I'm still starving!

Tarek: What do we need for your one-pot pasta? I don't think we have any meat.

Ava: We need pasta, veggies, tomatoes, herbs and spices. Let's see what you've got!

Tarek: All the spices are in the drawer over there. Lily, could you check what there is in the fridge? And could you please get the pasta from the cupboard, Ava?

Lily: There aren't many onions. But there are a lot of carrots and peppers and there's some cabbage. There isn't much cheese and not much milk. But there are many, many pots of yoghurt and a lot of chocolate – so no need to worry about dessert …

Tarek: Ava, do we need any cheese for the pasta?

Ava: We could add some cheese if you like. You can put in nearly anything. Oh, here are cans of chickpeas and tomatoes and a can of peas! But we need pasta and there is not much pasta left … Hm, there's a big jar with small yellow crumbs. What is it?

Tarek: It's couscous.

Ava: What is it like? Do you know how to cook it?

Tarek: It's really good, and it's super easy to prepare.

You just bring water to the boil, add the couscous and some salt, cover the pot and let it stand for five minutes. We often have it.

Harry: Cool! Can't we cook a dish from Egypt then, Tarek? What do you think?

Tarek: Couscous is NOT from Egypt, but we can try to cook a meal with it. We might need some onions and garlic, but I'm not sure how to put it all together and what spices we need.

Ava: Can't we search for a recipe online?

Lily: Sure, wait a second … Ah, here, I've

found something. It's a dish from Morocco. And here is a cook-along video. Shall we watch it? Look, it starts with a list of ingredients! It says we need couscous, veggies, an onion, garlic, chickpeas and a lot of spices: half a teaspoon of cumin, coriander, paprika, some cayenne pepper and vegetable stock. There is a mistake in the list: cinnamon. You put it in desserts and cakes!

Ava: Oh no, you can use it in savoury dishes, too. My dad even puts it on chicken with lemon and garlic. And it can be in curry powder! It's yummy!

7b

What is the children's first idea? What do the children decide to cook in the end?

7c　CHOOSE YOUR LEVEL　skill: reading p. 154, workbook p. 7/8

I　Read the dialogue again. Then complete the sentences and write them down.

1　One-pot pasta is quick and easy and …
2　All the spices are …
3　There aren't many …
4　There isn't much …
5　There are cans of …

II　Read the dialogue again. Then correct the sentences and write them down.

1　"Noah and I sometimes make it for lunch."
2　"We need pasta, veggies, tomatoes, ketchup and spices."
3　"There aren't many carrots."
4　"Do we need any meat for the pasta?"
5　"Can't we cook a dish from China?"

III　Read the dialogue again. Then put the sentences in the correct order and write them down.

A　Lily finds a recipe online.
B　There is not enough pasta but there is couscous.
C　Ava suggests making one-pot pasta because it is quick and easy to make.
D　Harry wants to cook a dish from Egypt.
E　Tarek would like to cook something with couscous but is not sure how.
F　Harry wants something quick and easy because he is still really hungry.
G　They look all over the kitchen for the ingredients for one-pot pasta.

A cook-along video

8a　video 1, skill: watching a video clip p. 156

Watch the video clip. What do you have to do after you have put the couscous in the pot?

8b

Watch the video clip again. Put the following verbs in the correct order:
chop, cut, heat, slice, cook, enjoy, cover, stir in

International food

9 CHOOSE YOUR TASK   wordbank: eating and eating out p. 160, skill: writing p. 153, C: media worksheet 13

A   **Write (and design) your dream menu for an international week at your school cafeteria.**

B   **Write a text message to a friend and describe a dish you ate in your holidays.**

C   **Describe a traditional dish from your family. You can add pictures if you like.**

Vegan Steven

10a   🔊 audio 1/5

Listen to the limerick. What is it about?

10b

What do you know about vegan and vegetarian diets? Talk about them.

10c   workbook p. 8/9

Learn the limerick by heart. In a group, think of an interesting way to present it.

> There was a young vegan called Steven,
>
> Who just would not kill for no reason,
>
> This kid would not eat
>
> No cheese or no meat
>
> And he hated the foxhunting season.
>
> *Benjamin Zephaniah*

PEOPLE & PLACES 1 🔊 video 2

Food in Great Britain

Traditional British dishes include fish and chips and a Sunday roast with Yorkshire pudding. Yorkshire pudding is made from the same ingredients as pancakes, but you bake it in the oven and eat it as a side with savoury dishes. The English word "pudding" does not mean the same as *Pudding* in German. It can refer to something savoury but it also means "dessert" in general. Some British dishes have unusual names, for example "toad in the hole" *(wörtlich: Kröte im Loch)*, which is simply sausages in a big Yorkshire pudding. "Bangers and mash" *(wörtlich: Knaller und Brei)* is sausages with mashed potato, and "bubble and squeak" *(wörtlich: Blase und Quieken)* is mashed potato mixed with cabbage or other veggies. But there is much more than traditional British food.

chicken tikka masala

You can get food from all over the world. Indian food, especially, has become very popular. One of the most popular dishes in Britain is "chicken tikka masala" – some people even say "chicken tikka masala" is Britain's number one national dish. Chicken tikka is an Indian dish, but when the British tried it, they wanted to have some sauce with the chicken. So Indian cooks added a sauce with yoghurt, coconut cream and a mix of different spices (masala).

Have you ever tried a traditional British dish or do you know any similar dishes?

    ACTIVATE   PRACTISE   **DEVELOP**   PRACTISE   APPLY

Dishes with funny names

11a
video 3, skill: watching a video clip p.156

Watch the video clip about dishes
with funny names.
Which name do you like best?

11b

Watch the video clip again. Make a list
with the names of the dishes. Which of
the dishes were real, which were fake?
Which dish would you like to try?

11c
workbook p.9/10-11

Do you know any dishes with funny names
in other languages? Try to translate the names
into English. Describe the dishes to the class.

You can say:

In Germany, there is a dish called "Arme Ritter".
That's "poor knights" in English.
It's white bread fried with milk and egg.

Foods invented by accident

12a
audio 1/8, skill: listening p.151

Listen to the podcast. What foods do the people talk about? Take notes.

12b   CHOOSE YOUR LEVEL   skill: mediation p.155, workbook p.10/12

A friend, who does not understand much English,
has some questions about the podcast.
Listen again, take notes and answer your friend's
questions in German.

I 1 Wie wurde denn das Sandwich erfunden?
   2 Was wurde von einem Kind erfunden?

II 1 Wer hat denn das Sandwich erfunden und warum?
   2 Wer hat das Eis am Stiel erfunden und wie kam es dazu?

III 1 Wer hat denn das Sandwich erfunden und warum?
    2 Wer hat das Eis am Stiel erfunden und wie kam es dazu?
    3 Wer hat die Kartoffelchips erfunden und warum?

Much or many?

13   grammar: quantifiers (R) p.174

Fill in 'much' or 'many' and write down the sentences.

1 I need ??? tomatoes for the sauce.
2 Have you got ??? favourite dishes?
3 How ??? ice cream have you eaten this week?

4 The boy is full. He has eaten too ??? cake.
5 I'd like to go to a restaurant, but I haven't got ??? money.

Cookbook language

14a

Complete the sentences with the correct verbs and write them down.

bring · mix · cook · add · cut · cover

1 ??? the water to the boil.
2 ??? the potatoes into cubes.
3 ??? the strawberries into the cream.

4 ??? the pasta for ten minutes.
5 ??? a pinch of salt to the tomatoes.
6 ??? the bowl and put it aside.

14b   workbook p.10/13

Read the recipe. Then explain to a friend who does not speak German how to cook spaghetti in English.

SPAGHETTI
Nimm pro Person 100-125 g Spaghetti. Erhitze in einem Topf ausreichend Wasser mit etwas Salz. Wenn das Wasser kocht, gib die Spaghetti in den Topf. Nach ca. 8 Minuten sind die Spaghetti fertig. Dazu passt zum Beispiel Tomatensoße.

Odd one out

15

Find the odd one out. Make more "odd one outs" with food words for a partner.

1 pot – fork – knife – spoon
2 carrot – potato – strawberry – pea

3 cumin – onion – salt – coriander
4 potatoes – chickpeas – rice – milk

Cooking

16   CHOOSE YOUR LEVEL   wordbank: eating and eating out p.160

Copy the word web.

❙ **Add three or more words to every branch.**
❙❙ **Add four or more words to every branch. Add another category.**
❙❙❙ **Add five or more words to every branch. Add two more categories.**

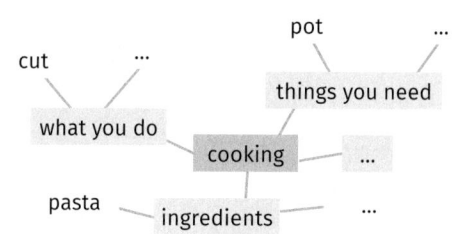

DIGITAL+ practise more 4-5

Our international cookbook TARGET TASK

17 ▨ ▣ workbook p. 11/14, wordbank: eating and eating out p. 160, media worksheet 1

Your task is to make an international cookbook in your class. You can work alone, with a partner or in small groups. Before you start, look at these steps:

STEP 1

In class, decide what kind of cookbook you want to create: a book, a digital cookbook, ...

STEP 2

Think of dishes from different countries. Then choose a dish. It can be ...
- a family recipe
- something you have eaten on holiday
- a dish you have tried in a restaurant
- ...

Find out: is there an English name for the dish? If not, use the original name.

STEP 3

Decide on how many people it should serve. Make a list of ingredients.

STEP 4

Write down how to prepare your dish.
You can add a photo for each step or even make a tutorial.

STEP 5

Put all the recipes together in your cookbook.
If you like, categorize the recipes in your cookbook: starters, main courses, desserts.
Try them out! You can organize a class party and serve your dishes!

VEGETABLE COUSCOUS FROM MOROCCO   *for two people*

Ingredients:
- *2 tablespoons olive oil*
- *1 medium red onion*
- *2 red peppers*
- *1 yellow pepper*
- *1 carrot*
- *2 cloves of garlic*
- *½ teaspoon paprika*
- *½ teaspoon coriander*
- *½ teaspoon cumin*
- *½ teaspoon cinnamon*
- *a pinch of cayenne pepper*
- *salt and pepper*
- *1 can of chickpeas*
- *1½ cups of vegetable stock*
- *1 cup of couscous*

Wash the vegetables and cut them into pieces. Chop the onion and slice the garlic. Heat the olive oil and cook the onion, peppers and carrots. Add the garlic. Mix in the spices. Add the chickpeas and the vegetable stock. Cook until the vegetables are soft. Stir in the couscous. Take the pot from the cooker, cover it and let it stand for five minutes. Enjoy!

Restaurants in your area

1 workbook p.12/1

What kinds of restaurants are there in your area? Talk about them.

You can say:

There is an Italian restaurant in my area.

You can eat … and … there.

You have to try …

… is the best …

Italian · Greek · Turkish · Chinese · Thai · Vietnamese · Lebanese · …

fast food restaurant · takeaway · …

Restaurant reviews

2a

Look at the pictures. Which restaurant would you like to go to or not like to go to? Say why.

You can say:

I would like to go to … because …

I wouldn't like to go to … because …

2b skill: reading p.154

Now skim the reviews. Would you still choose the same restaurant? Explain why or why not.

https://www.eatingout/reviewsxxxxx   × −

Sushi Blue

It's not cheap, but the food is very good!
The fish is the freshest that I've ever tasted.
The sushi looks beautiful. The service is very
quick and friendly. It is more expensive than
other sushi restaurants in the area, but you
get better quality.

I would go again.

https://www.eatingout/reviewsxxxx   × −

Pizza Extra Notting Hill

Stay away from this restaurant! I had the worst
pizza I've ever had in my life. The crust was
burnt, the toppings were disgusting and the
service was terrible! I waited over an hour for
the most disappointing pizza I've ever had.
My friend's pizza was as bad as mine.
We will never go back. There are other pizza
places nearby which are much better.

ACTIVATE PRACTISE DEVELOP PRACTISE APPLY

The Taj Mahal

This place has the hottest curry you can find in London! The vindaloo curry was so spicy that I could not finish it. The chicken tikka was also spicier than I expected, and even the vegetable korma was a bit too hot for my children. We had to add lots of yoghurt to finish our food. But the rice was perfect and the naan bread was yummy.

Only go there if you like *really* hot food!

The Black Horse

Very nice atmosphere, food OK. It's good value for money but not as tasty as the food we ate at The King's Head in North London the day before.
My fish was a bit overcooked, but the chips were delicious. My wife had a very juicy veggie burger with a side of chips.
The large choice of desserts was also great.
The pub is very cosy – we stayed for two hours and could have stayed longer!
The pub also has a beautiful garden with space for children to play.

2c CHOOSE YOUR LEVEL

ǀ Read the first two reviews and take notes for each restaurant.
  1 What did people like at Sushi Blue and Pizza Extra?
  2 What didn't they like? What makes one restaurant better than the other?

ǁ Read the first three reviews and take notes for each restaurant.
  1 What did people like at Sushi Blue, Pizza Extra and The Taj Mahal? What didn't they like?
  2 Rank the three restaurants according to the reviews.

ǁǁ Read the four reviews and take notes for each restaurant.
  1 What did people like at these restaurants? What didn't they like?
  2 Which restaurant do you think is the best, which is the worst? Why?

2d skill: talking with people p.152

What does a good restaurant need? Collect ideas.
What is most important to you? Talk to a partner.

GRAMMAR HELP the comparison of adjectives (R) p. 175

Erinnerst du dich noch daran, wie man im Englischen Dinge oder Personen miteinander vergleichen kann? Schau dir die Beispiele an und erkläre, wie die Formen gebildet und verwendet werden.

The service at Sushi Blue is better, quicker and friendlier than the service at Pizza Extra. The food at Sushi Blue is fresher and more expensive than the food at Pizza Extra. The fish is the freshest that I've ever tasted. Sushi Blue is the most expensive sushi restaurant in the area.	My friend's pizza was as bad as mine. The food at The Black Horse was not as tasty as the food at The King's Head.

Auf Seite 175 findest du weitere Beispiele und Erklärungen zur Steigerung von Adjektiven.

Tasty food

3a grammar: comparison of adjectives (R) p. 175

Compare different kinds of food. Write five or more comparisons with 'than' or 'as … as'. You can use the adjectives from the box.

tasty · good · healthy · delicious · spicy · …

You can write:

Hot dogs are as tasty as …

… are tastier than …

hot dog

chicken curry

salad

vegetable soup

?

…

3b grammar: comparison of adjectives (R) p. 175, wordbank: eating and eating out p. 160, workbook p. 12/2-4

Write five or more statements about your favourite food or restaurant. Use superlative forms. You can use the adjectives from the box.

tasty · good · fresh · delicious · cheap · …

You can write:

The pizza at … is the tastiest.

It's the … restaurant I know.

The restaurant has …

Where is the stress?

4a audio 1/10

Listen to the words and repeat them.

perfect · overcooked · dessert · vegetable · disgusting · expensive · restaurant · beautiful · delicious · atmosphere · disappointing

4b

Where is the stress? On the first, second or third syllable? Make three lists.

first syllable	second syllable	third syllable
<u>per</u>fect	de<u>ssert</u>	over<u>cooked</u>
…	…	…

DIGITAL+ practise more 6-7

ACTIVATE **PRACTISE** DEVELOP PRACTISE APPLY

Making plans

5a  audio 1/11

**Listen to Ava's mum Fiona talking to
Grandmother Edyta.
What are they talking about?**

5b CHOOSE YOUR LEVEL skill: listening p.151

**I   Listen again. Are the statements true or false? Take notes.
Then copy the true statements into your exercise book.**

1 The family is planning to go to a
   restaurant on Wednesday evening.
2 Grandma Edyta is allergic to raw fish.
3 Sushi is Grandma Edyta's favourite
   kind of food.

4 Joshua loves Turkish food.
5 There is a Chinese restaurant
   on Portobello Road.
6 Edyta likes the Indian restaurant
   near the station.

II   Listen again and take notes. Then correct these statements.

1 The family is planning to go to a
   restaurant on Tuesday evening.
2 Fiona is allergic to raw fish.
3 Grandma Edyta would like to go to
   a sushi restaurant.

4 Joshua loves Turkish food.
5 Fiona suggests a Vietnamese restaurant
   on Portobello Road.
6 The Indian restaurant doesn't have
   many vegetarian dishes.

III   Listen again and take notes. Then answer the questions.

1 When is the family planning to go to a restaurant?
2 Where does Fiona first suggest going?
3 What does Grandma Edyta say about sushi?
4 What doesn't Joshua like to eat?
5 Why don't they want to go to the Chinese restaurant?
6 Why is the Indian restaurant a good choice for Noah?
7 What is Ava's dad Sebastian looking forward to?

5c wordbank: eating and eating out p.160, workbook p.14/5

**Is there a restaurant you and your family
go to when you have a visitor or on special
occasions? Or do you prepare something
special to eat? Tell your class about it.**

You can say:
We always go to … on my dad's birthday.
My grandmother always cooks … when …
…

At The Palace of India – part one

6a   wordbank: talking about pictures p. 166, grammar: present progressive (R) p. 176

Look at the picture. What can you say about the scene? What are the people doing?

6b   audio 1/12

Listen to the dialogue and read along. What food does everybody order?

Waiter: Good evening and welcome to The Palace of India. Have you got a reservation?

Mrs Kogan: Hello, yes, the name is Kogan – a table for six.

Waiter: Certainly. Let me show you to your table. Please come this way. Take a seat.

* * *

Waiter: Here are your menus. Can I bring you some drinks to start with?

Mr Kogan: We'd like to look at the menu first, but can we please have a bottle of water for the table?

Waiter: Of course. May I offer you some recommendations for your meal?

Mrs Kogan: Yes please!

Waiter: Today we have a tikka masala with salmon and home-made mango ice cream for dessert.

Joshua: Fish? In a curry? I'm not sure that I would like that!

Waiter: It's a bit unusual, but it's one of our most popular dishes. I'll be back in a minute with your water and I'll take the rest of your order.

* * *

Waiter: So, have you decided what you would like to eat?

Mrs Kogan: Yes, that's two vegetable kormas for the boys and a chicken tikka masala for me. What are you having, Edyta?

Edyta: I'd like the tikka masala with salmon please, with rice on the side.

Waiter: What about the others, what would you like to eat?

Ava: I'm starving! I'll have the butter chicken with rice *and* some naan bread, please.

Waiter: Of course. And for you, sir?

Mr Kogan: I'll have the lamb vindaloo, please.

Waiter: Just to warn you, our vindaloo is extremely spicy.

Mr Kogan: I love hot food! I'll be OK.

Waiter: OK, great.

6c   workbook p. 14/6-7

These sentences are not very polite. Rewrite them in a more polite way. Look at the text for help.

1   Your table is over there. Sit down.
2   Do you want a drink?
3   We want a bottle of water.

4   Let me tell you what is good to eat here.
5   That sounds disgusting to me.
6   What do you want to eat?

The menu

7a

Read the menu of The Palace of India. What do they serve with all main courses?

DRINKS

Lemonade, cola, mineral water	£2.20
Juice (orange, apple, mango)	£2.50
Mango lassi	£3.00

*A cool yoghurt drink to enjoy
with a spicy curry*

STARTERS

Poppadoms with a selection of dips	£1.85

*Fried crackers made from
chickpea flour*

Onion bhaji	£2.30

Golden fried onions

Vegetable samosa	£3.95

*Fried pastry filled with potatoes,
onions, peas and sweetcorn*

MAIN COURSES

All main courses are served with rice or naan bread.

Butter chicken	£10.95

*Chicken cooked in a mild sauce
with garlic, tomato and coriander*

Korma	£13.95

*A mild curry with coriander and coconut cream.
Choose from vegetable, lamb or chicken.*

Tikka masala	£13.95

*A spicy curry with ginger, tomato, coriander and chilli.
Choose from vegetable, lamb, chicken or fish.*

Vindaloo	£9.95

*Our hottest curry with ginger, tomato, peppers and
lots of chilli. Choose from vegetable, lamb or chicken.*

Palak paneer	£7.95

Soft cheese cooked in a spinach curry

Mixed kebab plate	£11.95

Grilled lamb, chicken and beef skewers with salad

7b CHOOSE YOUR LEVEL   skill: mediation p. 155

▌ You are at The Palace of India with your grandmother. Answer her questions in German.

1 Was ist ein *mango lassi*?
2 Was gibt es denn alles als Vorspeise?
Ist da etwas ohne Zwiebeln dabei?

3 Bekommt man auch was zum Hauptgericht dazu, Kartoffeln oder so?

▌▌ You are at The Palace of India with your grandmother. Answer her questions in German.

1 Welche Vorspeise ist vegetarisch?
2 Was genau ist ein *vegetable samosa*?

3 Ich mag kein scharfes Essen. Welches
Hauptgericht wäre gut für mich?

▌▌▌ You are at The Palace of India with your grandmother. Answer her questions in German.

1 Was ist eigentlich *butter chicken*?
Ist da wirklich nur Butter in der Soße?
2 Ich habe Lust auf Fisch. Welche Gerichte
mit Fisch gibt es?

3 Ich mag sehr scharfes Essen. Welches
Hauptgericht sollte ich nehmen?
4 Welches Getränk passt gut zu scharfem
Essen?

7c

You have £20 to spend. What would you order? Make notes and talk to a partner.

At The Palace of India – part two

8a audio 1/13

Listen to the rest of the dialogue and read along. Who has not finished his or her food? Why?

Waiter: Is everything OK with your food? Can I get you any more drinks?
Noah: Really yummy, thank you.
Mrs Kogan: Yes, it's really good. I'm fine for drinks, thanks.
Mr Kogan: I'll have another mango lassi, please!
Waiter: Of course.
Mrs Kogan: How is the vindaloo?
Mr Kogan: It is really spicy!
Edyta: Are you OK?
Mr Kogan: Yes, yes, very good! I can handle it! And how is your salmon tikka?

***

Noah: I can't eat anymore. I'm full already! I'll have to leave the rest. Do you think I can take it home? It's a shame to waste it.
Edyta: I'm sure that will be OK. Sebastian, you haven't finished either! Was it too spicy for you?
Mr Kogan: Umm, no, err ... I just ... I'm getting full. But I think I'll have just one more mango lassi ...

***

Waiter: Would you like to see the dessert menu? We also have teas and coffee.
Mrs Kogan: No, thank you very much. We've all eaten too much already.

Mr Kogan: Can we get the bill, please?
Waiter: Of course. I'll be back in a minute. Would you like to pay with cash or card?
Mr Kogan: Card, please.
Waiter: OK. Just a minute. I'll bring the card machine over.

***

Edyta: What a great meal, thank you! I love coming here.
Mrs Kogan: I'm glad you enjoyed it! We like it here, too.
Mr Kogan: And the mango lassi is really excellent.
Mrs Kogan: We can take some home if you need some more ...

8b wordbank: eating and eating out p. 160, skill: writing p. 153, workbook p. 16/8-10

After the trip to the restaurant, Ava texts her friends.
Write down four or more sentences.

You can write:

Hi guys, I'm just back from ...

The food was ...

I had ...

...

ACTIVATE PRACTISE **DEVELOP** PRACTISE APPLY

Ordering food

9　GET TOGETHER　workbook p. 17/11

Get together with a partner.
Decide what you would like to order.

Partner A	Partner B
I Go to page 128.	I Go to page 137.
II Go to page 131.	II Go to page 140.
III Go to page 134.	III Go to page 143.

Eating out

10　CHOOSE YOUR TASK　wordbank: eating and eating out p. 160, C: skill: writing p. 153, media worksheet 9, workbook p. 17/12

A Write a menu for your dream restaurant.
B Create a phrase book for tourists: "Eating out in an English-speaking country"
C Write a review about a good or bad restaurant experience. You can write about a real experience or make one up.

A
STARTERS
small pancakes and chocolate soup

…

MAIN COURSES
chocolate cake with strawberries on the side

…

DESSERTS
ice cream with chocolate sauce

…

B
Eating out

Could I have a …, please?

I would like the …, please.

What is …?

Can I have chips with my burger?

A difficult customer

11a　📹 video 4, skill: watching a video clip p. 156

Watch the video clip. What is happening?
Describe the situation.

11b

How do you think the scene will end?
What is the lady going to eat?
Collect ideas for an ending.

11c　skill: writing p. 153, workbook p. 18/13

Later that evening the waiter and the lady both send text messages to a friend.
Choose one of them and write his or her text message.

What is going on?

12 CHOOSE YOUR LEVEL

I **Look at the pictures and read the texts. Then match the captions to the pictures.**

| A A disgusting experience | B Waiting for my lunch | C Sitting next to a famous person |

II **Look at the pictures and read the texts. Then choose one picture and think about what could happen next. Make notes.**

III **Look at the pictures and read the texts. Then write thought bubbles for the waiter, for Preppy Rappy and for the spider.**

1

Sorry, will be late. I'm still sitting here waiting for my lunch. It's taking longer than I expected.

2

OMG! Look who is sitting at the table right next to me!!! I can't believe I'm having dinner at the same restaurant as Preppy Rappy!!!

3

So disgusting! I actually found a spider in my soup!!! But at least I'm getting a free dessert now.

At the restaurant

13a   skill: mediation p. 155

You are at a restaurant with your family. Two English-speaking tourists at the table next to you ask you for help with the German menu. Can you help them?

Tourist: We would like soup, one vegetarian main course and one with meat.
We'd also like a dessert!
You: Then you could order …

13b   skill: performing a scene p. 159, workbook p. 18/14

Act out the conversation with a partner. Remember to be polite.

Ratsstübl

Vorspeisen und Suppen
Kleiner bunter Marktsalat
Feldsalat mit Speck
Kartoffelsuppe
Tomatensuppe
Gemüsesuppe Ratsstübl

⚜

Hauptgerichte
Schnitzel Ratsstübl mit Bratkartoffeln
Backfisch mit Salzkartoffeln
Spaghetti Bolognese
Bratwurst und Kartoffelpüree mit Salat
Gemüselasagne
Grillgemüse mit Käse überbacken

⚜

Nachtisch
Schokomousse hell und dunkel
Erdbeertörtchen
Vanilleeis mit heißen Früchten

DIGITAL+ practise more 8

Our restaurant role play TARGET TASK

14 ▧▨ workbook p.19/15, wordbank: eating and eating out p.160, skill: performing a scene p.159, media worksheet 2

Your task is to present a scene at a restaurant. Before you start, look at these steps:

STEP 1

Get together in small groups and plan your role play. Decide:
· What type of restaurant is it?
  (A fast food restaurant, an expensive 5-star restaurant, a takeaway, ...?)
· What can you eat there?
· What are your characters like?

STEP 2

What is going to happen in your scene? Think of an unusual event, for example:
· someone finds something disgusting in their food
· someone famous visits the restaurant
· someone chokes on their food
· ...

STEP 3
Decide who will play which part.

STEP 4

Make notes for your role play. Collect words and phrases you will need.
You do not have to write the complete scene but you can write cue cards for each character.

STEP 5

Practise your role play. You can use props or costumes if you like.

STEP 6

Perform your scene. If you like, you can film your scene and show it to the rest of the class.

Check out

Kannst du einen Blogeintrag zum Thema Essen verstehen?	Workbook, p. 20
Kannst du ein Gespräch zum Thema Kochen verstehen?	Workbook, p. 20
Kannst du über Gerichte sprechen, die du schon einmal probiert hast?	Workbook, p. 20
Kennst du wichtige Redewendungen, die man bei einem Restaurantbesuch braucht?	Workbook, p. 21
Kannst du jemandem sprachlich aushelfen, der eine Speisekarte nicht versteht?	Workbook, p. 21
Kannst du einen kurzen Text über ein Restaurant schreiben?	Workbook, p. 21

Delicious disaster

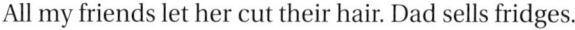

Hi, I'm Jamie and this is my sister Lucy. We live in Stoke-on-Trent with our mum and dad.

Well, he's not our *real* dad, but he behaves like one and we like him a lot. Our mum met him when I was three and Lucy was one. Our real dad lives in Birmingham and we don't see him that often. Sometimes he remembers our birthdays and sends presents but sometimes he doesn't.

Mum's a hairdresser. She works in the city centre and she's really good.

All my friends let her cut their hair. Dad sells fridges.

Last week, Dad's sister Sally came to our place for dinner. She's really cool and we like her a lot. She rides a motorbike and always wears a black leather jacket. She's also got a lot of tattoos. My favourite is the sunrise on her back.

That morning Mum said, "Tonight is going to be very busy. I've got a lot to do at work today, and Dad won't be home before seven. You'll have to let Sally in and then we'll order some pizza as soon as I'm home." Both my parents are quite bad at cooking so we order in a lot.

Or get takeaways. We're all really good at making sandwiches, though.

When I came home from school that day, no one was there and I went to the kitchen to get a snack. While I was searching for some cereal, I found this really fancy cookbook Mum has: *French cuisine: 300 traditional recipes.* I looked through it and there were lots of pictures of really yummy-looking food. The last part of the book was *Suggestions for menus.* There were ideas for three-, four- and even twelve-course menus!!!

Just at that moment Lucy came home and found me staring at something called *clafoutis aux cerises.* It looked like a very good cherry pie.

"What are you doing?" she asked and looked at the picture. "Oh, that looks yummy. Why do we never have anything like that?"

At that moment I had an idea. "Lucy," I said. "Why don't we cook our dinner for tonight? I'm sick and tired of pizza and pasta and takeaway meals. We're still growing; we should have some decent food." "But we can't cook," Lucy said.

"Well, that's what cookbooks are for," I said. "You have to start somewhere – why not with this 'classic French four-course meal for an informal dinner party'? It doesn't look too difficult. The main course is *poulet à la crème. Poulet* is chicken. Chicken can't be too difficult. Mum makes chicken nuggets all the time."

"OK, let's try it," Lucy said. "What do we do first?"

disaster = *Katastrophe*; cereal = *Frühstücksflocken*; fancy = *nobel*; course = *Gang*; decent = *anständig*; classic = *klassisch*

I looked at the cookbook. "I think we'll have to go shopping first," I said. "Let's take the pizza money; we won't need it anyway." So we took the cookbook and the pizza money and went shopping. To our great surprise, salad for the first course, some cheese and tomatoes for the second course, a chicken, potatoes and vegetables for the main course and fruit and cream for the dessert were cheaper than our usual pizza dinner.

"Right, let's do this," I said when we got home. "You could start washing and peeling the potatoes. I'll prepare the chicken." "Alright," Lucy said and put the potatoes in the kitchen sink.

About half an hour later we were in trouble. We found out that Lucy was not very good at peeling potatoes. There was not much left of the potatoes, but we had a huge load of peels. I was still trying to cut up the chicken, but it didn't look right at all. On the pictures in the cookbook there was a lot less blood and mess. "Maybe you could start whipping the cream for the dessert while I finish this," I told Lucy. "OK," she said and took out the mixer. Big mistake! Apparently, Lucy was as bad at whipping cream as she was at peeling potatoes. The cream just didn't stay inside the bowl. It went everywhere!

When Sally arrived at half past six, the kitchen looked like a battlefield. And we hadn't even started with the first two courses yet … There were bits of potato and chicken and whipped cream everywhere, and I was still holding the knife. Sally laughed so hard she almost cried.

We explained our plan to her and she said: "Oh, that's a lovely idea. But I don't think we have enough time to get that finished. How about we save that chicken, vegetables and potatoes for another day? I'll show you how to make a really good chicken soup at the weekend and we'll quickly make some pancakes for tonight?"

"But that's not French," Lucy said. "Well, then what about *crêpes au sucre*?" Sally asked. "What's that?" I asked. "Pancakes with sugar," Sally said. "Very French. Where's the flour? And a pan? And maybe we should clean the kitchen a bit?" She looked at the chicken and started laughing again. So we cleaned the kitchen and Oliva showed us how to make pancakes. With her help it was quite easy and we managed not to make any more mess. Well, apart from the one pancake that fell on the floor when Lucy flipped it.

When Mum and Dad came home, the kitchen was clean and there was a large stack of pancakes on the table. Mum and Dad were so surprised! Especially when they heard that Lucy and I had made dinner.

So we all sat down and had a lovely pancake dinner. I ate five, Lucy had three and Dad ate twelve!!! "That was sooooo good. Thank you guys," Mum said and put down her fork when we were all finished. "Maybe Jamie and Lucy could take over the cooking. Then we wouldn't always have to eat takeaways or sandwiches."

"That's a brilliant idea, dear," Dad said and licked his fingers. "They could learn to prepare some more dishes. Something with chicken maybe. Chicken's not too difficult."

surprise = *Überraschung*; sink = *Spüle*; peel = *Schale*; battlefield = *Schlachtfeld*; had made = *hatten gemacht*; take over = *übernehmen*

Curious about curry?

Curry is a traditional dish in many South Asian countries such as India, Pakistan and Bangladesh. The word 'curry' comes from the word 'kari' meaning 'sauce' in Tamil – a language spoken in South India and other parts of Asia.

There are many types of curries. They can be very spicy or mild, but they are all made using a combination of spices. In most curries you find chillies, coriander, cumin and turmeric. Many curries also include ginger, cardamom and garlic. A mix of some of these spices also goes into curry powder, a spice mix very popular in the Western world.

Note that 'curry' is the name of a dish, and 'curry powder' is the name of a mixture of spices.

curry powder

curry

a spice and tea stall at a market in India

So why is curry – and Indian food in general – so popular in the UK today? In the 17th century, British traders began trading goods like spices and tea with India.

At that time in Britain, Indian spices were very expensive, and only rich people could afford them. Nevertheless, people started to use Indian spices in their dishes. The first curry recipe that was published in Britain appeared in a cookbook in 1747. In 1773, at least one London coffee house had curry on the menu. In the 18th and 19th centuries, British influence in India grew, and the British East India Company, which controlled large parts of trade in India, became more and more powerful there.

In 1858, India officially became a British colony until it became independent in 1947. Many people from India have moved to Britain, bringing their culture and eating habits with them.

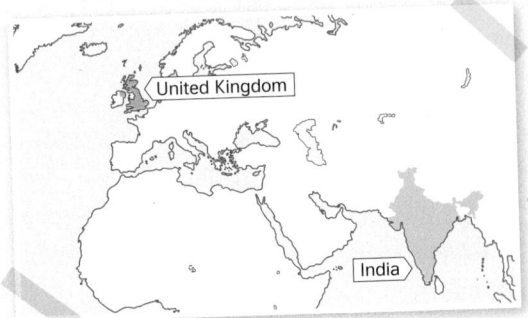

United Kingdom

India

Over time, curries have become increasingly popular in the UK, and today there are thousands of Indian restaurants all over the country.

Find out more about an Indian dish or spice and report your findings to the class.

2

1. Talk about the pictures. What are the people doing?
2. What do you think is important for a healthy lifestyle?
3. What sports do you like? Why?

Healthy living

Part A Keeping fit

- You will talk about different sports.
- You will listen to an interview.
- You will collect and present tips for a healthy lifestyle.

Part B At the doctor's

- You will talk about health issues.
- You will watch a video clip about cheering someone up who is ill.
- You will present a role play.

What's the right sport for you?

1a

Follow the flow chart and find out: what could be a good sport for you?

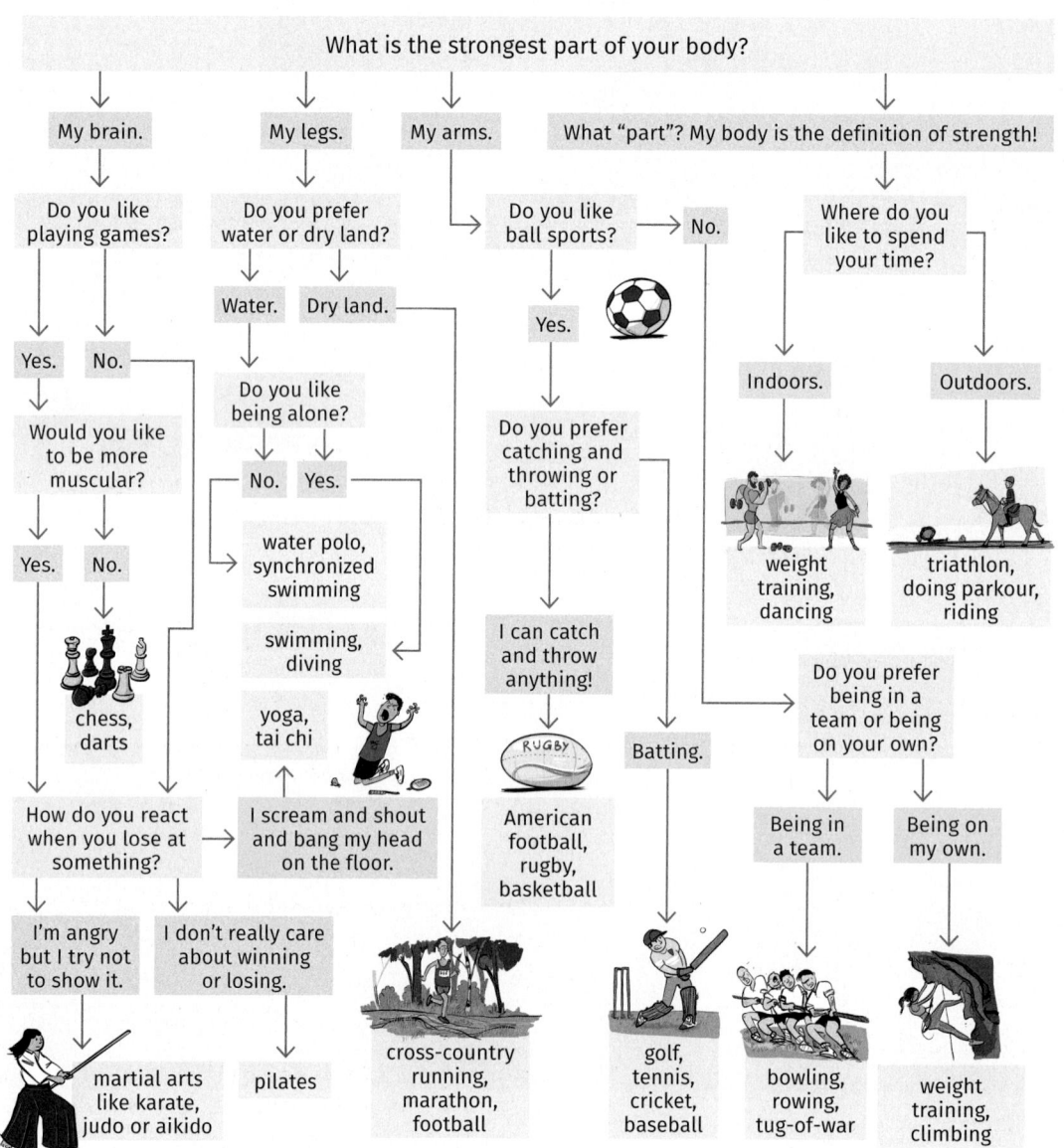

1b   workbook p. 22/1–3

Work with a partner. Talk about what the flow chart suggested for you.

You can say:

The flow chart suggested swimming or diving for me. I think swimming is a good idea because it keeps you fit and …

ACTIVATE   PRACTISE   DEVELOP   PRACTISE   APPLY

Finding the right sport

2a skill: reading p. 154

Scan the profiles and find out:

1 Who loves being in nature?
2 Who likes maths?

3 Who does not like being alone?
4 Who is not good at losing?

Hi, I'm Kristin. I just love being active and I'm not good at sitting still. My teachers always say I should calm down a bit. I like spending as much time as I can outside with my friends – that makes me really happy. I don't like being alone too much. Having people around me is very important to me, otherwise I feel lonely and bored.

Hi, I'm Ben. I like to choose when and where I train. I don't really like team sports because I like being on my own. I also love spending time outdoors in nature. Having a goal is very important to me. It feels great to reach a goal just by using my own skills and strengths. Living a healthy life is important to me, too, so I try to eat healthy food in order to stay fit.

Hi, I'm Amira. I don't like big groups of people. I prefer being indoors – on my own or with my best friend. I'm not much of an outdoor person. My favourite subject at school is maths. Logical thinking and solving puzzles and riddles is what I'm good at. I'm not a very good loser, I'm really competitive and it makes me really angry when I'm not the best at something. My best friend keeps telling me I should relax a little and take things a bit easier, but that's just not me.

2b CHOOSE YOUR LEVEL wordbank: keeping fit p. 162

I Read Kristin's profile. What does she like, what does she not like? Take notes in a table. What could be a good sport for her?

You can write:

Kristin likes:	Kristin doesn't like:
being …	being …

II Read Ben's profile. Take notes on what he likes and what he does not like. What could be a good sport for him? Write it down and explain why it would be a good sport for him.

You can write:

I think … could be a good sport for Ben
  because he likes …

III Read Amira's profile. Take notes on what she likes and dislikes and what she is good at. Think of a good sport for her and recommend it to her in a short message. Give reasons.

You can write:

Hi Amira, you say that you …
Maybe … because …
When you … you have to …
Why don't you …?

GRAMMAR HELP the gerund p. 177

Die *ing*-Form von Verben hast du schon beim *present progressive* kennengelernt, wie etwa in diesem Satz: *The children are playing football.* Schau dir nun folgende Sätze an. Wie werden die *ing*-Formen hier benutzt?

Swimming keeps you fit.
Do you like riding?
I'm good at climbing.

In diesen Fällen nennt man die Formen *gerund*. Auf Seite 177 findest du weitere Beispiele und Erklärungen.

A sport for Matilda

3   grammar: gerund p. 177, workbook p. 23/4

Read what Matilda said. Copy it and complete it with the words from the box.

swimming · playing ·
taking · sitting · going ·
spending · running

I don't like ??? at home. I want to find a sport that I really like. I've tried ???, but I stopped ??? to the pool after a few weeks.
Maybe ??? part in a team sport is better for me. I'm really good at ??? fast and I prefer ??? time outside. How about ??? rugby? Do you think it's a cool sport?

Doing sports

4   grammar: gerund p. 177, workbook p. 23/5

What do you think about different sports and activities? Write four or more sentences. You can use words from the boxes.

You can write:

Swimming is …
I think doing karate is not …
In my opinion … can be …
…

swimming · doing karate ·
running · playing … · cycling · …

exciting · dangerous · exhausting ·
fun · boring · easy · difficult · …

What are you good at?

5   grammar: gerund p. 177, wordbank: keeping fit p. 162, workbook p. 24/6

What sports and activities do you like doing? What are you good at? Write four or more sentences.

You can write:

I like …
I'm good at playing …
…

🖥 **DIGITAL+** practise more 9

ACTIVATE **PRACTISE** DEVELOP PRACTISE APPLY

An interview

6a skill: working with words p. 150, media worksheet 3

Match the definitions to the words. If necessary, look up words you do not know.

1 They tell you how to play a game.
2 What you need in order to do something well.
3 An action or strategy that is planned well in order to reach a certain goal.
4 If you always want to win, you are …
5 A series of games where the best team or player gets a prize at the end.
6 When you focus on something.
7 Doing something with your body.

A skill
B physical activity
C competitive
D rules
E tactic
F concentrate
G tournament

6b audio 1/19, skill: listening p. 151

You are going to hear the words from 6a in an interview. What do you think the interview is about? Collect ideas in class. Then listen to the interview. Were you right?

6c CHOOSE YOUR LEVEL

**I True or false? Listen again and take notes.
Copy the true statements and correct the false statements.**

1 Chess is sometimes called "the game of kings".
2 You can't play chess online.
3 Anna likes chess because it is relaxing.
4 There are four elements that make a sport a sport.

**II True or false? Listen again and take notes.
Copy the true statements and correct the false statements.**

1 Chess is probably 150 years old.
2 In Anna's opinion, chess is a game.
3 You have to learn different strategies.
4 Being fit does not help you in a game of chess.
5 Chess is very competitive.

**III What four elements make a sport a sport?
Listen again and take notes. Write a short text.**

6d wordbank: expressing opinions p. 165, media worksheet 15, workbook p. 24/7-9

Do you agree? Is chess a sport? What do you think? Say why.

Feeling good

7a skill: reading p.154

Scan the posts and write down what sports the teenagers do.

ELLIE, 13

I love dancing and I'm in a dance group. We have already performed at a small festival in my town. It's so much fun moving to the music and practising together as a team. The best part is that you exercise and have a great workout without even noticing it. After the training I'm really exhausted, but I always feel great. At school I really hate PE lessons. Our teacher thinks it's the most important subject ever, and most of my classmates seem to have fun. But I am not very good at running, jumping and playing football, so the traditional sports that we usually do are not for me. Why can't we do something like dancing?

RYAN, 15

I love playing wheelchair basketball. Playing in a team with your friends is great fun. I go to practice twice a week, and we play matches against other teams at the weekends. Our team was quite successful last year. My dream is to play for the national team some day.

In the summer holidays we always go to a special practice camp for a week to prepare for the season. There we also learn about things like mental strength and looking after ourselves – how to get enough sleep and what to eat and how not to stress too much. You can't be good at your sport if your mind is not in the game as well.

ALEX, 16

I feel that most sports are about competing against others and winning. I never liked that. At the same time I knew that doing something for my body was important. So I tried different things like running or cycling – but I didn't like that very much. I wanted to find an indoor activity. My mum has been doing yoga for a while, and one day I went to her class with her. That day changed my life! I do yoga regularly now and I love it. Yoga not only keeps me fit and flexible, it also helps me to learn about myself in new ways. I feel that I have more self-esteem and know how to relax when feeling stressed. Even my marks at school are better now. So, if you have the chance – why not try it out?

ACTIVATE   PRACTISE   **DEVELOP**   PRACTISE   APPLY

MIRA, 14

I've always been quite sporty – I was on my school's swimming team, and I used to ride my bike to school every day. But last year I broke my leg and was in hospital for some time. I had to have an operation. It was all quite complicated and it took ages until I could use my leg again. When I came out of the hospital, I spent a lot of time on the couch in front of a screen, watching TV or playing computer games. I also ate a lot of sweets. When my leg got better, I realized that the rest of me wasn't feeling too well. I had problems sleeping, and I felt tired and sad and in a bad mood most of the time. I talked to my mum, and she suggested that I should start swimming again and maybe eat less chocolate. It was so hard in the beginning, but after about three weeks I felt a lot better. The swimming helped my leg, and I can go to school by bike again. I also try to eat more fruit and vegetables because I can actually feel that that's better for me. Of course I still eat sweets but not as many as before.

7b CHOOSE YOUR LEVEL

▌ Read two or more of the teenagers' posts and answer the questions about them.
▌▌ Read three or more of the teenagers' posts and answer the questions about them.
▌▌▌ Read all of the teenagers' posts and answer the questions.

Questions on Ellie's post:
1 What does Ellie think about PE at school?
2 What does she like about dancing?

Questions on Ryan's post:
1 What does Ryan like about playing wheelchair basketball?
2 Apart from physical fitness – what does he need to be successful in his sport?

Questions on Alex's post:
1 What kinds of sports does Alex not like?
2 Why does yoga make him feel good?

Questions on Mira's post:
1 What happened when Mira had to stop doing sports?
2 What made her feel better?

7c workbook p. 25/10-11

What makes you feel good?
Make some notes, then talk to a partner
about it.

You can write:
- doing sports
- listening to music
…

PEOPLE & PLACES 2  video 5

School sport in the UK

Many schools in the UK have indoor and outdoor spaces for all kinds of sports. Students take part in lots of different sports during the school year, from well-known team sports like football and hockey to individual sports like badminton and cross-country running. Students wear a uniform for sport as well, so everybody can see what school they play for when different schools compete against each other. The uniform is normally a T-shirt, shorts and a pair of socks and is in the school colours.

During the summer term, most schools have a sports day. The students compete in different activities like running races and athletics.

At most schools there are four or five different houses, and every student belongs to one of these houses. On sports day, and during different events throughout the year, students can win points for their house. At the end of the year, the house with the most points wins a cup. House events are always very competitive!

Compare school sport in the UK to school sport at your school or schools in other countries you know about. What is the same? What is different?

Martin's favourite sport

8a  video 6, skill: watching a video clip p. 156, workbook p. 26/12

Watch the video clip. What is Martin's favourite sport and what does he like about it?

8b CHOOSE YOUR LEVEL skill: mediation p. 155

A friend, who does not speak English, wants to know what Martin is talking about. Read his or her questions. Then watch the video clip again.

| Take notes and answer three or more of the questions in German.
|| Take notes and answer four or more of the questions in German.
||| Take notes and answer the questions in German.

1 Wie lange betreibt Martin seinen Sport schon?
2 Wie oft ist er schon getaucht?
3 Warum braucht er manchmal einen „dry suit"?
4 Wieso hat er eine so große Uhr?
5 Was sind das für Fotos, die er zeigt?
6 Was ist ein „buddy check"?

Sports

9   CHOOSE YOUR TASK wordbank: keeping fit p.162, B: wordbank: presenting something p.168, workbook p.27/13

A Create a poster, a flyer or an advert for your favourite sport.

B Find out about an unusual sport. Give a one-minute talk about it.

C Write a post about a sport you like doing or watching.
     You can look at the posts on pages 36 and 37 again.

Sports poems

10a   audio 1/22-24

Listen to the poems and read along.

Choose your sports

Let's turn off our video games,
and run outside.
From so many sports,
we may choose and decide.

Baseball, soccer,
and basketball are fun.
Let's grab some friends,
and play in the sun.
(...)
Whatever sports,
you decide to play,
enjoy them with friends,
each and every day.

SKATEBOARDING

Knee pads, elbow pads,
start the show.
Grab your helmet;
Come on, let's go!

Margo L. Dill

What
Can You
Do With a
Football
?

Well...

You can
kick it - you can catch
it - you can bounce it - all
around. **YOU CAN GRAB IT** you can
pat it you can roll it - on the ground.
You can throw it *you can head it*
you can hit it - with a bat. You can
biff it you can boot it you can spin
it **you can shoot it.** You can
drop it you can stop it. **Just
like that!**

James Carter

10b

Which of the words in the poems are rhyming words? Collect them on the board.

10c

Think of more rhyming words and add them to your collection.

10d   wordbank: keeping fit p.162, workbook p.28/14

Be a poet.
Write a sports poem.

10e

Work with a partner or in small groups. Choose a poem (from this page or one of yours) and present it.

Word families

11 skill: working with words p. 150

How many other words that belong to each word family can you find? Write them down. You can use a dictionary to help you.

run · play · win ·
swim · dance · train

You can write:

run: runner, running, …

play: playground, …

…

A sports idol

12a audio 1/25

**Listen to the interview with Jada.
What does she say Tony Hawk wants to achieve with his "Skatepark Project"?**

12b CHOOSE YOUR LEVEL skill: listening p. 151, workbook p. 28/15

▌ Listen again and match the sentence parts.

1 Jada started competing	A Tony Hawk.
2 Looking out for each other is	B for keeping fit.
3 Skateboarding is a great sport	C when she was ten.
4 Jada's idol is	D important to skateboarders.

▌▌ Listen again and complete the sentences.

1 Jada started ??? when she was six years old.
2 Jada loves being able to do a new trick after hours of ???.
3 Tony Hawk is her ???.
4 Tony Hawk was really good at ??? new tricks.
5 Jada started ??? yoga because it helps her to ???.

**▌▌▌ Listen again and take notes.
Then answer the questions.**

1 When did Jada get her first skateboard?
2 What does she say about skaters?
3 What did her idol Tony Hawk have problems with?
4 What was he good at?
5 How did skateboarding help Jada?
6 How does the Skatepark Project help the skater community?
7 What do good skateboarders focus on when competing in a tournament?

12c wordbank: keeping fit p. 162, workbook p. 28/16

Who is your (sports) idol? Write four or more sentences about him or her.

You can write:

My idol is … He / She was born in …

DIGITAL+ practise more 10

ACTIVATE   PRACTISE   DEVELOP   **PRACTISE**   APPLY

Tips for a healthy lifestyle TARGET TASK

13 workbook p. 29/17, wordbank: keeping fit p. 162, presenting something p. 168, skill: presentations p. 158

Your task is to collect and present tips for keeping fit and healthy.
Before you start, look at these steps:

STEP 1
In class: think about how you would like to present the tips.
You could make:
· leaflets
· posters
· slides for a slide show
· a short video clip
· …

STEP 2
Get together with a partner or in a small group and collect information.
You can look at the unit again and / or search the Internet.
Make a list of 'dos and don'ts'.
Think about:
· sleep
· food
· sports
· …

STEP 3
Create your leaflet, poster, slide show, short video clip, …
Check it.

STEP 4
Present your work, for example in a gallery walk.
Which tips do you think are the most important ones?

STEP 5
Give each other feedback. Remember to be polite.

Tips for a healthy lifestyle

1. Get enough sleep
Make sure to …
Switch off your …
Don't …

2. Eat healthy food
Eat at least …

What's the matter?

1a

Look at the pictures. What do you think: what is the matter with the people?

1b   audio 1/26

Listen to the dialogues and read along. What is each patient's problem?

Matthew: Ow, my shoulder and my wrist hurt so much! And look, my wrist is swollen.
John: I know, but hopefully it won't be long until they call you in.
Matthew: What if my wrist is broken?
John: Don't worry too much. They'll probably take an X-ray, and if it is broken, you will get a cast.
Matthew: I don't want a cast! If I have a cast, I won't be able to play tennis and I'll miss the match next week! Ow – it really hurts!

Sarah: My tooth hurts so much!
Mum: Then I'll make an appointment at the dentist's for you.
Sarah: Oh no!
Mum: If it hurts so much, you'll have to go to the dentist. The toothache will only get worse if you don't go.
Sarah: I know. But I really hate going to the dentist.
Mum: I'll come with you, of course. Let me just give them a call.

Receptionist: Good morning, Dr Hill's practice. This is Jemima speaking. How can I help you?
Linda: Hello, this is Linda Miller. I think I've caught a cold. I've got a headache and a sore throat, and my nose just won't stop running. I also have a fever and a cough.
Receptionist: Oh yes, you don't sound too good. Are you a patient at this practice?
Linda: Yes, I am.
Receptionist: Ah yes, there you are. Let me see … If you come in at twelve o'clock, the doctor can see you just before his lunch break.
Linda: That sounds good. Thanks.

ACTIVATE   PRACTISE   DEVELOP   PRACTISE   APPLY

Mum: Oh dear. What's happened?
Tom: I tripped. I fell on my knee and it really hurts.
Mum: Let me have a look at it. Oh, it's bleeding. The first thing we have to do is to clean the wound. If we don't do that, you will get an infection. Then I'll put a plaster on it. If it doesn't get better soon, we'll go and see a doctor.

Nurse: Good morning, Demir. How are you feeling today?
Demir: My stomach still hurts.
Nurse: Well, it's no wonder you've still got a stomach ache. It's only been two days since they took out your appendix. But you're allowed to have some toast today.
Demir: Oh, great. I'm so hungry.
Nurse: Yes, I know. But make sure to eat slowly. It'll be quite painful if you eat too fast. And here is your medicine for today.

1c CHOOSE YOUR LEVEL skill: reading p. 154

▍ **Read the first three dialogues again. Collect words for body parts and words for health problems.**

You can write:
body part: shoulder, wrist, …
problem: hurt, …

▍▍ **Read the dialogues again. Collect words for body parts and words for health problems.**

▍▍▍ **Read the dialogues again and make notes. Then write about the people's problems.**

You can write:
Matthew's wrist hurts. Maybe it is …
The doctor will probably …
Sarah's …

1d skill: performing a scene p. 159, media worksheet 2, 5, workbook p. 30/1-2

Work with a partner. Try to imagine how the people are feeling in each situation and do a dramatic reading of one of the dialogues. You can record it if you like.

GRAMMAR HELP conditional clauses 1 p. 178

Wenn du sagen möchtest, was unter bestimmten Bedingungen geschehen wird, benutzt du Bedingungssätze. Diese Sätze bestehen aus zwei Teilen. Sieh dir die Beispiele an. In welchem Teil wird die Bedingung genannt und welcher Teil drückt aus, was passiert, wenn die Bedingung erfüllt ist?
Welche Zeitformen werden in den jeweiligen Teilen verwendet?

If you have a broken wrist, you will miss the tennis match.
The toothache will only get worse if you don't go to the dentist.
If it doesn't get better, we'll go and see a doctor.
It'll be quite painful if you eat too fast.

Auf Seite 178 findest du weitere Erklärungen zur Bildung und Verwendung von Bedingungssätzen.

If you …

2   grammar: conditional 1 p. 178

Match the sentence parts and write the sentences in your exercise book.

1 If you don't see a doctor,	A if you don't wear a warm jacket.
2 If you break your leg,	B it will only get worse.
3 If you stay in bed,	C if you eat too many sweets.
4 If you don't eat slowly,	D if you are in hospital.
5 You'll feel a lot better soon	E your stomach will hurt.
6 You will catch a cold	F if you take your medicine.
7 You'll get toothache	G you'll get well soon.
8 You won't be able to go to school	H you will get a cast.

What if …?

3a   grammar: conditional 1 p. 178

Write sentences. There can be more than one solution.

If you have a really bad cold, you ??? (must / will / can) stay at home.
If you stay at home, you ??? (must / will / can) play lots of video games.
If you play lots of video games, you ??? (must / will / can) become really good at it.
If you become really good at playing video games, you ??? (must / will / can) take part in competitions.

3b   grammar: conditional 1 p. 178, workbook p. 31/3

Choose one of the sentence beginnings below and write about a chain of events like in 3a. Write three or more sentences starting with "If …".

A If the weather is nice tomorrow, I'll go to the park. If I go to the park, …
B If it's rainy tomorrow, I will / I won't …
C If my brother / sister / mum / dad …
D If …

Tarek's accident

4a

Look at the picture. What can you see? Describe the situation. What do you think is going to happen next?

4b audio 1/28

Listen to the dialogue and read along. Who is Tarek's coach going to call?

Chris: Tarek, are you OK?

Tarek: Ow! I banged my head really hard.

Coach: Tarek, are you alright? Can you get up? Let me help you!

Tarek: Ow, I don't think I can! I can't move my foot, it hurts too much. I'm feeling dizzy, too.

Coach: OK, best stay down then. I'll call an ambulance. Could somebody call Tarek's dad, please?

Chris: I can call Mr Adil.

Coach: Thanks, Chris. Tell him not to worry and that I'll let him know which hospital we're at as soon as I know.

4c audio 1/29, skill: listening p.151

Listen to Tarek's coach calling the emergency services. What is going to happen next?

4d CHOOSE YOUR LEVEL workbook p.32/4-5

I Listen again. Choose the right words and write down what Tarek's coach explains to the operator.

There was an accident ??? (on the playing field / on the playground). During a hockey match, ??? (three / two) players ran ??? (into a wall / into each other). One of them can't stand on his ??? (left / right) foot and is feeling ??? (dizzy / cold). His head ??? (is bleeding / hurts).

II Listen again. Imagine you are Tarek's coach. Answer the operator's questions.

1 What is your emergency?
2 How many people are hurt?
3 Is the person able to talk?

4 What exactly is wrong with him?
5 How old is he?
6 Where are you exactly?

III Listen again. Imagine you are Tarek's coach and you are texting a friend. Write the message.

You can write:

Hi Tom, just imagine what happened today.
There was a / an ... this afternoon on the ...
I called ... and ...

At the hospital

5a skill: working with words p. 150, media worksheet 3

Look at the words and phrases in the box. If you do not know them, look them up in a dictionary. Write them down and add the German meanings.

injury · examine · sprained · put on a bandage · cool with an ice pack · advise · GP · X-ray

5b audio 1/32

Listen and read along. What do you find out about Tarek's injuries?

In the waiting room
Coach: Ah Tarek, there's your dad. Hello Mr Adil.
Dad: Tarek! Are you OK? Does it hurt? Have you seen a doctor yet?
Tarek: Calm down, Dad. It's not that bad.
Coach: Yes, we've already seen a doctor. She's examined his head, there is nothing wrong with it.
Tarek: I'm not feeling so dizzy anymore.
Dad: Phew.
Coach: Yes, that's what I thought. But the doctor wants to take an X-ray of his foot. We were just waiting for you, there are a few papers to sign.
Dad: Oh yes, of course. Where do I have to go?
Coach: Over there to the receptionist's desk. Is it OK if I go back to the team? They'll want to hear how Tarek is doing.
Dad: Yes sure, thanks for taking care of him. Tarek, I'll just go and sign those papers.
Tarek: OK, Dad.

***

In the doctor's practice
Dr Weston: Well, hello Mr Adil. I'm Doctor Weston and I've met your son already.
Dad: Hello.
Dr Weston: So, Tarek. How are you feeling now?
Tarek: My head is a lot better. But my foot still hurts really badly.

Dr Weston: Yes, I can imagine. But the good news is that it's not broken. You've got a sprained ankle. It's very important that you rest your ankle for the next few days. We'll put an elastic bandage on it and you'll have to keep it up as much as possible. You can also cool it with some ice.
Dad: What about school?
Dr Weston: I would advise him to stay at home for the next two days. And no sports for at least three weeks.
Tarek: No sports?
Dr Weston: Yes. If you start to use your foot too early, it'll only get worse.
Tarek: That'll be so boring. And I won't be able to play in our next hockey match.
Dad: I promise that I'll play that hockey video game with you if it gets too boring. And I'm sure your friends will visit to cheer you up. Thanks a lot, Doctor Weston.
Dr Weston: No problem. Please make an appointment for a check-up with your GP in about a week. But I'm sure everything will be fine. Bye, Tarek.
Tarek: Bye. And thank you.

ACTIVATE   PRACTISE   **DEVELOP**   PRACTISE   APPLY

5c CHOOSE YOUR LEVEL skill: reading p. 154

I   Read the dialogues again and write down the sentences in the correct order.

A Tarek's coach goes back to the team.

B Tarek's coach says that the doctor wants to take an X-ray.

C Tarek's ankle is only sprained.

D Tarek's dad arrives at the hospital.

II Read the dialogues again. Are the sentences true or false? Correct the false sentences.

1 Tarek's dad cannot come to the hospital.

2 Tarek's coach has gone back to the team before Tarek's dad arrives.

3 No one has examined Tarek's head yet.

4 Tarek's dad goes to the receptionist's desk to sign a few papers.

5 Tarek's ankle is broken.

6 Tarek should stay at home for two days.

III Read the dialogues again. Answer the questions.

1 What does the coach tell Tarek's dad?

2 Where does Tarek's coach go?

3 How is Tarek feeling when the doctor comes back?

4 What does the doctor say about Tarek's ankle?

5 What does she say about school and sports?

6 What does Tarek's dad promise to do?

5d skill: performing a scene p. 159, workbook p. 33/6-7

Work in groups of three. Practise reading out one or both of the two scenes.

What now?

6 grammar: modal verbs (R) p. 179, workbook p. 34/8-11

**Copy the sentences and fill in the gaps with the words from the box.
There can be more than one solution.**

will be allowed to · will be able to · will have to · won't be allowed to · won't be able to

1 Tarek's dad has arrived at the hospital. – Now he ??? find out what happened.

2 Tarek has a sprained ankle. – Now he ??? do sports for the next three weeks.

3 Tarek can't walk properly. – Now he ??? stay at home for two days.

4 Tarek can't do sport for three weeks. – But he ??? play video games with his dad.

5 Tarek has to rest his ankle for a few days. – Then he ??? walk properly again soon.

Cheering Tarek up

7a

Read the text message. What do you think: who is Ava writing to?

7b

What are Ava's ideas for cheering Tarek up?

7c   wordbank: health p. 163

Work with a partner and collect more ideas for cheering up someone who is ill.

7d

Talk about your ideas in class.
What are the three best ideas?

> 😟 **poorTarek**
>
> **Ava** Hi guys! I think we should try to cheer Tarek up a little. He didn't sound too good, did he? 😔 I was wondering if we should maybe get him some chocolate 🍫 or bake him a cake 🍰. And what do you think about one of those "Get well soon" balloons? 🎈 Or a card?
>
> Monday 7:17pm

Poor Ellie

8a   🎬 video 7, skill: watching a video clip p. 156

Watch the video clip.
What is wrong with Ellie?

8b

Watch the video clip again.
What do Ellie's family and friends do to cheer her up? Take notes.

8c   workbook p. 35/12-13

What is Ellie looking forward to when she can go back to school?

You can write:
Ellie is looking forward to meeting …
…

What do they miss?

9   GET TOGETHER 🔊 audio 1/34

Get together with a partner.
Listen to Ben and Jacob in hospital and find out what they are talking about.

Partner A	Partner B
I Go to page 129.	**I** Go to page 138.
II Go to page 132.	**II** Go to page 141.
III Go to page 135.	**III** Go to page 144.

Helping out at the doctor's

10a 🎧 audio 1/35, skill: listening p. 151

An exchange student called Sophie is staying with you. She does not speak much German. One day she wakes up in pain. Listen to Sophie. What is wrong with her? Take notes.

10b skill: mediation p. 155, workbook p. 36/14

You have to take Sophie to the doctor. Explain what is wrong to the German doctor.

What's wrong?

11 wordbank: health p. 163

Work in small groups.
Mime an injury or an illness.
The others have to guess what it is
and tell you what to do to get better.
Take turns.

You can say:
Have you got a … ?
You could …
You should …
…

Being ill and getting well

12 CHOOSE YOUR TASK   wordbank: health p. 163, C: skill: writing p. 153

A Design a "Get well soon" card.
B Look at the meme.
   Find a picture and create your own meme.
C Have you ever been ill or have you ever been to hospital?
   Write a short text about your experience.

A

B

Doctor, my back hurts when I wake up in the morning.

Wake up in the afternoon then.

C

Last year I had to go to hospital because they had to take out my appendix. I was a bit nervous because it was my first time staying in a hospital (and I was afraid it would be really boring). After the operation I didn't feel too well, but the girl in the bed next to me was really nice. We talked and played lots of different games. I definitely wasn't bored. We still hang out together sometimes, even now!

Who's asking?

13 CHOOSE YOUR LEVEL workbook p.36/15

I **Which of these questions does a doctor ask and which ones a patient? Make two lists.**

1 Where does it hurt?
2 How much chocolate have you eaten?
3 Will I have to stay at home for a week?
4 How exactly did it happen?
5 Will I be able to walk again soon?
6 How are you feeling?

II **Unscramble the questions. Which ones does a doctor ask and which ones does a patient ask? Make two lists.**

1 got – as well – have you – a fever
2 move – like this – can you – your fingers
3 hit you – the ball – did – where exactly
4 how long – in bed for – stay – will I have to
5 how long – a headache for – have you – had
6 will I – when – do sport – again – be able to

III **Who gives these answers? Doctor or patient? Make two lists. Then write the questions for the answers.**

1 You will have to stay at home for at least a week.
2 I've had a headache for the last two days.
3 No, I can't. Ouch!
4 Your ankle isn't broken, it's only sprained.
5 You won't be able to go to school for the next three days.
6 I tripped.

Can you hear the *r* ?

14a audio 1/36

Listen to the sentences. In which of the marked words can you hear the "r"? Can you explain why?

1 <u>There</u> are some papers to sign.
2 The waiting room is over <u>there</u>.
3 My <u>shoulder</u> and my wrist hurt.
4 Where does your <u>shoulder</u> hurt?
5 The <u>doctor</u> is in the office.
6 You can see the <u>doctor</u> now.
7 I'll put a <u>plaster</u> on your knee.
8 Don't remove the <u>plaster</u> too soon.

14b

Listen again and repeat the sentences.

Odd one out

15

Find the odd one out. Why is it the odd one out?

1 doctor – examine – dentist – nurse
2 leg – tooth – coach – ankle
3 stomach ache – pancake – toothache – headache
4 hospital – swollen – broken – sprained
5 swimming pool – gym – appointment – playing field
6 medicine – chocolate – cake – toast

DIGITAL+ practise more 12-13

ACTIVATE   PRACTISE   DEVELOP   **PRACTISE**   APPLY

A medical problem TARGET TASK

16 workbook p. 37/16, wordbank: health p. 163, skill: performing a scene p. 159, media worksheet 2

Your task is to do a role play about a medical problem.
Before you start, look at these steps:

STEP 1

Get together with a partner or in a small group and plan your role play.
Decide the following:

- What is the matter with the patient? What is the medical problem?

  - *I fell off … and hurt …*
  - *My … is swollen / is broken / hurts.*
  - *I have a …*

- Where does the scene take place? At the doctor's, at the hospital, at home, …?
- Who are the characters in your scene? What are they like? How are they feeling?

STEP 2

Collect ideas for your scene and make notes. You can also write cue cards.
Make sure each character has something to say.

STEP 3

Decide who will play which part and practise your role play.
You can use props or costumes if you like.

STEP 4

Act out your scene.
If you like, you can film your scene and
show it to the rest of the class.

Check out

Kannst du verstehen, wenn jemand darüber spricht, welchen Sport er oder sie mag?	Workbook, p. 38
Kannst du deine Meinung zu einer Sportart ausdrücken?	Workbook, p. 38
Kannst du Reimwörter finden und eigene Reime schreiben?	Workbook, p. 38
Kannst du darüber schreiben, was unter bestimmten Bedingungen passieren wird?	Workbook, p. 39
Kannst du wichtige Wörter und Redewendungen zum Thema Krankheit und Arztbesuch?	Workbook, p. 39
Kannst du jemandem beim Arzt sprachlich aushelfen?	Workbook, p. 39

Sports day

We finally had our sports day yesterday. I was so excited that I almost couldn't sleep the night before. This year I was going for the top! My training programme had been spot on, and I had signed up for as many events as I could.

I began the day with a healthy athlete's breakfast: a peanut butter and banana milkshake, fried eggs and porridge.

"Don't you think they meant you should have ONE of these for breakfast before a big event?" asked Dad, who was reading the newspaper at the kitchen table.

"Well, since I've signed up for ten events, this should be alright," I told him.

"You signed up for ten events? What were you thinking?" my brother Jamie asked. "We only have to take part in one. I only have the football match at eleven, and the rest of the day is free."

"I'm sorry we won't be there to cheer you on, darling," Mum said. "I just couldn't get out of work and Dad has this really important customer to visit."

If you ask me, no one in my family was showing much of the right spirit, as usual.

Our school looked brilliant that day. There were flags and streamers in our school colours everywhere, the sun was shining, and everyone was happy. Well, almost everyone.

"I hate sports day. All that running and sweating," my best friend Makena said. "I'm off to my chess game. I'm so glad the chess club managed to put chess down as a sport. See you later."

Since my day was about to get busy, I hurried to get to my first event – the mini javelin. Unfortunately, I could not wait for my javelin to land because I had to be on time for my second event, the 1500-metre race. During the run I was completely in the zone. I didn't look left or right. I just ran, ran, ran. When I crossed the finishing line, I just kept running to get to the long jump on time so I didn't hear who won. But since I didn't see any of my opponents anywhere near me, I was pretty sure I was first.

300-metre hurdles

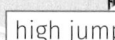

high jump

mini javelin

1500-metre race

long jump

At the long jump I did my three jumps, and then I had to leave in a hurry to be on time for the next event, the 300-metre hurdles. I didn't knock over any of the hurdles because of my careful technique.

had been spot on = *war genau richtig gewesen*; had signed up = *hatte angemeldet*; be in the zone = *in seinem Element sein*; opponent = *Gegner/in*

Luckily, the high jump was right next to the track for the 300-metre hurdles so I could walk over immediately after crossing the finishing line.

Once again, I left before they announced the winner. Next was the lunch break, and I wanted to be the first at the cafeteria. Us super athletes need our carbohydrates and I still had five more events to do.

I felt quite full after lunch so it was good that the next two disciplines were throwing rather than running: discus and softball throw. Once again, I did well – the other students' discuses and softballs landed nowhere near mine.

Seven events down, three to go. After the throwing events I was in great form again. I did the triple jump, and then I had to hurry to get to the relay in time. I was the first runner on my team, which was good because I could race over to my last event for the day as soon as I was finished.

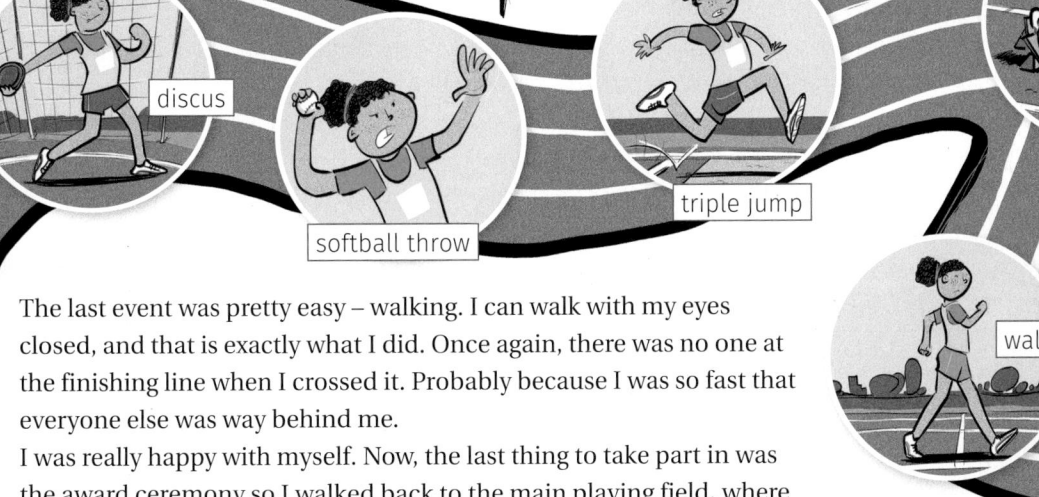

discus

softball throw

triple jump

relay

The last event was pretty easy – walking. I can walk with my eyes closed, and that is exactly what I did. Once again, there was no one at the finishing line when I crossed it. Probably because I was so fast that everyone else was way behind me.

I was really happy with myself. Now, the last thing to take part in was the award ceremony so I walked back to the main playing field, where there was a small stage.

walking

"Well done, Lucy," said Ms Fisher, my PE teacher, and handed me a large trophy. "You're the only student who managed to compete in ten disciplines. That's a new school record, and I'm very pleased to present you with this *School Champion of the Hearts* trophy."

I was so happy! I heard Jamie and Makena and my house cheer really loudly for me. I knew I was good, but I had never thought I might become school champion. What a success!

"Yes, very well done, Lucy," added Mr Dunkerley, our headteacher. "You came last in every single event, but what a remarkable display of spirit! We're really proud of you."

announce = *bekannt geben*; ...down, ...to go = *... vorbei, es bleiben noch...*; award ceremony = *Preisverleihung*; success = *Erfolg*; spirit = *hier: Kampfgeist*

Paralympics

Every four years thousands of athletes from all around the world come together and compete in the Paralympics. The Paralympics always take place in the same year as the Olympics, and there are summer and winter games. The city or region that hosts the Olympic Games usually also hosts the Paralympic Games.

In the Paralympics, athletes with a disability compete against each other. They may be blind or in wheelchairs or have other disabilities, perhaps since birth or after an accident. The first official Paralympic Games took place in Rome in 1960 with 400 athletes from 23 countries.

In the Tokyo 2020 Summer Paralympics, more than 4,000 athletes from over 160 countries competed in 22 different sports. Paralympic sports include archery, athletics, football 5-a-side (blind football), paratriathlon, sitting volleyball and wheelchair rugby.

Sitting volleyball

In sitting volleyball the players sit on the floor – so the net is much lower. Apart from that, the rules are similar to volleyball, for example there are also six players on a team.

Paratriathlon

A triathlon is made up of three sports – swimming, cycling and running. At the Paralympics it consists of 750m swimming, 20km cycling and a 5km wheelchair or running race.

Football 5-a-side

Football 5-a-side – or blind football – is an adaptation of football for athletes who have very little eyesight or who are blind. The sport uses modified FIFA rules. The field is smaller, and there are boards along the field to keep the ball inside. A team consists of five players, including the goalkeeper. Teams are allowed to have sighted goalkeepers and sighted guides. The guide has to stay off the field and assists the team by directing the players. The ball has bells inside so the players can locate it by sound.

Find out more about a Paralympic athlete or sport and present your findings to the class.

1 Look at the pictures. What do you think: where are the people?
2 What are the people doing?
3 Have you ever been to events like these? What was it like?

What's on?

Part A At the car boot sale

- You will talk about weekend activities.
- You will find out about car boot sales.
- You will do a role play about buying and selling second-hand items.

Part B Festivals

- You will find out about festivals in the UK.
- You will read an article about how festivals can become greener.
- You will create a poster about a festival.

Weekend activities

1

**Talk to a partner about weekend activities.
Think about where you can go, what you can
do there, if the activities are for free, …**

You can say:

At the weekend, I sometimes go to …

There's a / an … near my house / in my area.

… is free. / … not expensive. / … costs …

…

What's on in London?

2a skill: reading p. 154

**Read these tips for events in London at the weekend.
What can you do if you do not want to spend much money?**

LONDON WEEKEND TIPS
your guide to fun events in London

PORTOBELLO ROAD MARKET | Notting Hill   Saturday and Sunday 9am – 7pm

Find anything from clothes to arts & crafts at hundreds of shops and stalls.
There are some stalls which are only open on Saturdays, so come early to
discover the best finds and avoid the crowds.

CHARITY RUN | Finsbury Park   Saturday 11am

Run 5km for a good cause – this charity run is perfect for people who
like running and doing something good at the same time. All money
goes to charity. Registration fee: children £10, adults £14.99.

FAMILY FILM CLUB | The Barbican Cinema   Saturday 11am

Watch a family film at the Barbican Cinema.
Adults can only come if they bring a child, and children can
only come with an adult. Tickets cost £3.50.

CAR BOOT SALE | Notting Hill   Sunday 10am – 6pm

Visit the biggest car boot sale in Notting Hill and look for unique
second-hand items that you can't find anywhere else.
The entrance fee is only £1.50 and goes to a good cause.

THE LION KING | Lyceum Theatre   Sunday 2:30pm

A great show for people of all ages who love musicals. See the
famous musical now and remember it forever. Tickets from £23.50.

2b wordbank: what's on? p. 164, workbook p. 40 / 1-2

**Work with a partner and discuss each event. What would you like to do?
What would you not like to do? Give reasons.**

What to do?

3a 🔊 audio 2/2

Listen and read along. What are the friends talking about? What do they agree on in the end?

Ava: Hi guys, finally Friday! What are you up to this weekend? Would you like to do something together?

Tarek: Our coach cancelled the hockey tournament that he had planned for the weekend. I have no plans so far.

Lily: Me neither. Any ideas?

Ava: We could go to the cinema. We haven't been there for ages.

Harry: That's too expensive, I haven't got enough pocket money left.

Ava: We could go to the Family Film Club that they have at the Barbican. They have tickets which are just £3.50.

Tarek: Is that the one where you have to take an adult with you? I don't want that! Can we please find something else? Anyone up for the charity run on Saturday? Or a game of football?

Ava: Oh, Tarek. You always want to do sports. I'd rather do something that we don't do all the time. Actually, I really need a new hoodie. We could go shopping together.

Harry: Shopping would be OK. I'm sure I could get some money from our mums for new clothes. They keep telling me to get a new pair of jeans.

Lily: But you don't have to buy new things. I could help you with upcycling second-hand hoodies and jeans. We could go treasure hunting at a flea market! I need to get some inspiration for my next upcycling project anyway.

Ava: Should we go to Portobello Road Market then?

Harry: OK with me. Maybe that guy who sells those really funny T-shirts is still there.

Tarek: I only remember the funny guy that sells old cameras that nobody needs ... But Portobello Road Market is always so crowded at the weekend. And there are so many shops which are pretty expensive.

Lily: Hm, there's a car boot sale on Sunday. Shall we go there then?

Harry: Why not? And it's even for a good cause – I'll definitely get money for that.

Ava: That's a cool idea. Do you want to meet at 10:30 on Sunday?

Tarek: Yeah. Sounds great.

Ava: Great! See you on Sunday then!

3b CHOOSE YOUR LEVEL skill: reading p. 154

I Read again. Which events do the children talk about? Take notes.

II Read again. Who suggests what? Take notes for each person.

III Read again. Who suggests what? What arguments for and against the activities do the children mention? Take notes for each person.

3c workbook p. 41/3-4

Which of the events from the guide is your favourite?
Write a short text message in which you suggest the event to a friend.

GRAMMAR HELP
relative clauses p. 180

Wenn du Personen oder Dinge genauer beschreiben willst, kannst du Relativsätze benutzen.
Meist beginnt ein Relativsatz mit einem der Relativpronomen *who, which* oder *that*.
Sieh dir die Beispielsätze an. Wann verwendest du *which*? Wann verwendest du *who*? Auf welches Wort bezieht sich jeweils das Relativpronomen?

There are some stalls which are only open on Saturdays.
Maybe that guy who sells those really funny T-shirts is still there.

Nun schau dir die folgenden Sätze an. Wann kann man das Relativpronomen *that* verwenden?

There are stalls that sell unique second-hand items.
There is a funny guy that sells old cameras.

Auf Seite 180 findest du weitere Erklärungen und Beispiele, auch zur Verwendung des Relativpronomens *that*.

Tips for the weekend

4 grammar: relative clauses p. 180, workbook p. 42/5

Write sentences.

This is the flyer		takes place in Notting Hill.
There is a car boot sale		are especially interesting for children.
At the car boot sale there are people		like running.
There is a cinema	who	tells you what's on in London at the weekend.
You can see films there	which	has a Family Film Club.
At the theatre you can see a musical show		sell second-hand clothes.
On Saturday, there is a charity run for people		is very famous.

Making plans

5 grammar: relative clauses p. 180

Complete the sentences. Use 'who', 'which' or 'that'. Use each relative pronoun at least once.

1 The friends are talking about activities ??? they can do at the weekend.
2 Tarek suggests activities ??? have to do with sports.
3 Harry would like to see if the guy ??? sells funny T-shirts is still at Portobello Road Market.
4 The car boot sale ??? takes place on Saturday is the biggest in Notting Hill.

It's a person who …

6 grammar: relative clauses p. 180

Write four or more riddles for a partner.
He or she has to find out who or what it is.

You can write:

It's a person who acts on a stage or in films.
It's an object which you can use to take pictures.
It's a thing that …

DIGITAL+ practise more 14

ACTIVATE **PRACTISE** DEVELOP PRACTISE APPLY

PEOPLE & PLACES 3 📷 video 8

Second-hand shopping in the UK

Buying second-hand items has become more and more popular because it is not only cheaper than buying new things but also better for the environment. You can also use second-hand items for upcycling. In the UK you can find lots of flea markets, car boot sales and charity shops. In charity shops you can buy clothes, books, jewellery or even furniture from people who do not need these things anymore.
Mainly volunteers, who do not get any money for their work, run these shops. You can find good quality items at cheap prices, sometimes you can even find

At a car boot sale

interesting treasures. The money that people spend in charity shops goes to a good cause, for example to Oxfam, Cancer Research UK or the RSPCA (Royal Society for the Prevention of Cruelty to Animals).

Are there any charity shops in your area? Have you ever bought or sold second-hand items, for example at a flea market at your school? Talk about it in class.

Look at that!

7a 📷 audio 2/5

Listen to the four friends. Where are they?

7b CHOOSE YOUR LEVEL skill: listening p. 151, workbook p. 42/6-8

▌ **Listen again. Which of these things do the children talk about? Write them down.**

books

telephones

bicycle bells

vegetables

a singing fish

paintings

toys

clothes

▌▌ **Listen again. Who wants to buy what at the car boot sale? Take notes.**

You can write:

Ava: …

Lily: …

…

▌▌▌ **Listen again and write down what the children's plan is in the end.**

You can write:

First Ava and Lily want to go … while Tarek and Harry … Then …

Looking for bargains

8a   audio 2/6, skill: reading p. 154

Look at the pictures and the heading above. What do you think the dialogues are about? Then listen and read along. Were you right?

Harry: Look, there's a jeans stall. This pair looks alright, doesn't it?

Tarek: Yes, it does.

Seller 1: Hi guys. Good taste – those are original jeans from the 1950s, and I can sell them to you for just £249.

Harry: Oh, that's a bit more than I wanted to spend on a pair of jeans. I thought second-hand clothes are cheaper than new ones.

Seller 1: Well, why don't you look at the jeans over there then? They're all good quality and in excellent condition. They start from £5.

Harry: Great. Thanks.

Tarek: What do you think about these ones?

Harry: I like them. Excuse me, could I try these on?

Seller 1: Sure, just step behind that curtain.

Harry: What do you say, Tarek?

Tarek: They look good on you.

Seller 1: Do they fit?

Harry: Yes, they do. I think I'll take them. How much are they?

Seller 1: This pair is £7.

Harry: Great. Here you are.

Seller 1: £10, thanks. And here's £3 change.

Harry: Thank you. Bye.

Seller 1: Have a nice day! Bye.

Seller 2: Hello, can I help you?

Lily: We're just looking. But thank you.

Seller 2: All right then.

Lily: I really like this old flowerpot. It's only 50p and it would make a great lamp.

Tarek: Why don't you just buy a lamp? There's a nice one.

Lily: But that's not as much fun as looking for old stuff that can still be useful and making your own lamp. I also like this coffee grinder. Excuse me, how much is this? There's no price tag.

Seller 2: Oh, I got that from a man who was cleaning out his cellar. He lives in his grandparents' old house and keeps finding interesting things. His grandparents brought that back with them from a holiday in Italy because they liked Italian coffee so much. It's really old. There's also a coffee pot that came with it. See?

Lily: Oh, it's great. How much for both and this flowerpot?

Seller 2: I can give you the flowerpot for free if you take the other two things for £12, well, let's say £10.

Lily: That's a fair price. Here you are. Thank you! – Hey guys, I think I've just found a bargain!

Ava: Is there any more room on your shelves for new books?

Tarek: Not really. Now I have to get rid of some old ones.

Ava: If you want to get rid of old stuff, you could take it to a charity shop. There is a small one on Portobello Road.

Harry: I've got an idea! Why don't we sell some of our old things at a flea market?

Lily: I like Harry's idea. I think selling things at a flea market would be more fun than just taking them to the charity shop.

Harry: Yes! We have so many old board games that we don't play anymore. And Double and Trouble's old cage and …

Lily: Oh no, not the old cage. I've got an idea for that …

Lily: OK, that was a very successful day. I found lots of good things for my next lamp. Did you find anything, Tarek?

Tarek: Yes, I got five science fiction books for only £2.50. They're in my rucksack.

8b CHOOSE YOUR LEVEL

❙ Read the first two dialogues again. Complete the sentences and write them in your exercise book.

1 Harry and Tarek are at a …
2 Harry buys …
3 He spends …
4 Lily buys …
5 She spends …

❙❙ Read the dialogues again and answer the questions.

1 How much are the cheapest jeans at the jeans stall?
2 How much are the jeans that Harry buys?
3 What does Lily buy?
4 How much does Lily pay?
5 What kind of books has Tarek bought?
6 How much did he pay for them?

❙❙❙ Read the dialogues again and answer the questions.

1 What does Harry buy and how much does he pay for it?
2 Why is Lily interested in a flowerpot?
3 Where did the coffee grinder come from?
4 How much does Lily pay for the flowerpot?
5 Why does Tarek have to get rid of some old books?
6 What is Ava's idea for getting rid of old things?
7 What is Harry's idea for getting rid of old things and what does Lily think about it?

8c wordbank: expressing opinions p. 165, media worksheet 15, workbook p. 43/9

Lily says that buying a lamp is not as much fun as looking for old stuff that can still be useful and making your own lamp. Do you agree with her? Say why or why not.

How much is it?

9a wordbank: buying and selling p. 164

Look at the prices. Ask and answer questions with a partner. Take turns.

You can ask:

How much is the ...?
How much are the ...?

You can answer:

It's ...
They are ...

1
2
3
4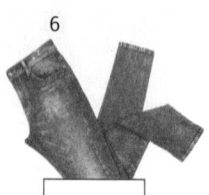
5
6

| £1.50 | 80p | £3.90 | £5.25 | £7 | £25.50 |

9b skill: searching the internet p. 157, workbook p. 44/10

How much do the items cost in euros?
You can find out on the Internet.

You can say:

One pound fifty is one euro ... cents.
...

Tom's day out

10a video 9, skill: watching a video clip p. 156

Watch the video clip. Where is Tom?
What is he doing?

10b CHOOSE YOUR LEVEL

Watch the video clip again.
Answer the questions.

▌ 1 What day is it?
2 What does Tom buy at the first stall?
3 How much does he pay for it?

▌▌ 1 What does Tom buy at the first stall?
2 At the second stall Tom buys several things. Why does he buy them?
3 What does Tom buy at the third stall?
4 How much does the woman want for it and how much does Tom pay for it in the end?

▌▌▌ 1 What information does Tom give about car boot sales?
2 How much money does Tom spend at each stall?
3 What would he love to buy at the last stall?
4 Why can't he buy it?
5 What did Tom particularly like about his day at the car boot sale?

ACTIVATE PRACTISE **DEVELOP** PRACTISE APPLY

At the market

11 skill: mediation p. 155

You are at a market in England with a friend who does not speak English very well. Help him or her. Write down what you say.

Your friend: Oh, schau mal da an dem Stand, da gibt es Marmelade und – Chutney? Könntest du mal fragen, was das ist?
(1) You: *Aber klar doch.*
Excuse me, what is …?

Seller: Chutney is really popular in the UK, especially mango chutney. It's a kind of sauce and originally from India. This one contains tomatoes and onions. You can eat it with vegetables, fish or meat.
(2) You: *Das ist … Man kann es …*

Your friend: Das hört sich gut an. Das könnte ich meinen Eltern mitbringen. Wie teuer ist denn ein Glas?
(3) You: …

Seller: £3.50. We've also got other kinds. This one contains pumpkin and carrots for example.
(4) You: …

Your friend: Super, mein Vater liebt Kürbis. Ich nehme beide. Dann habe ich zwei tolle Mitbringsel für meine Eltern.
(5) You: …

Seller: Great. That's £7 then.

Out and about

12 CHOOSE YOUR TASK A: wordbank: events p. 165, B: buying and selling p. 164, C: skill: writing p. 153

A **Create an event calendar for your dream weekend.**
B **Imagine you want to sell something really odd. Advertise it!**
C **Write a funny background story for an object.**
  Think about who owned it, what he or she used it for and why it is special.

Do you like fish?
Do you like music?

Then this is the **perfect item** for you!

This decorative fish sings one of 20 songs for you whenever you walk past it. It looks great in any room! So, what are you waiting for? Come and get your singing fish today for **only £35!**

B

This pair of unique roller skates will bring you endless hours of speedy fun!

Pre-owned by Birmingham's roller skate queen Emma Murpledale who rolled from victory to victory in them. They can be yours for only £15!

B

I'd like the blue one

13 grammar: prop words one and ones p. 181, workbook p. 44/11-12

Complete the sentences with 'one' or 'ones' and write them in your exercise book.

1 Which T-shirt do you like better?
   The red ??? or the green ????

2 I don't like these socks.
   The blue ??? are nicer.

3 This ring is too small for me.
   Have you got a bigger ????

4 Have you got another book like this ????

5 Which shoes are cheaper?
   The brown ??? or the black ????

6 This cup is broken.
   Have you got another ????

7 Let's look at the bags.
   I really need a new ???.

Buying and selling

14 CHOOSE YOUR LEVEL   workbook p. 46/13-16

▌ **Read the phrases. What does the customer say? What does the seller say? Make a table.**

You can write:

seller	customer
It's …	Excuse me, …
…	…

Excuse me, how much is this? ·
It's £6. · You can have it for £4.50. ·
Have you got another one of these? ·
I'll take it. · Here's your change. ·
Can I help you? ·
That's too much. I only have £4.

▌▌ **Match the sentence parts.**
   Then sort the sentences into two lists: one for the seller, one for the customer.

1 Excuse me, can
2 Hi there, are you
3 Do you need
4 This cap is quite expensive,
5 Thank you, we're just

A how much is that one?
B looking.
C looking for anything special?
D anything else?
E I try these on?

▌▌▌ **Unscramble the sentences.**
   Then sort them into two lists: one for the seller, one for the customer.

1 for these – how much – like – would you
2 I can – for free – this vase – give you
3 found – I think – I've just – a bargain
4 these six plates – I would – for 5 pounds – take
5 look – over there – at the jeans – why don't you
6 than I wanted to – that's – spend – a bit more
7 good quality – in excellent condition – they're all – and

DIGITAL+ practise more 15

ACTIVATE PRACTISE DEVELOP **PRACTISE** APPLY

Second-hand shopping TARGET TASK

15 workbook p. 47/17, wordbank: buying and selling p. 164, skill: performing a scene p. 159, media worksheet 2

Your task is to do a role play of a second-hand shopping situation.
Before you start, look at the following steps:

STEP 1

Get together in small groups and plan your role play.
Think about:
· Where does your role play take place?
· Who are your characters and what are they like?

STEP 2

What is going to happen in your shopping situation?
Collect ideas.
· Think of some objects that people could buy or sell.
· Make up an interesting story behind one or more of the objects.

STEP 3

Decide who will play which part.

STEP 4

Make notes for your role play. Collect words and phrases you will need.
You do not have to write the complete scene, but you can write cue cards for each character.

STEP 5

Practise your role play.
You can use your cue cards.

STEP 6

Present your role play.
Make a video recording or act it out in class.

Remember to be friendly and polite!

Good morning. / Hello.
Excuse me, could you …?
…, please.
Thank you.
You're welcome!
Have a nice day.
Thanks. Bye.

A festival

1a

Look at the poster. What information about the festival do you get?

1b

What do you know about the Vikings? Collect information in class.

1c

What do you think: why is there a Viking festival in York?

THE JORVIK VIKING FESTIVAL Join us in York for the largest Viking festival in Europe!

26ᵗʰ - 28ᵗʰ February
with an exciting programme of events

The Jorvik Viking festival

2a wordbank: talking about pictures p. 166

Describe the pictures in the blog entry in 2b. What are the people doing?

2b

Andy is a student in York. He likes travelling around the UK and writes a blog as *Adventuring Andy* about his experiences. Read his post about the Jorvik Viking Festival.

× −

1 March

Hey guys,

It's me, Adventuring Andy. Last weekend the *Jorvik Viking Festival* took place here in York. York has an interesting Viking past. The Vikings conquered York in 866. They lived here in the 9ᵗʰ and 10ᵗʰ centuries and had a big influence on everyday life. During the festival, the city of York seems to step back in time to remember its Viking past. What can I say? It was amazing. On my first day I checked out a show fight at the festival combat arena. When I arrived, two Viking warriors in authentic armour were fighting each other and hundreds of people were watching.

After that I was really hungry and I was glad to have a ticket for the *Banquet of the Voyagers*. When I walked into the dining room, lots of people were already eating delicious Viking food. Some people were listening to exciting adventure stories, too.

The next day, I watched the *Best Beard Competition*. That's a competition where men, women, children and even dogs – literally anyone – present their beards. The beards don't have to be real and I saw a lot of home-made beards. Although it was raining, everyone there had such a great time!

Then I went to the *Birds of Prey Show* at Barley Hall. While I was watching the birds, I listened to the bird trainer. He told us a lot about the role of birds in old Viking myths.

My personal highlight was the *Battle Spectacular* in which two Viking hordes fought against each other. Afterwards there was a breathtaking firework display for more peaceful minds. Throughout the festival, you could tell that all the visitors were really enjoying this trip to the Viking world.

Follow me for more interesting festival content. Coming soon: *Highland Games* and the *Notting Hill Carnival*.

2c CHOOSE YOUR LEVEL skill: reading p. 154

I **Read the post again. Put these pictures in the correct order and write captions for them.**

II **Read the post again. List all the events and activities that Andy mentions. What can you say about the activities?**

III **Read the post again. What do you learn about York's Viking past and the events and activities at the Jorvik Viking festival? Take notes.**

2d wordbank: events, expressing opinions p. 165

Which part of the Jorvik Viking festival do you find the most and the least interesting? Say why.

You can say:
I find the … the most interesting because …
I find it least interesting that …
…

2e workbook p. 48/1

Do you know any events that are similar to the Jorvik Viking Festival? Talk about them in class.

GRAMMAR HELP the past progressive p. 182-183

Du benutzt das *past progressive* um zu beschreiben, was zu einem bestimmten Zeitpunkt in der Vergangenheit gerade passierte.
Sieh dir die Beispiele an. Was fällt dir auf? Kennst du eine andere Zeitform, die ähnlich aussieht?

At 3 o'clock, two Viking warriors were fighting each other.
Although it was raining, everyone there had such a great time!
Throughout the festival, the visitors were enjoying this trip to the Viking world.

Auf den Seiten 182 und 183 findest du weitere Erklärungen, auch zu verneinten Sätzen und Fragen.

Preparing for the competition

3   grammar: past progressive p. 182

Joe is taking part in the Best Beard Competition. Write about what he was doing in the morning.

1   At 6:30, Joe ??? (have) breakfast.
2   At 7:00, he ??? (wash) his beard.
3   At 7:45, he ??? (style) his beard.

4   At 8:00, he ??? (put on) his costume.
5   At 8:20, he and his wife ??? (wait) for the bus to the festival.

What were they doing?

4a   grammar: past progressive p. 182

Look at the pictures. What was happening? Write sentences in your exercise book.

5pm, two Vikings

7pm, Andy

10am, men, women, children and dogs

2pm, Andy

9pm, visitors

You can write:
At 5pm, two Vikings were …
At 7pm, Andy …
…

4b   grammar: past progressive p. 182-183, workbook p. 49/2

What were you doing yesterday at 6pm, last Saturday at 10am, this morning at 7am, …?
Work with a partner. Ask and answer questions. Take turns.

You can ask:
What were you doing yesterday at 6pm?
…

You can answer:
I was talking to my dad.
…

DIGITAL+ practise more 16-17
ACTIVATE   **PRACTISE**   DEVELOP   PRACTISE   APPLY

Opinions

Listen to the three statements. Who is a fan of the Jorvik Viking Festival and who is not?

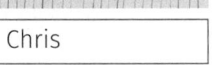
Chris

Cathy

Edward

5b CHOOSE YOUR LEVEL   skill: listening p. 151

I Listen to the three statements again. Complete three or more of the sentences.

Statement 1 (Chris)

1 Chris Cooper runs a ??? in York.
2 ??? is the best month of the year for the hotel.

Statement 2 (Cathy)

3 Cathy made her ??? from an old teddy bear.
4 She made a lot of new ??? from all over the world.

Statement 3 (Edward)

5 Edward has lived in York all his ???.
6 Last year, pickpockets stole Edward's ??? out of his pocket.

II Listen to the three statements again. Answer the questions.

1 What is the "Viking Lodge"?
2 Who stays there?
3 What is the best month of the year for the Viking Lodge?
4 What does Cathy say about her shoes?
5 What kind of competition does Cathy take part in every year?
6 How long has Edward lived in York?
7 Why is February not Edward's favourite month?

III Listen to the three statements again. Why do the people like or not like the festival? Take notes.

You can write:

Chris: many guests, ...
Cathy: ...
Edward: ...

5c wordbank: events p. 165, workbook p. 49/3-4

In class, collect positive and negative aspects of having a big festival in your area.

You can say:

In my opinion ...
On the one hand ..., on the other hand ...
...

More festivals

6a

Andy was on the road again and checked out three more festivals. Look at the photos. What can you see?

6b   skill: reading p. 154

Read Andy's blog posts. Which festival would you like to visit the most?

× −

29 June

Hey festival lovers,

Today I'm going to tell you about one of the biggest open-air music festivals in the world: the Glastonbury Festival in south-west England. It started in the 1970s and got bigger every year. At the Glastonbury Festival you sleep in tents, and when it rains everything is muddy at the end of the festival. But that doesn't bother anyone there. Every year, there are thousands of tents but it is not just a huge camping site, of course. At the festival itself there is so much to see.

At Glastonbury there are always world-famous musicians, and you get to listen to some really good live music. A lot of people bring their children with them, and there's even an area with activities just for children.

I definitely recommend going there.

The atmosphere is really special – it's like diving into another world.

4 August

Hey guys,

Adventuring Andy was on the road again.

This time I checked out the Notting Hill Carnival. It was impressive, loud and colourful! People from all over the world celebrate it in London every year in August. The carnival is a happy and cheerful event, but its beginnings in 1959 were quite serious. The organizers wanted to draw attention to the difficult situation of Caribbean immigrants.

If you like multicultural events, steel drums, colourful costumes and impressive parades, this is the right event for you. You can also taste a lot

ACTIVATE   PRACTISE   **DEVELOP**   PRACTISE   APPLY

of different Caribbean dishes and drinks. Make sure to try curried chicken and fresh coconut water. They are so delicious!

I had a really great time. I loved the final parade on Monday the most. Over 60 bands in fantastic costumes – where else can you see such a spectacle?

29 August

Hi there, lads and lasses!

Can you guess where I might be? That's right, I'm in Scotland, in Braemar! I came here to see the world-famous Highland Games. They take place every summer in lots of different places.

Well, let me tell you this: the Highland Games are worth the trip all the way up to Scotland. You'll hear a lot of bagpipes and see men in kilts.

There are many disciplines, for example Highland dancing, throwing the hammer or the most popular sport of all: tossing the caber.

Here, the contestants have to lift a big log and toss it so that it turns over and lands on its upper end. Aye, this way of moving logs is great to look at.

6c CHOOSE YOUR LEVEL workbook p.50/5-6

I Write down four or more questions about the Glastonbury Festival. Then work with a partner and ask and answer the questions. Take turns.

You can write:

What is the Glastonbury Festival?

What can you …?

Where …?

When …?

…

II Write down five or more questions about the Glastonbury Festival and the Notting Hill Carnival. Then work with a partner and ask and answer the questions. Take turns.

III Write down six or more questions about the Glastonbury Festival, the Notting Hill Carnival and the Highland Games. Then work with a partner and ask and answer the questions. Take turns.

Andy's picture show

7a   wordbank: talking about pictures p. 166

**Andy took a lot of pictures on his trips. Look at these four. What can you see?
Where do you think Andy took them?**

7b   ▶ video 10, skill: watching a video clip p. 156, workbook p. 51/7

**Andy is showing his pictures to a friend. Watch the video clip. What was new to you?
What did you find the most surprising? Say why.**

Party!

8   CHOOSE YOUR TASK   C: wordbank: events, expressing opinions p. 165, media worksheet 5, workbook p. 52/8

A   **Create your own look! How would you dress
if you went to a festival or a carnival?
Make a sketch of your look and label it.**

B   **Write slogans for one or more of the festivals.**

C   ▨ 🖥 **Festival fans look forward to the Glastonbury
Festival all year. What might the people
who live in Glastonbury think about it?
Make up a statement of a resident of Glastonbury.
Record it and present it in class.**

B

*FOR mud and music
LOVERS*

*Get the full experience
at the Glastonbury
Music Festival!*

ACTIVATE   PRACTISE   **DEVELOP**   PRACTISE   APPLY

Help the environment!

9a skill: reading p. 154

Read the newspaper article. What problem does it describe?

How to clear up Britain's biggest events

Over three million people attend UK festivals each year and produce 23,500 tons of waste, which means 2.8kg of waste per person, per day. It is the UK's plan to be plastic-free by 2042, and there is quite some pressure for festivals to become greener.

What's the plan?
In 2018, the British government published a plan on how to reduce waste over the next 25 years. Part of that plan was to abolish carrier bags, food packaging and plastic straws. These and other products made of plastic have been in use a lot at festivals across the country. For example, in the past visitors threw away more than one million plastic bottles at each Glastonbury Festival, and it cost organizers almost £800,000 to get rid of the waste every year. Since 2019, visitors are no longer allowed to bring plastic bottles in order to help protect the environment. Another problem at the festival is the large number of tents that people leave at the festival site. Paul Reed, CEO of The Association of Independent Festivals (AIF), appeals to festival goers to take their tents home and to reuse them. "Tents shouldn't be single-use items," he states.

Do green festivals exist?
At 'No Planet B', the UK's first 'zero waste' festival, there was a list of 'zero waste rules'. For example, festival guests had to bring their own bottles to help cut out plastic, and the organizers asked them to use digital tickets and not paper.

9b skill: mediation p. 155, workbook p. 53/9

Your sister has some questions. Read the article again and answer them in German.

1 Wieso ist denn da ein Bild von so vielen Zelten?
2 Was steht da über das Jahr 2042?
3 Was steht da mit 800.000?
4 Was steht in dem Artikel darüber, wie man Festivals umweltfreundlicher macht?

Which festival?

10 GET TOGETHER

Get together with a partner.
Read and talk about different festivals.

Partner A	Partner B
I Go to page 129.	I Go to page 138.
II Go to page 132.	II Go to page 141.
III Go to page 135.	III Go to page 144.

Check your spelling

11   grammar: past progressive p. 182

Look at the verbs in the box. What are their -ing forms?
Sort them into three lists in your exercise book.

run · have · watch ·
happen · put · talk ·
listen · make · sit ·
dance · drive · swim ·
play · stop · get

You can write:

run – running	have – having	watch – watching
...		

When it started to rain

12   CHOOSE YOUR LEVEL   grammar: past progressive p. 182, workbook p. 53/10-11

What were the people at the festival doing when it started to rain?

I   **Choose four or more of the situations**
    and write about them.

II   **Choose six or more of the situations**
    and write about them.

III   **Write about the situations.**

You can write:

Jill and Suzy were setting up their tent
   when it started to rain.
Becky ... when ...
...

Jill and Suzy

Becky

Levi

Sheree

Juan / the people

Marc

Murat

Writing about a festival

13   workbook p. 54/12-14

Match the sentence parts to make phrases. Sometimes there is more than one option.

1 First, I checked out   A another world.
2 It's like diving into   B the curried chicken.
3 My personal highlight was   C going there.
4 Make sure to try   D the show fight.
5 I can definitely recommend   E the food stalls.

A blog post TARGET TASK

14 🏁🖾 workbook p.55/15, wordbank: events p.165, skill: writing p.153, media worksheet 1, 10

Your task is to write a blog post about a festival or an event.
Before you start, look at these steps:

STEP 1
Think about what you would like to write about:
a carnival, a music festival, a street party, ...
It can be a festival or event you have been to
or would like to go to.
You can also make up an event or festival.

STEP 2
Collect ideas. Think about the following:
· Where did the event or festival take place?
· When did it take place? For how long?
· How much was it? Or was it free?
· What could you see or do there?
· Who was it for?
· What was special about it?
· What did / do you like about it?
· ...

STEP 3
Plan your post.

STEP 4
Write a first version of your post.
You can ask a classmate or your teacher to give you feedback.

STEP 5
Edit your post if necessary and write the final version.

3 March

Hi everyone,

It's me, ... again. Last weekend,
I was at ...

Look forward to next week's
blog – I'll write about ...

Your ...

Check out

Kannst du einem Flyer mit Veranstaltungstipps Informationen entnehmen?	Workbook, p. 56
Kannst du ein Verkaufsgespräch verstehen?	Workbook, p. 56
Kannst du jemandem in einer Einkaufssituation sprachlich aushelfen?	Workbook, p. 56
Kannst du einen Blogeintrag zu einem Festival verstehen?	Workbook, p. 57
Kannst du Fragen zu einem Blogeintrag formulieren und beantworten?	Workbook, p. 57
Kannst du einen Zeitungsbericht verstehen?	Workbook, p. 57

Medieval mischief

You can't imagine how glad I am to be back home! This weekend Mum forced us all to go to the *Medieval Weekend at Arundel Castle*. We had to sleep in a tent and wear funny costumes and I almost got killed.

But let me start at the beginning.

Two weeks ago, one of Mum's customers told her about this "really great event" which was "so much fun" and "a brilliant programme for children". Mum was like "it's going to be so educational" and "we never do things together" and "I'm sure it'll be good for us as a family".

My plan had been to spend the weekend at my best friend Joe's house. He's got a really good console and he has loads of games. His parents are fine with him gaming all the time and I was looking forward to finally improving my score.

But no. On Friday I found myself in the car, stuck between Lucy on one side and a spinning wheel and a sword on the other. Mum had borrowed those from her friend "to make it more authentic". The boot of the car was completely full of camping gear and costumes and tins of baked beans.

Lucy was really excited because there were going to be horses, and she had always wanted to go horse riding.

When we arrived, a guy dressed like a knight showed us where to park the car and where to put up the tent. There were people dressed in medieval clothing everywhere. Some of them even had medieval-style tents. Ours just looked old.

The next morning, Mum woke us up and served porridge in wooden bowls. Except she called it "gruel". More authentic, you know. After breakfast, Lucy wanted to go and see the horses.

"But first, let's get dressed," Mum said and handed me something that looked like a brown curtain. "What's that?" I asked, "and what should I do with it?" "It's a tunic. And I've got woollen socks for you, too," Mum said happily. "Just put them all on. You'll look just like a medieval teenager." Then she handed Lucy another curtain (beige) and grabbed the spinning wheel. "Why are you taking the spinning wheel with you?" Lucy asked "Isn't it a bit heavy for an accessory?" "I'm not going to carry it around all the time," Mum replied. "It's for the mother-daughter living picture competition I've registered us for." "You've done WHAT?" Lucy asked. "I thought we were going horse riding and then I could go back to the tent and read my book." "Oh no, dear," Mum said. "And now let's go and make some beautiful memories."

medieval = *mittelalterlich*; mischief = *Unfug*; force = *zwingen*; had been = *war gewesen*; spinning wheel = *Spinnrad*; sword = *Schwert*; had borrowed = *hatte ausgeliehen*; camping gear = *Campingausrüstung*; gruel = *Grütze*; tunic = *Tunika*

"That's a great idea," Dad said and looked like he was trying really hard not to laugh. But Mum didn't notice. She just smiled at him. "It is, isn't it?" she said.

So we all followed Mum to the stage in the middle of the festival ground. She set herself and Lucy and the spinning wheel up, and a jury came by and looked at all the mothers and daughters spinning and baking and doing all that other stuff women did in the Middle Ages. Then the jury went off to decide who had created the best living picture.

"OK," Lucy said, "that's it. I'm off to find the horses now." And she was gone.

"I want to have a look at the medieval soap and cosmetics stalls now," Mum said. "I'll come with you," Dad said, "I guess there are some food stalls in that direction, too."

Since there were posters all over the place advertising a show fight in the combat arena somewhere near our tent, I thought it might be a good idea to offer to take the spinning wheel back to the tent and check out the arena. Mum was happy with that, too.

I was nearly at our tent when someone behind me suddenly shouted: "Careful! Get out of the way everyone!!!" I turned around and saw the biggest horse I'd ever seen galloping towards me. On its back was my sister, barely hanging on. "Lucy!" I shouted.

"Help!" Lucy shouted.

I jumped out of the way, stumbled over a stone and fell on my left knee. It really hurt, but I saved the spinning wheel! Meanwhile, the giant horse with Lucy on its back was galloping into the distance.

But another horse was already on its way. Someone who was obviously a lot better at riding than my little sister was trying to catch her up.

He was in full armour and he jingled and jangled as he went flying by.

Behind him came Mum and Dad, running and out of breath and clearly panicking. Dad panicked even more when the sword the knight was wearing on his belt almost cut my ear off. That was the moment when I decided I liked the 21st century very much. Not so many swords and less gruel, much safer. I don't know how, but the knight managed to bring Lucy and the horse back. Lucy was fine and she wanted to get back on her horse and try again, but my knee hurt so much that they had to take me to the emergency tent first. The doctor there bandaged my knee, told me to keep it up and gave me some painkillers.

When we came out of the emergency tent, Mum said, "Alright, that was a bit too authentic. Even for me. I'm so glad they invented modern medicine. I think I'm ready to go home, order some pizza and watch TV on the couch in our living room."

Just at that moment, Mum and Lucy were called back to the stage and the jury announced that they had won the mother-daughter living picture competition. They got the first prize: a week at a Middle Ages Camp in the Cotswolds for the whole family.

the Middle Ages = *das Mittelalter*; had seen = *gesehen hatte*; gallop = *galoppieren*; stumble = *stolpern*; meanwhile = *inzwischen*

Glastonbury and the legend of King Arthur

Glastonbury is not only famous for its music festival, it is also connected with the legend of King Arthur. Allegedly, King Arthur was buried in Glastonbury. Visitors can see the site of his tomb at the ruins of Glastonbury Abbey. Another place connected with King Arthur is Glastonbury Tor, a tall hill with a tower. Some people say that it is the mythical island of Avalon. According to the legend, King Arthur's sword Excalibur was made in Avalon.

There are different versions of the legend of King Arthur, and it is not clear if King Arthur really existed and what the historical background of the legend exactly is. However, there are many stories about King Arthur and also about the wizard Merlin, Arthur's loyal friend and counsellor. A well-known part of the legend is the story about the sword in the stone and how Arthur became king.

Once upon a time, Britain was suffering greatly. Their king, Uther Pendragon, had died, and there was no heir to the throne. For years, the kingdom was without a king and there were many battles to take the throne. But no one succeeded and still there was no new king. This was a cause of great worry to everyone in the country.
In one corner of this kingdom lived a young man, Arthur. He lived in the castle of Sir Ector and his son, Sir Kay. They had taken in Arthur when he was a baby and raised him well. Now Arthur was sixteen years old. One morning, in the middle of the town, a great stone with a sword appeared. On the stone there were these words:

"He who pulls this sword from its stone shall be the rightful King of Britain."

The town was buzzing with talk of this stone. Who had put it there? Where did it come from? Who would be the next king? For days people tried to pull the sword from the stone, but it did not move one bit. When Sir Ector and his sons walked past, Sir Kay took great interest in the matter and even took a turn himself, but Arthur paid little attention.
Later, when Kay was preparing for a tournament, he realized that he couldn't find his sword and asked Arthur to search for it. Sir Ector and Kay waited and finally, Arthur came rushing back with a sword. "That … that's not Kay's sword! Wh-where did you find this?" stuttered Sir Ector, already recognizing the sword. Arthur took them back to see the stone, now without the sword. Arthur explained that he had taken the sword out of the stone because he couldn't find Kay's sword, and he promised to return it. "You are our new king! My brother is king!" cried Sir Kay.
Later, the great wizard Merlin appeared, and he explained to Arthur who Arthur really was. "Your real father was the great King Uther, but he could not raise you and I gave you to Ector to raise you like his own child. So finally, his heir is here to be the greatest king that Britain has ever had." And so Arthur ruled Britain, kindly and bravely, and the people were finally happy, for they knew that their new king was truly the greatest.

Do you know any stories, books or films about the legend of King Arthur? Search the Internet for more information and present your findings to the class.

1. Describe the photos.
2. How do you think the people are feeling?
3. Choose one photo and collect ideas for a possible story behind the photo.

You are not alone

Part A Exploring roots

- You will find out about different people's family roots and life stories.
- You will talk about what is special to you in the town or village where you live.
- You will present a life story.

Part B Giving a helping hand

- You will practise describing feelings and situations.
- You will learn how to seek and give advice.
- You will present a scene about giving a helping hand.

The place where you live

1 workbook p. 58/1

**What do you like about the place where you live? What is special about it?
Make notes and share your thoughts in class.**

Living in London

2a

**Read what four people from London posted on this website.
Why did they come to London? Where in London do they live now? Take notes.**

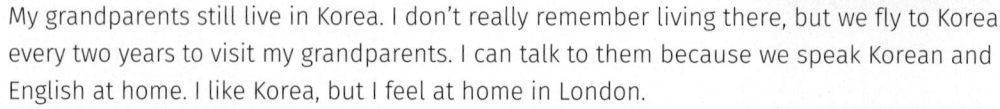

× −

* * * * * * * * * * * * * * * * * * * LIVING IN LONDON * * * * * * * * * * * * * * * * * *

1 My name is Jenna, and I am 16 years old. I was born in Korea,
but my parents moved to London when I was four because they
found better jobs here.
I have one brother and we live in south-west London, in Merton.
5 There's a Korean church in our neighbourhood and we go there
every Sunday. I like going to church because I always meet my
friends there.
My first memory of London was when I went on the London Eye.
It was lots of fun, and the view was amazing! The riverside near
10 the London Eye is my favourite place in London.
My grandparents still live in Korea. I don't really remember living there, but we fly to Korea
every two years to visit my grandparents. I can talk to them because we speak Korean and
English at home. I like Korea, but I feel at home in London.

Hi, I'm Leon. I'm from Spain, but we moved to Bayswater last
15 year because my mum got a job here in London. We lived in
northern Spain, in the countryside, and I loved it there! My
hobby is mountain biking, and it's hard to find a good place for
that around here.
I don't really feel at home in London, and I would like to go back
20 to Spain as soon as possible. I had to leave all my friends there,
and I miss them very much. I text them all the time, but that's
just not the same. I also don't like my school here.
When I first came here, I didn't understand much of what people
said, and sometimes people thought I was stupid just because of my accent.
25 The only thing I like about London is that there are a lot of parks here – Hyde Park is
my favourite.

My name is Sam. I live in Hammersmith with my best friend, Josh. I grew up in Battersea. As far as I know my family has always lived in London. My parents run a pub that my great-

30 great-grandfather opened in 1920. The plan is that my brother takes over the family business when my parents retire.
I lived in Bristol for three years when I went to university, but I didn't like it very much because I missed London so much. There are so many things to do here. You can go shopping, visit

35 museums, spend time in parks, go to lots of concerts and shows … My favourite place in London is definitely the Science Museum. There are always new exhibitions and I often go there. I love London. I don't want to live anywhere else!

Hello, I'm Erika. I'm originally from Sweden, and I came to London in 2006 to go to university here. That's where I met my

40 husband. He's from Ghana and we both liked London's lively atmosphere so much that we decided to stay here. We got married in 2014 and moved to Elephant & Castle in 2016. What I like most about this part of London are the people. I often meet someone I know in the street! There is a very strong

45 community here.
My husband and I have a son and a daughter and we talk to them a lot about our family roots – both the West African side and the Swedish side. We all like cooking and we often prepare dishes that are a mixture of West African, Swedish and British cuisine.

2b CHOOSE YOUR LEVEL skill: reading p. 154

I Read the first three texts again. What do Jenna, Leon and Sam like about London? Take notes. In which lines did you find the information?

You can write:
Jenna: … (line 6) and …
Leon: …

II Read the texts again. What do the people like about London? Take notes. In which lines did you find the information?

You can write:
Jenna likes …
In line … she says: "…"

III Read the texts again. Do the people like or not like living in London? Write down two or more sentences about each person. Quote from the texts to support your answer.

2c skill: talking to people p. 152, workbook p. 58/2-3

If you could live anywhere in the world, where would you like to live? Why?
Get together in small groups and talk about your dream places to live.

| in the country | in a big city | in a small village | where I live now | in London | … |

GRAMMAR HELP   the simple past (R) p. 184-185

Die Zeitform *simple past* kennst du schon. Du benutzt sie, wenn du über etwas sprechen möchtest, das in der Vergangenheit liegt und abgeschlossen ist. Sieh dir die Beispielsätze an. Erinnerst du dich? Wie bildest du die Formen? Worauf musst du bei der Verneinung und bei Fragen im *simple past* besonders achten?

My parents moved to London when I was four.
They found better jobs here.

I didn't like Bristol very much.
Why did the people come to London?

Auf den Seiten 184 und 185 sind die wichtigsten Punkte zum *simple past* noch einmal zusammengefasst.

Writing about the past

3a   grammar: simple past (R) p. 184

Write down the simple past forms of these verbs and use them to write four or more true or false statements about the people from pages 80 and 81.

1 move   2 live   3 love   4 be   5 like
6 grow up   7 meet   8 get   9 go

You can write:

Jenna's parents moved to Korea from London.
Leon ...

3b   grammar: simple past (R) p. 184, workbook p. 59/4

Work with a partner. Your partner has to correct the false statements. Take turns.

Who, what, when, where?

4a   grammar: simple past (R) p. 185

Unscramble the questions and write them down.

1 move to – where – Jenna's parents – did
2 what – in Spain – did – about living – Leon – like
3 was – in London – born – who
4 Sam – did – to university – go – where
5 to study – went – who – to London
6 did – when – come to London – Erika
7 when – get married – did – Erika

4b   grammar: simple past (R) p. 184

Look at pages 80 and 81 again and write down the answers to the questions from 4a.

4c   grammar: simple past (R) p. 184, workbank: family history p. 166, workbook p. 60/5

Write three or more statements about yourself and your family.

You can write:

I was born in ...
My great-grandmother came from ...
...

DIGITAL+ practise more 19

ACTIVATE   **PRACTISE**   DEVELOP   PRACTISE   APPLY

London neighbourhoods

5a 🔊 audio 2/15

Listen to the podcast.
Match the neighbourhoods with the pictures.

A Golders Green	B Southall
C Chinatown	D Brixton

5b CHOOSE YOUR LEVEL skill: listening p. 151, workbook p. 60/6-8

I Listen to the podcast again and take notes. Complete the sentences and write them down.

1 Many tourists visit ???.
2 In ??? you can try dishes from many South Asian countries.
3 Many people in ??? have an African or Caribbean background.
4 The largest Jewish community in London lives in ???.

II Listen to the podcast again. Choose the correct information and write it down.

1 Chinatown
  A Chinese immigrants have lived here for over 200 years.
  B There is no parade for Chinese New Year in Chinatown in December.

2 Southall
  A Southall is in South London.
  B Many people who live here have an Indian background.

3 Brixton
  A You can hear more than 130 different languages here.
  B Over 50% of the population in Brixton has an African or Caribbean background.

4 Golders Green
  A Only Jewish people live here.
  B Many of the people who live in Golders Green have German or Polish roots.

III Listen to the podcast again. What do you learn about each neighbourhood?
Write down two or more facts for each.

PEOPLE & PLACES 4 video 11

Multicultural London

Britain has always been multicultural and people from different countries have moved there for centuries. After the Second World War, many people came to Britain from former British colonies, for example from India, Pakistan, Hong Kong and some African countries. Many people came to Britain – and especially to London – because they hoped to find better jobs there. The people who came to Britain brought their cultures and languages with them. London is the melting pot of these cultures and is one of the most multicultural cities in the world. You can hear more than three hundred different languages in London. In some parts of London you can see the strong influence of the different groups. For example, many people from Bangladesh live in East London. The most famous area there is Brick Lane where you can even see street signs in Bengali, a language that is mainly spoken in Bangladesh and India. Other languages that a large number of people in London speak include Polish, Turkish, Gujarati, Punjabi or Urdu.

What languages do your classmates speak? Make a survey in your class.

The Grandparent Project

6a

What do you think: what is "The Grandparent Project"?

6b   skill: mediation p. 155

Your grandparents have found this website. Tell them in German what it is about.

---
    x   –

Connecting children & grandparents all over the world

This programme helps children all over the world to write their grandparents' stories and learn about their family history.

→ Interview your grandparents and listen to their story.
→ Write your grandparents' story. If you like, you can put it into a digital or printed book format, make a drawing or create a multimedia series.
→ Learn important creative storytelling and life skills.

6c

What questions would you ask in an interview for the Grandparent Project? Collect ideas in class.

Edyta's life story – part one

7a audio 2/18

Ava has decided to take part in the Grandparent Project and talks to her grandmother Edyta in Poland on the phone. Listen and read along. Who do they talk about?

Ava: Hi Grandma. Thanks for helping me with this project.

Edyta: Of course. I'm looking forward to talking to you about our family history. Where would you like to start?

Ava: Maybe with your parents? I know that my great-grandfather left Poland and came to England. Can you tell me more about it?

Edyta: Of course. My father, your great-grandfather Radek, was a pilot. When World War II began in 1939, he and many other Polish pilots went to England and joined the Royal Air Force to help fight the Nazis.

Ava: That sounds very dangerous. Did he often talk about it?

Edyta: To tell you the truth, my father didn't really talk a lot about the war. Only that it was a terrible time and that he was lucky to be alive.

Ava: And what happened after the war?

Edyta: He decided that he wanted to stay in Britain.

Ava: And how did he meet your mother?

Edyta: Oh, he knew her already. She was from the same town in Poland as he was. They had kept in touch over the years. So, in 1946 my mother – your great-grandmother Agata – left Poland and emigrated to Great Britain to marry him and start a new life in London.

Ava: How did she feel about it? Was it hard for her to move to a foreign country?

Edyta: It wasn't easy at first. She didn't speak any English and she was homesick. But they lived in a neighbourhood with a lot of Polish people, so she could manage. She also learnt to speak English, and after a while she felt at home. And then my oldest brother, Pavel, was born in 1951.

Ava: And when was your brother Jan born?

Edyta: Jan was born in 1955 and then I was born in 1958 …

7b CHOOSE YOUR LEVEL skill: reading p. 154, workbook p. 61/9-10

I **Read the dialogue again. What do you learn about Edyta's mother Agata? Take notes.**

II **Read the dialogue again. What do you learn about Edyta's father Radek? Take notes.**

III **Read the dialogue again. What do you learn about Edyta's parents? Take notes.**

Edyta's life story – part two

8a wordbank: talking about pictures p. 166

Look at the pictures. What do you think happened in Edyta's life?

8b audio 2/19, skill: reading p. 154

Listen to the dialogue and read along. What does Edyta say about speaking Polish?

Ava: You looked so cute when you were a baby. I remember the old photo of you in your funny baby dress …

Edyta: Ha, ha. That was the latest fashion for babies then! But I had a wonderful childhood. We lived in a nice house and I loved playing in our garden.

Ava: You speak English and Polish. How did you learn to speak both languages?

Edyta: Well, at school I always spoke English, and at home we mostly spoke Polish. It was very important to my parents that my brothers and I were able to speak Polish with our relatives in Poland.

Ava: It's a shame that I don't speak Polish that well. When I want to talk to people in Poland, we have to mix English and Polish. Did you have Polish lessons at school?

Edyta: No, I didn't. But I went to a Polish

theatre group once a week. That's where I met your grandad Filip.

Ava: He was Polish, too, wasn't he?

Edyta: Actually, we were both British. We just came from Polish families.

Ava: Oh. Right. But you still spoke Polish at home. That's why Dad can speak Polish a lot better than Noah, Joshua and me.

Edyta: Yes, we both wanted to keep that part of our family history and heritage alive. We often spent the summer holidays in Poland when your father was little.

Ava: Yes, he told us about that. He really liked it there. But back to you. What about your job? Did you like it?

Edyta: Yes, I did. I very much liked working as a nurse, and when your father was old enough, I went back to my job.

Ava: Grandpa Filip died when Dad was still

ACTIVATE PRACTISE **DEVELOP** PRACTISE APPLY

quite young, didn't he? What was that like for you?

Edyta: Oh, that was a very sad time for all of us. Your father was at university in Manchester and I felt a bit lonely at that time, but then I began to visit my family in Poland more often.

Ava: And how did you get the idea to move to Poland?

Edyta: I liked it there. Life is short and I didn't want to think "what if …?" for the rest of my life. So, when my cousin in Warsaw suggested I should move to Poland, I thought "why not?" It felt right and like a new beginning.

Ava: Do you miss anything about London?

Edyta: Sure. I miss you. That's why I come to visit as often as I can. But Warsaw feels as much like home as London. I feel like I have two homes.

Ava: "Two homes". That's a good title for my story for the Grandparent Project. I think I have a lot to write about now.

Edyta: I really enjoyed talking to you. Just let me know if you want to know anything else about our family.

Ava: Thanks for answering all my questions.

Edyta: You're welcome, darling.

8c   CHOOSE YOUR LEVEL   skill: writing p. 153, media worksheet 11

I Choose three or more of the pictures from 8a and write speech or thought bubbles for Edyta.

II Choose two or more of the pictures from 8a and write Edyta's diary entries for those days.

You can write:

Dear diary,

Today was a great day. I …

…

III Choose three or more of the pictures from 8a and write letters that Edyta wrote to friends on those days.

> *London, 24 March 1982*
>
> *Dear Janina,*
>
> *Today, I …*
>
> *Love,*
> *Edyta*

8d   wordbank: family history p. 166, workbook p. 63/11–13

What does 'home' mean to you? Is it a place? A feeling? People? Share your thoughts in class.

Tell us more

9 CHOOSE YOUR TASK   A+B: wordbank: family history p. 166, C: skill: searching the Internet p. 157, media worksheet 6

A **Create a picture or collage about what 'home' means to you and label it. You can also include sayings like "Home is where the heart is".**

B **What were important events in your own life? Make a timeline.**

C **Find a map of London on the Internet. Choose a neighbourhood that looks interesting to you. Find out more about it. Then write a fact file.**

Interviewing grandparents

10 CHOOSE YOUR LEVEL grammar: simple past (R) p. 185, workbook p. 64/14-15

Read the following answers to interview questions. Write questions to the answers.

I
1 My father was from Italy.
2 My mother had two brothers.
3 My parents got married in 1952.
4 I went to school in Exeter.

You can write:
Where was ...?
How many ... did ...?
When did ...?

II
1 My mother was born in Egypt.
2 My father had two brothers and a sister.
3 My parents moved to Liverpool in 1955.
4 Yes, I did. I liked going to school a lot.

III
1 My parents were both born in Turkey.
2 My parents left Turkey in 1953.
3 We moved to York when I was eight years old.
4 Yes, they did. My parents always spoke Turkish with us children.
5 No, we didn't. We never went on holiday.

Adjectives and nouns

11a

Match all the adjectives to the nouns. There can be more than one solution.

better · first · foreign · happy ·
Polish · friendly · best · sad ·
wonderful · good · strong

job · memory · place · relatives · time ·
accent · language · roots · family · childhood ·
life · part · people · country · background

11b

Use your expressions from 11a and write five or more sentences.

How to pronounce the letter *s*

12a   audio 2/21

Listen and repeat.

parks · things · roots · parents ·
brothers · neighbourhoods · exhibitions ·
towns · accents · relatives · bikes ·
groups · immigrants · friends

12b

Make two lists in your exercise book and listen again. Write the words in your lists.

/s/	/z/
parks	things
...	...

12c   audio 2/22

Listen and check your lists.

DIGITAL+ practise more 20

ACTIVATE   PRACTISE   DEVELOP   **PRACTISE**   APPLY

A life story TARGET TASK

13 ▨ ▣ workbook p.65/16, wordbank: family history p.166, media worksheet 1

Your task is to present someone's life story.
Before you start, look at these steps:

STEP 1

Decide whose life story you want to present. You could choose:
· yourself
· someone from your family
· a famous person
· someone from a book or film
· …

STEP 2

Think of questions you would like to ask the person
and decide how you want to present his or her life story.
You could:
· create a poster
· create a photo story with speech and thought bubbles
· create a collage with labels
· create a timeline with photos
· write a text about the person's life
· …

My great-grandmother's
life story

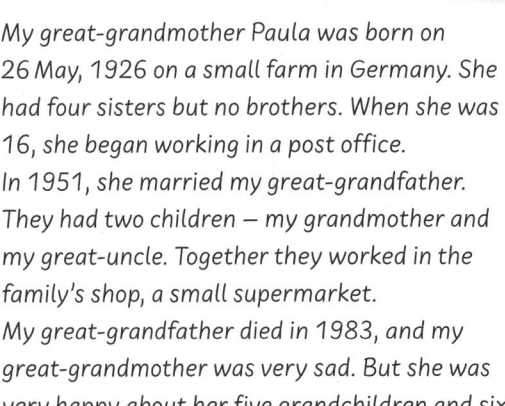

My great-grandmother Paula was born on
26 May, 1926 on a small farm in Germany. She
had four sisters but no brothers. When she was
16, she began working in a post office.
In 1951, she married my great-grandfather.
They had two children — my grandmother and
my great-uncle. Together they worked in the
family's shop, a small supermarket.
My great-grandfather died in 1983, and my
great-grandmother was very sad. But she was
very happy about her five grandchildren and six
great-grandchildren. She died when she was 96.

STEP 3

Find out as much as you can about the person's life story.
Think about:
· his or her family background (parents, grandparents, …)
· different places where the person lived
· important people in the person's life
· the person's school, university, job, …
· …

STEP 4

Create your work.

STEP 5

Present your work.

How are you today?

1 skill: talking with people p. 152, wordbank: feelings p. 167, workbook p. 66/1

Work in small groups.
How are you feeling today?
Talk to each other.

You can say:

I'm happy today because …
I'm a bit sad because …
I feel OK. How about you?

What's up?

2a wordbank: talking about pictures p. 166

Look at the pictures. Describe the situations. What do you think: how are the people feeling?

You can say:

In picture A, there are …
They are …
The boy looks …
I think the girl on the left is feeling …
…

2b audio 3/1, skill: listening p. 151

Listen to the dialogues. Which picture from 2a goes with which dialogue?

2c

Read the three dialogues. What are the problems?

1 **Louise:** Hi Emily! What's wrong? You look sad.
Emily: Hi Louise. Oh, it's about Chloe. We had an argument.
Louise: Why, what happened?
Emily: She wanted to copy my French homework. But I said no because I know that Mr Henderson always notices, and that she should do her homework herself.
Louise: Yeah, he is a very strict teacher.
Emily: But now Chloe is so angry with me that she won't even talk to me anymore.
Louise: Don't worry. I'm sure she'll soon realize that she is wrong. Should I try to talk to her?
Emily: Thanks, Louise – that would be great!

2 Toby: Hi guys. Anyone up for hanging out at my place this afternoon?
Paul: Er – what day is it today?
Jack: It's Tuesday. I'm in!
Paul: Aw man – I have maths tuition.
Toby: Why don't you ask your mum if you can skip the lesson?
Paul: I don't think that she will let me. She always says that it is important for me to go. She's not happy with my marks. Just because I got a D in my last test …
Jack: And what does your dad say?
Paul: Oh, no chance, he is even stricter! He always tells me that I have to follow through with everything. No skipping allowed! It's really annoying. What if I join you guys later?
Toby: Yeah, good idea. We'll save some snacks for you!
Paul: That would be great. Thanks, guys.

3 Faisal: Guys, have you heard about James and Delia? Delia invited James to her party, but she says that he won't come.
Linda: Why not? What happened? We're all going to the party!
Faisal: She says that he says that her party will be lame – because she didn't invite his rugby friends.
Matt: But Delia doesn't even know his rugby friends!
Faisal: Exactly. Why should she invite people that she doesn't know?
Matt: I think she's right. Why should she?
Faisal: Now James is angry and says that he doesn't even want to go to Delia's party. He's telling everybody that he'll have his own party on that day – with HIS friends only!
Linda: That's so silly. Delia must be really upset. I'll go and talk to her.

2d CHOOSE YOUR LEVEL skill: reading p.154

I Match the sentence parts. Write the sentences in your exercise book.

1 Emily tells Louise that
2 Louise thinks that
3 Paul explains to his friends that
4 Delia says that

A he has to go to maths tuition before he can join them.
B James won't come to her party.
C Chloe is wrong.
D she is sad because she had an argument with Chloe.

II Are the sentences true or false? Copy the true sentences and correct the false sentences.

1 Emily tells Louise that she is sad because she got a bad mark in maths.
2 Louise thinks that Chloe is right.
3 Paul has to go to maths tuition on Fridays.
4 Paul says that his mum is even stricter than his dad.
5 Delia wants to invite James's rugby friends to her party.

III Complete the sentences.

1 Emily tells Louise that she … because …
2 Chloe is angry because Emily …
3 Paul has to go to maths tuition because … and …
4 Paul's dad always tells Paul that he …
5 Delia says that she … and that James …
6 James is … and plans to have …

2e workbook p.66/2

Choose one of the situations from 2c and write down what you think will happen next.

GRAMMAR HELP reported speech 1 p. 186

Wenn du wiedergeben möchtest, was jemand anderes sagt, benutzt du indirekte Rede *(reported speech)*.
Schau dir die Sätze an und achte dabei vor allem auf die Pronomen und die Verbformen. Was fällt dir auf?

Direkte Rede:
Louise: "You look sad."
Emily: "We had an argument."
Emily: "Chloe wanted to copy my French homework."

Paul: "I have maths tuition."

Indirekte Rede:
Louise tells Emily <u>that</u> she looks sad.
Emily says <u>that</u> they had an argument.
Emily says <u>that</u> Chloe wanted to copy her French homework.
Paul says <u>that</u> he has maths tuition.

Auf Seite 186 findest du weitere Beispiele und Erklärungen zur indirekten Rede.

Text messages

3   grammar: reported speech 1 p. 186, workbook p. 66/3-4   DIGITAL+ practise more

What do the people say in their text messages? Write it down.

1 James
Hi everyone, my party will be at my house this Saturday. We start at four! James

2 Matt
Hi James, I'm really sorry. I can't come to your party. I've already said yes to Delia's party. Matt

3 Faisal
Hi guys, I can get the present for Delia. It's OK if you all give me the money on Monday at school. Faisal

4 Phil
Hi James, I'll definitely be there and I'll bring my friends from the football team as well. Phil

5 James
Hi Phil, you can't bring your football friends! There are 12 rugby players here already. My parents say that's enough. James

You can write:
James says that …
Matt …
…

Feelings

4a   wordbank: feelings p. 167

How do you think the people are feeling? Make notes.

Mia

Eric

Michelle

Oliver

4b   audio 3/2, skill: listening p. 151, grammar: reported speech 1 p. 186

Listen to the statements and write down what the people say. Compare with your notes in 4a.

You can write:
Mia says that …
…

DIGITAL+ practise more 21

ACTIVATE   **PRACTISE**   DEVELOP   PRACTISE   APPLY

Lily's problem

5a

Read the text messages. Why does Lily want to talk to Noah?

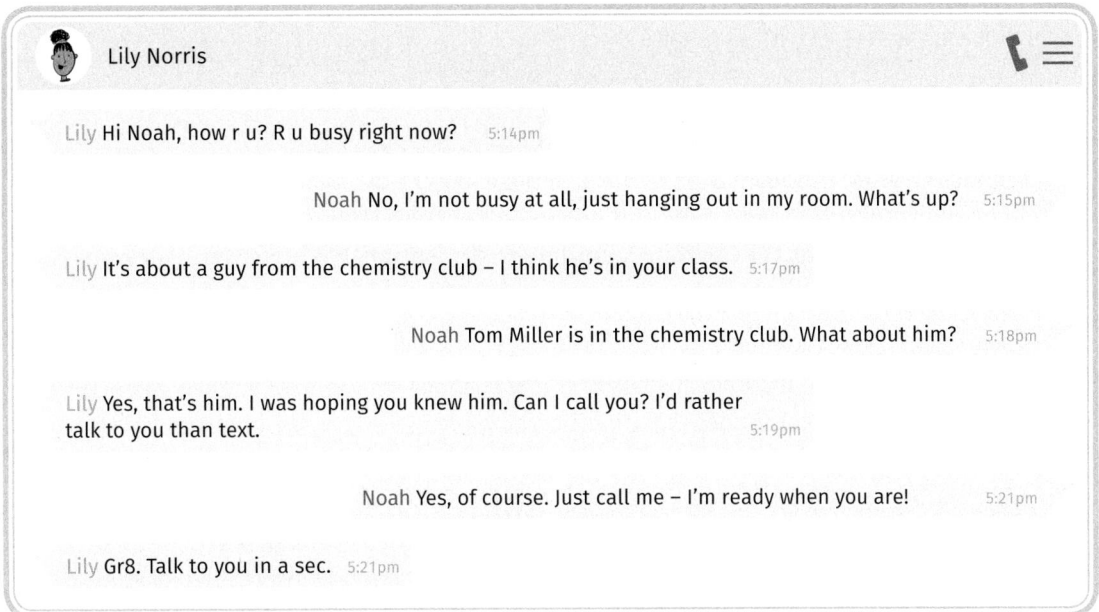

> **Lily Norris**
>
> Lily Hi Noah, how r u? R u busy right now? 5:14pm
>
> Noah No, I'm not busy at all, just hanging out in my room. What's up? 5:15pm
>
> Lily It's about a guy from the chemistry club – I think he's in your class. 5:17pm
>
> Noah Tom Miller is in the chemistry club. What about him? 5:18pm
>
> Lily Yes, that's him. I was hoping you knew him. Can I call you? I'd rather talk to you than text. 5:19pm
>
> Noah Yes, of course. Just call me – I'm ready when you are! 5:21pm
>
> Lily Gr8. Talk to you in a sec. 5:21pm

5b audio 3/3

Listen to Lily talking to Noah on the phone. What is Lily's problem?

5c CHOOSE YOUR LEVEL skill: listening p. 151

I Listen again.
Then write down Noah's ideas.

You can write:
Noah offers to …
He says that Lily could …

II Listen again and answer the questions.

1 Why did Lily tell Tom to delete the photo?
2 What was Tom's reaction when Lily asked him to delete the photo?
3 What do Lily's mums always say about the Internet?
4 What does Noah say Lily could do now?

III Listen again and answer the questions.

1 What is the problem with putting photos on the Internet?
2 What does Noah suggest Lily could do?
3 What does Noah say about such websites?
4 How does Lily feel at the end of the phone call?

5d skill: talking with people p. 152, workbook p. 68/5

Imagine you have a problem at school or at home. What could you do? Who could you talk to? Talk about it with a partner.

Seeking advice

6a

Look at the headline of the website.
What kind of content do you expect?

6b   skill: reading p. 154

Read the texts. Who is writing?
Who is the website for?

× –

✴ ✴ ✴ ✴ ✴ ✴ ✴ LONDON TEEN HELP – ASK OUR EXPERTS ONLINE ✴ ✴ ✴ ✴ ✴ ✴ ✴

1   **School, parents, friends – there's a lot that teenagers can feel worried about. If you
need advice, we're here to help and not to judge. Send your questions to our team
of trained experts at the London Teen Help Organisation. We'll answer every single
question and post some of them anonymously with our answers on this website.**

5   **Q** Dear expert,
I have a problem with this boy in the year above me. He took a photo of me with
his phone after school the other day. I look really silly in the photo and I told him
to delete it, but he said no. He says that the photo is his and that he can keep it and do
whatever he wants with it – even put it on the Internet. I really don't want that and I tried
10   to talk to him about it, but he only laughs at me. Now I don't know what else I can do to
stop him. He used to be really friendly, but I'm not talking to him at the moment. Can you
give me a piece of advice? Thanks a lot,
Sunnyday

  A *Dear Sunnyday,*
15   *I'm sorry to hear about your situation, but I'm sure there's a solution to your
problem. That boy has absolutely no right to keep or publish that photo. You did
not officially agree to anything so he must delete it if you say so. I suppose that he does not
know that he is doing something wrong. I suggest that you talk to him as soon as possible
to make that really clear to him. I would also suggest that you ask a parent or a teacher to*
20   *come with you to make sure that he realizes how serious the problem is.
All the best and good luck!
Your expert*

  Q Dear expert,
I am 13 years old and I have a problem with my parents. This is the situation:
25   my parents are very strict when it comes to online time. I am not allowed to be
online more than an hour per day which is not enough at all! That's just enough time to
do some work for school, check my messages and answer them. All my friends are online
all day. They chat and play online video games. I am completely left out unless I go to a
friend's house and go online with them. The reason my parents won't let me be online
30   more is that they worry about my marks. They think I won't do my homework if I spend
more time online, and they don't even listen to my arguments. Help! What can I do?
Lonelygirl

---

35 *Hi Lonelygirl,*
I know exactly how important it can be to be online. I'm sure that your parents
spend quite a bit of time online as well. Teenagers today live in a very digital world
– you use laptops or tablets at school and at home. Have you explained to them that you're
not only online for fun but that you also communicate with your classmates about school
matters, hand in school work online, do research and so on? Maybe you could keep a diary
to show your parents how much time you need for your online school work alone? You could
40 *also ask them for a trial phase in which you are allowed more time online, but you will also*
have to prove to them that your marks won't get worse. There are also official websites that
give parents an idea of how much screen time is OK for children and teenagers. I wish you
good luck!
Your expert

45 Dear expert,
I am 14 and I have a problem that I can't solve. There is this girl in the chemistry
club at my school and I really like her – but I am too shy to tell her. Last week,
after school, we walked home together and were joking around, taking funny pictures of
each other with our phones. She did not like one of the photos that I took of her – but I
50 think she looks cute in it, so I didn't want to delete it when she asked me to. I thought it
was really funny and told her that I might put the photo on the Internet. I just wanted to
tease her, but she got so angry with me that she doesn't look at me or talk to me anymore.
What can I do now? I really want her to like me again. Can you help me?
Anonymous

55 *Dear Anonymous,*
Why don't you talk to her again and apologize? You are definitely not allowed to keep
that photo or put it on the Internet – she has the right to make you delete it, you
know? And don't you think she might be happy if you tell her the real reason for keeping the
picture? Teasing her is definitely the wrong way. Just tell her that you like her. Good luck!
60 *Your expert*

6c CHOOSE YOUR LEVEL

I In your own words, describe Sunnyday's problem. Write three or more sentences.
Can you guess who Sunnyday is?

II In your own words, describe Sunnyday and Lonelygirl's problems.
Write three or more sentences for each person. Can you guess who Sunnyday is?

III In your own words, describe the people's problems. Write three or more sentences
for each person. Can you guess who Sunnyday and Anonymous are?

6d wordbank: expressing opinions p.165, skill: talking with people p.152, workbook p.68/6-9

Work in small groups and talk about the solutions that the experts suggest.
What do you think about their answers? Are they helpful? Have you got any other ideas?

Solving the problem

7 skill: writing p. 153, workbook p. 70/10-11

Work with a partner. Write a dialogue between Tom and Lily in which they try to solve the problem.

You can write:

Tom: I wanted to talk to you about …
Please listen to me and …
I'm sorry that … / I didn't mean to …
Lily: But you …
It's important to me that …
Tom / Lily: Why don't we …?
Let's …
…

A person to talk to

8a video 12, skill: watching a video clip p. 156

Watch the video clip.
Where does the woman work?

8b workbook p. 71/12

Watch the video clip again.
Who is the woman?
What does she talk about?

8c wordbank: expressing opinions p. 165

Do you think that talking to a school counsellor can be helpful? Why or why not?
Work with a partner and collect arguments.

8d

Use your arguments and have a discussion in class.

Sheree's problems

9 GET TOGETHER   audio 3/5

Get together with a partner.
Listen to Sheree's call to the teen helpline.

Partner A	Partner B
I Go to page 130.	I Go to page 139.
II Go to page 133.	II Go to page 142.
III Go to page 136.	III Go to page 145.

ACTIVATE PRACTISE **DEVELOP** PRACTISE APPLY

Dealing with feelings

10 CHOOSE YOUR TASK A: skill: performing a scene p. 159, media worksheet 2, 5, B: wordbank: feelings p. 167

A Work in groups or pairs and read out one of the dialogues from pages 90/91.
You can record your reading.

B Make a word search for a partner with words for feelings.

C Write a list of dos and don'ts for parents of teenagers. Think about the following aspects:
what to say or not to say to them, how to react to strong feelings, what to cook for them,
what to do about screen time etc.

Helping out

11 skill: mediation p. 155, workbook p. 71/13

**Bob is an exchange student at your school, and he does not speak much German.
He is upset because he has lost his rucksack. Help him to get it back.**

Bob: I can't find my rucksack! I think I left it
on the bus yesterday when we were on the
school trip. Could we call the bus company
and ask if they have found my rucksack?
(1) You: *Yes, sure. Let's look them up on the
Internet. Here they are. I'll call their office.
Guten Tag, ...*

Office manager: Wie spät war das denn?
Und wo genau hat er gesessen und welche
Farbe hat der Rucksack?
(2) You: *What time ...? And ...? What ...?*

Bob: It was about three in the afternoon
and I was sitting in the middle of the bus on
the left. It's a red rucksack
(3) You: ...

Office manager: Alles klar. Da muss ich mal
eben mit einem Kollegen sprechen, einen
Moment bitte. (...)
Ich habe eine gute Nachricht! Sie haben
einen roten Rucksack gefunden. Das muss
seiner sein. Ihr könntet ihn heute Nachmittag
abholen.
(4) You: ...

Bob: Oh great. Thank you very much.
Where do we have to pick it up?
(5) You: ...

Office manager: In der Husarenstraße 10.
Direkt beim Busbahnhof.
(6) You: ...

Your problem or mine?

12 workbook p. 72/14-15

Copy the sentences and fill in the correct words from the brackets.

1 Your brother is wrong: it's not your problem, it's ???. (he / our / his)
2 The photo belongs to me, it's ??? and I can do whatever I want with it. (mine / me / my)
3 She took my cap and now she says that it's ???. (she / my / hers)
4 Who left the dirty T-shirt in the living room? Is it ???? (your / yours / they)
5 The TV belongs to all of us, it's ???. (ours / us / our)
6 Do you think the rubbish in our garden belongs to our neighbours? - Yes, I think it's ???.
   (their / theirs / they)

Linking parts

13 CHOOSE YOUR LEVEL

▌ Match the sentence parts and write down the sentences.

1 I feel stressed   A and don't allow me to stay up late.
2 My parents are really strict   B when I have too much homework.
3 I'm angry with my brother   C because I can't go to my friend's party.
4 I'm really sad   D but he only laughs at me.

▌▌ Choose the correct linking word and write down the sentences.

1 I always feel sad when / but my parents have an argument.
2 My friend is angry because / and I forgot her birthday.
3 I got a very rude message from a classmate when / and I definitely won't answer it.
4 My sister can stay up late because / but I have to be in bed by nine.

▌▌▌ Make one sentence out of two. Choose a linking word from the   but · and · before ·
    box. There are more than you need. Write down your sentences.   when · so that · because

1 I got a really bad mark. I didn't have enough time to prepare for the test.
2 I don't like my new classmate. She doesn't like me either.
3 My parents don't like it. I spend too much time online.
4 My parents are usually very strict. Sometimes they let me stay up late.

How to pronounce the letters *th*

14 audio 3/10

Listen to the words and repeat them. Then sort them into two lists:
words with /ð/ as in "this" and words with /θ/ as in "thanks".

this · thanks · that · think · thought · then · through · there · they

DIGITAL+ practise more 21

ACTIVATE   PRACTISE   DEVELOP   **PRACTISE**   APPLY

Giving a helping hand TARGET TASK

15 🔲 🔲 workbook p. 73/16, wordbank: seeking and giving advice p. 167, skill: performing a scene p. 159, media worksheet 2

Your task is to prepare a scene about helping somebody.
Before you start, look at these steps:

STEP 1

Work in small groups. Choose a situation in which you can give advice or help, for example:
· A friend always panics before tests.
· A classmate tells you that his or her best friend says bad things behind his or her back.
· The new pupil in your class looks very sad and lonely.
· ...

STEP 2

Make notes for your scene. You can look at the box for help. You do not have to write the complete script but you can write cue cards for each character.

Think about what you can do.	You can sit next to him or her. · You can spend time with him or her. · You can try to talk to ... · ...
Think about what you can say.	You are not alone. · It's not your fault. · Maybe you could ... · Maybe it would help to ... · ...
Ask questions to find out more.	What exactly is the problem? · Why ...? · Do you think ...? · Are you afraid of ...? · ...
Talk about your experience.	When I had this problem, I ... · I've tried ... · I know someone who ... · He / She ... · ...
Think about who else could help.	What about the school counsellor? · Could you talk to your parents? · Could you ask a teacher for advice? · ...

STEP 3

Decide who will play which part and practise your scene.

STEP 4

Perform your scene. If you like, you can film your scene and show it to the rest of the class.

Check out

Kannst du einem Blogeintrag Informationen entnehmen?	Workbook, p. 74
Kannst du über vergangene Ereignisse schreiben?	Workbook, p. 74
Kannst du einen Podcast über Stadtteile in London verstehen?	Workbook, p. 74
Kannst du verstehen, worum es geht, wenn jemand über ein Problem spricht?	Workbook, p. 75
Kannst du wiedergeben, was jemand sagt?	Workbook, p. 75
Kannst du deine Meinung zu einem Problem äußern?	Workbook, p. 75

Wrong impressions

A couple of months ago, my English teacher, Mr Rogers, kept me behind after class and asked me if I could help a student from another class with her work for English Literature because she didn't like to read and wasn't doing well in her exams.

I wasn't too happy about that, especially when he said, "It's Marianne Hamilton from your year."

Until that day I had talked to Marianne exactly three times.
The first time was in the queue at lunch break. She said, "Oh, could you pass me a fork, please? I forgot to take one," and I said, "Yeah sure. Here you are." The second time was during the music project all the students in our year did together. She said, "Could you move your chair, please?" and I said, "Yeah sure. Sorry."

The third time was in our school library. I was there with my friends having fun when she said, "Could you please be quiet? Some people are actually trying to work here," and I said, "Yeah sure."
Well, anyway, I had always been a bit shy around Marianne, but because of how she behaved in the library, I decided that she was probably quite boring and one of those students who are good at everything and always on time and always do their homework and always study for hours before exams. I don't like studying too much. I'm good at English by accident. I just like reading and writing about what I've read. That helps a lot.

"If you help Marianne for about one hour every week, I can let that count as your group project for this year," Mr Rogers went on. At my school we have to do one group project in English every year. I like reading but I hate doing group projects. It's always a lot of work, and we have to do a presentation at the end. I wasn't sure what was worse, but then I thought I may as well give it a try so I said, "Yeah, OK, I'll help her."
"Brilliant!" Mr Rogers said and seemed very happy. He told me to come back to his room at the end of the school day. Marianne would be there, too, and we would work out a plan together. In the afternoon, Marianne was there, but she didn't seem to be too excited about Mr Rogers' idea, either. All she said was, "Yes. OK. Yes, Saturday works for me. We can meet at my house. Just give me your phone number and I'll text you my address." Which she did.
On Saturday, Marianne's mum let me in. The house was really nice – lots of comfy chairs and pictures on the walls. Marianne's mum seemed nice, too. She gave us a plate of biscuits and some lemonade and told us to have fun. I wasn't sure I'd have much fun in the next hour but at least there were biscuits. Really good chocolate biscuits.
We went upstairs and Marianne opened the door to her room. It was full of books!

impression = *Eindruck*; exam = *Prüfung*; queue = *Schlange*; to behave = *sich verhalten*; to count = *zählen*; upstairs = *nach oben*

Really, there were books all over the place! In shelves on the walls, in piles on the floor, next to her bed, on her bed, on her desk – everywhere.

"Whoa," I said, "I thought you didn't like reading?"

"Who says I don't like reading?" she said, "I LOVE reading. It's just that I didn't like the first book we had to read in Year 7. I hated it. I don't like books with animals as the main characters. I think they're silly. I think we should read books about real people. So I wrote what I thought was bad about the book. But apparently, it is Mr Rogers' favourite book of all time and ever since then he has had it in his head that I don't get literature and that I'm not good with books. I can say and write and do whatever I want – he has this image of me and I can't change it. I've tried to get into Ms Williams' English Literature class, but I seem to be stuck with Mr Rogers."

"That's not fair of him," I said, "I liked the book but maybe only because my dad read it to my sister and me when we were younger. I'm not sure I would like it as much otherwise. But now Mr Rogers seems to like me and I get good marks."

"See?" Marianne said, "He's got this opinion and it's really hard to change it. I really like the book we're reading now, but I'm sure he won't give me anything better than a C. So, why bother? What are you reading at the moment?"

"*Noah can't even*," I said, "It's about a boy who's …"

"Oh, I've read it," Marianne interrupted me, "I loved it. Have you ever read this one?" and she pulled a book from the pile next to her bed.

We spent the next three hours discussing books, and Marianne let me borrow five of her books that I hadn't read yet. I didn't help her with her homework at all, but we had a good time and set a date for Marianne to come to my place so that she could borrow some of my books.

From then on, we spent all our "lessons" talking about books and reading. When Mr Rogers asked how it was going, we always smiled and told him that we were working hard and that Marianne was doing very well.

The day before her next exam, we studied a little but not too much. Then we went out for ice cream. The next day Marianne told me that the exam questions had been quite easy and that she had answered all of them.

Three days later Marianne got her very first A in an English exam. She told me that Mr Rogers had smiled at her when he returned her exam paper and said: "That was very well done. I'm happy that my plan worked out so well."

pile = *Stapel, Haufen*; image = *Bild*; to be stuck = *festhängen*; to bother = *sich Mühe geben*; to interrupt = *unterbrechen*

On the Move Again

You know
You gotta go.
No time to grieve
You just gotta leave.

Get away from the pain
On the move again.

Take the train.
Catch a plane.

Make the trip
In a ship.

Take a hike
Ride a bike.

Go by car.
Going far.

Use your feet
On the street.

Get stuck
In a truck.

Then you arrive
And you're alive.

What you leave behind
Won't leave your mind.

But home is where you find it.
Home is where you find it.
Home is where you find it.
Home is where you find it.

Michael Rosen

1. Look at the pictures. What can you see?
2. What can you do with the objects?
3. Which of the objects do you use? Which of them would you like to use? Why?

Everyday science

Part A Inventions

- You will read about different inventions.
- You will learn how to write about inventions and their inventors.
- You will present your ideas for a new invention.

Part B Communication

- You will read about a project week at Holland Park School.
- You will watch a presentation.
- You will give a three-minute talk about one aspect of the history of communication.

Everyday objects

1a

What objects from your everyday life could you not live without? Talk about them in class.

You can say:
I couldn't live without ...
I really need ...

1b

Look at these pictures. Match them to the definitions.

1
2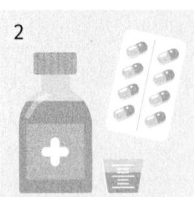
3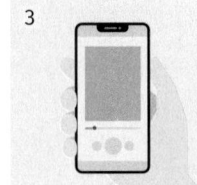
4
5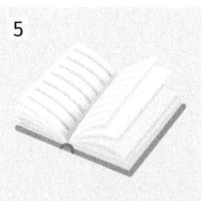
6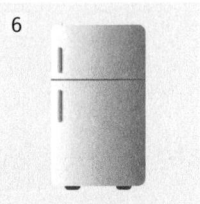

A A telephone that has apps for entertainment, education and more.
B A type of transport which has two wheels and needs muscle power to move.
C Lots of pages with text that was written by an author.
D A small computer that you can take with you.
E An electric cupboard which you use to keep your food cool.
F Something that helps you to get better when you are ill.

1c skill: talking with people p. 152, workbook p. 76/1

Which of the objects from 1b do you find most important? Why? Share your thoughts with a partner.

You can say:
I think the ... is most important because ...
In my opinion, ... is not very important.

British inventions

2a

Look at the pictures. Which invention do you think came first, which came last? Work with a partner. Try to put the inventions in the correct order.

telephone

toothbrush

TV

steam locomotive

ACTIVATE PRACTISE DEVELOP PRACTISE APPLY

2b

Read the article. Did you put the inventions in the correct order?

British inventions

British inventors are very creative. Let's have a closer look at some of their inventions.

The toothbrush

People have always found ways to clean their teeth, but toothbrushes as we know them today were invented in 1780 by a man named William Addis. His toothbrush was made of horsehair and cow bone. The basic design of the toothbrush has not changed much, but today other materials, such as plastic, are used.

The steam locomotive

In 1802, the first high-pressure steam engine for locomotives was invented by Richard Trevithick. In the 1820s Robert and George Stephenson built a steam locomotive that could pull passenger trains. Soon this invention was used all over the world. Today, most trains are pulled by locomotives with electric or diesel engines.

The telephone

The telephone was invented in 1876. It was patented by Alexander Graham Bell from Scotland, but the American Thomas Watson helped him with his invention. The first phone call was made between the two men in the same building. Soon long-distance phone calls were possible as well, but they were extremely expensive. In 1927, the first three minutes of the first transatlantic telephone call cost $75 – half the price of a car at that time.

The television

Many scientists are credited with inventing the television, but the first working television was presented in London in 1927 by John Logie Baird.

2c CHOOSE YOUR LEVEL skill: reading p.154, workbook p.76/2

▌ Match the sentence parts and write down the sentences.

1 William Addis invented a toothbrush that	A could pull passenger trains.
2 Steam locomotives	B were extremely expensive.
3 The first telephone calls	C was made of horsehair and cow bone.

▌▌ Copy the sentences and complete them.

1 The basic design of the ??? has not changed much.
2 Steam locomotives were used all over the ???.
3 The first ??? was made between Bell and Watson in the same building.
4 The first working ??? was presented in London in 1927.

▌▌▌ Read again and take notes for each invention. What was invented?
Who invented it and when? Write one statement or more about each invention.

GRAMMAR HELP the passive p. 187

Aktivsätze stellen den oder die Handelnden in den Vordergrund. Bei Passivsätzen dagegen ist es nebensächlich oder nicht bekannt, wer oder was handelt. Die Handlung selbst steht im Vordergrund. Sieh dir die Beispielsätze an. Was fällt dir auf?

An author wrote lots of pages.	Lots of pages were written by an author.
Many people used this invention.	This invention was used by many people.
Today, electric engines pull many trains.	Today, many trains are pulled by electric engines.

Weitere Erklärungen findest du auf Seite 187.
Die Liste mit den unregelmäßigen Verbformen findest du auf den Seiten 255 bis 257.

Inventions

3a   grammar: passive p. 187

Unscramble the sentences and write them down.

1 invented – a lot of things – by British inventors – were
2 by William Addis – was – the first toothbrush – invented
3 was – the first steam locomotive – in Britain – built
4 in Scotland – of the telephone – born – the inventor – was
5 was – Alexander Graham Bell – patented – the telephone – by

3b   grammar: passive p. 187, workbook p. 76/3

Copy the sentences and complete them with words from the box.

1 Many scientists ??? with inventing the television.
2 The fridge ??? to keep your food cool.
3 A laptop is a small computer that ??? anywhere.
4 Steam locomotives ??? by railway companies.
5 Before the telephone ???, more letters ???.

> is used · were used · was invented ·
> can be taken · are credited · were written

Important inventions

4   grammar: passive p. 187, workbook p. 77/4-5

Rewrite the sentences in the passive.

1 Doctors give medicine to sick people.
2 A British inventor invented the telescope.
3 William Addis made the modern toothbrush.
4 In the 1820s, steam locomotives pulled trains.
5 Thomas Watson helped Alexander Graham Bell.
6 Many people around the world watch TV programmes.

You can write:

Medicine is given to sick people by …
…

A day out

5a

Look at Ava's computer screen.
What is on at the London Science Museum?

London Science Museum

- Section on science and medicine
- Exhibition about clock design
- Display about Stephen Hawking
- Everyday technology section

5b 🎵 audio 3/12

Listen to Ava, Lily and Harry. What are they talking about?

5c   CHOOSE YOUR LEVEL   skill: listening p. 151

▌ **Listen again and choose the correct answer.**

1 Which section of the London Science Museum ist Ava excited about?
   A science and medicine   B everyday technology   C clock design

2 Who was Stephen Hawking?
   A Ava's neighbour   B an inventor   C a scientist

3 What is the everyday technology section about?
   A inventions that have changed our lives   B the history of computers   C space travel

▌▌ **Listen again. Match the sentence parts and write down the sentences.**

1 Ava's mum is going to take Ava and her brothers   A on different topics or people.
2 Ava is really excited   B inventions that have changed our lives.
3 There are always special exhibitions   C to the London Science Museum.
4 The everyday technology section is about   D about the everyday technology section.

▌▌▌ **Listen again and answer the questions.**

1 What is Ava's opinion about art and science museums?
2 What can you see at the London Science Museum?
3 Who was Stephen Hawking and what did he discover?
4 What is Ava really excited about?
5 What do Lily and Harry think about Ava's day out and what do they decide to do?

5d 🎵 🖼 skill: searching the Internet p. 157, media worksheet 6, workbook p. 78/6

What would you like to see at the London Science Museum?
Find out more on the Internet and tell your class.

ACTIVATE   PRACTISE   **DEVELOP**   PRACTISE   APPLY

Visiting the London Science Museum

6   skill: mediation p. 155

You are at the London Science Museum. A German family does not understand the visitor information. Help them and answer their questions in German.

TICKETS

The museum is free to visit.
To avoid long waits, we recommend you book a free ticket online in advance.

OPENING TIMES

The museum is open from Wednesday to Sunday from 10am to 6pm.
Exhibition areas start to close 30 minutes before the museum closes.

FOOD AND DRINK

1. There are several cafés in the museum.
2. You are welcome to bring your own food and drink, which can be eaten in the picnic area outside.
3. Eating in the exhibition rooms is not allowed.

GETTING HERE

The museum is located on Exhibition Road in South Kensington. The nearest tube station is South Kensington.

PLEASE NOTE

We are currently rebuilding and renovating some of our exhibitions. To find out which exhibitions are closed, please see our home page.

1   Was muss man zum Thema Tickets wissen?
2   Wie sieht es mit den Öffnungszeiten aus?
3   Wo im Museum kann man etwas essen?

4   Wie kommt man zum Museum?
5   Was muss man sonst noch beachten?

Everyday technology

7a

**Read the info texts that Ava and her friends saw at the London Science Museum.
What objects did they look at?**

Everyday technology that ... *saves time and is practical*

Zip

When you look around you – how many zips can you count?
They are everywhere! On trousers, jackets, bags, rucksacks, ...
Just imagine how long it would take to button all these things.
But that's what people did until the 1930s when zips were first
used for clothes. Although early versions of the zip appeared
from the 1870s onwards, it took until then for the clothes
industry to discover how useful zips can be.

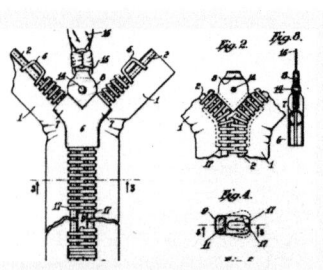

construction drawing for one of the first zips

Everyday technology that ... *saves lives*
Seat belts

Before the invention of the modern seat belt, people either used a very uncomfortable version of a seat belt or no seat belt at all. Early seat belts were simple straps of leather that you fastened in front of you like a belt. They kept you in your seat but did not really prevent injuries. But in the 1950s, Swedish engineer Nils Bohlin invented the kind of seat belt that looks like the letter Y. It is a lot more comfortable and safer and is still used in cars today.

Nils Bohlin presenting his invention in 1958

Everyday technology that ... *keeps food fresh*
Tins and tin openers

For centuries, people looked for ways to keep food from going bad, especially meat and fish. To solve this problem, Peter Durand came up with the idea of the tin in 1810. If you put food inside tins, close them very tightly and then heat them, the food inside the tins can be stored for a long time and the food inside can still be eaten years later. Unfortunately, the tin opener was only invented in 1870. Until then, people had to use other tools to open their tins.

an early tin

Everyday technology that ... *was invented by accident*
Penicillin

Until 1942, a small wound or scratch could actually kill you if it became infected with bacteria. But in 1928, Alexander Fleming accidentally discovered penicillin, the first antibiotic that helped cure these infections. He was tidying up some Petri dishes with different bacteria in his lab when he noticed something unusual on one dish – there were bacteria all over the dish except for one area where some mould was growing. Apparently, the mould was killing the bacteria. This discovery was the beginning of modern antibiotics. It is estimated that penicillin has saved at least 200 million lives since its first use as a medicine in 1942.

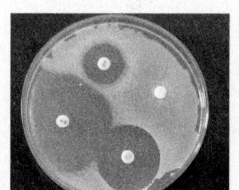
antibiotic mould killing bacteria

7b CHOOSE YOUR LEVEL skill: reading p. 154, workbook p. 78/7

Ⅰ Read the info texts again and match the sentence parts.

1 First versions of a zip
2 Until the 1930s,
3 The first seat belts
4 The tin opener

A did not prevent injuries.
B was only invented in 1870.
C zips were not used on clothes.
D appeared from the 1870s onwards.

Ⅱ Read the info texts again and complete the sentences.

1 The clothes industry discovered very late how ???.
2 Early ??? were simple straps of ???.
3 For centuries, ??? had problems ???.
4 You can store food for a long time if you ???.

Ⅲ Read the info texts again and answer the questions.

1 When was the zip invented and when did the clothes industry start using it?
2 What is the difference between early seat belts and modern ones?
3 Why did Peter Durand invent the tin?
4 How did Alexander Fleming discover penicillin?

PEOPLE & PLACES 5   video 13

The Industrial Revolution

What we call the "Industrial Revolution" began about 300 years ago in the UK. From the 1730s on, a lot of new inventions in different fields such as farming, travelling and industry changed everyday life dramatically. These inventions were soon adopted all over the world. One of the most important inventions was probably the steam engine that was improved by James Watt in 1765. This modified steam engine made production processes quicker and cheaper – more things could be produced in less time by fewer people. Of course, these inventions had and still have

both positive and negative impacts on people's lives, but without them, life as we know it is impossible to imagine.

What positive and negative aspects of the Industrial Revolution can you think of? Share your thoughts in class.

Useful inventions?

8a   video 14, skill: watching a video clip p. 156

Watch the video clip. What is George watching on TV and why? What inventions are presented? You can take notes in German.

8b   wordbank: inventions p. 168, workbook p. 79/8-9

How useful are the inventions to you and why? Rate each one from 1 (not useful at all) to 10 (very useful). Compare your ratings with a partner.

Writing about inventions

9   CHOOSE YOUR TASK   A+B: wordbank: inventions p. 168, C: skill: writing p. 153, workbook p. 80/10

A   **Make a list of inventions that you could live without. You can use a dictionary.**

B   **Write quiz cards for a partner. Describe an invention. Your partner has to guess what it is. Take turns.**

You can write:

You use it to see when it is dark.

You can use it when there is no electricity.

…

C   **Imagine there was no electricity last Tuesday. Write about your day.**

There was no electricity last Tuesday. In the morning, I got up really late because my mobile didn't work. I couldn't listen to music while I had breakfast. Then …

Visiting a German museum

10 skill: mediation p. 155, media worksheet 2, 5

You want to take a British friend to the Technik Museum in Speyer. Look at the brochure and work with a partner. He or she plays the role of your friend and asks you two or more questions in English about the museum. Take turns. You can record your dialogues.

TECHNIK MUSEUM SPEYER

Im nahe der Innenstadt von Speyer gelegenen Technik Museum erwarten Sie mehr als 3000 Ausstellungsstücke: Flugzeuge, klassische Automobile, Lokomotiven, U-Boote, Schiffe und viele andere technische Meisterleistungen. Zu den größten Attraktionen zählen eine Boeing 747, die russische Raumfähre BURAN und das voll zugängliche U-Boot U9.

Wir haben **365 Tage im Jahr geöffnet**.
Montag bis Freitag: 9–18 Uhr
Samstag, Sonntag, Feiertage: 9–19 Uhr
+ +
Unser **Restaurant** bietet jeweils von 9 bis 18 Uhr eine Auswahl an kalten und warmen Speisen.
+ +
Die **Buslinien 564 und 565** bringen Sie direkt vom Bahnhof zum Museum.

Eintrittspreise
Kinder 5–14 J.   15,00 €
Erwachsene   19,00 €

Funny inventions

11a

Look at the pictures and guess what you can do with the inventions.

11b

Match the descriptions to the pictures. Were you right in 11a?

Emma: "My invention is just the thing for birthday parties. All I do is watch my biscuit baker making biscuits."

Leona: "My invention is practical. With my cleaning skates I can clean the floor and have fun at the same time."

Chris and Claire: "With our invention we always know the answers to the homework. We can read the teacher's book with our X-ray glasses."

11c skill: writing p. 153, media worksheet 13, workbook p. 81/11-13

▌ Choose one of the inventions from the box below and write about it.

▌▌ Choose two of the inventions from the box below and write about them.

▌▌▌ Choose three of the inventions from the box below and write about them.

close-your-eyes lamp · singing toilet roll · homework butler · shrink-and-grow lunchbox

More inventions

12   CHOOSE YOUR LEVEL   grammar: passive p. 187

I   **Unscramble the sentences and write them down.**

1   in 1860. – invented – Dog biscuits – were
2   by Levi Strauss. – Blue jeans – designed – were
3   made – cornflakes – in 1894. – were – The first
4   was – The raincoat – by Charles Macintosh. – invented
5   teddy bear – The first – made – in 1902. – was

II   **Unscramble the two texts about dog biscuits and cornflakes. Copy one of them into your exercise book.**

III   **Unscramble the two texts and copy them into your exercise book. Find headings for them.**

For a long time, dogs were given almost exactly the same food as their owners ate: meat, vegetables and bread. Cornflakes were first made in 1894 by John Harvey Kellogg. They were originally created as a healthy food for the patients at the hospital where he worked. In 1860, James Spratt came up with the idea to produce special biscuits for dogs. Although there was no sugar in the first recipe and they probably tasted like paper, they soon became very popular as a breakfast cereal. They were made of flour, vegetables and a little meat and became an immediate success with rich dog owners.

Nouns and verbs

13a

Copy the verbs from the box. Add the nouns. You can find help in a dictionary.

begin · collect · invent · spell ·
invite · build · meet · celebrate · end

You can write:
begin — beginning
collect — ...

13b   workbook p. 82/14–15

Look at the endings of the nouns. What do you notice? Sort them into two lists. Add more nouns.

Where is the stress?

14a   audio 3/18

Listen to the words and repeat them.

vegetarian · invention · television ·
vegetable · toothbrush · information ·
smartphone · communicate · inventor ·
computer · modern · understand

14b

Where is the stress? On the first, second or third syllable? Make three lists.

first syllable	second syllable	third syllable
television	*invention*	*vegetarian*
...	...	...

Ideas for a new invention TARGET TASK

15 🔲 🔲 workbook p. 83/16, skill: giving a presentation p. 158, wordbank: inventions, presenting something p. 168, media worksheet 13

Your task is to present your ideas for a new invention.
Before you start, look at these steps:

STEP 1

Work with a partner or in a small group.

STEP 2

Think of objects that should be invented or objects that you would like to improve.
You can think of something from the following categories:
· food
· school
· tasks at home
· free time and holidays
· medicine
· travel
· ...

STEP 3

Agree on one object and be creative: what should the object be able to do?
How could it help people? Which problem should it solve?
Make notes and make a draft.

STEP 4

Decide how you would like to present your idea. You can:
· make a collage and label it
· draw a picture and label it
· write a text
· ...

STEP 5

Create your collage, picture, text, ...
Check it.

STEP 6

Present your ideas in class.

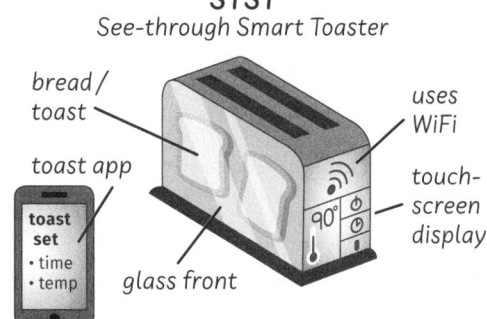

STST
See-through Smart Toaster

bread / toast
uses WiFi
toast app
touch-screen display
toast set · time · temp
glass front

Communication

1 workbook p. 84/1

How do people communicate with each other? Collect ideas in class.

Project week at Holland Park School

2a skill: reading p. 154

Scan the noticeboard. What is the topic of the project week? What workshops are offered?

PROJECT WEEK – COMMUNICATION IN THE PAST AND PRESENT

Workshop 1: Written communication – from hieroglyphs to emojis

From hieroglyphs on stone tablets and papyrus in ancient Egypt to then writing postcards and letters on paper to sending texts with your smartphone – in this workshop we are going to look at the development of writing and explore the history of written communication. For the presentation we are going to learn different ways to do a digital presentation.

Workshop 2: The history of the telephone

From the beginnings with Alexander Graham Bell to your smartphone – in this workshop we are going to focus on the technological development of the telephone and what role it played in war and peace. We are going to build models of low-tech telephones that work without electricity. At the end of the workshop we are going to present our results on different posters.

Workshop 3: Radio and TV

No streaming, no video on demand, no podcasts – can you imagine life in the early days of radio and TV? In this workshop we are going to look at the history of radio and TV and record our own radio or TV show to present our findings.

GENERAL INFORMATION

All groups have to do research at the library.

At the end of the week all students are going to display their results in the assembly hall and give short presentations on their topic.

All groups have to write handouts for the other students.

ACTIVATE PRACTISE DEVELOP PRACTISE APPLY

2b CHOOSE YOUR LEVEL workbook p.84/2

Ⅰ Read the texts on the noticeboard and correct the statements.

1 In workshop 1, students are going to learn how to do a poster presentation.
2 The students in workshop 2 are going to focus on the technological development of radios.
3 In workshop 3, students are going to look at the history of writing.

Ⅱ Are the statements true or false?
Read the texts on the noticeboard and correct the false statements.

1 Students can explore the future of written communication in workshop 1.
2 In workshop 1, students are going to make paper.
3 In workshop 2, students are going to look at the beginnings of the telephone.
4 They are going to build models of high-tech telephones in workshop 2.
5 In workshop 3, students are going to create posters about their findings.

Ⅲ Read the texts on the noticeboard and answer the questions.

1 What materials did people use to write on in the past?
2 What kind of presentation are the students in workshop 1 going to do?
3 How are the students going to present the results of workshop 2?
4 What are the newer developments in the area of radio and TV that people in the early days of radio and TV did not have?
5 Where are all students going to present the results of the workshops?
6 What do all groups have to prepare for the other students?

Talking about the workshops

3a 🔲 audio 3/19, skill: listening p.151

Listen to Ava, Lily, Harry and Tarek.
Who is going to sign up for which workshop?

3b skill: talking with people p.152, workbook p.84/3

Which workshop would you be interested in?
Talk to a partner.

You can say:

I would choose … because …

To me, workshop … is the most interesting.

…

GRAMMAR HELP   the going to-future (R) p. 188-189

Wenn du sagen möchtest, was jemand für die Zukunft plant oder beabsichtigt, benutzt du das *going to-future*. Du benutzt es auch, wenn du ausdrücken möchtest, dass etwas mit großer Wahrscheinlichkeit passieren wird. Schau dir die Beispiele an. Beschreibe, wie Aussagesätze und Fragen gebildet werden.

Harry thinks the workshop is going to be a bit boring.
We are going to produce our own TV show.
I am not going to choose the workshop on the history of the telephone.

Are you going to present your findings?
Which workshop are you going to take?

Auf den Seiten 188 und 189 findest du weitere Erklärungen und Beispiele zum *going to-future*.

They are going to …

4   grammar: going to-future p. 188, workbook p. 85/4

Write down what is going to happen.

| Anna: get dirty | Tim and Bob: miss bus | Suzy: fall off horse | Dan: wake up soon |

You can write:

Anna is going to …
Tim and Bob …

Plans

5a   grammar: going to-future p. 188

Read Lily's planner and write down what she is going to or not going to do next week.

You can write:

Next Monday afternoon, Lily is going to …
Next Tuesday, Lily is not …

> Monday afternoon: meet Ava
> Tuesday: ~~do yoga with Olivia~~
> Wednesday: hand in English homework
> Thursday: do research (school library)
> Friday afternoon: ~~do some upcycling,~~
> go skateboarding (park)

5b   grammar: going to-future p. 188-189, workbook p. 85/5

Work with a partner. Ask and answer questions about his or her plans for next week.

You can ask:

Are you going to … next Monday afternoon?
Are you going to …?

You can answer:

Yes, I am.
No, I'm not. I'm going to …

DIGITAL+ practise more 23

ACTIVATE **PRACTISE** DEVELOP PRACTISE APPLY

At the library

6a  audio 3/20

**Listen to the dialogue and read along.
Why are the friends at the library?**

Tarek: Lily, why did you bring your tablet?
I thought we came here for the books.
Lily: Yes, we did. But I'm going to take notes
on my tablet.
Harry: That sounds smart to me. But you're
connected to the school network and the
Internet, too, aren't you?
Lily: Yes, I am.
Harry: Cool. Can I maybe use your tablet
when you're done with it, Lily?
Lily: Sure. I'm going to have a look at the
books first, so you can use the tablet now.
I hope they have some useful books on
ancient Egypt.

Ava: Hey guys, look. I've found all these
books on the history of TV and radio. Harry,
come on! You're in my workshop, too.
Harry: No, thanks, Ava. I'm going to use
modern methods and research online.
Tarek: But Mr Patel told us to use books.
Harry: No, he didn't. He told us to go to
the library to do research. And where are
we now? Right. I'm going to find all the
information I need on the Internet.

6b audio 3/21

Listen to the rest of the dialogue. What are the friends talking about?

6c CHOOSE YOUR LEVEL skill: listening p. 151

❙ Listen again. Complete the sentences.

1 Harry copied all the ??? into his document.
2 He has no idea what is ??? and what is
  not.
3 Lily says that he has to ??? his sources
  and save the ??? to the pages where he
  found his information.
4 Ava gives Harry a ??? and Tarek suggests
  that he should make a poster about
  his findings.

**❙❙ Listen again. Copy the true sentences
and correct the false sentences.**

1 Harry used a search engine and has
  59 pages of information now.
2 Harry understands all the texts and knows
  exactly what is important.
3 Lily says that they have to name their
  sources.
4 Harry has saved the links of the pages
  where he found his information.

**❙❙❙ What did Harry do wrong when doing his research on the Internet? Listen again and take
notes. Then write a short text.**

6d workbook p. 86/6-7

**Listen to the rest of the dialogue again and take notes on what is important when doing
research online. Use your notes and write down tips in German.**

The history of communication

7a skill: reading p. 154

Lily found some information for her project. Skim the texts to find the main pieces of information.

7b

Write headings for the texts.

1. From pictures to letters and back to pictures, the history of writing has been a long one. The beginning of writing can be seen in rock art – pictures that people all over the world painted on stone. Some of these pictures are as old as 28,000 years and there are different theories on why people created them. Maybe they wanted to remember special events or tell a story or the pictures had a religious function.

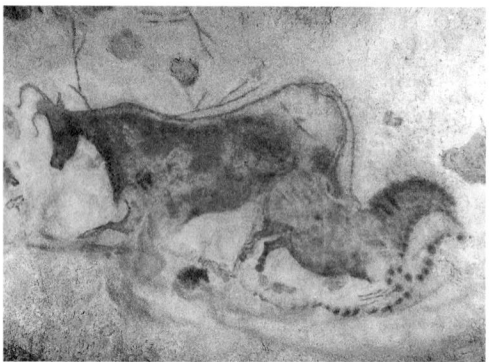

2. As early as 9,000 BC, people used pictures and signs on stone tablets to make notes. But the first "real" letters were hieroglyphs. They were invented by people in ancient Egypt about 3,000 BC. The ancient Egyptians were the first to tell longer stories in writing, and they also invented papyrus, which made writing a lot easier.

3. Before papyrus and paper were invented, people used stone or clay tablets to write on. Paper as we know it was first used by the Chinese around 105 AD. From then on paper was used for all kinds of things. In communication it was used for letters and – probably even more important – books. With the invention of the modern printing press in the 15th century, information could travel faster and wider than ever before.

ACTIVATE   PRACTISE   **DEVELOP**   PRACTISE   APPLY

4. After 2,000 years of text on paper, the invention of the computer changed the way we communicate once more. ☺ The first email was sent in 1971 by computer engineer Raymond Tomlinson. The rise of the Internet began in the 1990s and smartphones appeared in the 2000s. ☺ Texting, messaging and emojis 😊 have made it even easier and quicker to keep in touch with each other. Some people mourn the lost art of writing a letter, 😟 ✎ but many also appreciate a simple and uncomplicated 'thumbs up'. 👍

7c CHOOSE YOUR LEVEL

Ⅰ Choose one or more of the texts and read it. Take notes on the most important facts.

Ⅱ Choose two or more of the texts and read them. Take notes on the most important facts.

Ⅲ Read the texts. Take notes on the most important facts.

7d workbook p.87/8-9

Share your findings in class. Organize them in a table.

What?	When?	Where?	Who?	Other information
pictures on stone	…	…	…	…
…	…	…	…	…

An interview

8 skill: talking with people p.152, wordbank: communication p.169, workbook p.87/10

Work with a partner. Interview each other about your communication habits.

You can ask:

How often do you text someone?

Do you write letters?

Have you ever written a postcard?

How do you communicate with your grandparents?

Have you ever made a video call?

What's your favourite way to communicate?

…

You can answer:

I often / sometimes …

Yes, I do. / No, I don't. I …

…

A challenge

9a video 15

Watch the video clip.
What is Zara's challenge?

9b skill: watching a video clip p. 156, workbook p. 88/11

Watch the video clip again.
What are difficult situations for Zara?
How does she solve her problems?

Modern technology

10 CHOOSE YOUR TASK C: wordbank: inventions p. 168, media worksheet 13

A There are emojis for almost every situation. Design your own emoji and explain exactly what it means.

B Imagine a day without your phone, your tablet and your console. Describe the situations in which you would miss your devices. Think of alternatives.

> On a day without my phone,
>
> I wouldn't be able to …
>
> I could …
>
> My friends would …
>
> …

C Design an app that solves one of your everyday problems. Write down what problem you want to solve and how the app can help.

Two inventions

11 GET TOGETHER   workbook p. 88/12-14

Get together with a partner.
Read and talk about two different inventions.

Partner A	Partner B
I Go to page 130.	I Go to page 139.
II Go to page 133.	II Go to page 142.
III Go to page 136.	III Go to page 145.

ACTIVATE PRACTISE **DEVELOP** PRACTISE APPLY

Being online

12a skill: mediation p. 155

Read this list from a British magazine. Tell a partner in German what the rules say.

SIX DOS AND DON'TS FOR USING THE INTERNET

1. Only give your password to your parents, not to anyone else.

2. Don't post personal information like your name, address, phone number etc.

3. Be careful what you download. Check links before clicking on them and don't trust just anybody.

4. Don't befriend people online that you don't know in real life.

5. If someone bullies you on the Internet, don't react to the person. Show their messages to your parents or a teacher.

6. Internet behaviour has consequences in real life – so always treat other people on the Internet in the way you would like to be treated and use respectful language.

12b wordbank: going online p. 169, media worksheet 7, workbook p. 89/15

Work with a partner. Can you think of any more dos and don'ts for using the Internet? Collect as many as you can and share your ideas in class.

A presentation

13a video 16

Watch Jason's presentation. What is it about?

13b skill: watching a video clip p. 156

Go to www.westermann.de/webcode and enter the webcode WES-128202-001 to find the feedback sheet. Watch the presentation again and fill it in.

13c wordbank: presenting something p. 168, workbook p. 90/16

Give some written feedback. Do not forget to mention the positive aspects.

You can write:

At the beginning, you spoke loudly and clearly. That was good.

You could use more …

Your summary was …

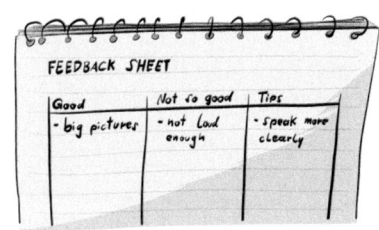

FEEDBACK SHEET

Good	Not so good	Tips
- big pictures	- not loud enough	- speak more clearly

Mr Patel's feedback

14 audio 3/25, skill: listening p.151, workbook p.90/17

**Listen to Mr Patel giving feedback on another presentation.
Is he happy with the student?
Say why or why not.**

Giving feedback

15 CHOOSE YOUR LEVEL

I Match the German and the English sentences. Write them down.

1 Deine Präsentation war sehr interessant.
2 Du hast etwas zu schnell gesprochen.
3 Ich konnte einige der Bilder nicht richtig sehen, weil sie zu klein waren.
4 Du hast frei vorgetragen.

A You spoke a bit too fast.
B You spoke freely.
C Your presentation was very interesting.
D I couldn't see some of the pictures because they were too small.

II Match the sentence parts. Write down the sentences.

1 It was good that you spoke
2 I liked your
3 Why don't you use
4 You could
5 You were very well

A add some more pictures.
B prepared. You could answer all the questions.
C loudly and clearly.
D introduction. It gave me an idea about what to expect.
E more linking words the next time?

III You would like to give feedback in English. What do you say in the following situations? Add one or more tips.

1 Die Präsentation war interessant, du konntest aber keins der Bilder erkennen, weil sie alle zu klein waren.
2 Der / Die Präsentierende hat zu leise gesprochen.
3 Die Bilder in der Präsentation waren gut ausgesucht.
4 Der / Die Vortragende hat nur abgelesen und die Zuhörenden nicht angeschaut.
5 Einige der Folien waren sehr unübersichtlich gestaltet und zu voll.

DIGITAL+ practise more 24

ACTIVATE PRACTISE DEVELOP **PRACTISE** APPLY

A three-minute talk TARGET TASK

16 workbook p.91/18, skill: searching the Internet p.157, presentations p.158, media worksheet 4, 6

Your task is to give a three-minute talk.
Before you start, look at these steps:

STEP 1

Decide what you would like to talk about. Think about:
· an invention you find interesting or useful
· one aspect of the history of communication
· …

STEP 2

Do your research.
· Do some research on your topic using books or the Internet.
  Find some good pictures. Do not forget to list your sources.
· Choose texts which are easy to understand.
  Write down the most important facts in your own words.

STEP 3

Prepare your presentation.
· Read through your findings and organize the information. What is important? What is not?
· In which order do you want to present the facts? Decide on a structure for your presentation.
· You can make a digital presentation or a poster.
· Write down what you are going to say.
· Write the most important facts of your presentation on cue cards.

STEP 4

Practise your presentation with a partner.
· Use your cue cards.
· Give each other feedback.

In my presentation, I'm going to talk about
…
This is a picture of …
Now I'd like to talk about …
If you look closely at this …, you'll see …
My next point is …
Finally, …

STEP 5

Give your presentation.

Check out

1. Kannst du über Erfindungen sprechen?	Workbook, p. 92
2. Kannst du einem Gespräch Informationen entnehmen?	Workbook, p. 92
3. Kannst du Informationen aus einem deutschen Museumsflyer auf Englisch wiedergeben?	Workbook, p. 92
4. Kannst du einem Aushang die wichtigsten Inhalte entnehmen?	Workbook, p. 93
5. Kannst du über Zukünftiges schreiben?	Workbook, p. 93
6. Kannst du Feedback formulieren?	Workbook, p. 93

A field trip

Last Tuesday, all the students at my school in years 8 to 10 went to the Science and Industry Museum in Manchester for the Science of the Future exhibition. I love science, and the museum looked really good on the Internet so I was quite excited to go. Jamie wasn't that excited, but he said it would be better than a day at school. We went to Manchester by train, but I didn't see Jamie at all because there were so many of us, and we were divided into year groups.

My group almost lost Daniel Thomas from my class twice before we even got to the museum. The first time was at the station in Manchester. Ms Barlow, one of the teachers who was with us, counted us to make sure no one was missing. "40, 41, 42," Ms Barlow went. "42, 42, wait, where's 43? There should be 43 of us. MS KERSHAAAAAAW!"

Ms Kershaw is the other teacher who went with us because 43 students were about 42 too many for Ms Barlow, who is always a bit nervous. Also, Ms Barlow doesn't usually teach our class so she didn't know Daniel Thomas. She didn't know that he always gets lost. When we went to the zoo last year, we had to search for him for over two hours. Sometimes he gets lost at school on his way to class … But anyway, Ms Barlow was getting really nervous: "Ms Kershaw! There's one student missing. WHO IS MISSING? HAVE WE LEFT SOMEONE ON THE TRAIN? WHO IS …?" Suddenly, Daniel Thomas appeared behind her and said, "I'm here. I'm 43. I just needed the loo. Everything is OK." Daniel Thomas knows that he always gets lost and that he has to calm people down when they find him. "Oh," Ms Barlow said. "Yeah, alright. Let's go then."

The museum was not too far from the station so we walked there because Ms Barlow and Ms Kershaw thought it would be good for us to get some exercise. But maybe that wasn't such a good idea because that's how we lost Daniel Thomas for the second time. On the way he met this very nice little old lady who asked him where Manchester Cathedral was. Daniel Thomas told her that he didn't know because he was from London, and then the lady told him that she liked London a

lot, and then they talked about London for a bit. Ms Kershaw, who counted us at the entrance of the museum, didn't get as nervous as Ms Barlow at the station, but when Daniel Thomas appeared, she wasn't very friendly to him.

When we were finally ready and could go inside, there were soooo many cool things. We started with a guided tour of the exhibition.

"Hi, I'm Ben," the guide said. "I study mechanical engineering at the University of Manchester, and I'll show you around our Science of the Future exhibition today. This way please, we'll begin with the section on drones."

---

field trip = *Exkursion*; divide = *(auf)teilen*; make sure = *achten auf*; get lost = *verloren gehen*; loo = *Klo*; drone = *Drohne*

Ben was really nice and funny, and he told us about how science and technology and inventions might develop in the future. We were allowed to try things out, and he asked me to control a robot just by moving my eyeballs. The robot followed my eyeballs, and I could give it simple orders by opening and closing my eyes. That was brilliant.

Daniel Thomas almost got lost again at the station with the VR glasses. He put on a pair and then just wandered off. We found him when he crashed into one of the tables where you could do experiments with sound and light somewhere at the back of the exhibition hall. Ben was really glad that the VR glasses were still working. He continued to be friendly, but he seemed to become a bit nervous, too. He did the rest of the tour a lot faster than the first bit. But that was good, actually, because after the tour we were allowed to walk around the museum by ourselves.

"But remember to be back at the meeting point near the main entrance at two o'clock for our lunch break. Don't break anything and stay inside the exhibition area. Don't leave the museum and don't go anywhere you're not allowed to go. Is that clear?" Ms Kershaw asked.

"Yes, Ms Kershaw," we all said.

I wandered around and came across Jamie at the Textiles Gallery. Jamie doesn't like science that much, but he's always reading books about the past so this part of the museum was exactly right for him. There wasn't anything about the future, but there was a lot about Manchester's past as the centre of the cotton industry. There was a real Spinning Jenny, and one of the people working at the museum showed us how it worked. She even let us try it. I wasn't very good at spinning, but Jamie was really talented. The next time Mum takes us to anything medieval, HE gets the spinning wheel! Then we read about how slaves had to pick the cotton and how children had to work in the mills and couldn't go to school. We learnt that a few people became really rich, but a lot were poor and had to live in horrible small houses and never had enough to eat.

Just when we were about to leave the Textiles Gallery, I saw Daniel Thomas walking through a door with a sign on it that said "NO ENTRY!"

"Oh no," I thought. "Not again."

I knew exactly what was going to happen:
we would get together at the meeting point, Ms Kershaw would count again, Daniel Thomas would be missing, we would have to search for him, Ms Barlow would be first nervous and then hysterical, we might even have to miss lunch and maybe our train, then someone would call the police … but I would not let that happen!

"Come on, Jamie," I said and pulled him with me through the door and down the stairs that were right behind the door. "Hey! What …?" Jamie said, "Lucy, we can't just go there. We're not allowed here. There might be … Wow!"

eyeball = *Augapfel*; order = *Befehl*; wander off = *weggehen*; spinning wheel = *Spinnrad*; pick = *pflücken*; mill = *Mühle*; entry = *Zutritt*

"Wow!" was about right. We were standing in a huge hall with shelves everywhere. On the shelves were collections of about everything you can imagine. There were old machines, furniture, books and paintings.

Then I saw Daniel Thomas. He was looking at a huge machine which had a wheel and something that looked like a hammer. "Look, I've found a medieval torture machine," he said.

"That's an early steam engine," Jamie said. "Oh no, it's a medieval torture machine that was used to hammer your enemies to death," Daniel Thomas replied. "And over there is a time travelling machine. Unfortunately it's broken so we now have visitors from the future in Manchester. But they don't show themselves."

"But that's a …" Jamie began.

"Oh, and there's a telescope that lets you see the people who live on Mars," Daniel Thomas went on.

"Oh yes," I said. "Look, that over there is a stuffed Mastederontomtom. It lived about 100,000 years ago and went extinct because there were so few of them that they simply didn't find each other."

Jamie looked at me as if he thought I was crazy. "No, that's a …" he tried to say again. But then he seemed to get it – that this was the best part of the museum because there was no one there to tell us what everything was. We could make up our own stories!

"Oh yes," he said and pointed at something that looked like a collage of newspapers, umbrellas and shoes, "that's a piece of art from a group of people who live on the underground in London. They travel on the Tube all the time and collect the things that people forget. They take everything to a secret tunnel, which they call "the place where it happens", and they create art." Daniel Thomas was looking at Jamie as if he thought Jamie was the cleverest person he had ever met. "Whoa, you're really good at this. Let's go on," he said.

We had so much fun! We found a calculator for numbers that haven't been invented yet, the last egg of the last British dragon, an accordion that only bats can hear and a lot of other interesting things. Sometimes you find the best places when you are lost!

Luckily, at quarter to two, we found a clock that was still working and showed the correct time. We were on time for the lunch break so Ms Barlow didn't have to get nervous again.

After lunch we did some class activities, which was good because Daniel Thomas had to stay with our group the whole time and I could keep an eye on him. On the way back to the station, I made sure that I could always see him. But when we were finally safely on the train, I relaxed a little. At the station in Stoke-on-Trent Ms Barlow counted us again.

"40, 41, 42," she went. "42, 42, WHERE IS 43?"

torture = *Folter*; enemy = *Feind/in*; stuffed = *ausgestopft*; crazy = *verrückt*; bat = *Fledermaus*; be lost = *sich verirrt haben*; on time = *pünktlich*

Inventions inspired by nature

burdock plant

Velcro®

Did you know that the hook-and-loop fastener, commonly known as Velcro®, was inspired by the burdock plant?
The seeds of the plant easily stick to clothes because they have lots of little hooks.

bat

walking stick for the blind

Bats can fly in complete darkness because they give off sounds that echo back. Scientists invented a walking stick for the blind that was inspired by bats. Like a bat, the UltraCane can send and receive sound waves. The stick 'sees' objects on the ground and warns the user.

kingfisher

The first Japanese high-speed train could travel over 200 km/h. But going that fast caused a loud "boom" when the train left a tunnel. To solve the problem, engineers turned to nature for inspiration. The high-speed train was inspired by the kingfisher. Kingfishers dive down into the water to catch fish. Their beaks hardly make a ripple when they hit the water. Today, Japan's high-speed trains have long, beak-like noses and exit tunnels quietly.

high-speed train

Find out more about one of the inventions or find out about another invention that was inspired by nature. Report your findings to the class.

Ordering food

9a UNIT 1, p. 25 PARTNER A

You and your partner would like to order some food. You are looking at menus from two different restaurants. Tell your partner about your restaurant and agree on one menu.

Paolo's Pizza Palace – Italian restaurant

SPECIAL OFFER FOR 2
- 2 Pizzas
- 2 Drinks   for just £29.99
- 2 Desserts

DRINKS
Water, lemonade, cola £2.20
Juice (orange, apple) £2.50

STARTERS
Garlic bread £1.85
Fresh bread with garlic
Mixed salad £6.30
Salad with our special dressing
Tomato soup £5.95
Home-made tomato soup with freshly-baked bread

PIZZAS
Margherita £10.95
tomatoes, mozzarella, basil
Fresh from the sea £13.95
tomato sauce, octopus
Farmhouse £13.95
tomato sauce, bacon, mushrooms, onions
Spinach £11.95
mozzarella, spinach, garlic
Ham-ster £11.95
tomato sauce, ham, onions

DESSERTS
Tiramisu £3.95
Ice cream £2.95
Sorbet £2.95

You can say:
I've got a menu from an Italian restaurant.
They have ...
I really like ...
I don't like ...
Let's order ...
...

You can ask:
What menu have you got?
Have they got ... at your place?
Do you like ...?
How much is ...?
What about ...?
...

9b UNIT 1 p. 25 PARTNER A

Look at the menu you agreed on. Write down what you would like to order.

9c UNIT 1 p. 25 PARTNER A

Do a role play – you call the restaurant and order your food.
Your partner answers the phone.
You can record your dialogue if you like.

You can say:
I would like to order ...
How long will it take?
...

What do they miss?

9a UNIT 2, p. 48 📖 PARTNER A, audio 1/34, skill: listening p. 151

❚❚ Copy the table. Then listen to Jacob and Ben in hospital. What does Ben miss?
Complete the table for Ben.

Ben				ice hockey practice	sleeping in
Jacob				going swimming	playing the guitar with his band

9b UNIT 2, p. 48 PARTNER A

❚❚ Work with your partner. Find out what Jacob is missing. Ask and answer questions and
complete the table for Jacob. What activity do both of the boys miss?

Which festival?

10a UNIT 3, p. 73 PARTNER A

❚❚ Read the table. Then ask and answer questions with your partner and write down the
information for the gaps.

You can ask:

Which festival is ...?

Where is the ...?

When is the ...?

You can answer:

The ... is in ...

It's in / on ...

It costs ... pounds (and ... pence).

What?	Where?	When?	How much?	Other information
1	2	usually in February	different fees for different events	three days packed with Viking events all around York
The Garlic Festival	Isle of Wight	third weekend in August	one day for adults: £12.50 for children: £7.50	garlic lovers from around the world come to the Isle of Wight to get a taste.
The Children's Festival	Edinburgh	27 May to 4 June	adult or child as part of family: £9.00	12 performances at different places, lots of additional activities
The Big Feastival	the Cotswolds	3	weekend for adults: £187.95, weekend for children: £41.80	a family-friendly festival with great music, great food and lots of activities for children

10b UNIT 3, p. 73 PARTNER A, wordbank: what's on? p. 164

❚❚ Which festival would you like to go to?
Why? Tell your partner.

You can say:

I would like to go to the ... because I like ...

...

Sheree's problems

9a UNIT 4, p. 96 — PARTNER A, audio 3/5, skill: listening p. 151

Listen to Sheree's call to the teen helpline. Which of these problems does Sheree have? Write down the correct sentences.

1 Her parents are very strict.
2 She is not allowed to play video games.
3 She is really bad at school.

4 She has to do too many chores.
5 Her sister never has to help.

9b UNIT 4, p. 96 — PARTNER A

Tell your partner about Sheree's problems. Then listen to your partner. What advice does Gemma from the teen helpline offer? Take notes.

9c UNIT 4, p. 96 — PARTNER A

Work with your partner and match Gemma's tips to Sheree's problems.

You can say:

When Sheree says …, Gemma suggests …

…

Two inventions

11a UNIT 5, p. 120 — PARTNER A, skill: reading p. 154

Read the text about the hippo roller. Take notes about the most important facts.

The hippo roller

The problem: many people have to walk very far to get clean water. The traditional way is to carry the water on your head. That means that one person cannot transport a lot of water.

The idea: the hippo roller. You fill it with water and pull or push it, so you do not have to carry all the weight. Getting water is a lot easier because you can transport more water in one go, which saves a lot of time and energy.

11b UNIT 5, p. 120 — PARTNER A

Use your notes and tell your partner about the hippo roller.

You can say:

Many people have to …

That means that …

When you use the hippo roller you can …

…

Ordering food

9a UNIT 1, p. 25 PARTNER A

▌▌ You and your partner would like to order some food. You are looking at menus from two different restaurants. Tell your partner about your restaurant and agree on where to order.

Paolo's Pizza Palace – Italian restaurant

SPECIAL OFFER FOR 2
- 2 Pizzas
- 2 Drinks   for just £29.99
- 2 Desserts

PIZZAS

Margherita	£10.95
tomatoes, mozzarella, basil	
Fresh from the sea	£13.95
tomato sauce, octopus	
Farmhouse	£13.95
tomato sauce, bacon, mushrooms, onions	
Cheer for cheese	£12.95
tomato sauce, four different kinds of cheese	
Spinach	£11.95
mozzarella, spinach, garlic	
Ham-ster	£11.95
tomato sauce, ham, onions	

DRINKS

Water, lemonade, cola	£2.20
Juice (orange, apple)	£2.50

STARTERS

Garlic bread	£1.85
Fresh bread with olive oil and garlic	
Mixed salad	£6.30
Salad with fresh tomatos and our special dressing	
Tomato soup	£5.95
Home-made tomato soup with freshly-baked bread	

DESSERTS

Tiramisu	£3.95
Ice cream	£2.95
Sorbet	£2.95

You can say:

I've got a menu from an Italian restaurant.

They have …

I really like …

I don't like …

Let's order …

…

You can ask:

What menu have you got?

Have they got … at your place?

Do you like …?

How much is …?

What about …?

…

9b UNIT 1 p. 25 PARTNER A

▌▌ Look at the menu you agreed on. Write down what you would like to order.

9c UNIT 1 p. 25 PARTNER A

▌▌ Do a role play – you call the restaurant and order your food.
Your partner answers the phone.
You can record your dialogue if you like.

You can say:

I would like to order …

How long will it take?

…

What do they miss?

9a UNIT 2, p. 48 ▣ PARTNER A, audio 1/34, skill: listening p. 151

‖ Copy the table. Then listen to Jacob and Ben in hospital. What does Ben miss?
Complete the table for Ben.

Ben					sleeping in
Jacob					playing the guitar with his band

9b UNIT 2, p. 48 PARTNER A

‖ Work with your partner. Find out what Jacob is missing. Ask and answer questions and
complete the table for Jacob. What activity do both of the boys miss?

Which festival?

10a UNIT 3, p. 73 PARTNER A

‖ Read the table. Then ask and answer questions with your partner and write down the
information for the gaps.

You can ask:
Which festival is on / in ...?
Have you got any other information on ...?
...

You can answer:
It's ...
Yes, there is / are ...
...

What?	Where?	When?	How much?	Other information
1	2	usually in February	3	three days packed with Viking events all around York
The Garlic Festival	Isle of Wight	third weekend in August	one day for adults: £12.50, for children: £7.50	garlic lovers from around the world come to the Isle of Wight to get a taste.
The Children's Festival	Edinburgh	27 May to 4 June	4	12 performances at different places, lots of additional activities
The Big Feastival	the Cotswolds	5	weekend for adults: £187.95, weekend for children: £41.80	a family-friendly festival with great music, great food and lots of activities for children

10b UNIT 3, p. 73 PARTNER A, wordbank: what's on? p. 164

‖ Which festival would you like to go to? Why? Tell your partner.

Sheree's problems

9a UNIT 4, p. 96 🖭 PARTNER A, audio 3/5, skill: listening p. 151

‖ Listen to Sheree's call to the teen helpline. What are her problems? Take notes.

You can write:

Her parents …

She is not allowed to …

She has to …

9b UNIT 4, p. 96 PARTNER A

‖ Tell your partner about Sheree's problems. Then listen to your partner. What advice does Gemma from the teen helpline offer? Take notes.

9c UNIT 4, p. 96 PARTNER A

‖ Work with your partner and match Gemma's tips to Sheree's problems.

You can say:

When Sheree says …, Gemma suggests …

…

Two inventions

11a UNIT 5, p. 120 PARTNER A, skill: reading p. 154

‖ Read the text about the hippo roller. Take notes about the most important facts.

The hippo roller

The problem: in a lot of African countries, people have to walk long distances to get clean water. The traditional way is to carry the water on your head. But that means that one person cannot transport a lot of water. Often children have to do this chore. This chore takes up a lot of their time, so they cannot go to school.

The idea: the hippo roller. You fill it with water and push or pull it, so you do not have to carry all the weight. Getting water is a lot easier when you use it because you can transport more water in one go, which saves a lot of time and energy.

Unfortunately, it does not solve the problem that there is not enough clean water for everyone.

11b UNIT 5, p. 120 PARTNER A

‖ Use your notes and tell your partner about the hippo roller.

Ordering food

9a UNIT 1, p. 25 PARTNER A

III You and your partner would like to order some food. You are looking at menus from two different restaurants. Tell your partner about your restaurant and agree on where to order.

Paolo's Pizza Palace – Italian restaurant

SPECIAL OFFER FOR 2
- 2 Pizzas
- 2 Drinks   for just £29.99
- 2 Desserts

DRINKS

Water, lemonade, cola	£2.20
Juice (orange, apple)	£2.50

STARTERS

Garlic bread £1.85
Fresh bread with olive oil and garlic

Mixed salad £6.30
Salad with fresh tomatos, onions, cucumber, peppers, egg and our special dressing

Tomato soup £5.95
Home-made tomato soup with a side of freshly baked bread

PIZZAS

Margherita £10.95
tomatoes, mozzarella, basil

Fresh from the sea £13.95
tomato sauce, octopus

Farmhouse £13.95
tomato sauce, bacon, mushrooms, onions

Cheer for cheese £12.95
tomato sauce, four different kinds of cheese

Vegetariana £9.95
tomato sauce, onions, mushrooms, peppers, olives

Sausage Supreme £14.95
tomato sauce, onions, sausage

Spinach £11.95
mozzarella, spinach, garlic

Ham-ster £11.95
tomato sauce, ham, onions

DESSERTS

Tiramisu	£3.95
Ice cream	£2.95
Sorbet	£2.95

9b UNIT 1 p. 25 PARTNER A

III Look at the menu you agreed on. Write down what you would like to order.

You can say:

I've got a menu from an Italian restaurant.

They have …

I really like …

I don't like …

Let's order …

…

You can ask:

What menu have you got?

Have they got … at your place?

Do you like …?

How much is …?

What about …?

…

9c UNIT 1 p. 25 PARTNER A

III Do a role play – you call the restaurant and order your food.
Your partner answers the phone.
You can record your dialogue if you like.

You can say:

I would like to order …

The address is …

How long will it take?

What do they miss?

9a UNIT 2, p. 48 🔲 PARTNER A, audio 1/34, skill: listening p. 151

||| Copy the table. Then listen to Jacob and Ben in hospital. What does Ben miss?
Fill in the table for Ben.

Ben					
Jacob					

9b UNIT 2, p. 48 PARTNER A

||| Work with your partner. Find out what Jacob is missing. Ask and answer questions and fill in
the table for Jacob. What activity do both of the boys miss?

Which festival?

10a UNIT 3, p. 73 PARTNER A

||| Read the table. Then ask and answer questions with your partner
and write down the information for the gaps.

What?	Where?	When?	How much?	Other information
1	2	usually in February	3	three days packed with Viking events all around York
The Garlic Festival	Isle of Wight	third weekend in August	one day for adults: £12.50, for children: £7.50	4
The Children's Festival	Edinburgh	27 May to 4 June	5	12 performances at different places, lots of additional activities
The Big Feastival	the Cotswolds	6	Weekend for adults: £187.95, weekend for children: £41.80	7

10b UNIT 3, p. 73 PARTNER A, wordbank: what's on? p. 164

||| Which festival would you like to go to? Why? Tell your partner.

Sheree's problems

9a UNIT 4, p. 96 🖳 PARTNER A, audio 3/5, skill: listening p. 151

||| Listen to Sheree's call to the teen helpline. What are her problems? Take notes.

9b UNIT 4, p. 96 PARTNER A

||| Tell your partner about Sheree's problems. Then listen to your partner.
What advice does Gemma from the teen helpline offer? Take notes.

9c UNIT 4, p. 96 PARTNER A

||| Work with your partner and match Gemma's tips to Sheree's problems.

Two inventions

11a UNIT 5, p. 120 PARTNER A, skill: reading p. 154

||| Read the text about the hippo roller. Take notes about the most important facts.

The hippo roller

In a lot of African countries and other places all over the world it is a big problem that people have to walk long distances to get clean water. The traditional way is to carry the water on your head. But that means that one person can only transport a limited amount of water. Often children have to do this chore. This chore takes up a lot of their time, so they cannot go to school.

One idea to solve the problem is the hippo roller. You fill it with water and it rolls when you push or pull it, so you do not have to carry all the weight. Getting water is a lot easier when you use it because you can transport more water in one go – almost five times as much as with a traditional container – which saves a lot of time and energy. Unfortunately, it does not solve the problem that in some areas there is not enough clean water for everyone.

11b UNIT 5, p. 120 PARTNER A

||| Use your notes and tell your partner about the hippo roller.

Ordering food

9a UNIT 1, p. 25 PARTNER B

You and your partner would like to order some food. You are looking at menus from two different restaurants. Tell your partner about your restaurant and agree on one menu.

The Wonton Wok – the best Chinese restaurant in town

Special offer for just £25.50
- 2 soups
- 2 main courses
- 2 Desserts

DRINKS

Water, lemonade, cola	£2.20
Juice (lychee, apple)	£2.50
Green tea	£1.95

SOUPS

Chicken soup	£5.40
Delicious hot soup	
Spring soup	£2.30
Vegetable soup	
Fish and tofu soup	£3.95
Fresh fish, tofu and vegetables	

MAIN COURSES

Sweet and sour pork	£13.95
Pork in a sweet and sour sauce	
Spring rolls	£9.95
Five large spring rolls with meat	
Vegetarian spring rolls	£7.95
Five large spring rolls with vegetables	
Mango chilli chicken	£11.95
Chicken cooked with mango and chilli	
Dim Sum	£11.95
A selection of traditional Chinese food	

DESSERTS

Baked banana with honey	£3.95
Lychees	£4.95
Ice cream	£2.95

You can say:

I've got a menu from a Chinese restaurant.

They have …

I really like …

I don't like …

Let's order …

…

You can ask:

What menu have you got?

Have they got … at your place?

Do you like …?

How much is …?

What about …?

…

9b UNIT 1 p. 25 PARTNER B

Look at the menu you agreed on. Write down what you would like to order.

9c UNIT 1 p. 25 PARTNER B

Do a role play – your partner calls the restaurant and orders your food.
You answer the phone.
You can record your dialogue if you like.

You can say:

Hello, this is the Wonton Wok.

What can I do for you?

It's … pounds …

It will take … minutes.

…

What do they miss?

9a UNIT 2, p. 48   PARTNER B audio 1/34, skill: listening p. 151

Copy the table. Then listen to Jacob and Ben in hospital. What does Jacob miss?
Complete the table for Jacob.

Jacob				going swimming	playing the guitar with his band
Ben				ice hockey practice	sleeping in

9b UNIT 2, p. 48   PARTNER B

Work with your partner. Find out what Ben is missing. Ask and answer questions and
complete the table for Ben. What activity do both of the boys miss?

Which festival?

10a UNIT 3, p. 73   PARTNER B

Read the table. Then ask and answer questions with your partner and write down the
information for the gaps.

You can ask:

When is the ...?

Which festival is ...?

Where is the ...?

You can answer:

The ... is in ...

It's in / on ...

It costs ... pounds (and ... pence).

What?	Where?	When?	How much?	Other information
The Viking Festival	York	usually in February	different fees for different events	three days packed with Viking events all around York
The Garlic Festival	Isle of Wight	1	one day for adults: £12.50, for children: £7.50	garlic lovers from around the world come to the Isle of Wight to get a taste
2	Edinburgh	27 May to 4 June	adult or child as part of family: £9.00	12 performances at different places, lots of additional activities
The Big Feastival	3	August	weekend for adults: £187.95, weekend for children: £41.80	a family-friendly festival with great music, great food and lots of activities for children

10b UNIT 3, p. 73   PARTNER B, wordbank: what's on? p. 164

Which festival would you like to go to?
Why? Tell your partner.

You can say:

I would like to go to the ... because I like ...

...

Sheree's problems

9a UNIT 4, p. 96 📷 PARTNER B, audio 3/5, skill: listening p. 151

Listen to Sheree's call to the teen helpline. Which of these solutions does Gemma from the teen helpline suggest? Write down the correct sentences.

1 Talk to her parents.
2 Ask her parents to look at an official website about screen time for teenagers.

3 Do everything her parents say.
4 Have a family meeting.
5 Move out.

9b UNIT 4, p. 96 PARTNER B

Tell your partner about Sheree's problems. Then listen to your partner. What advice does Gemma from the teen helpline offer? Take notes.

9c UNIT 4, p. 96 PARTNER B

Work with your partner and match Gemma's tips to Sheree's problems.

You can say:

When Sheree says ..., Gemma suggests ...

...

Two inventions

11a UNIT 5, p. 120 PARTNER B, skill: reading p. 154

Read the text about the pot-in-pot fridge. Take notes about the most important facts.

The pot-in-pot fridge

The problem: in many places people in the country have no electricity. That means they cannot use electrical fridges to keep their food fresh.
The idea: you only need two pots, sand and a little water to build a fridge that works without electricity. You put the smaller pot inside the bigger pot and fill the gap between the pots with wet sand. You put your food inside the smaller pot. When the water in the sand evaporates[1], the smaller pot becomes cooler, and fresh vegetables stay fresh for three to four weeks.

1 (to) evaporate = verdunsten

11b UNIT 5, p. 120 PARTNER B

Use your notes and tell your partner about the pot-in-pot fridge.

You can say:

Many people don't have ...

So they cannot ...

But you only need ... to build ...

...

Ordering food

9a UNIT 1, p. 25 PARTNER B

|| **You and your partner would like to order some food. You are looking at menus from two different restaurants. Tell your partner about your restaurant and agree on where to order.**

The Wonton Wok – the best Chinese restaurant in town

Special offer for just £25.50
- 2 soups
- 2 main courses
- 2 Desserts

DRINKS

Water, lemonade, cola	£2.20
Juice (lychee, apple)	£2.50
Green tea	£1.95

SOUPS

Chicken soup	£5.40
Delicious hot soup with chicken and noodles	
Spring soup	£2.30
Vegetable soup	
Fish and tofu soup	£3.95
Fresh fish, tofu and different vegetables	

MAIN COURSES

Sweet and sour pork	£13.95
Pork in a sweet and sour sauce	
Spring rolls	£9.95
Five large spring rolls with different vegetables and meat	
Vegetarian spring rolls	£7.95
Five large spring rolls with different vegetables	
Garlic soy beef	£11.95
Tender beef cooked in a soy sauce with garlic	
Mango chilli chicken	£11.95
Chicken cooked with mango and just enough chilli	
Dim Sum	£11.95
A delicious selection of traditional Chinese food	

DESSERTS

Baked banana with honey	£3.95
Lychees	£4.95
Ice cream	£2.95

You can say:

I've got a menu from a Chinese restaurant.

They have …

I really like …

I don't like …

Let's order …

…

You can ask:

What menu have you got?

Have they got … at your place?

Do you like …?

How much is …?

What about …?

…

9b UNIT 1 p. 25 PARTNER B

|| **Look at the menu you agreed on. Write down what you would like to order.**

9c UNIT 1 p. 25 PARTNER B

|| **Do a role play – your partner calls the restaurant and orders your food.**
You answer the phone.
You can record your dialogue if you like.

You can say:

Hello, this is the Wonton Wok.

What can I do for you?

It's … pounds …

It will take … minutes.

…

What do they miss?

9a UNIT 2, p. 48 PARTNER B, audio 1/34, skill: listening p. 151

|| Copy the table. Then listen to Jacob and Ben in hospital. What does Jacob miss?
Complete the table for Jacob.

Jacob					playing the guitar with his band
Ben					sleeping in

9b UNIT 2, p. 48 PARTNER B

|| Work with your partner. Find out what Ben is missing. Ask and answer questions and complete the table for Ben. What activity do both of the boys miss?

Which festival?

10a UNIT 3, p. 73 PARTNER B

|| Read the table. Then ask and answer questions with your partner and write down the information for the gaps.

You can ask:

Which festival is ...?

How much is the ...?

...

You can answer:

It's ...

There is / are ...

...

What?	Where?	When?	How much?	Other information
The Viking Festival	York	usually in February	different fees for different events	three days packed with Viking events all around York
1	Isle of Wight	2	3	garlic lovers from around the world come to the Isle of Wight to get a taste
4	Edinburgh	27 May to 4 June	adult or child as part of family: £9.00	12 performances at different places, lots of additional activities
The Big Feastival	5	August	6	a family-friendly festival with great music, great food and lots of activities for children

10b UNIT 3, p. 73 PARTNER B, wordbank: what's on? p. 164

|| Which festival would you like to go to? Why? Tell your partner.

Sheree's problems

9a UNIT 4, p. 96 PARTNER B, audio 3/5, skill: listening p. 151

‖ Listen to Sheree's call to the teen helpline. What solutions does Gemma from the teen helpline suggest? Take notes.

You can write:

Gemma suggests that Sheree should …

She says that Sheree could try …

…

9b UNIT 4, p. 96 PARTNER B

‖ Listen to your partner. What are Sheree's problems? Take notes. Then tell your partner what Gemma suggests.

9c UNIT 4, p. 96 PARTNER B

‖ Work with your partner and match Gemma's tips to Sheree's problems.

You can say:

When Sheree says …, Gemma suggests …

…

Two inventions

11a UNIT 5, p. 120 PARTNER B, skill: reading p. 154

‖ Read the text about the pot-in-pot fridge. Take notes about the most important facts.

The pot-in-pot fridge

The problem: in many countries people in rural areas have no electricity. That means they cannot use electrical fridges to keep their food fresh.
The idea: you only need two clay pots, sand and a little water to build a fridge that works without electricity. You put the smaller pot inside the bigger pot and fill the gap between the pots with wet sand. You put your food inside the smaller pot. When the water in the sand evaporates[1], the smaller pot becomes cooler. Fresh vegetables stay fresh for three to four weeks in the smaller pot – and people do not have to spend money on electricity!

1 (to) evaporate = verdunsten

11b UNIT 5, p. 120 PARTNER B

‖ Use your notes and tell your partner about the pot-in-pot fridge.

Ordering food

9a UNIT 1, p. 25 PARTNER B

You and your partner would like to order some food. You are looking at menus from two different restaurants. Tell your partner about your restaurant and agree on where to order.

The Wonton Wok – the best Chinese restaurant in town

Special offer for just £25.50
- 2 soups
- 2 main courses
- 2 Desserts

DRINKS
Water, lemonade, cola	£2.20
Juice (lychee, apple)	£2.50
Green tea	£1.95

SOUPS
Chicken soup — £5.40
Delicious hot soup with chicken and noodles

Spring soup — £2.30
Vegetable soup with mushrooms, peppers and broccoli

Fish and tofu soup — £3.95
Fresh fish with tofu and different vegetables

RICE AND NOODLES
Egg fried noodles — £7.95
Noodles and vegetables fried with egg

Egg fried rice — £7.95
Rice and vegetables fried with egg

MAIN COURSES
All main courses are served with rice

Sweet and sour pork — £13.95
Pork in a sweet and sour sauce

Spring rolls — £9.95
Five large spring rolls filled with different vegetables and meat

Vegetarian spring rolls — £7.95
Five large spring rolls filled with different vegetables

Kung Pao chicken — £12.95
Diced chicken with dried chilli, cucumber, and fried cashews

Garlic soy beef — £11.95
Tender beef cooked in a soy sauce with garlic

Mango chilli chicken — £11.95
Chicken cooked with mango and just enough chilli

Dim Sum — £11.95
A selection of traditional Chinese food

DESSERTS
Baked banana with honey	£3.95
Lychees	£4.95
Ice cream	£2.95

9b UNIT 1 p. 25 PARTNER B

Look at the menu you agreed on. Write down what you would like to order.

9c UNIT 1 p. 25 PARTNER B

Do a role play – your partner calls the restaurant and orders your food.
You answer the phone.
You can record your dialogue if you like.

You can say:
Hello, this is the Wonton Wok.
What can I do for you?
Would you like anything else?
It's … pounds …
It will take forty minutes.
…

What do they miss?

9a UNIT 2, p. 48 PARTNER B, audio 1/34, skill: listening p. 151

||| Copy the table. Then listen to Jacob and Ben in hospital. What does Jacob miss?
Fill in the table for Jacob.

Jacob					
Ben					

9b UNIT 2, p. 48 PARTNER B

||| Work with your partner. Find out what Ben is missing. Ask and answer questions and fill in
the table for Ben. What activity do both of the boys miss?

Which festival?

10a UNIT 3, p. 73 PARTNER B

||| Read the table. Then ask and answer questions with your partner and write down the
information for the gaps.

What?	Where?	When?	How much?	Other information
The Viking Festival	York	usually in February	different fees for different events	1
2	Isle of Wight	3	4	garlic lovers from around the world come to the Isle of Wight to get a taste
5	Edinburgh	27 May to 4 June	adult or child as part of family: £9.00	6
The Big Feastival	7	August	8	a family-friendly festival with great music, great food and lots of activities for children

10b UNIT 3, p. 73 PARTNER B, wordbank: what's on? p. 164

||| Which festival would you like to go to? Why? Tell your partner.

Sheree's problems

9a UNIT 4, p. 96 PARTNER B, audio 3/5, skill: listening p. 151

Ⅲ Listen to Sheree's call to the teen helpline. What solutions does Gemma from the teen helpline suggest? Take notes.

9b UNIT 4, p. 96 PARTNER B

Ⅲ Listen to your partner. What are Sheree's problems? Take notes.
Then tell your partner what Gemma suggests.

9c UNIT 4, p. 96 PARTNER B

Ⅲ Work with your partner and match Gemma's tips to Sheree's problems.

Two inventions

11 UNIT 5, p. 120 PARTNER B, skill: reading p. 154

Ⅲ Read the text about the pot-in-pot fridge. Take notes about the most important facts.

The pot-in-pot fridge

The problem: In many countries people in rural areas have no or only unreliable electricity. That means they cannot use electrical fridges to keep their food from going bad.

The idea: you only need two clay pots, sand and a little water to build a fridge that works without electricity. You put the smaller pot inside the bigger pot and fill the gap between the pots with wet sand. You put your food inside the smaller pot. When the water in the sand evaporates[1], you have a cooling effect in the smaller pot. Fresh vegetables stay fresh for three to four weeks in the smaller pot – and people do not have to spend money on electricity!

1 (to) evaporate = verdunsten

11b UNIT 5, p. 120 PARTNER B

Ⅲ Use your notes and tell your partner about the pot-in-pot fridge.

A country profile: India ⬛ DIGITAL+

Introduction

India is one of the biggest countries in the world. What do you already know about India and what else would you like to know?

These are some questions you may find interesting:

· What famous sights and places are there?
· What sports are popular in India?
· What animals live in India?
· What languages are spoken in India?
· What is the historical connection with the UK?

Find answers to these and other interesting questions in a project about India!

Plan it

1 In class, collect ideas for topics you could work on. You can make notes in a word web. Here is an example:

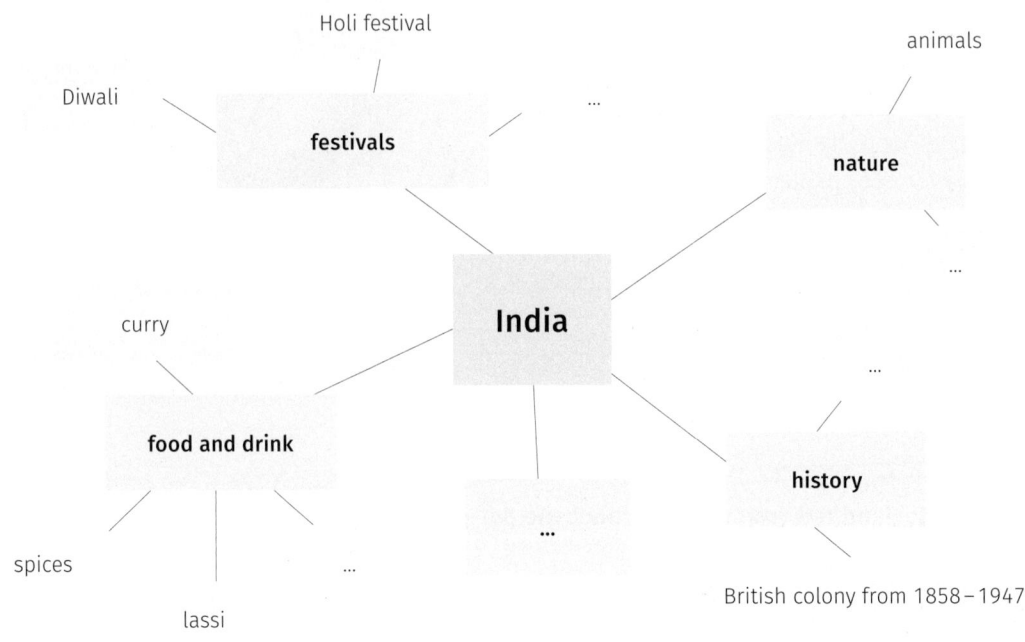

2 **Now collect ideas about what you could create. For example:**

- ▸ fact files
- ▸ posters
- ▸ pages for a computer presentation
- ▸ podcasts
- ▸ ...

Tip

You can make a class product, for example a brochure: every group creates one page and you put everything together in the end.

India
- capital: New Delhi
- population: about 1.4 billion
- languages: English, Hindi, ...
- ...

3 **Now get together in small groups and make a detailed plan. Write down:**

- ▸ what information you need
- ▸ how you can find information
- ▸ how you want to present your work
- ▸ what material you need for your project work (for example: computer, paper, glue, ...)
- ▸ who does what and when

Tip

When you as a group have a plan about what to do and how to present your work, you can ask your classmates from other groups for feedback on your plan.

Do it skill: searching the Internet p. 157, media worksheet 4, 6

And ... action! Do research, collect pictures, write texts, ... and create an interesting fact file, poster, computer presentation, ...

Check it

Check everything. Are there any spelling or grammar mistakes? Are the pictures big enough?
Is everything easy to understand? If you want to give a presentation, practise it before you give it.

Present it skill: presentations p. 158

Present your work. You can ask your classmates for feedback after the presentation.

Music 🎵 DIGITAL+

Introduction

Music plays an important role in many people's lives. What about you?
What does music mean to you?
What bands or singers do you like?
Do you play an instrument?

Think about the role of music in your life and explore the world of music in a project.

Plan it

1 In class, think about what you would like to do in your project.
You can collect ideas in a list, for example:

▶ Prepare a presentation or a podcast on a band or singer.
▶ Present a song you like and give some background information on it.
▶ Write about a concert you have been to.
▶ Create a poster for a concert or music festival.
▶ Interview classmates about what music they like or what instruments they play.
▶ Collect quotations about music and present them in a creative way.
▶ …

2 Now collect ideas about what you could create. For example:

- fact files
- posters
- pages for a computer presentation
- podcasts
- …

Tip

You can make a class product, for example a music magazine: every group creates one page and you put everything together in the end.

Billie Eilish
- Birthday: 18 December 2001
- Birthplace: Los Angeles, USA
- Famous songs: Bad guy, …
- …

3 Now get together in small groups and make a detailed plan. Write down:

- what information you need
- how you can get the information
- how you want to present your work
- what material you need for your project work (for example: computer, paper, glue, …)
- who does what and when

Tip

When you as a group have a plan about what to do and how to present your work, you can ask your classmates from other groups for feedback on your plan.

Do it skill: searching the Internet p. 157, media worksheet 4, 6

And … action! Do research, collect pictures, write texts, … and create an interesting fact file, poster, computer presentation, …

Check it

Check everything. Are there any spelling or grammar mistakes? Are the pictures big enough? Is everything easy to understand? If you want to give a presentation, practise it before you give it.

Present it skill: presentations p. 158

Present your work. You can ask your classmates for feedback after the presentation.

1 WORKING WITH WORDS
Wortschatzarbeit

Im *Dictionary* ab Seite 219 kannst du die Wörter nachschlagen, die in diesem Buch vorkommen. Dort findest du auch die Lernwörter aus den vorigen Bänden. Wenn du ein Wort suchst, das dort nicht steht und das du dir nicht aus dem Zusammenhang erschließen kannst, kannst du ein Wörterbuch benutzen. Hier findest du einige Tipps zum Umgang mit Wörterbüchern.

1. Wörterbücher

▸ Wörterbücher haben oben auf jeder Seite Leitwörter, die den jeweils ersten oder letzten Eintrag auf der Seite anzeigen.

▸ Die Wörter sind alphabetisch geordnet. Du darfst nicht nur auf den ersten Buchstaben achten, sondern musst auch die folgenden Buchstaben angucken: *face* steht beispielsweise vor *false*.

▸ Hinter den fett gedruckten Einträgen stehen Lautschrift und Wortart. Dann folgen in einsprachigen Wörterbüchern eine Definition oder Erklärung des Wortes, in zweisprachigen Wörterbüchern die Übersetzung und Beispiele zur Verwendung des Wortes.

2. Die richtige Übersetzung finden

▸ Angenommen, du suchst ein Wort aus einem Rezept, beispielsweise *season*.

▸ Was bedeutet hier *season*? Schau im Wörterbuch nach:

Method:
1. Cut the chicken into slices. Then season the chicken with salt, pepper and curry powder.

Betonungszeichen —— ┌ **Lautschrift**

Wortart (hier Verb)   ┌── **Wortart (hier Substantiv/Nomen)**

sea•son /'siːzn/ **I** *s.* **1.** (Jahres)Zeit *f.;* **2.** (Reife- *etc.*)Zeit *f.,* rechte Zeit *(für et.);* **3.** Saison *f.;* **II** *v/t* **4.** *Speisen* würzen; **III** *v/i* **5.** reifen; **6.** ablagern

▸ *season* als Nomen mit der Bedeutung „Jahreszeit" oder „Saison" ergibt hier keinen Sinn. Außerdem ist *season* in deinem Beispiel ein Verb.
Du kannst also nicht immer gleich beim ersten Eintrag aufhören zu lesen, du musst immer alle Einträge durchlesen. Dann entscheidest du, welche Übersetzung am besten passt.

▸ Unter dem Eintrag des Verbs *season* findest du unter anderem den Eintrag „würzen" – das ist hier die passende Übersetzung.

▨ 🖥 **Tipp: Nutze elektronische Hilfsmittel!** (media worksheet 3)

· Im Internet gibt es viele Seiten, auf denen du Wörter nachschlagen und dir die richtige Aussprache anhören kannst. Oft gibt es ausführliche Erklärungen zu den unterschiedlichen Bedeutungen in verschiedenen Zusammenhängen.

2 LISTENING
Hören

In Klasse 5 und 6 hast du schon einige Strategien für
Hörübungen kennengelernt.
Hier ist eine Zusammenfassung der wichtigsten Punkte:

1. Vor dem Hören

▶ Gibt es eine Höraufgabe im Buch? Dann lies sie dir genau durch. Was sollst du herausfinden?

▶ Wie lautet die Überschrift des Hörtextes? Welche Hinweise gibt sie dir?

▶ Gibt es Bilder? Was ist darauf zu sehen? Vielleicht kannst du vor dem Hören schon etwas über die Situation herausfinden.

▶ Überlege: Worum könnte es gehen? Was weißt du schon über das Thema?

2. Während des Hörens

▶ Höre dir den Hörtext einmal ganz an und verschaffe dir einen Überblick.
Wer ist beteiligt? Was ist passiert? Vielleicht kannst du auch schon etwas heraushören,
das du für die Bearbeitung der Aufgabe brauchst.

▶ Dabei musst du nicht jedes einzelne Wort verstehen. Versuche erst einmal herauszufinden,
worum es ganz allgemein geht *(listening for gist)*.

▶ Achte auch auf die Stimmen der Sprechenden. Selbst Hintergrundgeräusche können dir
helfen zu verstehen, worum es geht.

▶ Sieh dir noch einmal an, was du herausfinden sollst. Dann höre wieder zu. Achte diesmal auch
auf Details *(listening for detail)* und mache dir Notizen. Notiere nur Stichwörter, keine ganzen
Sätze.

Who?	Where?	When?	What?
Wer spricht? Um wen geht es?	Wo findet das Gespräch / die Geschichte statt?	Wann findet das Gespräch / die Geschichte statt?	Was wird besprochen? Was passiert?

3. Nach dem Hören

▶ Vergleicht eure Ergebnisse. Was habt ihr herausgefunden?

🔲 **Tipp: Nutze jede Gelegenheit, um Englisch zu hören!**

· Alle Hörtexte zum Buch findest du, wenn du auf www.westermann.de/webcode den Webcode
  WES-128202-001 eingibst oder den QR-Code scannst, den du auf Seite 2 findest.

· Versuch doch mal, dein Lieblingsbuch als Hörbuch auf Englisch anzuhören.

· Es gibt verschiedene Möglichkeiten, sich Texte in verschiedenen Geschwindigkeiten vorlesen
  zu lassen. Du kannst probieren, das Tempo nach und nach zu erhöhen.

3 TALKING WITH PEOPLE
Mit anderen sprechen

Um dein Englisch zu trainieren, solltest du jede Gelegenheit nutzen, Englisch zu sprechen. Auch wenn es dir vielleicht komisch vorkommt – sprich so viel Englisch wie möglich mit deinen Mitschülerinnen und Mitschülern.

---

1. Versuche, so viel wie möglich auf Englisch auszudrücken

▶ Wenn du über ein bestimmtes Thema sprechen willst, überlege dir vorher einige Ausdrücke, die du im Gespräch verwenden kannst. Die *wordbanks* ab Seite 160 können dir dabei helfen.

▶ Wenn du etwas nicht verstanden hast, bitte darum, dass es wiederholt wird:
   „*Can you say that again, please?*" oder: „*Can you repeat that, please?*"

▶ Wenn dir ein Wort nicht einfällt, kannst du es umschreiben:
   „*Excuse me, could you pass me the … erm … it's not a fork or a knife. You can eat soup with it.*"

2. Präge dir Redewendungen und Sätze ein

▶ Es gibt eine Reihe von Redewendungen und Sätzen, die du im Englischunterricht häufig verwenden kannst.

▶ Viele davon findest du bei den *classroom phrases* auf den Seiten 170-171.

3. Wenn du Interviews durchführst

▶ Schreibe deine Fragen auf und überlege, was mögliche Antworten sein könnten.

▶ Stelle offene Fragen, die mehr als ein Wort als Antwort erfordern.
   Verwende Fragewörter wie *what, when, where, who, how* oder *why*.

▶ Wenn etwas unklar ist oder du es nicht richtig verstanden hast, stelle weitere Fragen oder bitte um Wiederholung.

4. Sprich so oft Englisch, wie du kannst

▶ Höre dir die Hörtexte aus deinem Englischbuch an und lies die Texte laut mit. Versuche, die Aussprache der Sprecherinnen und Sprecher nachzuahmen.

▶ Singe englischsprachige Lieder mit.

▶ Unterhalte dich auf Englisch mit jemandem, der ebenfalls Englisch sprechen kann.

Tipp: Nimm dich auf! (media worksheet 5)

· Lies einen Text aus dem Buch laut vor oder sprich Englisch und nimm dich auf.
  Dann kannst du dich selbst anhören und überprüfen, wie dein Englisch klingt.

· Wenn ihr zu zweit zusammenarbeitet, könnt ihr Dialoge und Interviews aufnehmen und gemeinsam prüfen, ob es noch etwas zu verbessern gibt.

4 WRITING
Schreiben

Auch zum Erstellen unterschiedlicher Texte hast du schon einige Methoden kennengelernt. Wichtig ist, dass du deinen Text planst und nicht einfach losschreibst. Hier sind die wichtigsten Schritte:

1. Planen

▸ Überlege: Was für einen Text willst du schreiben – eine E-Mail, eine Textnachricht, eine Geschichte, einen Brief? Auf www.westermann.de/webcode kannst du den Webcode WES-128202-001 eingeben und dort Anleitungen zu verschiedenen Textsorten finden.

▸ Wenn du eine Geschichte schreiben willst, kannst du mithilfe von *who, what, where, when* und *why* Ideen sammeln und die Geschichte planen.

▸ Außerdem kann es helfen, in einem *word web* oder einer Liste passende Wörter zu sammeln. Du kannst auch in den *wordbanks* im Buch oder in einem Wörterbuch nachschauen.

▸ Überlege: Was sollte am Anfang stehen, wie weckst du Interesse? Was folgt darauf? Wie könnte das Ende der Geschichte sein?

▸ Auch wenn du einen Artikel oder Bericht schreibst, solltest du dir vorher überlegen, wie du ihn gliedern möchtest und wichtige Wörter sammeln.

2. Schreiben und überarbeiten

▸ Bei jeder Art von Texten gilt, dass du zunächst einen Entwurf *(draft)* schreiben solltest – entweder handschriftlich oder am Computer.

▸ Überlege dir eine passende Überschrift. Möchtest du Bilder einfügen? Falls ja, suche passende und vergiss nicht, anzugeben, wo du sie gefunden hast.

▸ Überarbeite und verbessere *(edit)* dann deinen Text. Du kannst auch andere nach ihrer Meinung zu deinem Text und nach Verbesserungsvorschlägen fragen.

▸ Wenn dein Text fertig ist, schreibe ihn ins Reine. Das kannst du handschriftlich oder mithilfe eines Textverarbeitungsprogramms am Computer machen.

3. Veröffentlichen

▸ Dein fertiger Text sollte „veröffentlicht" werden *(publish)*. Zeige ihn deiner Lehrkraft, einem Mitschüler, einer Mitschülerin oder der Klasse.

▸ Du kannst deinen Text in deinem (digitalen) Portfolio aufbewahren.

Tipp: Texte digital erstellen und veröffentlichen (media worksheet 1, 9-15)

· Wenn du einen Text mithilfe eines Textverarbeitungsprogramms am Computer schreibst, kannst du zunächst Ideen und nützliche Wörter in einem Dokument sammeln und speichern. Du kannst deine Ideensammlung und deinen Text dann jederzeit bearbeiten, ändern und ergänzen.

· Oft könnt ihr Texte, die in Einzel- oder Partnerarbeit entstanden sind, zu einem Klassenprodukt zusammenfügen. Vielleicht gibt es die Möglichkeit, dieses Produkt auf der Schul- oder Klassenwebseite zu veröffentlichen.

5 READING
Lesen

Es gibt viele Strategien, die dir helfen können, einen englischen Text zu verstehen. Hier sind drei der wichtigsten:

1. Skimming

Beim *skimming* überfliegst du den Text erst einmal. Du versuchst, dir schnell einen Überblick zu verschaffen: Worum geht es? Was passiert? Wer ist beteiligt?
Dafür brauchst du nicht jedes Wort zu verstehen.

2. Reading for detail

Du liest den Text gründlich, um möglichst viele Details herauszufinden. Mit den *wh*-Fragen kannst du die wichtigsten Informationen herausbekommen: Who? Where? When? What?

SWIMMING IS HIS LIFE

He's young, he's fast, he's great! This young man is going to make it to the top. Leroy Haffner will soon be one of Britain's best swimmers! Leroy was born in Bristol, UK. Swimming has always been his greatest love. He started swimming at the age of four. Three years later he had already won medals for his local club. The pool became the centre of his life and he took part in one national competition after another. Then last year, Leroy had an injury and couldn't swim for nearly two months. It was the worst time of his life. But Leroy is a fighter and he didn't give up. He started swimming again – and with great success.
Next week, Leroy will participate in the National Championships. His coach, Ted Henley, knows that "Leroy will do really, really well".

Mache dir Notizen. Auf Kopien oder in deinen eigenen Büchern kannst du auch wichtige Textstellen markieren.

3. Scanning

Beim *scanning* suchst du einen Text gezielt nach ganz bestimmten Informationen ab, zum Beispiel nach speziellen Fakten.

Tipp: Suche dir englische Texte zu Themen, die dich interessieren!

- Du kannst im Internet und in Büchereien nach interessanten Texten auf Englisch suchen.
- Lies so viel du kannst. Am Ende jeder Unit in diesem Buch findest du eine Kurzgeschichte und einen Sachtext oder ein Gedicht.

6 MEDIATION
Sprachmittlung

Manchmal gibt es Situationen, in denen du jemandem helfen musst, der deine Muttersprache oder eine Fremdsprache nicht so gut kann wie du. Hier erfährst du, wie das funktioniert:

1. Gib den Sinn wieder

Es kommt nicht darauf an, dass du alles Wort für Wort übersetzt. Wichtiger ist es, den Sinn wiederzugeben. Es muss klar werden, worum es geht.

Was gibt es heute Besonderes?

Our special recommendation today is fresh fish. Our chef was able to get some fresh trout that was caught this morning. We serve it with a lemon cream sauce, a side dish of rice and a light salad.

Es gibt frischen Fisch in Zitronensauce mit Reis und Salat.

2. Fasse dich kurz

Bilde einfache, kurze Sätze. Unwichtige Einzelheiten kannst du weglassen.

Was steht denn da?

**Science Museum –
New section open now**
Don't miss our brand new exhibition section on the history of the computer. From a model of Konrad Zuse's Z3, the first working computer in the world, to the latest tablets, there's a lot to see, learn and try out.

Sie haben eine neue Abteilung zur Geschichte des Computers eröffnet.

Tipp: Keine Angst vor Fehlern!

- Wenn dir ein wichtiges Wort nicht einfällt, kannst du es umschreiben.
- Versuche, dich an Redewendungen zu erinnern. Zum Beispiel kannst du mit „What about …?" Vorschläge machen oder mit „There is … / There are …" etwas beschreiben.

7 WATCHING A VIDEO CLIP
Videoclips verstehen

Englischsprachige Videoclips anzuschauen macht Spaß und ist eine tolle Möglichkeit, die Sprache noch besser zu lernen. Dabei solltest du einige Dinge beachten:

1. Bevor es losgeht
▸ Gibt es Bilder aus dem Videoclip in deinem Buch? Was ist zu sehen?
▸ Lies den Titel des Videoclips. Welche Hinweise gibt er auf den Inhalt?
▸ Worum könnte es gehen? Stelle Vermutungen an. Weißt du vielleicht schon etwas über das Thema?

2. Währenddessen
▸ Schaue dir den Videoclip in Ruhe an. Konzentriere dich dabei zunächst vor allem auf das, was du siehst.
  Who?   Wer ist zu sehen? Um wen geht es?
  Where? Wo findet das Geschehen statt?
  When? Wann findet das Geschehen statt?
  What? Worum geht es? Was passiert?
▸ Was ist dein erster Eindruck? Mache dir Notizen. Es ist nicht schlimm, wenn du nicht alles verstehst. Achte auf die Stimmen, Körpersprache und Gesichtsausdrücke der Personen im Videoclip.
▸ Gibt es eine Aufgabe zu dem Videoclip in deinem Buch? Was sollst du herausfinden? Behalte die Fragen im Kopf, während du ein zweites Mal zuschaust. Konzentriere dich stärker auf das, was du hörst. Kannst du jetzt schon mehr verstehen? Gibt es Wörter, die immer wieder vorkommen? Notiere sie dir.
▸ Versuche, gleich danach die Fragen zu beantworten. Wenn nötig, schaue dir dann den Clip ein weiteres Mal an. Überprüfe dabei deine Antworten.

3. Hinterher
▸ Tausche dich mit deinen Mitschülerinnen und Mitschülern aus.
  Welche Eindrücke habt ihr bekommen? Was habt ihr herausgefunden?

Tipp: Schaue dir Videoclips und Filme auf Englisch an (media worksheet 8)

- Alle Videoclips zum Buch findest du, wenn du auf www.westermann.de/webcode den Webcode WES-128202-001 eingibst oder den QR-Code scannst, den du auf Seite 2 findest.
- Sieh dir Filme, Serien oder Berichte zu Themen, die dich interessieren, auf Englisch an.
- Auf DVDs oder bei Streaming-Diensten kannst du fast immer den englischen Ton und englische Untertitel einschalten. Nach und nach lernst du so besser zu verstehen, was gesagt wird.

8 SEARCHING THE INTERNET
Im Internet recherchieren

Hier erfährst du, wie du im Internet zu einem Thema recherchieren kannst.

---

1. Benutze eine Suchmaschine

▷ Gute Suchbegriffe erleichtern dir die Suche im Internet. Versuche, möglichst genau zu formulieren, wonach du suchst – und zwar auf Englisch.

▷ Gib die Suchbegriffe in eine Suchmaschine ein.

▷ Es kann sein, dass die Suchmaschine eine riesige Anzahl an Treffern anzeigt. Oft genügt es, sich die ersten 10 bis 20 Suchergebnisse anzuschauen.

---

2. Suche auf englischsprachigen Seiten

▷ Suche am besten direkt auf englischsprachigen Seiten – dann steht dir der nötige Wortschatz gleich zur Verfügung. Bei vielen Suchmaschinen kannst du Englisch als Sprache wählen.

▷ Es gibt Webseiten, auf denen du Informationen in einfacherem Englisch finden kannst. Deine Lehrkraft kann dir helfen, sie zu finden.

---

3. Halte nützliche Informationen fest

▷ Überfliege erst einmal die Seiten, die dir interessant erscheinen. Dafür brauchst du nicht jedes Wort zu verstehen.

▷ Wenn du interessante Webseiten gefunden hast, kannst du dir Notizen zu den Inhalten machen.

▷ Denke daran, dir auch das Datum deiner Recherche aufzuschreiben und die Quelle zu sichern. So weißt du später noch, wo du die Informationen gefunden hast.

▷ Wenn du Textausschnitte für deine eigenen Texte unverändert aus dem Internet übernimmst, musst du zeigen, dass es Zitate sind. Setze sie in Anführungszeichen und gib die Quelle an, sowie das Datum, an dem du sie gefunden hast.

---

4. Sei kritisch

▷ Informationen, die du im Internet findest, sind nicht immer richtig.

▷ Sei deshalb kritisch und überprüfe die Informationen noch einmal auf anderen Seiten oder in einem Lexikon.

Tipp: Nutze digitale Tools (media worksheet 6, 7)

· Es gibt viele sinnvolle Tools im Internet. Du kannst zum Beispiel Währungen und Maßeinheiten umrechnen oder dir Entfernungen anzeigen lassen.

· Viele englischsprachige Einrichtungen, vor allem Museen, bieten virtuelle Rundgänge an.

· Du kannst auch virtuell durch britische Städte spazieren.

9 PRESENTATIONS
Präsentationen halten

Hier findest du einige Tipps und Tricks für gelungene Präsentationen.

---

1. Bevor du etwas präsentierst

▸ Überlege: Was möchtest du zu deinem Thema sagen? Wie viel Zeit hast du für deinen Vortrag?

▸ Bei einer sehr kurzen Präsentation, zum Beispiel einem *one-minute talk*, musst du dich auf das absolut Notwendige beschränken.

▸ Gliedere deinen Vortrag: Überlege, in welcher Reihenfolge du deine Ideen vorstellen und wie du anfangen möchtest.

▸ Fertige ein Poster oder eine Computerpräsentation an, um deinen Vortrag anschaulich zu machen. Wenn du Bilder oder Texte aus dem Internet oder aus einem Buch kopiert hast, dann vermerke immer, wo und wann du sie gefunden hast.

▸ Notiere Stichpunkte zu dem, was du sagen möchtest, auf Karteikarten.

▸ Übe deinen Vortrag vor dem Spiegel, vor Freunden oder vor deiner Familie.

---

2. Während du präsentierst

▸ Sprich langsam und deutlich.

▸ Sieh deine Zuhörerinnen und Zuhörer an, wenn du sprichst. Achte zum Beispiel bei einer Computerpräsentation darauf, nicht ständig auf den Bildschirm zu schauen.

▸ Versuche, frei zu sprechen. Du kannst die wichtigsten Punkte von deinen Notizen oder deinem Poster ablesen. Nützliche Redewendungen findest du in der *wordbank* auf Seite 168.

3. So wird dein Vortrag spannend und lebendig

▸ Musik, Videoclips, interessante Bilder oder Zitate machen deinen Vortrag abwechslungsreich.

▸ Achte auf eine lebendige Mimik, Gestik und Stimme.

▸ Zeige deinen Zuhörerinnen und Zuhörern auf deinem Poster oder auf den Seiten deiner Computerpräsentation, worüber du gerade sprichst. So wird dein Vortrag für die Klasse noch interessanter.

So sieht ein gelungenes Vortragsposter aus

▸ *ansprechende Überschrift*

▸ *interessante Informationen*

▸ *verständliche Sätze, aber nicht zu viel Text*

▸ *große Bilder und Schrift: Jeder im Raum muss sie sehen und lesen können.*

▸ *saubere Schrift*

▸ *Bilder mit Bildunterschriften*

Tipp: Schau dir Tutorials an (media worksheet 4)

• Zum Präsentieren gibt es viele Tutorials im Internet. Schau dir einige an und überlege, was bei dir schon gut klappt und was du noch verbessern könntest.

• Zum Thema Computerpräsentationen kannst du dir ein passendes Arbeitsblatt herunterladen und dir Tutorials anschauen. Gehe dazu auf www.westermann.de/webcode und gib den Webcode WES-128202-001 ein.

10 PERFORMING A SCENE
Eine Szene vorspielen

Szenische Lesungen, Rollenspiele und Theaterstücke sind eine gute Methode, um dein Englisch zu trainieren. Hier findest du einige Tipps, damit du deine Rolle erfolgreich spielen kannst.

1. Szenische Lesung

▸ Für ein *dramatic reading* musst du deinen Text nicht auswendig lernen. Du solltest ihn aber so gut kennen, dass du auf Aussprache, Betonung und Mimik achten kannst, ohne den Faden zu verlieren.

▸ Achte darauf, dass Betonung, Lautstärke und Aussprache zu dem passen, was du liest.

2. Rollenspiele

▸ Mit der Methode *read – look up – speak* kannst du deine Rolle auswendig lernen: Du liest deinen Satz still, siehst dann auf und sprichst ihn.

▸ Halte beim Sprechen Augenkontakt zu deinem Gegenüber.

▸ Wechselt auch mal die Rollen und übt mit anderen Partnern. So lernt ihr, spontan zu reagieren.

▸ Wenn ihr *cue cards* verwendet, denkt daran, nur Stichworte zu notieren, keine ganzen Sätze!

3. Theaterstücke

▸ Bei Theaterstücken geht es noch mehr als bei Rollenspielen um das Schauspielern. Du solltest deinen Text gut auswendig lernen, damit du dich besser auf das Spielen konzentrieren kannst.

▸ Versetze dich in die Person hinein, die du darstellst. Überlege, in welcher Stimmung die Person ist. Denke beim Sprechen an die passende Mimik und Gestik.

▸ Mit Requisiten *(props)* und Kostümen fällt es leichter, richtig in eine Rolle hineinzuschlüpfen.

▸ Denke immer daran, laut und deutlich und nicht zu schnell zu sprechen, damit das Publikum dich gut verstehen kann.

4. Präsentieren

▸ Rollenspiele, kleine Szenen, Sketche und Theaterstücke sind gute Mittel, um auch anderen zu zeigen, wie viel Englisch ihr schon könnt. Bei einem Schulfest oder an einem Tag der offenen Tür könnt ihr Eltern oder andere Klassen zu einer Vorführung einladen.

 Tipp: Schaut euch selbst zu (media worksheet 2)

· Rollenspiele könnt ihr aufnehmen und so gemeinsam überprüfen, ob es noch etwas zu verbessern gibt.

Eating and eating out

I have never eaten octopus.
But I would like to try it.

My family's traditional dish
is Sunday roast.

I tried sushi but I didn't
like it.

On special occasions we go out
for a meal. We often go to a
traditional British restaurant.

My favourite food is mashed
potatoes with bacon and chips.

Food can be …

savoury · sweet · tasty · yummy · perfect · delicious · vegetarian · nice ·
spicy · good · bad · special · disgusting · fried · healthy ·
fresh · traditional · vegan · hot · grilled · overcooked

Preparing a meal

- *Heat two tablespoons of oil / butter /…*
- *Chop the tomatoes / vegetables /…*
- *Slice the onion / cucumber /…*
- *Cut the potatoes / carrots /… in half.*
- *Put the vegetables in the pot / pan /…*
- *Add a teaspoon of salt / sugar /…*
- *Boil for 10 minutes / half an hour /…*
- *Stir in the flour / the milk /…*
- *Add a cup of yoghurt /…*
- *Cover the pot / pan /…*
- *Bake for 20 minutes / one hour /…*

Ingredients

a bag of potatoes · some tomatoes ·
many carrots · a lot of peppers ·
a few onions · 500g of cabbage ·
one cup of chickpeas · 3 cloves of garlic

a little water · some couscous ·
a bit of bread · a cup of rice

a bottle of milk · a little yoghurt ·
a piece of cheese

some cumin · a little coriander ·
pepper · a teaspoon of paprika ·
a pinch of cayenne pepper · cinnamon ·
not too much salt

At a restaurant

On a menu you can find …

starters · main courses · desserts ·
drinks · sides · soups · salads

Restaurants can be …

expensive · good · bad · nice · cosy ·
lovely · cheap · delicious · vegetarian ·
traditional · perfect · vegan

A restaurant review

My favourite restaurant is …
The service was quick / good / bad / …
I had the …
The food was tasty / healthy / cheap /
good value for money / disgusting /
spicy / overcooked / burnt / …
I had the best / worst … I have ever eaten.
The atmosphere was friendly / cosy /
relaxed / busy / …
It is not as … as other restaurants.
It is … / more … than other restaurants.

Keeping fit

My favourite sport is swimming. I'm really strong and I like being on my own. I like being indoors and outdoors, so I go swimming at the swimming pool but also in the sea.

I love dancing! I don't like being outdoors, so climbing, cycling and going hiking are not my favourite sports. I prefer indoor sports. Dancing is perfect for me because I like music, too.

I enjoy diving because I like being in the water and watching fish. I love outdoor sports. I just can't be indoors all the time. Being outside makes me happy and I feel less stressed.

Sports

rowing · cross-country running · climbing · swimming · weight training · running · riding · dancing · diving · marathon · triathlon

play: cricket · football · ball sports · rugby · games · golf · chess · tennis · water polo · baseball

do: athletics · martial arts · yoga · judo · gymnastics · karate · aikido · parkour

I don't really know what sport I would like.

You should play / go / do …

Sports can be …

fun · exciting · exhausting · difficult · easy · good for you · dangerous · fast

I'm always stressed.

I think doing yoga would be a good idea because it is so relaxing.

My sports idol

My favourite sportsperson is … because he / she is fast / good at … / …
He / She respects other players and is friendly / funny / …
He / She trains hard and gives a lot of money to charity.

I have never tried playing football.

I think you would be good at it because you can run very fast.

Health

To stay healthy, it is important to …

do sport regularly · get enough sleep · eat healthily · spend time outdoors · drink enough water ·
don't eat too many sweets · make sure you are not too stressed · do things that make you happy · relax ·
eat enough fruit and vegetables

At the doctor's

What's the matter?

Where does it hurt?

When did you fall?

Does your toe hurt?

Have you got a headache?

How long have you had a headache for?

You should rest until you feel better.

You will have to stay at home for a week.

There is something wrong with my leg.

It is swollen and painful.

My knee is bleeding.

I hurt my ankle.

What do I have to do?

How soon will I feel better?

When will I be able to do sports again?

You can have …

a sore throat · a fever · a cough · a cold ·
a headache · an infection · a running nose ·
a toothache · a broken arm · an injury ·
a sprained ankle · a stomach ache

You can feel …

ill · sick · dizzy · tired · well again

You need …

a plaster · a cast · some medicine ·
an ambulance · to go to the dentist's ·
to rest · to see a doctor · an X-ray ·
to make an appointment for a check-up with
your GP · to cool your leg and keep it up

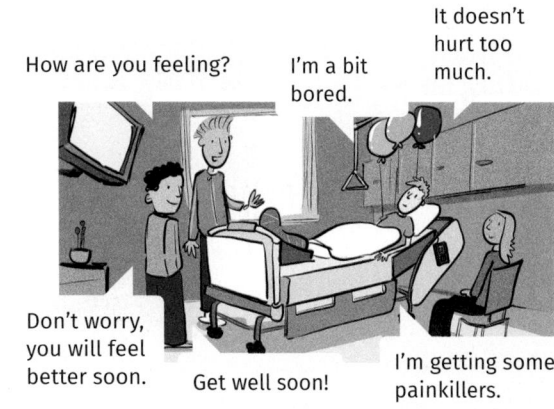

How are you feeling?

I'm a bit bored.

It doesn't hurt too much.

Don't worry, you will feel better soon.

Get well soon!

I'm getting some painkillers.

What's on?

What shall we do in London this weekend?
Where could we go?

My favourite event is the Notting Hill Carnival.
I would like to see the costumes and listen to
the music. Do you want to go there?

Portobello Market is not really quiet.
What about going to the cinema?

There is a summer festival in
St James's Park. What about that?

Why don't we go to Portobello Market? You can
buy lots of different things there, try food from
all over the world and meet interesting people.

That's always so loud and there are so many
people. I really don't want to go there.
I would prefer something more quiet.

It's so warm and sunny, why don't we do
something outside?

That sounds good. Let's do that!
I've never been to an outdoor festival before.

When is it?

this weekend · next month · on 3 July · Sunday morning ·
Monday afternoon · in the evening · at twelve o'clock

Buying and selling

Can I help you?

Excuse me, I'm looking for a pair of jeans.

Why don't you try it on?

Do you have any
dark blue ones?

I can give it to you
for £25.50.

How much does
this pair cost?

Anything else?

How much are these?

That'll be £30.80.

Here's your change.

Für die Schreibung von
Geldbeträgen wird im
Englischen zuerst das
Währungssymbol geschrieben,
dann – ohne Leerzeichen –
der Betrag in Ziffern. Es wird
ein Punkt und kein Komma
verwendet! Zum Beispiel:
£4.50 / €3.45

Advertising things

For just £2.50 you can get a ...

It's ideal for ...

This is the perfect ... for you!

Are you looking for a ...?

Events

When you go to a music festival, you can listen to lots of different bands.

You can watch many different actors perform at a theatre festival.

When you take part in a charity run, you can do something good while you're having fun.

At a flea market you can sell things you don't need anymore and buy things that other people don't need anymore.

If you like going to the cinema, a film festival is the event for you!

At the Notting Hill Carnival you can watch a brilliant parade.

Events can be …

loud · crowded · free · exciting · fun · for children · world-famous · interesting

---

For or against big events?

I think big events are great. You can meet new people and have new experiences. Sometimes you can learn something new.

I don't like big events because there are so many people. It gets very crowded and loud.

Big events are good for shopkeepers because they get more customers.

Many visitors come by car and they leave their rubbish everywhere. That's bad for the environment.

Events are good for the people who work at them – for example musicians and actors who perform there.

Sometimes they are even free.

Those events are only about making money. The entrance fee can be really expensive.

Expressing opinions

In my opinion, …

I think that …

If you ask me, …

I agree that …

On the one hand,…

On the other hand,…

I would say that …

Family history

I am originally from Brighton. I moved when I was 19 and went to university in Leeds.

My parents met in London when they were studying there.

My mother spent her childhood in Edinburgh. When she was a teenager, her family moved to Wales.

My brother was born in London. My family moved to Brighton when he was three.

My great-grandfather grew up in Trinidad. He started working when he was 16 years old and he met my great-grandmother when he was 18.

Two years later my parents got married.

They had four children and emigrated to Great Britain in the 1950s.

When did it happen?

in the 1990s · in 2005 · around 2010 · on 22nd October 1999 · in the early 1930s · in the late 1960s · in March 1981

Family

mother · father · son · daughter · child · brother · sister · uncle · aunt · cousin · wife · husband · partner · grandmother · grandfather

Home

For me, home is where my family is.
I don't feel at home without friends and family.
I feel at home when I know everyone in my neighbourhood.
My home is in London / …
I used to live in a small village in the countryside but I like big cities more, so now I live in London.

Talking about pictures

In the picture, there are two children. The girl is sitting on a couch on the left and the boy is sitting on a chair on the right.

I think it's a very old picture. It's black and white and the machine on the table looks funny.

There is a table between them. On the table I can see a vase with flowers.

The girl could be older than the boy. She seems to be a bit afraid.

They might be listening to the radio.

The boy doesn't look very happy.

Maybe the children are brother and sister.

Feelings

I am feeling ...

angry

afraid

worried

bored

... **excited** because I'm going to a music festival at the weekend.

... **lonely** because all my friends are on holiday.

... **upset** about an argument with my mum.

... **stressed** because I have a problem at school.

... **proud** because I was very good at my maths test.

... **shy** because I have to start a new school.

... **scared** because there's a big black spider in my room.

... **nervous** about my next English test.

happy

sad

Seeking and giving advice

I have a problem with my parents.
They are so strict. Do you have any tips?
What do you think I should do? Can you help?
How shall I deal with them?
I don't know what to do. I need some advice.
Can you help me, / give me some advice,
please?

What's the problem? What happened?
Why are you feeling so sad?

I'm sorry to hear that. Why don't
you try to talk to them again?

How about you ask your brothers for help?

I think you should wait for a while and then try again.

Why do you think you can't talk to them?

Have you tried asking your grandma for advice?
Maybe you could speak to her.

I suggest that you talk to the school counsellor.

Inventions

I proudly present my latest invention. It will solve a lot of problems.

You can save a lot of time and money with this machine.

It can improve people's lives because it helps them with different tasks.

It can work for hours without electricity.

It can be used anywhere at any time.

You only have to switch it on.

My invention is very useful if you haven't got enough time.

It was invented in 1982. · It was invented by James Watt. · It can be used to pull heavy objects. · It can be seen all over the world. · It is used by many people every day. · It was built in 1895. · First versions of this invention appeared in 1723. · It was invented to cure people.

Presenting something

Hello and welcome to my presentation about …
First I would like to introduce the topic of …
In the second part of my presentation, I will …
After that I will talk about …
Finally, I will look at …
I will first give some information on …
Here is an example of …
On this slide you can see …
This is a photo of …
This picture shows that …
It is also important to mention that …
The last aspect is …
Thanks for listening. Are there any questions?

Giving feedback

I enjoyed your presentation because you talked about all aspects of the topic.

There was a good summary at the end.

My favourite part of your presentation was when you talked about …

The best part were the pictures on the third slide.

I think it was a good / fantastic / well-researched / … presentation.

Well done for giving a good presentation.

You could improve by speaking more loudly / more clearly / more slowly / …

You need to improve on your time management / research more facts / …

Next time you should have a clearer structure / more pictures / less … / a handout / …

The presentation was a little hard to understand.

Communication

How do you communicate with your friends and family?

How often do you text your best friend?

What is the best way to communicate with your grandparents?

Have you ever been on a video chat?

I write text messages to my friends.

I send letters or emails to my grandparents.

I send postcards when I am on holiday.

I often call my best friend.

I react with a heart or a smiley to comment on my friend's social media post.

Dear Mr Kogan,
Dear Mrs Norris,
Dear Grandma,
Hi Ava,

How are you? I'm …

Yours sincerely, …
Lots of love, … / Love, …
I look forward to hearing from you.
Please write to me soon!

Olivia Norris
Lexham Gardens 2A
London W8 5JL
UK

Going online

I'm online for about two hours every day. I chat with my friends, watch videos or play games.

I don't post anything that I don't want to go on the Internet.

My password is strong. Nobody knows it but me and my parents.

I don't share things with people I don't know.

I always ask people for their permission before I take pictures of them.

I delete photos when the person in them asks me to.

Classroom phrases

Wenn man ankommt oder geht

Good morning.	Guten Morgen.
What's for homework?	Was haben wir als Hausaufgabe auf?
See you tomorrow.	Bis morgen.
Bye.	Tschüs.

Wenn es ein Problem gibt

Sorry I'm late.	Tut mir leid, dass ich zu spät bin.
Sorry, I haven't got my exercise book with me.	Tut mir leid, ich habe mein Heft nicht dabei.
Sorry, I haven't got my homework with me.	Tut mir leid, ich habe meine Hausaufgaben nicht dabei.
What's the matter?	Was ist los?
I'm fine.	Mir geht's gut.
I feel sick.	Mir ist schlecht.
I've got a headache.	Ich habe Kopfschmerzen.
Can I open the window, please?	Kann ich bitte das Fenster öffnen?
Can I go to the toilet, please?	Kann ich bitte zur Toilette gehen?

Wenn man Hilfe braucht

Can you help me, please?	Können Sie / Kannst du mir bitte helfen?
I've got a question.	Ich habe eine Frage.
I don't understand this.	Ich verstehe das hier nicht.
How can I do this exercise?	Wie kann ich diese Aufgabe machen?
What's … in English / German?	Was heißt … auf Englisch / Deutsch?
What does … mean?	Was bedeutet …?
Is that correct?	Ist das richtig?
Can you write that on the board, please?	Können Sie das bitte an die Tafel schreiben?
Can you spell that, please?	Können Sie das bitte buchstabieren?
Can you say that again, please?	Können Sie / Kannst du das bitte noch einmal sagen?
Can we listen to the audio track again, please?	Können wir den Audiotrack bitte noch einmal hören?
Sorry, I don't know.	Tut mir leid, das weiß ich nicht.
What page, please?	Auf welcher Seite bitte?

Wenn man zusammen arbeitet oder spielt

Whose turn is it?	Wer ist dran?
Do you want to work with me?	Möchtest du mit mir arbeiten?
Let's check …	Lass uns … überprüfen.
Let's compare …	Lass uns … vergleichen.
Let's talk about …	Lass uns über … sprechen.

Wenn man mit dem Computer arbeitet

What's your email address?	Wie ist deine E-Mail-Adresse?
You can click on this link.	Du kannst auf diesen Link klicken.
Can I print that out?	Kann ich das ausdrucken?
Can I download it?	Kann ich es herunterladen?
I saved the links to name the sources.	Ich habe die Links gespeichert, um die Quellen anzugeben.
I did research online. I used a search engine.	Ich habe online recherchiert. Ich habe eine Suchmaschine benutzt.

Was die Lehrerin oder der Lehrer sagt

Open your books at page …	Öffnet eure Bücher auf Seite …
Turn to page …	Blättert zu Seite …
Look at line …	Seht euch Zeile … an.
Look at the next paragraph.	Seht euch den nächsten Absatz an.
Read the text on page …	Lies / Lest den Text auf Seite …
Work in pairs / in groups of four.	Arbeitet zu zweit / zu viert.
Listen to the audio track.	Hör dir / Hört euch den Audiotrack an.
Listen to audio track number …	Hör dir / Hört euch Audiotrack Nummer … an.
Write about …	Schreibe / Schreibt über …
Talk about …	Sprich / Sprecht über …
Ask questions about …	Stelle / Stellt Fragen zu …
Answer the question, please.	Beantworte / Beantwortet bitte die Frage.
Match the sentences.	Ordne / Ordnet die Sätze zu.
Who wants to read out the text?	Wer möchte den Text vorlesen?
Write down the answers.	Schreibt die Antworten auf.
Act out the dialogue.	Spielt den Dialog vor.
Change roles.	Tauscht die Rollen.
Make your own dialogue / conversation.	Entwirf / Entwerft selbst einen Dialog / ein Gespräch.
Take a card.	Nimm / Nehmt eine Karte.
Come to the board, please.	Komm / Kommt bitte zur Tafel.
Do this exercise at home, please.	Mache / Macht diese Aufgabe bitte zu Hause.
Be quiet, please.	Sei / Seid bitte ruhig.
Sit down, please.	Setz dich bitte. / Setzt euch bitte.
Please speak up.	Sprich / Sprecht bitte lauter.
You can do better.	Das kannst du / könnt ihr besser.
Try again.	Versuch / Versucht es noch einmal.
Well done.	Gut gemacht.

1 THE PRESENT PERFECT: STATEMENTS (REVISION)
Das Perfekt: Aussagen *(revision)*

Das *present perfect* verwendest du, wenn etwas irgendwann in einem Zeitraum von der Vergangenheit bis zur Gegenwart passiert ist. Der genaue Zeitpunkt ist dabei nicht wichtig.
Du verwendest es auch, wenn ein Vorgang in der Vergangenheit noch Auswirkungen auf die Gegenwart hat.

I *have* already finished my homework. Can I go out now?

a) Bejahte Aussagesätze im *present perfect*

DIGITAL+ video 17

Das *present perfect* bildest du mit *have / has* + Partizip Perfekt *(past participle)*.
Statt *have* bzw. *has* kannst du auch die entsprechende Kurzform benutzen.

*I **have cleaned** the kitchen.*
*I**'ve done** the shopping.*
*He **has finished** his dinner.*
*He**'s tidied** his room.*

Bei regelmäßigen Verben bildest du das Partizip Perfekt, indem du an die Grundform des Verbs die Endung *-ed* anhängst. Beachte auch die Besonderheiten bei der Schreibung und Aussprache der *ed*-Endungen (s. auch Grammatik-Kapitel 13 auf Seite 184).

Grundform	*simple past*	*past participle*
clean	cleaned	cleaned
help	helped	helped
play	played	played
tidy	tidied	tidied
visit	visited	visited

Die Formen der unregelmäßigen Verben musst du wie Vokabeln auswendig lernen.

Auf den Seiten 255–257 findest du hierzu eine Liste und auf Seite 257 einen Tipp, wie du die unregelmäßigen Formen gruppieren kannst, um sie dir leichter einzuprägen.

Grundform	*simple past*	*past participle*
be	was / were	been
do	did	done
have	had	had
buy	bought	bought

b) Verneinte Aussagesätze im *present perfect*

Die Verneinung bildest du mit *have not / has not* + Partizip Perfekt bzw. mit den Kurzformen *haven't / hasn't* + Partizip Perfekt.

*I **have not cleaned** the kitchen yet.*
*He **hasn't finished** his homework.*
*We **haven't eaten** lunch yet.*

2 THE PRESENT PERFECT: QUESTIONS (REVISION)
2 Das Perfekt: Fragen *(revision)*

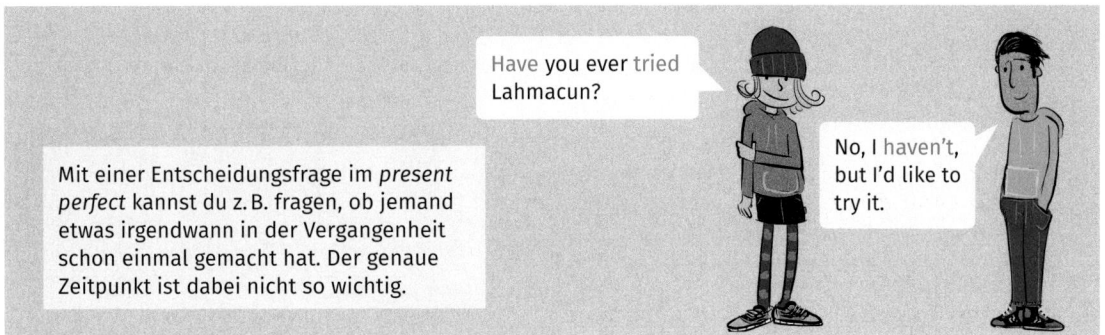

Mit einer Entscheidungsfrage im *present perfect* kannst du z. B. fragen, ob jemand etwas irgendwann in der Vergangenheit schon einmal gemacht hat. Der genaue Zeitpunkt ist dabei nicht so wichtig.

Have you ever tried Lahmacun?

No, I haven't, but I'd like to try it.

a) Entscheidungsfragen und Kurzantworten im *present perfect*

DIGITAL+ video 17

Entscheidungsfragen im *present perfect* bildest du, indem du *have* bzw. *has* an den Satzanfang stellst.

Entscheidungsfrage	Kurzantwort	Kurzantwort
Have you ever been to a Chinese restaurant?	Yes, I have.	No, I haven't.
Has Ava ever eaten a Sunday roast?	Yes, she has.	No, she hasn't.
Have the children finished their dinner?	Yes, they have.	No, they haven't.

b) Fragen mit Fragewort im *present perfect*

Bei Fragen mit Fragewort steht das Fragewort am Satzanfang.

What have you done?
Where have you been?
Why hasn't she called yet?

c) Adverbien der unbestimmten Zeit

Beim *present perfect* ist es nicht wichtig, wann genau in der Vergangenheit etwas passiert ist. Man betrachtet stattdessen den Zeitraum von der Vergangenheit bis zur Gegenwart. Daher werden bei Fragen und Aussagen im *present perfect* häufig Adverbien der unbestimmten Zeit verwendet, z. B. *ever* (= jemals), *never* (= nie), *already* (= schon), *just* (= gerade), *yet* (= schon) und *not yet* (= noch nicht).

Die meisten Adverbien stehen dann direkt vor dem Partizip Perfekt.

*Have you **ever** been to London? – No, I've **never** been there.*
*Has Ava **already** taken Ollie for a walk? – Yes, she has **just** come back.*

Beachte die Ausnahme: *yet* steht am Satzende.

*Have you been to the new Turkish restaurant in town **yet**? – No, I haven't been there **yet**.*

3 QUANTIFIERS (REVISION)
Mengenangaben *(revision)*

There aren't many onions. But there are a lot of carrots and peppers and there's some cabbage. There isn't much cheese ...

Mengenangaben wie *some* und *any* verwendest du, wenn du keine genaue Menge oder Anzahl von etwas angeben möchtest. Auch *much, many* und *a lot of* sind Mengenangaben.

a) Die Mengenangaben *some* und *any*

Some und *any* bedeuten auf Deutsch so viel wie „einige", „ein paar" oder „etwas". In bejahten Aussagesätzen benutzt du *some*.

DIGITAL+ video 18

*There are **some** apples in the kitchen.*
*I need **some** milk for my cornflakes.*

In verneinten Aussagesätzen und in den meisten Fragen verwendest du *any*.
Die Mengenangabe *not ... any* bedeutet „kein" oder „keine".

*Are there **any** apples?*   *We haven't got **any** apples.*
*Have you got **any** milk?*   *There isn't **any** milk.*

Wenn du höflich um etwas bittest oder etwas anbietest, benutzt du *some* auch in Fragen:

*Can I have **some** milk, please?*
*Would you like **some** tea?*

b) Die Mengenangaben *much, many* und *a lot of*

Much (auf Deutsch „viel") wird mit Nomen verwendet, die nicht zählbar sind (z. B. *water, milk, juice, time, money, ...*). Die Nomen stehen daher in der Einzahl.

*We haven't got **much** milk.*
*How **much** cheese have we got?*

Many (auf Deutsch „viele") wird dagegen mit Nomen verwendet, die zählbar sind (z. B. *apples, eggs, tomatoes, ...*). Die Nomen stehen in der Mehrzahl.

*We haven't got **many** apples.*
*How **many** tomatoes have we got?*

Much und *many* werden vor allem in Fragen und verneinten Aussagesätzen verwendet, in bejahten Aussagesätzen eher *a lot of* oder *lots of*. Hier braucht man nicht zwischen zählbaren und nicht zählbaren Nomen zu unterscheiden.

*We need **lots of** juice and **lots of** snacks for the party.*

4 THE COMPARISON OF ADJECTIVES (REVISION)
Die Steigerung von Adjektiven *(revision)*

Wenn du Personen oder Dinge näher beschreiben möchtest, verwendest du Adjektive. Wenn du Personen oder Dinge miteinander vergleichen möchtest, kannst du diese Adjektive steigern. Die erste Steigerungsform heißt Komparativ, die zweite Steigerungsform heißt Superlativ.

This is a very nice restaurant, don't you think?

Yes, much nicer than the other one. Actually, I think it's the nicest in Notting Hill.

a) Steigerung von Adjektiven mit *-er* und *-est*
Einsilbige Adjektive (z. B. *cheap* und *old*) werden durch das Anhängen von *-er* und *-est* gesteigert.

Bei manchen Adjektiven ändert sich die Schreibweise.

Auch einige zweisilbige Adjektive können mit *-er* und *-est* gesteigert werden, z. B. Adjektive, die auf *-er, -le, -ow* und *-y* enden.
Vorsicht: Bei Adjektiven auf *-y* wird dabei aus dem *-y* ein *-i*.

Einige Adjektive haben unregelmäßige Steigerungsformen. Diese Formen musst du wie Vokabeln lernen.

DIGITAL+ video 19

	Komparativ	Superlativ
cheap	cheaper	(the) cheapest
old	older	(the) oldest
big	bigger	(the) biggest
nice	nicer	(the) nicest
clever	cleverer	(the) cleverest
easy	easier	(the) easiest
good	better	(the) best
bad	worse	(the) worst

b) Steigerung von Adjektiven mit *more* und *most*
Mehrsilbige Adjektive werden mit *more* und *most* gesteigert.
Du stellst dabei *more* oder *most* vor das Adjektiv. Das Adjektiv bleibt unverändert.

	Komparativ	Superlativ
useful	more useful	(the) most useful
beautiful	more beautiful	(the) most beautiful
interesting	more interesting	(the) most interesting

c) Vergleichssätze
Willst du Personen oder Dinge miteinander vergleichen, dann benutzt du den Komparativ mit *than*.

*Noah is older **than** Ava.*
*The jacket is more expensive **than** the T-shirt.*

Sind die Eigenschaften gleich, benutzt du *as ... as*.

*Lily is **as** old **as** Harry.*
*The jeans are **as** expensive **as** the jacket.*

5 THE PRESENT PROGRESSIVE (REVISION)
Die Verlaufsform der Gegenwart *(revision)*

Mit dem *present progressive* kannst du beschreiben, was gerade passiert oder was auf einem Bild zu sehen ist. Du kannst es auch verwenden, um über Pläne für die (nähere) Zukunft zu sprechen.

The man **is waiting** for his food.

a) Bejahte Aussagesätze im *present progressive*

So bildest du das *present progressive*:

Form von *be (am, is, are)* + Grundform des Verbs + Endung *-ing*.

I **am** starv**ing**!
The waiter **is** show**ing** the Kogans to their table.
The Kogans **are** order**ing** their food.

Beachte: Endet das Verb auf ein stummes *-e*, dann fällt das *-e* in der *ing*-Form weg.

write → writ**ing**   dance → danc**ing**   take → tak**ing**

Endet das Verb auf einem kurzen betonten Vokal + Konsonant, wird der Konsonant verdoppelt.

put → putt**ing**   run → runn**ing**   get → gett**ing**

b) Verneinte Aussagesätze im *present progressive*

Für die Verneinung fügst du *not* hinter der Form von *be* ein. Oft wird die Kurzform verwendet:

I **am not** making pizza.   I**'m not** making pizza.
Harry **is not** dancing.   Harry **isn't** dancing.
They **are not** watching TV.   They **aren't** watching TV.

c) Fragen im *present progressive*

Bei Entscheidungsfragen stellst du die Form von *be* (also *am, is* oder *are*) an den Satzanfang. In den Kurzantworten wird die Form von *be* aufgegriffen.

Is Ava enjoying her food?   Yes, she **is**. / No, she **isn't**.
Are the Kogans eating at home?   Yes, they **are**. / No, they **aren't**.

Bei Fragen mit Fragewort steht das Fragewort am Satzanfang:

What are you having for dinner?

DIGITAL+ video 20

6 THE GERUND
Das Gerundium

I love playing football!
Playing football is my favourite activity.

Wird ein Verb wie ein Nomen verwendet, nennt man die Form Gerundium *(gerund)*. Im Englischen benutzt man dafür die *ing*-Form des Verbs.

a) Das Gerundium als Subjekt

DIGITAL+ video 21

Wie die *ing*-Form eines Verbs gebildet wird, hast du schon im Zusammenhang mit dem *present progressive* gesehen. Achte bei der Bildung der *ing*-Form auf die Besonderheiten bei der Schreibweise (siehe Seite 176). Ein Gerundium kann Subjekt eines Satzes sein.

Swimming keeps you fit.
Cycling is fun.
Playing the guitar is my favourite hobby.

b) Das Gerundium nach bestimmten Verben

Das Gerundium folgt oft nach bestimmten Verben, z. B. *like, love, hate, enjoy, suggest, try* und *prefer*. Es ist dann das Objekt des Satzes.

*I **like being** outdoors.*
*I don't **like being** alone.*
*We **enjoy playing** games.*
*Do you **prefer running** or **swimming**?*

c) Das Gerundium nach bestimmten Präpositionen

Auch bei verschiedenen Ausdrücken mit Präpositionen wird das Gerundium verwendet, z. B. *be good at, be interested in, care about* und *look forward to*.

*Are you **good at playing** basketball?*
*I'm **interested in playing** hockey.*
*I don't really **care about winning** or **losing**.*
*We're **looking forward to going** to the football match.*

7 CONDITIONAL CLAUSES 1
Bedingungssätze 1

Mit Bedingungssätzen kannst du sagen, was unter bestimmten Bedingungen passieren wird bzw. passieren kann.

If your knee doesn't get better soon, we'll see a doctor.

Ein Bedingungssatz besteht aus einem *if*-Satz und einem Hauptsatz.
Der *if*-Satz nennt eine Bedingung. Der Hauptsatz drückt aus, was passiert, wenn die Bedingung erfüllt ist.
Im *if*-Satz steht das *simple present*, im Hauptsatz meist das *will-future*.

DIGITAL+ video 22

if-Satz (Bedingung: **Wenn …**)	**Hauptsatz** (Folge: … **dann** …)
If you miss the bus,	you will be late.
If it rains,	the children won't go outside.

Bedingungssätze können entweder mit dem *if*-Satz oder mit dem Hauptsatz beginnen.
Wenn sie mit dem *if*-Satz beginnen, werden sie mit einem Komma getrennt.
Wenn sie mit dem Hauptsatz beginnen, verwendest du kein Komma.

If you go to the cinema, I'll come with you.
I'll come with you if you go to the cinema.

Im Hauptsatz kannst du auch Modalverben (z. B. *can, must*) oder den Imperativ verwenden.

*If you feel sick, you **can stay** at home.*
*If you have broken your leg, you **must get** an X-ray.*
*If you need help, **ask** your mum or dad.*

8 MODAL VERBS (REVISION)
8 Modalverben *(revision)*

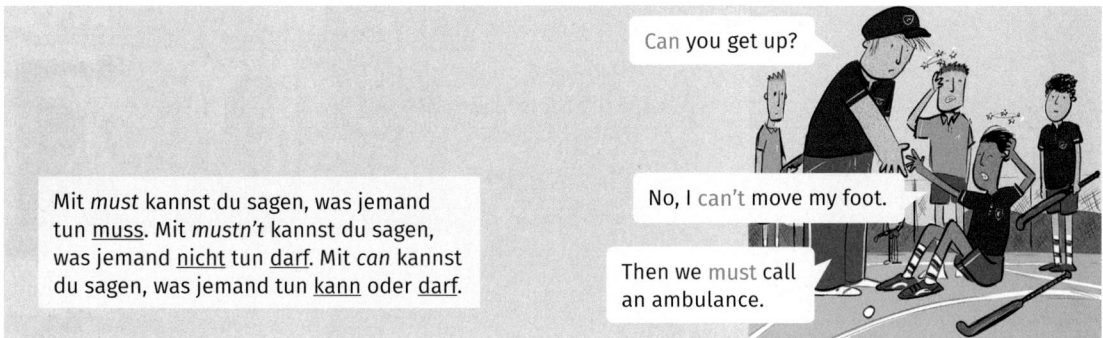

Can you get up?

No, I **can't** move my foot.

Then we **must** call an ambulance.

Mit *must* kannst du sagen, was jemand tun <u>muss</u>. Mit *mustn't* kannst du sagen, was jemand <u>nicht</u> tun <u>darf</u>. Mit *can* kannst du sagen, was jemand tun <u>kann</u> oder <u>darf</u>.

a) *Must / have to*
Must bedeutet „müssen". Die Form ist bei allen Personen gleich.
Hinter *must* steht die Grundform des Hauptverbs.
In der Regel kannst du *must* auch durch *have to* bzw. *has to* ersetzen.

*Demir **must** take his medicine. = Demir **has to** take his medicine.*

Die Form *must* gibt es nur im *simple present*. Um z. B. auszudrücken, was jemand in der Vergangenheit tun musste oder in Zukunft wird tun müssen, brauchst du eine Form von *have to*.

*Last week, Demir **had to** go to hospital.*
*Tarek **will have to** stay at home for two days.*

b) *Mustn't / not be allowed to*
Mit *mustn't* kannst du sagen, was jemand nicht tun darf. *Mustn't* gibt es nur im *simple present*.
In anderen Zeitformen als dem *simple present* verwendest du die Ersatzform *not be allowed to*.

*Tarek **mustn't** do sports at the moment. = Tarek **isn't allowed to** do sports at the moment.*
*Tarek **won't be allowed to** do sports for three weeks.*
*Tarek **wasn't allowed to** play video games yesterday.*

c) *Can / be able to / be allowed to*
Can bedeutet „können" oder „dürfen". Für einige Zeitformen, wie z. B. dem *will-future*, brauchst du eine Ersatzform. Die Ersatzform für *can* mit der Bedeutung „können" ist *be able to*.

*John **can** play tennis and he is really good at it, but he broke his arm today.*
*He **will be able to** play tennis again in a few months, but he **won't be able to** play next week.*

Im *simple past* kannst du *could* oder *was able to* verwenden.
*John **could** play tennis yesterday. = John **was able to** play tennis yesterday.*

Wenn du *can* mit der Bedeutung „dürfen" z. B. im *will-future* verwenden willst, dann benutzt du die Ersatzform *be allowed to*.

*Tarek **will be allowed to** play video games while he is ill.*

9 RELATIVE CLAUSES
Relativsätze

> We could go to Portobello Road Market at the weekend.

> Mit Relativsätzen kannst du Personen oder Dinge näher beschreiben.

> Maybe that guy who sells those really funny T-shirts is still there.

Relativsätze sind Nebensätze, die Personen oder Dinge näher beschreiben. Ein Relativsatz beginnt meist mit einem Relativpronomen, also z. B. mit *who*, *which* oder *that*. Dabei verwendest du *who* für Personen und *which* für Dinge. *That* kannst du sowohl für Dinge als auch für Personen benutzen.

🖳 **DIGITAL+** video 23

	Relativsatz
There is a <u>man</u>	**who** sells old cameras.
There is a <u>car boot sale</u>	**which** takes place on Sunday.

	Relativsatz
Tarek bought some <u>books</u>	**that** were really cheap.
There are many <u>people</u>	**that** sell things at the car boot sale.

Relativsätze können auch in der Mitte eines Satzes stehen:

*The man **who is selling old cameras** is funny.*

TIPP

Übrigens: Man kann das Relativpronomen weglassen, wenn es das Objekt des Relativsatzes ist.

These are the books that Tarek bought.   oder:
These are the books Tarek bought.

Relativsätze ohne Relativpronomen heißen *contact clauses*.

10 THE PROP WORDS ONE AND ONES
Die Stützwörter *one* und *ones*

I'm also looking for a teapot.

Wenn du ein Nomen ersetzen willst, das vorher schon genannt wurde, benutzt du stattdessen *one* bzw. *ones*.

How do you like this one?

Das Stützwort *one* bzw. *ones* kann für ein Nomen stehen, das schon erwähnt wurde und deshalb nicht wiederholt werden muss.

Du benutzt *one*, um ein Nomen im Singular zu ersetzen.

Englisch	Deutsch
Which <u>T-shirt</u> do you like? The red **one** or the blue **one**?	Welches T-Shirt magst du? Das rote oder das blaue?

Du benutzt *ones*, um ein Nomen im Plural zu ersetzen.

Englisch	Deutsch
Tarek bought some new <u>books</u> and now has to get rid of some old **ones**.	Tarek hat ein paar neue Bücher gekauft und muss nun ein paar alte loswerden.

Im Deutschen kannst du in diesen Fällen das Nomen einfach weglassen, wenn du es nicht wiederholen möchtest. Im Englischen ist das nicht möglich, hier musst du stattdessen *one* oder *ones* benutzten.

11 THE PAST PROGRESSIVE: STATEMENTS
Die Verlaufsform der Vergangenheit: Aussagen

Mit dem *past progressive* kannst du ausdrücken, was zu einem bestimmten Zeitpunkt in der Vergangenheit gerade passierte.

5pm

At 5pm, two Vikings were fighting.

a) Bejahte Aussagesätze im *past progressive*

🖥 DIGITAL+ video 24

Auch für die Vergangenheit gibt es eine *progressive form*, das *past progressive*. Es drückt aus,

· was jemand zu einem bestimmten Zeitpunkt in der Vergangenheit gerade tat oder was gerade passierte.

· was gerade vor sich ging, als plötzlich etwas anderes geschah.

Das *past progressive* wird ganz ähnlich gebildet wie das *present progressive*, nur dass die Form von *be* im *simple past* steht.
Simple past-Form von *be (was / were)* + Grundform des Verbs + Endung *-ing*.

*Andy **was watching** a show.*
*The people **were eating**.*

Wenn du beschreiben möchtest, was gerade vor sich ging, als etwas anderes geschah, kannst du das so tun:

past progressive	simple past
While Andy **was looking** at a stall, The people **were** already **eating**	it **started** to rain. when Andy **came** in.

was gerade passierte:
past progressive

neues Ereignis:
simple past

b) Verneinte Aussagesätze im *past progressive*

Für die Verneinung fügst du einfach **not** hinter die Form von *be* (**was** bzw. **were**) ein:

*Andy **wasn't** dancing.*
*Some people **weren't** listening to the stories.*

12 THE PAST PROGRESSIVE: QUESTIONS
Die Verlaufsform der Vergangenheit: Fragen

Bei einer Entscheidungsfrage im *past progressive* steht *was* bzw. *were* am Satzanfang. Bei einer Frage mit Fragewort steht das Fragewort am Satzanfang.

What was **Andy** doing yesterday at 7pm?

a) Entscheidungsfragen und Kurzantworten im *past progressive*

Entscheidungsfragen im *past progressive* bildest du, indem du *was* bzw. *were* an den Satzanfang stellst. In der Kurzantwort wird *was* bzw. *were* aufgegriffen.

DIGITAL+ video 24

*Was Andy **having** dinner at 7pm?*	–	*Yes, he **was**. / No, he **wasn't**.*
*Were the people **dancing**?*	–	*Yes, they **were**. / No, they **weren't**.*

b) Fragen mit Fragewort im *past progressive*

Bei Fragen mit Fragewörtern stellst du das Fragewort an den Satzanfang:

*What **were** you **doing** yesterday at 7pm?*
*What **was** Andy **doing**?*
*Why **were** the people **laughing**?*
*Who **was** taking pictures?*

13 THE SIMPLE PAST: STATEMENTS (REVISION)
Die einfache Vergangenheit: Aussagen *(revision)*

> In the holidays, I went to Poland with my family. We visited my grandma. It was great!

> We didn't go abroad, we stayed in the UK. The weather wasn't bad so we went outside a lot.

> Das *simple past* verwendet man, wenn man über etwas spricht, das in der Vergangenheit liegt und abgeschlossen ist.

a) Formen und bejahte Aussagesätze im *simple past*

🖥 **DIGITAL+** video 25, 26

Bei den regelmäßigen Verben hängst du -ed an die Grundform an:

stay + **ed** → sta**yed** /steɪd/   look + **ed** → look**ed** /lʊkt/   visit + **ed** → visit**ed** /ˈvɪzɪtɪd/

Achte auf die Rechtschreibung: Endet die Grundform des Verbs auf -e, dann wird nur -d angehängt.

arrive → arrive**d** /əˈraɪvd/

Endet das Verb auf einen kurzen betonten **Vokal + Konsonant**, dann wird der Konsonant verdoppelt.

stop → sto**pped** /stɒpt/

Endet das Verb auf **Konsonant + y**, dann wird aus dem -y ein -i und die Endung lautet -ied.

tidy → tid**ied** /ˈtaɪdɪd/

Unregelmäßige Verben haben im *simple past* eine eigene Form (siehe Seite 255–257).

have → **had**   Tarek **had** a great holiday.
go → **went**   He **went** to Wales with his father.
do → **did**   They **did** lots of things together.

Das Verb *be* hat zwei Formen im *simple past*: I / he / she / it was – you / we / they **were**

I **was** in London last week, but my friends **were** in Paris.

b) Verneinte Aussagesätze im *simple past*

Sätze im *simple past* verneinst du im Allgemeinen mit *didn't (= did not)*.
Didn't ist bei allen Personen gleich. Danach kommt dann das Verb in der Grundform.

I **didn't go** to Paris last week.

Bei *was* und *were* hängst du nur *not* oder die Kurzform *n't* an.

I **wasn't** in Paris last week, and my friends **weren't** in London.

14 THE SIMPLE PAST: QUESTIONS (REVISION)
Die einfache Vergangenheit: Fragen *(revision)*

Did you go to Bristol in the holidays?

Yes, I did.

Was it good?

Yes, it was.

Fragen im *simple past* bildest du in den meisten Fällen mit *did*. Eine Ausnahme sind Sätze mit *was* oder *were*.

a) Entscheidungsfragen und Kurzantworten im *simple past*

Bei Entscheidungsfragen im *simple past* stellst du *did* an den Satzanfang.
Did ist bei allen Personen gleich.
Achte auch hier darauf, das Verb danach in der Grundform zu verwenden.
In der Kurzantwort wird *did* wieder aufgegriffen.

🖥 **DIGITAL+** video 25, 26

Entscheidungsfrage	Kurzantwort	Kurzantwort
Did you go on holiday?	Yes, I did.	No, I didn't.
Did Harry visit his grandparents?	Yes, he did.	No, he didn't.

Bei Fragen mit *was* und *were* brauchst du kein *did*.
Hier steht *was* oder *were* am Satzanfang.
In der Kurzantwort wird *was* bzw. *were* wieder aufgegriffen.

Entscheidungsfrage	Kurzantwort	Kurzantwort
Were your parents in Paris last year?	Yes, they were.	No, they weren't.
Was the weather good?	Yes, it was.	No, it wasn't.

b) Fragen mit Fragewort im *simple past*

Bei Sätzen mit Fragewort steht das Fragewort am Satzanfang. Es steht vor *did*.

What did you do in the holidays?
Where did you go?

Bei Fragen mit *who* braucht man kein zusätzliches *did*, wenn *who* nach dem Subjekt fragt.

Who went to Poland? – Ava went to Poland.

Bei Fragen mit *was* oder *were* brauchst du ebenfalls kein *did*.

How was your holiday?
What were your favourite places?

15 REPORTED SPEECH 1
Indirekte Rede 1

Wenn du berichten willst, was jemand anderes sagt, benutzt du indirekte Rede.

My mum says that I have to go home now.

Indirekte Rede besteht aus einem Begleitsatz und der wiedergegebenen Aussage. Beide Satzteile können, müssen aber nicht unbedingt durch *that* verbunden werden.

DIGITAL+ video 27

	Begleitsatz	wiedergegebene Aussage
Paul: "I have maths tuition."	Paul says (that)	he has maths tuition.
Linda: "Delia is really angry."	Linda says (that)	Delia is really angry.

Wenn der Begleitsatz in der Gegenwart steht, verändern sich die Zeiten in der wiedergegebenen Aussage nicht.

Wenn die Originalaussage Wörter enthält, die nur aus dem Zusammenhang richtig zu verstehen sind, musst du sie in der wiedergegebenen Aussage anpassen.

James: "**I** will have **my** own party."   James says (that) **he** will have **his** own party.
Emily: "**We** had an argument."   Emily says (that) **they** had an argument.
Emily: "Chloe is angry with **me**."   Emily says (that) Chloe is angry with **her**.
Tom: "The dog is **here**."   Tom says (that) the dog is **there**.

16 THE PASSIVE
Das Passiv

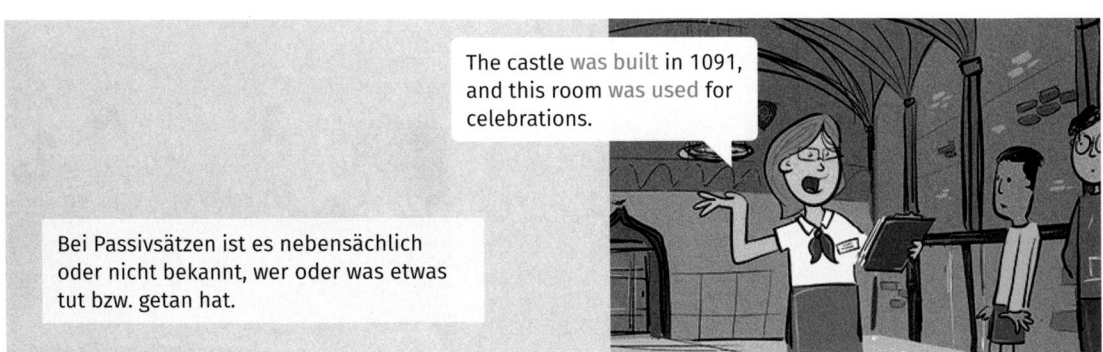

The castle was built in 1091, and this room was used for celebrations.

Bei Passivsätzen ist es nebensächlich oder nicht bekannt, wer oder was etwas tut bzw. getan hat.

Aktivsätze sagen uns, wer oder was handelt bzw. gehandelt hat. In folgendem Beispiel ist das *William Addis*.

DIGITAL+ video 28

*William Addis **invented** the toothbrush in 1780.*

Wenn aber nicht betont werden soll oder wenn nicht bekannt ist, wer etwas tut oder getan hat, kannst du einen Passivsatz verwenden.

*The toothbrush **was invented** in 1780.*

Das Objekt aus dem Aktivsatz, hier *the toothbrush*, wird zum Subjekt des Passivsatzes.

	Subjekt	Verb	Objekt	
Aktivsatz:	William Addis	invented	the toothbrush	in 1780.
Passivsatz:	The toothbrush	was invented		in 1780.

Das Passiv bildest du so:
Form von **be** + Partizip Perfekt *(past participle)*

Englisch	Deutsch
English **is spoken** all over the world.	Englisch wird überall auf der Welt gesprochen.
Matches **are used** to make fire.	Streichhölzer werden zum Feuermachen benutzt.
My computer **was made** in China.	Mein Computer wurde in China hergestellt.
These books **were written** in Germany.	Diese Bücher wurden in Deutschland geschrieben.

In der Liste mit den unregelmäßigen Verben auf den Seiten 255–257 findest du das Partizip Perfekt *(past participle)* in der dritten Spalte.

Wenn du in einem Passivsatz doch einmal die handelnde Person oder die Ursache für etwas nennen willst, hängst du sie mit **by** („von", „durch") an den Satz an:

*The toothbrush was invented **by** William Addis in 1780.*
*The house was destroyed **by** a fire.*

17 THE GOING TO-FUTURE: STATEMENTS (REVISION)
Das Futur mit *going to*: Aussagen *(revision)*

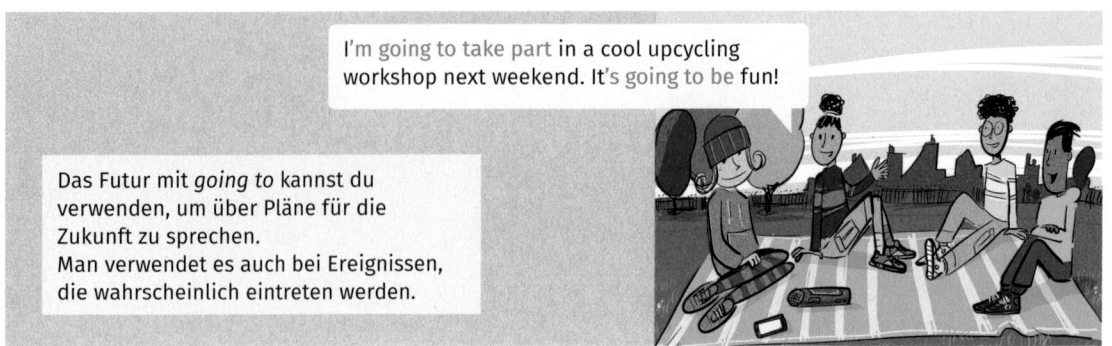

I'm going to take part in a cool upcycling workshop next weekend. It's going to be fun!

Das Futur mit *going to* kannst du verwenden, um über Pläne für die Zukunft zu sprechen.
Man verwendet es auch bei Ereignissen, die wahrscheinlich eintreten werden.

a) Bejahte Aussagesätze im *going to-future*

Im Deutschen gibt es keine Zeitform, die dem *going to-future* entspricht.
Du hast aber verschiedene Möglichkeiten, es im Deutschen wiederzugeben.

DIGITAL+ video 29

Englisch	Deutsch
I'm going to do a drama workshop.	Ich **werde** einen Theaterworkshop **machen**. Ich **möchte / will** einen Theaterworkshop **machen**. Ich **plane / habe vor**, einen Theaterworkshop **zu machen**.

Du bildest das Futur mit *going to* mit einer Form von *be* + *going to* + Grundform des Verbs.

	Langform	Kurzform			
Singular	I am	I'm			
	You are	You're			
	He/She is	He's/She's	going to	do	a drama workshop.
Plural	We are	We're			
	You are	You're			
	They are	They're			

b) Verneinte Aussagesätze im *going to-future*

Für die Verneinung stellst du *not* hinter die Form von *be*. Oft benutzt man Kurzformen.

	Langform	Kurzform			
Singular	I am not	I'm not			
	You are not	You aren't			
	He/She is not	He/She isn't	going to	do	a cooking workshop.
Plural	We are not	We aren't			
	You are not	You aren't			
	They are not	They aren't			

18 THE GOING TO-FUTURE: QUESTIONS (REVISION)
Das Futur mit *going to*: Fragen *(revision)*

Are you going to go to Poland in the holidays, Ava?

Mit einer Frage im *going to-future* kannst du z. B. danach fragen, was jemand für die Zukunft plant.

Yes, I am.

How long are you going to stay?

a) Entscheidungsfragen und Kurzantworten im *going to-future*

DIGITAL+ video 29

Bei Entscheidungsfragen rückt im *going to-future* die Form von *be (am, is, are)* an den Satzanfang.
In der Kurzantwort steht dann die entsprechende Form von *be*.

Entscheidungsfrage	Kurzantwort	Kurzantwort
Are you going to do a cooking workshop?	Yes, I am.	No, I'm not.
Is Ava going to visit her grandmother?	Yes, she is.	No, she isn't.
Are the children going to take part in a workshop?	Yes, they are.	No, they aren't.

b) Fragen mit Fragewort im *going to-future*

Bei Fragen mit Fragewort steht das Fragewort an erster Stelle.

What are you going to do in the holidays?
When is the workshop going to start?
Where is it going to take place?

Nach Vokabeln suchen

Alphabetische Wortliste *(Dictionary)*: Du suchst nach der Bedeutung eines einzelnen englischen Wortes, das im Textbook vorgekommen ist? Dann nutze die alphabetische Wortliste ab Seite 219. Hier findest du auch die Wörter aus der *Story*, aus den Projekten, aus den *Wordbanks* und von den *Get together-* und *Challenge*-Seiten. Einige englische Wörter, die im Englischen und im Deutschen gleich sind, findest du auf Seite 192.

Wortlisten nach Kapiteln *(Vocabulary)*: Du möchtest die Vokabeln zu einem ganzen Abschnitt im Buch lernen? Dann nutze die chronologische Wortliste ab Seite 193. Nach Kapiteln und Seitenzahlen sortiert findest du hier alle Wörter, die neu im Buch vorkommen.

Vokabeln finden
Hier siehst du, zu welcher Aufgabe eines Kapitels die Vokabeln gehören. Die Seitenzahl hilft dabei.

Wichtige Vokabeln erkennen
Wichtige Vokabeln sind fett schwarz gedruckt und farbig markiert. Die solltest du dir merken.

Vokabeln richtig aussprechen
Die Lautschrift zeigt dir, wie die Wörter richtig ausgesprochen werden.

Unit

p. 36, 1	**englische Vokabel** /Lautschrift/	deutsche Übersetzung
	englische Vokabel /Lautschrift/	deutsche Übersetzung
	englische Vokabel /Lautschrift/	deutsche Übersetzung
	englische Vokabel /Lautschrift/	deutsche Übersetzung
	englische Vokabel /Lautschrift/	deutsche Übersetzung
	englische Vokabel /Lautschrift/	deutsche Übersetzung
	englische Vokabel /Lautschrift/	deutsche Übersetzung
	englische Vokabel *(Hinweis)* /Lautschrift/	deutsche Übersetzung

Beispielsätze und Bilder helfen dir dabei, dir Vokabeln einzuprägen.

In farbigen Kästen findest du nützliche Informationen.

Passiver Wortschatz
Vokabeln, die nicht zum Lernwortschatz gehören, sind grau gedruckt. Die brauchst du dir nicht zu merken.

Besondere Hinweise
Zu einigen Vokabeln findest du Angaben, die dir wichtige Hinweise zu ihrem Gebrauch geben:

(pl)   Das Wort kommt hier in seiner Pluralform vor bzw. hat eine unregelmäßige Pluralform.

(no pl)   Dieses Wort hat keine Pluralform.

(informal) Dieses Wort oder dieser Ausdruck ist umgangssprachlich.

(AE)   Dieses Wort oder dieser Ausdruck kommt aus dem amerikanischen Englisch.

(irr)   Dieses Verb ist unregelmäßig. Du findest eine Liste mit unregelmäßigen Verben auf den Seiten 255-257.

Die richtige Aussprache

Im Englischen spricht man Wörter oft anders aus als man sie schreibt.
Die Aussprache der Wörter wird mithilfe der Lautschrift in jedem Wörterbuch angegeben.
Man kann so auch neue Wörter richtig aussprechen, ohne sie vorher gehört zu haben.
Die Lautschrift ist eine Schrift, deren Symbole jeden Laut genau bezeichnen.
Hier ist eine Liste mit den Symbolen dieser Lautschrift zusammen mit Beispielwörtern.

The English alphabet

a	/eɪ/
b	/biː/
c	/siː/
d	/diː/
e	/iː/
f	/ef/
g	/dʒiː/
h	/eɪtʃ/
i	/aɪ/
j	/dʒeɪ/
k	/keɪ/
l	/el/
m	/em/
n	/en/
o	/əʊ/
p	/piː/
q	/kjuː/
r	/ɑː/
s	/es/
t	/tiː/
u	/juː/
v	/viː/
w	/ˈdʌbljuː/
x	/eks/
y	/waɪ/
z	/zed/

English sounds

Vokale

/ɑː/	arm
/ʌ/	but
/e/	desk
/ə/	a, an
/ɜː/	girl, bird
/æ/	apple
/ɪ/	in, it
/i/	happy
/iː/	easy, eat
/ɒ/	orange, sorry
/ɔː/	all, call
/ʊ/	look
/u/	January
/uː/	boot

Doppellaute

/aɪ/	eye, by, buy
/aʊ/	our
/eə/	air, there
/eɪ/	take, they
/ɪə/	here
/ɔɪ/	boy
/əʊ/	go, old
/ʊə/	tour

Konsonanten

/b/	bag, club
/d/	duck, card
/f/	fish, laugh
/g/	get, dog
/h/	hot
/j/	you
/k/	can, duck
/l/	lot, small
/m/	more, mum
/n/	now, sun
/ŋ/	song, long
/p/	present, top
/r/	red, around
/s/	sister, class (stimmlos)
/z/	nose, dogs (stimmhaft)
/t/	time, cat
/ʒ/	television
/dʒ/	sausage
/ʃ/	fresh
/tʃ/	child, cheese
/ð/	these, mother (stimmhaft)
/θ/	bathroom, think (stimmlos)
/v/	very, have
/w/	what, word

Betonungszeichen für die folgende Silbe

/ˈ/	Hauptbetonung
/ˌ/	Nebenbetonung

Bekannte Wörter

Viele Wörter sind im Englischen und im Deutschen so gut wie gleich. Manche unterscheiden sich nur durch die Groß- bzw. Kleinschreibung – im Englischen werden die meisten Nomen kleingeschrieben. Viele dieser Wörter, die in deinem Buch vorkommen, findest du hier. Bei denen, die anders ausgesprochen werden als im Deutschen, ist die Lautschrift farbig hervorgehoben.

aikido /aɪˈkiːdəʊ/
alternative /ɔːlˈtɜːnətɪv/
app /æp/
arm /ɑːm/
audio /ˈɔːdiəʊ/
baby /ˈbeɪbi/
badminton /ˈbædmɪntən/
ball /bɔːl/
band /bænd/
baseball /ˈbeɪsbɔːl/
basketball /ˈbɑːskɪtbɔːl/
beige /beɪʒ/
blind /blaɪnd/
blog post /ˈblɒɡ pəʊst/
bowling /ˈbəʊlɪŋ/
burger /ˈbɜːɡə/
bus /bʌs/
butler /ˈbʌtlə/
butter /ˈbʌtə/
café, cafeteria /ˈkæfeɪ, ˌkæfəˈtɪəriə/
cashew /ˈkæʃuː/
cent /sent/
champion /ˈtʃæmpjən/
chance /tʃɑːns/
chat /tʃæt/
cola /ˈkəʊlə/
collage /ˈkɒlɑːʒ/
computer /kəmˈpjuːtə/
cool /kuːl/
cornflakes /ˈkɔːnfleɪks/
couch /kaʊtʃ/
couscous /ˈkuːskuːs/
currywurst /ˈkʌriwɜːst/
darts /dɑːts/
definition /ˌdefəˈnɪʃn/
diesel /ˈdiːzl/
digital /ˈdɪdʒɪtl/
dip /dɪp/
display /dɪˈspleɪ/
dressing /ˈdresɪŋ/
element /ˈelɪmənt/
email /ˈiːmeɪl/
emoji /ɪˈməʊdʒi/
etc. (= etcetera) /et ˈsetrə/
euro /ˈjʊərəʊ/
fair /feə/
fan /fæn/
fast food /ˌfɑːst ˈfuːd/

film /fɪlm/
finger /ˈfɪŋɡə/
fit, fitness /fɪt, ˈfɪtnəs/
flyer /ˈflaɪə/
form /fɔːm/
format /ˈfɔːmæt/
front /frʌnt/
golden /ˈɡəʊldn/
golf /ɡɒlf/
hammer /ˈhæmə/
handout /ˈhændaʊt/
hieroglyph /ˈhaɪrəɡlɪf/
high-tech /ˌhaɪ ˈtek/
hobby /ˈhɒbi/
hockey /ˈhɒki/
home page /ˈhəʊm peɪdʒ/
hoodie /ˈhʊdi/
horde /hɔːd/
hot dog /ˌhɒt ˈdɒɡ/
hotel /həʊˈtel/
ideal /aɪˈdɪəl/
idol /ˈaɪdl/
info /ˈɪnfəʊ/
instrument /ˈɪnstrʊmənt/
international /ˌɪntəˈnæʃnəl/
Internet /ˈɪntəˌnet/
interview /ˈɪntəˌvjuː/
jeans /dʒiːnz/
judo /ˈdʒuːdəʊ/
jury /ˈdʒʊəri/
karate /kəˈrɑːti/
ketchup /ˈketʃəp/
kilt /kɪlt/
land /lænd/
laptop /ˈlæpˌtɒp/
limerick /ˈlɪmərɪk/
link /lɪŋk/
live /laɪv/
mango /ˈmæŋɡəʊ/
marathon /ˈmærəθn/
material /məˈtɪəriəl/
meme /miːm/
mild /maɪld/
million /ˈmɪljən/
mini /ˈmɪni/
minute /ˈmɪnɪt/
mixer /ˈmɪksə/
modern /ˈmɒdən/
moment /ˈməʊmənt/

mozzarella /ˌmɒtsəˈrelə/
multimedia /ˌmʌltiˈmiːdiə/
museum /mjuːˈziːəm/
musical /ˈmjuːzɪkl/
name /neɪm/
national /ˈnæʃnəl/
OK (= okay) /ˌəʊˈkeɪ/
olive /ˈɒlɪv/
online /ˈɒnlaɪn/
operation /ˌɒpəˈreɪʃn/
organisation /ˌɔːɡənaɪˈzeɪʃn/
papyrus /pəˈpaɪrəs/
parade /pəˈreɪd/
paratriathlon /ˌpærətraɪˈæθlən/
park /pɑːk/
partner /ˈpɑːtnə/
party /ˈpɑːti/
patient /ˈpeɪʃnt/
penicillin /ˌpenəˈsɪlɪn/
person /ˈpɜːsn/
pilates /pɪˈlɑːtiːz/
pilot /ˈpaɪlət/
pizza /ˈpiːtsə/
plan /plæn/
planet /ˈplænɪt/
podcast /ˈpɒdˌkɑːst/
pool /puːl/
portion /ˈpɔːʃn/
post, poster /pəʊst, ˈpəʊstə/
problem /ˈprɒbləm/
quiz /kwɪz/
radio /ˈreɪdiəʊ/
region /ˈriːdʒn/
rest /rest/
restaurant /ˈrestrɒnt/
revolution /ˌrevəˈluːʃn/
ring /rɪŋ/
roller skate /ˈrəʊlə skeɪt/
rucksack /ˈrʌkˌsæk/
rugby /ˈrʌɡbi/
sand /sænd/
sandwich /ˈsænwɪdʒ/
science fiction /ˌsaɪəns ˈfɪkʃn/
service /ˈsɜːvɪs/
shorts /ʃɔːts/
show /ʃəʊ/
situation /ˌsɪtʃuˈeɪʃn/

skateboarder /ˈskeɪtbɔːdə/
skater /ˈskeɪtə/
slogan /ˈsləʊɡən/
smartphone /ˈsmɑːtˌfəʊn/
smiley /ˈsmaɪli/
snack /snæk/
so /səʊ/
softball /ˈsɒftˌbɔːl/
sorbet /ˈsɔːbeɪ/
spaghetti /spəˈɡeti/
streaming /ˈstriːmɪŋ/
super /ˈsuːpə/
sushi /ˈsuːʃi/
T-shirt /ˈtiː ʃɜːt/
tablet /ˈtæblət/
tai chi /ˌtaɪ ˈtʃiː/
tattoo /tæˈtuː/
team /tiːm/
teenager /ˈtiːnˌeɪdʒə/
tennis /ˈtenɪs/
test /test/
text /tekst/
ticket /ˈtɪkɪt/
toast, toaster /təʊst, ˈtəʊstə/
tofu /ˈtəʊfuː/
touch-screen /ˈtʌtʃskriːn/
tour, tourist /tʊə, ˈtʊərɪst/
training /ˈtreɪnɪŋ/
triathlon /traɪˈæθlən/
tunnel /ˈtʌnl/
tutorial /tjuːˈtɔːriəl/
uniform /ˈjuːnɪfɔːm/
upcycling /ˈʌpˌsaɪklɪŋ/
vase /vɑːz/
verb /vɜːb/
video clip /ˈvɪdiəʊ klɪp/
volleyball /ˈvɒlibɔːl/
warm /wɔːm/
webcode /ˈwebˌkəʊd/
website /ˈwebˌsaɪt/
winter /ˈwɪntə/
wok /wɒk/
workshop /ˈwɜːkˌʃɒp/
yoga /ˈjəʊɡə/
yoghurt /ˈjɒɡət/

p. 6	**grandma** *(informal)* /ˈɡrænˌmɑ:/	(die) Oma	
	original, originally /əˈrɪdʒnəl, əˈrɪdʒnəli/	ursprünglich	**originally** = at first
	Egypt /ˈiːdʒɪpt/	Ägypten	

Unit 1 | Part A Delicious dishes

p. 7	**dish** *(pl* **dishes)** /dɪʃ, ˈdɪʃɪz/	(das) Gericht, (die) Speise	
	from (all) around the world /frɒmˌɔːlˌəˌraʊnd ðə ˈwɜːld/	aus der (ganzen) Welt	
	(to) **eat out** *(irr)* /ˌiːtˈaʊt/	auswärts essen; im Restaurant essen	
	cookbook /ˈkʊkˌbʊk/	(das) Kochbuch	
p. 8, 2	(to) **order (in)** /ˈɔːdə, ˌɔːdərˈɪn/	bestellen	
	salad /ˈsæləd/	(der) Salat	When you are **full**, you don't want to eat or drink anything.
	full /fʊl/	satt	
	(to) **finish** /ˈfɪnɪʃ/	aufessen	
	absolutely /ˈæbsəluːtli/	absolut	
	vegetable /ˈvedʒtəbl/	(das) Gemüse	
	potato *(pl* **potatoes)** /pəˈteɪtəʊ, pəˈteɪtəʊz/	(die) Kartoffel	
	vegetarian /ˌvedʒəˈteəriən/	(der/die) Vegetarier/in; vegetarisch	
	savoury /ˈseɪvəri/	pikant, salzig	
	thin /θɪn/	dünn	There is a **thin** slice of cheese in the burger.
	onion /ˈʌnjən/	(die) Zwiebel	
	spicy /ˈspaɪsi/	würzig, scharf	
	speciality /ˌspeʃiˈæləti/	(die) Spezialität	**speciality** = a type of food that a place is famous for
	BFF (= best friends forever) *(informal)* /ˌbiːefˈef, best ˌfrendz fərˈevə/	allerbeste Freunde/Freundinnen	
	greetings *(pl)* /ˈɡriːtɪŋz/	(die) Grüße	
	Greece /ɡriːs/	Griechenland	
	fisherman *(pl* fishermen) /ˈfɪʃəmən/	(der) Fischer, (der) Angler	
	octopus /ˈɒktəpəs/	(der) Tintenfisch	**octopus**
	cucumber /ˈkjuːˌkʌmbə/	(die) Salatgurke	
	grilled /ɡrɪld/	gegrillt	
	roast /rəʊst/	(der) Braten; gebraten, geröstet	
	mashed potatoes *(pl)* /ˌmæʃt pəˈteɪtəʊz/	(der) Kartoffelbrei	
	gravy /ˈɡreɪvi/	(die) (Braten)soße	**Gravy** is a type of sauce.
	lamb /læm/	(das) Lamm	
	beef /biːf/	(das) Rindfleisch	
	Yorkshire pudding /ˌjɔːkʃə ˈpʊdɪŋ/	*britische gebackene Beilage*	
	comfort food /ˈkʌmfət fuːd/	(das) Wohlfühlessen	
	Lahmacun /ˌlaməˈdʒuːn/	*traditionelles türkisches Gericht*	
	rolled /rəʊld/	gerollt	
	flatbread /ˈflætbred/	(der) Fladen	
	minced meat /ˌmɪnst ˈmiːt/	(das) Hackfleisch	
	Turkey /ˈtɜːki/	die Türkei	

	Lebanon /ˈlebənən/	der Libanon
p. 9, 2	**any** /ˈeni/	jede(r, s); alle
	sauce /sɔːs/	(die) Soße
	pepper /ˈpepə/	(die) Paprika; (der) Pfeffer
	(to) **serve** /sɜːv/	servieren; reichen für
	soft /sɒft/	weich
	(to) **contain** /kənˈteɪn/	enthalten
	selection /sɪˈlekʃn/	(die) Auswahl
	meat /miːt/	(das) Fleisch
	vegan /ˈviːgən/	(der/die) Veganer/in; vegan
	option /ˈɒpʃn/	(die) Wahlmöglichkeit
	hot /hɒt/	scharf
	Poutine /ˌpuːˈtiːn/	*traditionelles kanadisches Gericht*
	Canada /ˈkænədə/	Kanada
	fried /fraɪd/	gebraten
	topping /ˈtɒpɪŋ/	(der) Belag
	mushroom /ˈmʌʃruːm/	(der) Pilz
	chilli (*pl* chillies) /ˈtʃɪli, ˈtʃɪliz/	(der) Chili, (die) Peperoni
	cream cheese /kriːm ˈtʃiːz/	(der) Frischkäse
	Shakshuka /ʃəkˈʃuːkə/	*traditionelles israelisches und nordafrikanisches Gericht*
	North Africa /ˌnɔːθ ˈæfrɪkə/	Nordafrika
	garlic /ˈgɑːlɪk/	(der) Knoblauch
	Dim Sum /ˌdɪm ˈsʌm/	*traditionelles chinesisches Gericht*
	spring roll /ˈsprɪŋ rəʊl/	(die) Frühlingsrolle
	cabbage /ˈkæbɪdʒ/	(der) Kohl
p. 11, 6	web page /ˈweb ˌpeɪdʒ/	(die) Webseite, (die) Internetseite
	noodle /ˈnuːdl/	(die) Nudel
	(chicken) tikka masala, (chicken) tikka /ˌtʃɪkɪn ˌtiːkə məˈsɑːlə, ˌtʃɪkɪn ˈtiːkə/	*britisch-indisches (Hühnchen-)Gericht*
	India /ˈɪndiə/	Indien
p. 12, 7	**pot** /pɒt/	(der) Topf
	pasta /ˈpæstə/	(die) Nudeln
	quick /kwɪk/	schnell, kurz
	veggie *(informal)* /ˈvedʒi/	(das) Gemüse
	herb /hɜːb/	(das) (Gewürz)kraut
	spice /spaɪs/	(das) Gewürz
	fridge /frɪdʒ/	(der) Kühlschrank
	cupboard /ˈkʌbəd/	(der) Schrank
	dessert /dɪˈzɜːt/	(der) Nachtisch
	(to) **put in** *(irr)* /ˌpʊt ˈɪn/	hineintun, hinzufügen
	nearly /ˈnɪəli/	fast, beinahe
	can /kæn/	(die) Dose, (die) Büchse
	left /left/	übrig

Pepper is a vegetable and a spice.

soft ≠ hard

A **vegan** doesn't eat meat or drink milk.

hot = spicy

mushrooms

The man is cooking food in a **pot**.

There are lots of **spices** in a curry.

A **dessert** is sweet.

(to) **prepare** /prɪˈpeə/	zubereiten	Everybody can learn to cook with the help of a **recipe**.
recipe /ˈresəpi/	(das) Rezept	
(to) starve /stɑːv/	verhungern	I**'m starving**! Ich habe einen Bärenhunger!, Ich habe riesigen Hunger!
drawer /ˈdrɔːə/	(die) Schublade	
No need to worry. /nəʊ ˈniːd̮ tə ˌwʌri/	Wir müssen uns keine Sorgen machen.	
chickpea /ˈtʃɪkˌpiː/	(die) Kichererbse	
pea /piː/	(die) Erbse	
jar /dʒɑː/	(das) (Glas)gefäß	
crumb /krʌm/	(der) Krümel	
(to) bring to the boil *(irr)* /ˌbrɪŋ tə ðə ˈbɔɪl/	zum Kochen bringen	

shall /ʃæl/	sollen; werden	
ingredient /ɪnˈɡriːdiənt/	(die) Zutat	
teaspoon /ˈtiːˌspuːn/	(der) Teelöffel	**teaspoon**
mistake /mɪˈsteɪk/	(der) Fehler	
Morocco /məˈrɒkəʊ/	Marokko	
cook-along video /ˈkʊk_əˌlɒŋ ˌvɪdiəʊ/	*(das) Mitmach-Koch-Video*	
cumin /ˈkjuːmɪn/	(der) Kreuzkümmel	**Cumin** and **coriander** are spices.
coriander /ˌkɒriˈændə/	(der) Koriander	
paprika /ˈpæprɪkə/	(das) Paprikapulver	
cayenne pepper /ˌkeɪen ˈpepə/	(der) Cayennepfeffer	
vegetable stock /ˈvedʒtəbl stɒk/	(die) Gemüsebrühe	
cinnamon /ˈsɪnəmən/	(der) Zimt	
curry powder /ˈkʌri ˌpaʊdə/	(das) Currypulver	
yummy *(informal)* /ˈjʌmi/	lecker	

p. 13, 7 (shall → mistake); People and Places info text.

(to) **chop** /tʃɒp/	hacken	
(to) **heat** /hiːt/	erhitzen	
(to) **slice** /slaɪs/	in Scheiben schneiden	to **slice** a cucumber
(to) **stir in** /ˌstɜːr_ˈɪn/	einrühren, unterrühren	

diet /ˈdaɪət/	(die) Ernährung; (die) Diät	
by heart /ˌbaɪ ˈhɑːt/	auswendig	
(to) **kill** /kɪl/	töten	
season /ˈsiːzn/	(die) Saison	
for no reason /fə ˌnəʊ ˈriːzn/	ohne Grund, grundlos	
foxhunting *(no pl)* /ˈfɒks ˌhʌntɪŋ/	(die) Fuchsjagd	

Great Britain /ˌɡreɪt ˈbrɪtn/	Großbritannien	A **side dish** is food that you get at the same time as the main course.
(is) made /ˌɪz ˈmeɪd/	(wird) gemacht, (wird) hergestellt	
side (dish) /ˈsaɪd_dɪʃ/	(die) Beilage	
(to) **refer to** /rɪˈfɜː tu/	hinweisen auf, gelten für	
in general /ɪn ˈdʒenrəl/	im Allgemeinen	
fish and chips /ˌfɪʃ_ən ˈtʃɪps/	*Fisch mit Pommes*	
pancake /ˈpænˌkeɪk/	(der) Pfannkuchen	
oven /ˈʌvn/	(der) Ofen	
pudding /ˈpʊdɪŋ/	(die) Nachspeise	

Margin labels: p. 13, 7 · p. 13, 8 · p. 14, 10 · People and Places 1

	toad in the hole /ˌtəʊd‿ɪn ðə ˈhəʊl/	Bratwürste in einem Yorkshire Pudding
	sausage /ˈsɒsɪdʒ/	(die) Wurst, (das) Würstchen
	bangers and mash /ˌbæŋəz‿ən ˈmæʃ/	Würstchen mit Kartoffelbrei
	bubble and squeak /ˌbʌbl‿ən ˈskwiːk/	Resteessen aus gebratenem Kartoffelbrei und zerstampftem Gemüse
	Indian /ˈɪndiən/	(der/die) Inder/in; indisch
	cook /kʊk/	(der/die) Koch/Köchin
	coconut cream /ˈkəʊkəˌnʌt kriːm/	(die) Kokosmilch
	mix /mɪks/	(die) Mischung
	masala /məˈsɑːlə/	Gewürzmischung
p. 15, 11	**bread** /bred/	(das) Brot
	fake /feɪk/	gefälscht, falsch
	knight /naɪt/	(der) Ritter
p. 15, 12	**invented** /ɪnˈventɪd/	erfunden
	by accident /ˌbaɪ‿ˈæksɪdnt/	zufällig, aus Versehen
p. 16, 14	cube /kjuːb/	(der) Würfel
	strawberry /ˈstrɔːbri/	(die) Erdbeere
	cream /kriːm/	(die) Sahne
	pinch (pl pinches) /pɪntʃ, ˈpɪntʃɪz/	(die) Prise
	(to) put aside (irr) /ˌpʊt‿əˈsaɪd/	beiseitelegen
p. 16, 15	odd one out /ˌɒd wʌn‿ˈaʊt/	(das) Wort, das nicht zu den anderen passt
p. 16, 16	branch /brɑːntʃ/	(der) Zweig, (der) Ast
p. 17, 17	**starter** /ˈstɑːtə/	(die) Vorspeise
	main (course) /ˈmeɪn kɔːs/	(das) Hauptgericht
	(to) **try out** /ˌtraɪ‿ˈaʊt/	ausprobieren
	tablespoon /ˈteɪblˌspuːn/	(der) Esslöffel
	oil /ɔɪl/	(das) Öl
	medium /ˈmiːdiəm/	mittel(groß)
	(to) categorize /ˈkætɪɡəraɪz/	kategorisieren, in Gruppen unterteilen
	clove of garlic /ˌkləʊv‿əvˈɡɑːlɪk/	(die) Knoblauchzehe
	(to) mix in /ˌmɪks‿ˈɪn/	untermischen
	cooker /ˈkʊkə/	(der) Herd
	Enjoy! /ɪnˈdʒɔɪ/	Guten Appetit!

Germany is famous for its **bread**.

by accident = not planned

strawberry

A **tablespoon** is bigger than a teaspoon.

medium = between large and small in size

Unit 1 | Part B At a restaurant

p. 18, 1	**takeaway** /ˈteɪkəˌweɪ/	(das) Essen zum Mitnehmen, (die) Imbissbude
	Italian /ɪˈtæljən/	(der/die) Italiener/in; italienisch
	Turkish /ˈtɜːkɪʃ/	türkisch
	Thai /taɪ/	(der/die) Thailänder/in; thailändisch
	Vietnamese /viˌetnəˈmiːz/	(der/die) Vietnamese/Vietnamesin; vietnamesisch
	Lebanese /ˌlebəˈniːz/	(der/die) Libanese/Libanesin; libanesisch
p. 18, 2	**review** /rɪˈvjuː/	(die) Kritik, (die) Rezension

A **takeaway** is a meal that you buy and take home.

(to) **skim** /skɪm/	überfliegen	
cheap /tʃiːp/	billig	**cheap** ≠ expensive
quality /ˈkwɒləti/	(die) Qualität	
(to) **stay away from** /ˌsteɪ_əˈweɪ frɒm/	meiden; sich fernhalten von	
disgusting /dɪsˈɡʌstɪŋ/	widerlich	
disappointing /ˌdɪsəˈpɔɪntɪŋ/	enttäuschend	
mine /maɪn/	meine(r, s)	
nearby /ˌnɪəˈbaɪ/	in der Nähe (gelegen)	**nearby** ≠ far away
crust /krʌst/	(die) Kruste	
burnt /bɜːnt/	verbrannt, angebrannt	
curry /ˈkʌri/	(das) Curry(gericht)	
atmosphere /ˈætməsˌfɪə/	(die) Atmosphäre	
tasty /ˈteɪsti/	lecker	
north /nɔːθ/	(der) Norden; Nord-	If you can choose between different things, you have a **choice**.
choice /tʃɔɪs/	(die) Auswahl, (die) Wahl	
pub /pʌb/	(die) Kneipe	
according to /əˈkɔːdɪŋ ˌtuː/	nach, gemäß	
vindaloo /ˌvɪndəˈluː/	*indisches Gericht*	
korma /ˈkɔːmə/	*indisches Gericht*	
naan bread /ˈnɑːn bred/	*indisches Fladenbrot*	
(to) be good value for money *(irr)* /ˌbiː ɡʊd ˌvæljuː fə ˈmʌni/	sein Geld wert sein	
overcooked /ˌəʊvəˈkʊkt/	verkocht	
juicy /ˈdʒuːsi/	saftig	
cosy /ˈkəʊzi/	gemütlich	
(to) rank /ræŋk/	einstufen, anordnen	There is a tablespoon in the **soup**.
soup /suːp/	(die) Suppe	
superlative /sʊˈpɜːlətɪv/	(der) Superlativ	
syllable /ˈsɪləbl/	(die) Silbe	
(to) **be allergic to** *(irr)* /ˌbi_əˈlɜːdʒɪk tʊ/	allergisch sein auf	
occasion /əˈkeɪʒn/	(die) Gelegenheit, (der) Anlass	
raw /rɔː/	roh	
waiter / waitress /ˈweɪtə, ˈweɪtrəs/	(der/die) Kellner/in	
reservation /ˌrezəˈveɪʃn/	(die) Reservierung	
certainly /ˈsɜːtnli/	sicher, gerne	
this way /ˈðɪs weɪ/	hier entlang	They **have taken a seat** in a restaurant.
(to) **take a seat** *(irr)* /ˌteɪk_əˈsiːt/	sich setzen	
recommendation /ˌrekəmenˈdeɪʃn/	(die) Empfehlung	
home-made /ˌhəʊmˈmeɪd/	hausgemacht, selbst gemacht	
(to) **take an order** *(irr)* /ˌteɪk_ənˈɔːdə/	eine Bestellung aufnehmen	
on the side /ˌɒn ðə ˈsaɪd/	als Beilage	**on the side** = as a side dish
sir / Sir /sɜː/	Sir; Herr *(Anrede vor Vornamen)*	
(to) **warn** /wɔːn/	warnen	

Left-margin references: p. 19, 2 (curry); p. 20, 3 (soup); p. 20, 4 (syllable); p. 21, 5 (be allergic to); p. 22, 6 (waiter / waitress)

	extremely /ɪkˈstriːmli/	äußerst, höchst, außerordentlich	
	palace /ˈpæləs/	(der) Palast	
	(to) show to the table *(irr)* /ˌʃəʊ tə ðə ˈteɪbl/	zum Tisch führen	
	salmon /ˈsæmən/	(der) Lachs	
	order /ˈɔːdə/	(die) Bestellung	to **rewrite** = to change a piece of writing
	(to) rewrite *(irr)* /ˌriːˈraɪt/	überarbeiten, umschreiben	
p. 23, 7	**lemonade** /ˌleməˈneɪd/	(die) Limonade	
	mineral water /ˈmɪnrəl ˌwɔːtə/	(das) Mineralwasser	
	lassi /ˈlæsi/	*Joghurtgetränk*	
	poppadom /ˈpɒpədəm/	*dünnes indisches Brot*	
	cracker /ˈkrækə/	(der) Kräcker	**filled** / fɪld/ gefüllt
	flour /ˈflaʊə/	(das) Mehl	**cooked** /kʊkt/ gekocht
	bhaji /ˈbɑːdʒi/	*indisches Gericht*	**mixed** /mɪkst/ gemischt
	samosa /səˈməʊsə/	*indische gefüllte Teigtasche*	
	pastry /ˈpeɪstri/	(der) Brandteig, (der) Blätterteig	**are served** /ˌɑː ˈsɜːvd/ werden serviert
	sweetcorn /ˈswiːtˌkɔːn/	(der) Mais	
	ginger /ˈdʒɪndʒə/	(der) Ingwer	
	palak paneer /ˌpɑːlək pəˈnɪə/	*indisches Gericht*	
	spinach /ˈspɪnɪdʒ/	(der) Spinat	
	skewer /ˈskjuːə/	(der) Spieß	
p. 24, 8	(to) **get** *(irr)* /get/	bringen	
	any more /ˌeni ˈmɔː/	noch mehr	
	(to) **be a shame** *(irr)* /ˌbi ə ˈʃeɪm/	schade sein	
	(to) **waste** /weɪst/	verschwenden	
	not ... either /ˌnɒt ˈaɪðə/	auch nicht	The mother is not happy. The father is **not** happy **either**.
	bill /bɪl/	(die) Rechnung	
	cash /kæʃ/	(das) Geld, (das) Bargeld	
	(to) **bring over** *(irr)* /ˌbrɪŋ ˈəʊvə/	herbeibringen	
	glad /glæd/	glücklich, froh	
	(to) **handle** /ˈhændl/	bewältigen, umgehen mit	Wales and Scotland are **English-speaking** countries.
p. 25, 10	**English-speaking** /ˈɪŋglɪʃ ˌspiːkɪŋ/	englischsprachig	
	phrase book /ˈfreɪz bʊk/	*Sammlung von Redewendungen*	OMG! (= Oh my God!) *(informal)* Oh mein Gott!
p. 25, 11	**lady** /ˈleɪdi/	(die) Frau, (die) Dame	
	both /bəʊθ/	beide	
p. 26, 12	(to) **go on** *(irr)* /ˌgəʊ ˈɒn/	passieren; weitergehen, weiterreden	
	caption /ˈkæpʃn/	(die) Bildunterschrift	
	thought bubble /ˈθɔːt ˌbʌbl/	(die) Gedankenblase	
	spider /ˈspaɪdə/	(die) Spinne	
p. 26, 13	**conversation** /ˌkɒnvəˈseɪʃn/	(das) Gespräch, (die) Unterhaltung	There are usually lots of **props** on a theatre stage.
p. 27, 14	**prop** /prɒp/	(die) Requisite	
	(to) choke on /ˈtʃəʊk ɒn/	sich verschlucken	

Unit 2 | Part A Keeping fit

p. 31	**living** /ˈlɪvɪŋ/	(der) Lebensstil
	lifestyle /ˈlaɪfˌstaɪl/	(der) Lebensstil
	(to) **keep fit** *(irr)* /ˌkiːp ˈfɪt/	fit bleiben, (sich) fit halten
	doctor /ˈdɒktə/	(der/die) Arzt / Ärztin
	health /helθ/	(die) Gesundheit
	issue /ˈɪʃuː/	(die) Frage, (das) Thema
	(to) cheer up /ˌtʃɪərˈʌp/	aufmuntern, aufheitern
p. 32, 1	**strong** /strɒŋ/	stark
	brain /breɪn/	(das) Gehirn
	strength /streŋθ/	(die) Kraft, (die) Stärke
	(to) **prefer** /prɪˈfɜː/	vorziehen, bevorzugen
	indoors /ˌɪnˈdɔːz/	drinnen, im Haus
	outdoors /ˌaʊtˈdɔːz/	draußen, im Freien
	diving /ˈdaɪvɪŋ/	(das) Tauchen
	chess /tʃes/	(das) Schach
	(to) **lose** *(irr)* /luːz/	verlieren
	(to) **scream** /skriːm/	schreien
	(to) **win** *(irr)* /wɪn/	gewinnen
	flow chart /ˈfləʊ tʃɑːt/	(das) Flussdiagramm
	muscular /ˈmʌskjʊlə/	muskulös
	(to) bat /bæt/	schlagen *(Ball)*
	water polo /ˈwɔːtə ˌpəʊləʊ/	(der) Wasserball *(Sportart)*
	synchronized swimming /ˌsɪŋkrənaɪzd ˈswɪmɪŋ/	(das) Synchronschwimmen
	weight training /ˈweɪtˌtreɪnɪŋ/	Krafttraining
	riding /ˈraɪdɪŋ/	(das) Reiten
	(to) bang /bæŋ/	schlagen
	(to) care about (doing something) /ˈkeərˌəbaʊt/	sich etwas machen aus
	martial arts *(pl)* /ˌmɑːʃl̩ˈɑːts/	(der) Kampfsport
	cross-country running /ˌkrɒs ˌkʌntri ˈrʌnɪŋ/	(der) Geländelauf
	cricket /ˈkrɪkɪt/	(das) Kricket
	rowing /ˈrəʊɪŋ/	(das) Rudern
	tug-of-war /ˌtʌg‿əv ˈwɔː/	(das) Tauziehen
	climbing /ˈklaɪmɪŋ/	(das) Klettern
p. 33, 2	(to) **scan** /skæn/	absuchen, überfliegen
	profile /ˈprəʊfaɪl/	(das) Profil, (das) Porträt
	active /ˈæktɪv/	aktiv
	(to) **sit** *(irr)* /sɪt/	sitzen
	(to) **calm down** /ˌkɑːm ˈdaʊn/	sich beruhigen
	otherwise /ˈʌðəˌwaɪz/	sonst, im Übrigen

When I was younger, I **kept fit** by playing football.

Wenn man den Ort und nicht die Person meint, sagt man „at the doctor**'s**" – beim Arzt / bei der Ärztin.

chess

to **win** ≠ to **lose**

Cross-country running is an outdoor sport.

They **are sitting** on the sofa.

(to) **train** /treɪn/	trainieren	
(to) **reach** /riːtʃ/	erreichen	
skill /skɪl/	(die) Fähigkeit, (das) Geschick	
in order to /ˌɪn_ˈɔːdə tʊ/	um zu	Camping is an **outdoor** activity.
outdoor /ˌaʊtˈdɔː/	im Freien; Outdoor-	
(to) **keep doing something** *(irr)* /ˌkiːp ˈduːɪŋ sʌmθɪŋ/	etwas weiter tun	
(to) **dislike** /dɪsˈlaɪk/	nicht mögen	to **dislike** = to not like
still /stɪl/	still, bewegungslos	
logical thinking /ˌlɒdʒɪkl ˈθɪŋkɪŋ/	(das) logische Denken	
puzzle /ˈpʌzl/	(das) Rätsel	
riddle /ˈrɪdl/	(das) Rätsel	
loser /ˈluːzə/	(der/die) Verlierer/in	
competitive /kəmˈpetətɪv/	*von Konkurrenzdenken geprägt*	
(to) **take things easy** *(informal, irr)* /ˌteɪk θɪŋz_ˈiːzi/	sich keinen Stress machen	
exhausting /ɪgˈzɔːstɪŋ/	anstrengend	Training hard is very **exhausting**.
(to) **look up** /ˌlʊk_ˈʌp/	hochschauen; nachschlagen	
strategy /ˈstrætədʒi/	(die) Strategie	
certain /ˈsɜːtn/	bestimmt, gewiss	
series /ˈsɪəriːz/	(die) Folge, (die) Serie	When you win something, you often get a **prize**.
prize /praɪz/	(der) Preis, (der) Gewinn	
physical /ˈfɪzɪkl/	körperlich	
(to) **concentrate** /ˈkɒnsnˌtreɪt/	sich konzentrieren	
relaxing /rɪˈlæksɪŋ/	entspannend	
(to) **agree** /əˈgriː/	zustimmen	
tactic /ˈtæktɪk/	(die) Taktik	
tournament /ˈtʊənəmənt/	(das) Turnier	Their **dance** is very beautiful.
dance /dɑːns/	(der) Tanz	
(to) **move** /muːv/	(sich) bewegen	
(to) **seem** /siːm/	scheinen	
wheelchair /ˈwiːltʃeə/	(der) Rollstuhl	
twice /twaɪs/	zweimal	
successful /səkˈsesfl/	erfolgreich	
some day /ˈsʌmˌdeɪ/	eines Tages	
ourselves /aʊəˈselvz/	uns; wir selbst	
sleep /sliːp/	(der) Schlaf	The girl has a good **sleep**.
(to) **stress** /stres/	stressen	
mind /maɪnd/	(der) Geist, (der) Verstand	
(to) **compete** /kəmˈpiːt/	an einem Wettkampf teilnehmen; kämpfen	
at the same time /ˌæt_ðə ˌseɪm ˈtaɪm/	gleichzeitig, zur gleichen Zeit	
indoor /ˌɪnˈdɔː/	Hallen-	

p. 34, 4 · p. 35, 6 · p. 36, 7

	for a while /fər_ə ˈwaɪl/	eine Weile	
	regularly /ˈregjʊləli/	regelmäßig	
	flexible /ˈfleksəbl/	biegsam, gelenkig	The boy is very **flexible**.
	myself /maɪˈself/	mir/mich/ich (selbst)	
	self-esteem /ˌself_ɪˈstiːm/	(das) Selbstwertgefühl	
	stressed /strest/	gestresst	
	chance /tʃɑːns/	(die) Möglichkeit, (die) Gelegenheit	
	(to) exercise /ˈeksəsaɪz/	trainieren	
	workout /ˈwɜːkaʊt/	(das) Training	
	exhausted /ɪgˈzɔːstɪd/	erschöpft	
	mental /ˈmentl/	geistig, mental	
p. 37, 7	**complicated** /ˈkɒmplɪˌkeɪtɪd/	kompliziert	**complicated** = not easy
	(to) **get better** *(irr)* /ˌget ˈbetə/	besser werden; gesund werden	
	most of the time /ˈməʊst_əv ðə ˌtaɪm/	meistens	
	apart from /əˈpɑːt frəm/	abgesehen von	
	(to) **make somebody do something** *(irr)* /ˌmeɪk ˌsʌmbədi ˈduː ˌsʌmθɪŋ/	jemanden dazu bringen, etwas zu tun	My mum **made** me **do** my homework.
	sporty /ˈspɔːti/	sportlich	
	for some time /fə ˌsʌm ˈtaɪm/	eine Zeitlang	
	(to) take ages *(informal, irr)* /ˌteɪk_ˈeɪdʒɪz/	ewig dauern	
People and Places 2	**well-known** /ˌwelˈnəʊn/	bekannt, berühmt	
	individual /ˌɪndɪˈvɪdʒuəl/	individuell; einzeln	
	normally /ˈnɔːmli/	normalerweise	
	sock /sɒk/	(die) Socke	
	(to) **compete in** /kəmˈpiːt_ɪn/	teilnehmen an	
	race /reɪs/	(das) Rennen	
	(to) **belong** (to) /bɪˈlɒŋ/	gehören (zu)	
	cup /kʌp/	(der) Pokal	The winner is holding a **cup** in her hands.
	sports day /ˈspɔːts deɪ/	*(das) Sportfest*	
	athletics *(no pl)* /æθˈletɪks/	(die) Leichtathletik	
	throughout /θruːˈaʊt/	während	
p. 38, 8	**check** /tʃek/	(die) Überprüfung, (die) Kontrolle	
	dry suit /ˈdraɪsuːt/	(der) Taucheranzug	
	buddy *(informal)* /ˈbʌdi/	(der) Kumpel	
p. 39, 9	**advert (= ad)** /ˈædvɜːt, æd/	(die) Werbung, (die) Anzeige	**advert**
	(to) **give a talk** *(irr)* /ˌgɪv_ə ˈtɔːk/	einen Vortrag halten	
	talk /tɔːk/	(das) Gespräch, (der) Vortrag	
	one-minute /ˌwʌnˈmɪnɪt/	einminütig	
p. 39, 10	(to) **turn off** /ˌtɜːn_ˈɒf/	ausschalten	
	helmet /ˈhelmɪt/	(der) Helm	**helmet**
	(to) **roll** /rəʊl/	rollen	
	(to) **shoot** *(irr)* /ʃuːt/	schießen	

like that /ˌlaɪk ˈðæt/	so	
rhyming word /ˈraɪmɪŋ wɜ:d/	(das) Reimwort	Poems often have **rhyming words**.
poet /ˈpəʊɪt/	(der/die) Dichter/in	
soccer *(AE)* /ˈsɒkə/	(der) Fußball	**soccer** *(AE)* = football
(to) grab /græb/	sich schnappen, greifen	
each and every /ˈi:tʃˌənˌˈevri/	jede(r, s) einzelne	
knee pad /ˈni: ˌpæd/	(der) Knieschützer	
elbow pad /ˈelbəʊ ˌpæd/	(der) Ellenbogenschützer	
Come on! /ˌkʌmˈɒn/	Komm(t) schon!	
(to) bounce /baʊns/	(auf)springen	
all around /ˌɔ:lˌəˈraʊnd/	überall (in)	**all around** = everywhere
(to) pat /pæt/	einen Klaps geben	
(to) head /hed/	(einen Ball) köpfen	
bat /bæt/	(der) Schläger	
(to) biff *(informal)* /bɪf/	hauen, schlagen	**bat**
(to) boot /bu:t/	einen Tritt geben	
(to) spin *(irr)* /spɪn/	drehen, einen Drall geben	
(to) drop /drɒp/	fallen lassen	
(to) achieve /əˈtʃi:v/	erreichen	to **achieve** something = to be successful when you do something
community /kəˈmju:nəti/	(die) Gemeinschaft, (die) Gemeinde	
(to) **be born** *(irr)* /ˌbi: ˈbɔ:n/	geboren werden	
(to) **look out for** /ˌlʊkˈaʊt fə/	*hier:* sich kümmern um	
slide /ˈju:nɪt/	(die) Folie	
unit /ˈju:nɪt/	(das) Kapitel	
(to) **switch off** /ˌswɪtʃˈɒf/	ausschalten	It is dark when you **switch off** the light at night.
leaflet /ˈli:flət/	(der) Prospekt, (die) Broschüre	
slide show /ˈslaɪd ʃəʊ/	(die) Bildschirmpräsentation	the most important ones /ðə ˌməʊstˌɪmˈpɔ:tnt wʌnz/ **die wichtigsten**
gallery walk /ˈgæləri wɔ:k/	*(die) Gruppendiskussion in Stationsarbeit*	

p. 40, 12 *(to the left of "(to) achieve")*
p. 41, 13 *(to the left of "slide")*

Unit 2 | Part B At the doctor's

What's the matter? /ˌwɒts ˌðə ˈmætə/	Was ist los?	
shoulder /ˈʃəʊldə/	(die) Schulter	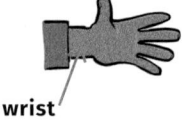
wrist /rɪst/	(das) Handgelenk	**wrist**
(to) **hurt** *(irr)* /hɜ:t/	wehtun, schmerzen; verletzen	
swollen /ˈswəʊlən/	geschwollen	Wenn man den Ort und nicht die Person meint, sagt man „at the dentist**'s**" – „beim Zahnarzt / bei der Zahnärztin/ in der Zahnarztpraxis" oder „to the dentist**'s**" – „zum Zahnarzt / zur Zahnärztin".
broken /ˈbrəʊkən/	gebrochen	
(to) **take an X-ray** *(irr)* /ˌteɪkˌən ˈeksreɪ/	eine Röntgenaufnahme machen	
cast /kɑ:st/	(der) Gips	
tooth *(pl* **teeth***)* /tu:θ, ti:θ/	(der) Zahn	
appointment /əˈpɔɪntmənt/	(der) Termin	
dentist /ˈdentɪst/	(der/die) Zahnarzt / Zahnärztin	

p. 42, 1 *(to the left of "What's the matter?")*

toothache *(no pl)* /ˈtuːθeɪk/	(die) Zahnschmerzen	
(to) **give somebody a call** *(irr)* /ˌgɪv ˌsʌmbədi_ə ˈkɔːl/	jemanden anrufen	
practice /ˈpræktɪs/	(die) Praxis	
This is ... speaking. /ðɪs_ɪz ... ˈspiːkɪŋ/	Hier spricht ...	
(to) **catch a cold** *(irr)* /ˌkætʃ_ə ˈkəʊld/	sich erkälten	
cold /kəʊld/	(die) Erkältung	
headache /ˈhedeɪk/	(die) Kopfschmerzen	
sore throat /ˌsɔː ˈθrəʊt/	(die) Halsschmerzen	
fever /ˈfiːvə/	(das) Fieber	
cough /kɒf/	(der) Husten	
(to) **come in** *(irr)* /ˌkʌm_ˈɪn/	hereinkommen	
(to) **see** *(irr)* /siː/	empfangen, drannehmen	
ow (= ouch) *(informal)* /aʊ, aʊtʃ/	aua, autsch	
hopefully /ˈhəʊpfli/	hoffentlich	
(to) **call in** /ˌkɔːl_ˈɪn/	rufen, hereinbitten	
receptionist /rɪˈsepʃnɪst/	(die) Empfangsdame / (der) Empfangschef	

She has a **cold** and a **sore throat** and is making an appointment with the doctor.

p. 43, 1

(to) **trip** /trɪp/	stolpern
(to) **fall** *(irr)* /fɔːl/	fallen
(to) **bleed** *(irr)* /bliːd/	bluten
wound /wuːnd/	(die) Wunde
infection /ɪnˈfekʃn/	(die) Infektion
plaster /ˈplɑːstə/	(der) Gips, (das) Pflaster
soon /suːn/	bald
(to) **see a doctor** *(irr)* /ˌsiː_ə ˈdɒktə/	einen Arzt / eine Ärztin aufsuchen
stomach /ˈstʌmək/	(der) Magen, (der) Bauch
stomach ache *(no pl)* /ˈstʌmək_ˌeɪk/	(die) Bauchschmerzen
(to) **take out** *(irr)* /ˌteɪk_ˈaʊt/	herausnehmen
medicine /ˈmedsn/	(die) Medizin, (die) Medikamente
dramatic /drəˈmætɪk/	dramatisch
reading /ˈriːdɪŋ/	(die) Lesung
oh dear *(informal)* /əʊ ˈdɪə/	oje
wonder /ˈwʌndə/	(das) Wunder
appendix /əˈpendɪks/	(der) Blinddarm
painful /ˈpeɪnfl/	schmerzhaft

The girl **is seeing** her **doctor**.

p. 45, 4

accident /ˈæksɪdnt/	(der) Unfall
coach /kəʊtʃ/	(der/die) Trainer/in
hard /hɑːd/	fest, kräftig
(to) **call an ambulance** /ˌkɔːl_ən_ˈæmbjʊləns/	einen Krankenwagen rufen
emergency /ɪˈmɜːdʒnsi/	(der) Notfall
(to) **bang one's head** /ˌbæŋ wʌnz ˈhed/	sich den Kopf anschlagen
alright /ɔːlˈraɪt/	in Ordnung

They had to go to the hospital after the **accident**.

	dizzy /ˈdɪzi/	schwindlig
	emergency services *(pl)* /ɪˈmɜːdʒnsi ˌsɜːvɪsɪz/	(der) Notdienst, (der) Rettungsdienst
	operator /ˈɒpəˌreɪtə/	(der/die) Telefonist/in
	playing field /ˈpleɪɪŋ ˌfiːld/	(der) Sportplatz
p. 46, 5	**meaning** /ˈmiːnɪŋ/	(die) Bedeutung
	injury /ˈɪndʒəri/	(die) Verletzung
	(to) **examine** /ɪɡˈzæmɪn/	untersuchen
	sprained /spreɪnd/	verstaucht
	(to) **put on** *(irr)* /ˌpʊt_ˈɒn/	anlegen, auftragen
	bandage /ˈbændɪdʒ/	(der) Verband
	(to) **cool** /kuːl/	kühlen
	(to) **advise** /ədˈvaɪz/	raten, beraten
	waiting room /ˈweɪtɪŋ ˌruːm/	(das) Wartezimmer
	yet /jet/	schon; noch
	(to) **sign** /saɪn/	unterschreiben
	news *(no pl)* /njuːz/	(die) Neuigkeit, (die) Nachrichten
	ankle /ˈæŋkl/	(der) (Fuß)knöchel
	(to) **rest** /rest/	ausruhen
	possible /ˈpɒsəbl/	möglich
	(to) **promise** /ˈprɒmɪs/	versprechen
	GP (= General Practitioner) /ˌdʒiː ˈpiː, ˌdʒenrəl prækˈtɪʃnə/	(der/die) Hausarzt / Hausärztin
	X-ray /ˈeksreɪ/	(das) Röntgenbild
	phew *(informal)* /fjuː/	puh
	receptionist's desk /rɪˈsepʃnɪsts desk/	(die) Rezeption
	doctor's practice /ˈdɒktəz ˌpræktɪs/	(die) Arztpraxis
	elastic /ɪˈlæstɪk/	elastisch, flexibel
	(to) **keep up** *(irr)* /ˌkiːp_ˈʌp/	*hier:* hochlegen
	No problem. /ˌnəʊ ˈprɒbləm/	*hier:* Keine Ursache.
	check-up /ˈtʃek_ʌp/	(die) Untersuchung
p. 47, 5	(to) **read out** *(irr)* /ˌriːd_ˈaʊt/	(laut) vorlesen
p. 47, 6	**properly** /ˈprɒpəli/	richtig
p. 48, 7	**Get well soon!** /ˌɡet ˌwel ˈsuːn/	Gute Besserung!
p. 48, 8	(to) **be wrong (with)** *(irr)* /ˌbiː ˈrɒŋ wɪθ/	nicht in Ordnung sein (mit)
p. 49, 10	(to) **help out** /ˌhelp_ˈaʊt/	aushelfen
	exchange student /ɪksˈtʃeɪndʒ ˌstjuːdnt/	(der/die) Austauschschüler/in
	in pain /ˌɪn ˈpeɪn/	unter/mit Schmerzen
p. 49, 11	**illness** /ˈɪlnəs/	(die) Krankheit
	(to) **mime** /maɪm/	mimen, pantomimisch darstellen
p. 49, 12	(to) **get well** *(irr)* /ˌɡet ˈwel/	gesund werden
	(to) **hang out** *(informal, irr)* /ˌhæŋ_ˈaʊt/	Zeit mit jemandem verbringen

She **is examining** his knee **injury**.

'To **advise**' means to tell somebody what you think they should do.

When you **promise** something, you tell someone that you will definitely do something.

He is **reading out** a story.

An **exchange student** goes to school in another country for some time.

When you are ill, you want to **get well** soon.

p. 50, 13	(to) unscramble /ʌnˈskræmbl/	ordnen, in die richtige Reihenfolge bringen
p. 50, 14	(to) **mark** /mɑːk/	markieren, kennzeichnen
p. 51, 16	(to) **fall off** *(irr)* /ˌfɔːlˈɒf/	(herunter)fallen
	medical /ˈmedɪkl/	medizinisch

Unit 3 | Part A At the car boot sale

People sell **second-hand items** at a **car boot sale**.

p. 55	**car boot sale** /ˌkɑː ˈbuːt seɪl/	*(der) Kofferraum-Flohmarkt*
	second-hand /ˌsekənd ˈhænd/	gebraucht
	item /ˈaɪtəm/	(der) Gegenstand
	green /griːn/	umweltfreundlich, ökologisch
p. 56, 2	**stall** /stɔːl/	(der) Stand
	(to) **avoid** /əˈvɔɪd/	meiden, vermeiden
	crowd /kraʊd/	(die) Menschenmenge
	charity /ˈtʃærəti/	(die) Wohltätigkeitsorganisation
	run /rʌn/	(der) Lauf
	km (= kilometre) /ˈkɪləˌmiːtə/	(der) Kilometer
	unique /juˈniːk/	einzigartig
	anywhere /ˈeniˌweə/	irgendwo
	fee /fiː/	(die) Gebühr, (das) Geld
	age /eɪdʒ/	(das) Alter
	guide /gaɪd/	(der) Führer *(Buch)*
	arts and crafts /ˌɑːrts ən ˈkrɑːfts/	(das) Basteln, (die) Bastelarbeit
	find /faɪnd/	(der) Fund
	charity run /ˈtʃærəti rʌn/	(der) Wohltätigkeitslauf
	a good cause /ə ˌgʊd ˈkɔːz/	eine gute Sache, ein guter Zweck
	registration fee /ˌredʒɪˈstreɪʃn fiː/	(die) Anmeldegebühr
	forever /fərˈevə/	ewig, für immer
	(to) give a reason *(irr)* /ˌgɪv ə ˈriːzn/	einen Grund nennen
p. 57, 3	(to) **agree on** /əˈgriː ɒn/	sich einigen auf
	finally /ˈfaɪnli/	schließlich, endlich
	(to) **cancel** /ˈkænsl/	absagen, streichen
	neither /ˈnaɪðə, ˈniːðə/	auch nicht
	pocket money /ˈpɒkɪt ˌmʌni/	(das) Taschengeld
	flea market /ˈfliː ˌmɑːkɪt/	(der) Flohmarkt
	anyway /ˈeniweɪ/	sowieso
	(to) **sell** *(irr)* /sel/	verkaufen
	nobody /ˈnəʊbədi/	niemand, keiner
	crowded /ˈkraʊdɪd/	überfüllt
	argument /ˈɑːgjʊmənt/	(das) Argument; (der) Streit
	(to) **mention** /ˈmenʃn/	erwähnen
	(to) **be up to something** *(irr)* /ˌbiː ˌʌp tə ˈsʌmθɪŋ/	etwas vorhaben
	had planned /ˌhæd ˈplænd/	hatte(n) geplant

There are one thousand metres in a **kilometre**.
1 **km** = 0.6214 miles

Your **age** is how old you are.

finally = in the end

The concert was **crowded**.

	for ages *(informal)* /fər ˈeɪdʒɪz/	seit einer Ewigkeit
	(to) have something left *(irr)* /ˌhæv sʌmθɪŋ ˈleft/	etwas übrig haben
	the one /ðə ˈwʌn/	der/die/das
	(to) be up for something *(informal, irr)* /ˌbi ˌʌp fɔː ˈsʌmθɪŋ/	Lust zu etwas haben
	treasure hunting /ˈtreʒə ˌhʌntɪŋ/	(das) Schatzsuchen
	inspiration /ˌɪnspəˈreɪʃn/	(die) Inspiration, (die) Idee
p. 58, 5	**once** /wʌns/	einmal
	relative pronoun /ˌrelətɪv ˈprəʊnaʊn/	(das) Relativpronomen
p. 58, 6	relative clause /ˌrelətɪv ˈklɔːz/	(der) Relativsatz
People and Places 3	**mainly** /ˈmeɪnli/	hauptsächlich
	(to) **run** *(irr)* /rʌn/	leiten, betreiben
	price /praɪs/	(der) Preis (Kosten)
	charity shop /ˈtʃærəti ʃɒp/	*(der) Laden, in dem gebrauchte Dinge zu Wohltätigkeitszwecken verkauft werden*
	volunteer /ˌvɒlənˈtɪə/	(der/die) ehrenamtliche Mitarbeiter/in
	treasure /ˈtreʒə/	(der) Schatz
p. 59, 7	bicycle bell /ˈbaɪsɪkl bel/	(die) Fahrradklingel
	singing /ˈsɪŋɪŋ/	singend
p. 60, 8	**bargain** /ˈbɑːgɪn/	(das) Schnäppchen
	above /əˈbʌv/	oben, oberhalb
	seller /ˈselə/	(der/die) Verkäufer/in
	taste /teɪst/	(der) Geschmack
	condition /kənˈdɪʃn/	(der) Zustand
	(to) **try on** /ˌtraɪ ˈɒn/	anprobieren
	all right /ˌɔːl ˈraɪt/	in Ordnung
	cellar /ˈselə/	(der) Keller
	much /mʌtʃ/	sehr
	..., doesn't it? /ˈdʌznt ɪt/	..., nicht wahr?
	curtain /ˈkɜːtn/	(der) Vorhang
	flowerpot /ˈflaʊəˌpɒt/	(der) Blumentopf
	lamp /læmp/	(die) Lampe
	coffee grinder /ˈkɒfi ˌgraɪndə/	(die) Kaffeemühle
	price tag /ˈpraɪs tæg/	(das) Preisschild
	(to) clean out /ˌkliːn ˈaʊt/	ausräumen, entrümpeln
	coffee pot /ˈkɒfi pɒt/	(die) Kaffeekanne
p. 61, 8	(to) **get rid of** *(irr)* /ˌget ˈrɪd əv/	loswerden
	(to) **be interested in** *(irr)* /ˌbi ˈɪntrəstɪd ɪn/	interessiert sein an
	some old ones /səm ˈəʊld wʌnz/	ein paar alte
	a small one /ə ˈsmɔːl wʌn/	ein kleiner/eine kleine/ein kleines
p. 62, 10	**several** /ˈsevrəl/	einige, verschiedene
	particularly /pəˈtɪkjʊləli/	besonders, vor allem

once = one time

People **mainly** speak English in an English-speaking country.

When people go **treasure hunting**, they want to find **treasures**.

A **bargain** is something you can buy that costs much less than normal.

A **cellar** is a room under a building. It is usually dark in a cellar.

curtain

new ones /ˈnjuː wʌnz/ neue
these ones /ˈðiːz wʌnz/ diese

The boy **is interested in** buying a T-shirt.

several = more than two but not very many

p. 63, 11	chutney /ˈtʃʌtni/	*würzige indische Soße*	
p. 63, 12	(to) **own** /əʊn/	besitzen	this one /ˈðɪs wʌn/ diese(r, s)
	out and about /ˌaʊt̬_ən_əˈbaʊt/	unterwegs	the blue / red / green one /ðə ˈbluː / ˈred / ˈɡriːn wʌn/ der / die / das blaue / rote / grüne
	odd /ɒd/	merkwürdig, seltsam	
	(to) advertise /ˈædvətaɪz/	für etwas Werbung machen	
p. 64, 13	**one** /wʌn/	eine(r, s)	
	broken /ˈbrəʊkən/	zerbrochen; kaputt	the blue / brown / black ones /ðə ˈbluː / ˈbraʊn / ˈblæk wʌnz/ die blauen / braunen / schwarzen
p. 65, 15	**part** /pɑːt/	(die) Rolle	
	complete /kəmˈpliːt/	vollständig, komplett	another one /əˈnʌðə wʌn/ noch ein/e; ein anderer / ein anderes / eine andere
	You're welcome. /jɔː ˈwelkəm/	Gern geschehen., Keine Ursache.	

Unit 3 | Part B Festivals

p. 66, 1	Viking /ˈvaɪkɪŋ/	(der/die) Wikinger/in; Wikinger-	
p. 66, 2	**entry** /ˈentri/	(der) Eintrag	
	student /ˈstjuːdnt/	(der/die) Student/in	
	influence /ˈɪnfluəns/	(der) Einfluss	
	(to) **check out** *(informal)* /ˌtʃek_ˈaʊt/	sich ansehen; ausprobieren	
	fight /faɪt/	(der) Kampf, (der) Streit	
	after that /ˌɑːftə ˈðæt/	danach	first → **after that**
	(to) conquer /ˈkɒŋkə/	erobern	
	(to) step back in time /ˌstep_ˌbæk_ˌɪn ˈtaɪm/	sich in die Vergangenheit zurückversetzen	
	combat arena /ˈkɒmbæt_əˌriːnə/	(die) Wettkampfarena	
	warrior /ˈwɒriə/	(der/die) Krieger/in	
	authentic /ɔːˈθentɪk/	authentisch	There is a show **fight** with men in **authentic armour** in a **combat arena**.
	armour /ˈɑːmə/	(die) Rüstung	
	banquet /ˈbæŋkwɪt/	(das) Bankett, (das) Festessen	
	voyager /ˈvɔɪɪdʒə/	(der/die) Reisende/r	
	dining room /ˈdaɪnɪŋ ruːm/	*hier:* (der) Speisesaal	
p. 67, 2	**beard** /bɪəd/	(der) Bart	
	anyone /ˈeniˌwʌn/	jede(r, s); (irgend)jemand	the **highlight** = the best part of an event
	highlight /ˈhaɪˌlaɪt/	(der) Höhepunkt	
	battle /ˈbætl/	(der) Kampf	
	spectacular /spekˈtækjʊlə/	atemberaubend, spektakulär	
	peaceful /ˈpiːsfl/	friedlich, friedfertig	
	content /ˈkɒntent/	(der) Inhalt	
	least /liːst/	am wenigsten	
	literally /ˈlɪtrəli/	buchstäblich, wirklich	
	bird of prey /ˌbɜːd_əv ˈpreɪ/	(der) Raubvogel	a **bird of prey**
	trainer /ˈtreɪnə/	(der/die) Trainer/in	
	myth /mɪθ/	(der) Mythos	
	breathtaking /ˈbreθˌteɪkɪŋ/	atemberaubend	
	firework display /ˈfaɪəˌwɜːk dɪˌspleɪ/	(das) Feuerwerk	
	coming soon /ˌkʌmɪŋ ˈsuːn/	in Kürze erscheinend	

p. 68, 3	(to) **prepare for** /prɪˈpeə fɔː/	sich vorbereiten auf
	(to) **put on** *(irr)* /ˌpʊt‿ˈɒn/	anziehen *(Kleidung)*
	(to) style /staɪl/	frisieren
p. 69, 5	(to) **steal** *(irr)* /stiːl/	stehlen
	pocket /ˈpɒkɪt/	(die) (Hosen)tasche
	aspect /ˈæspekt/	(der) Aspekt, (der) Gesichtspunkt
	on the one hand ... /ˌɒn ðə ˈwʌn hænd/	einerseits ...
	on the other hand ... /ˌɒn ðɪ‿ˈʌðə hænd/	andererseits ...
	teddy bear /ˈtedi beə/	(der) Teddybär
	pickpocket /ˈpɪkˌpɒkɪt/	(der/die) Taschendieb/in
p. 70, 6	(to) **bother** /ˈbɒðə/	stören, belästigen
	not anyone /ˌnɒt‿ˈeniwʌn/	niemand
	itself /ɪtˈself/	selbst, sich selbst
	world-famous /ˌwɜːld ˈfeɪməs/	weltberühmt
	(to) **dive** /daɪv/	tauchen
	impressive /ɪmˈpresɪv/	beeindruckend
	colourful /ˈkʌləfl/	farbenfroh, bunt
	cheerful /ˈtʃɪəfl/	fröhlich, vergnügt
	serious /ˈsɪəriəs/	ernst
	(to) **draw attention to** *(irr)* /ˌdrɔː‿əˈtenʃn tə/	Aufmerksamkeit lenken auf
	immigrant /ˈɪmɪɡrənt/	(der/die) Einwanderer/in, (der/die) Immigrant/in
	multicultural /ˌmʌltiˈkʌltʃərəl/	multikulturell
	lover /ˈlʌvə/	(der/die) Liebhaber/in
	open-air /ˌəʊpənˈ‿eə/	im Freien
	south-west /ˌsaʊθˈwest/	Südwest-
	tent /tent/	(das) Zelt
	muddy /ˈmʌdi/	matschig, schlammig
	camping site /ˈkæmpɪŋ ˌsaɪt/	(der) Campingplatz
	organizer /ˈɔːɡəˌnaɪzə/	(der/die) Organisator/in
	Caribbean /ˌkærɪˈbiən/	karibisch
	steel drum /ˌstiːl ˈdrʌm/	*Steeldrum*
p. 71, 6	**such** /sʌtʃ/	so, solch
	(to) **be worth** *(irr)* /ˌbiː ˈwɜːθ/	(sich) lohnen, wert sein
	discipline /ˈdɪsəplɪn/	(die) Disziplin
	(to) **lift** /lɪft/	(hoch)heben
	(to) **turn over** /ˌtɜːn‿ˈəʊvə/	(sich) umdrehen
	(to) **land** /lænd/	landen
	upper /ˈʌpə/	obere(r, s)
	curried chicken /ˌkʌrid ˈtʃɪkɪn/	*Hühnchenfleisch in Curry*
	coconut /ˈkəʊkəˌnʌt/	(die) Kokosnuss
	spectacle /ˈspektəkl/	(das) Spektakel

You can **put on** a costume for a party or a carnival.

teddy bear

The chair is very **colourful**.

A **multicultural** class is a class with pupils from many different cultures.

tent

Früher war die britische Schreibweise von Wörtern mit '-ise', 'isation' oder '-iser' eindeutig die mit 's', nur im amerikanischen Englisch wurden alle diese Wörter mit 'z' geschrieben. Mittlerweile werden kaum noch Unterschiede gemacht. Viele Briten schreiben 'organize, organizer, realize, ...'.
In vielen Wörterbüchern wird sogar die Schreibweise mit 'z' als die häufiger vorkommende gelistet.

	lad *(informal, Scottish)* /læd/	(der) Junge
	lass *(informal, Scottish)* /læs/	(das) Mädchen
	bagpipes *(pl)* /ˈbæɡˌpaɪps/	(der) Dudelsack
	tossing the caber /ˌtɒsɪŋ ðə ˈkeɪbə/	(das) Baumstammwerfen
	contestant /kənˈtestənt/	(der/die) Wettbewerbsteilnehmer/in
	log /lɒɡ/	(der) Baumstamm
	(to) toss /tɒs/	werfen
	aye *(informal, Scottish)* /aɪ/	ja
p. 72, 8	**look** /lʊk/	(das) Aussehen, (der) Look
	(to) **dress** /dres/	sich anziehen, sich kleiden
	resident /ˈrezɪdnt/	(der/die) Bewohner/in
	carnival /ˈkɑːnɪvl/	(das) Volksfest, (der) Karneval
	sketch *(pl sketches)* /sketʃ, ˈsketʃɪz/	(die) Skizze
p. 73, 9	(to) **attend** /əˈtend/	besuchen
	(to) **produce** /prəˈdjuːs/	produzieren
	waste /weɪst/	(der) Abfall
	pressure /ˈpreʃə/	(der) Druck
	government /ˈɡʌvənmənt/	(die) Regierung
	(to) **reduce** /rɪˈdjuːs/	reduzieren
	packaging /ˈpækɪdʒɪŋ/	(die) Verpackung
	use /juːs/	(die) Verwendung; (der) Einsatz
	no longer /ˌnəʊ ˈlɒŋɡə/	nicht mehr
	site /saɪt/	(die) Stelle, (der) Platz
	association /əˌsəʊsiˈeɪʃn/	(die) Vereinigung
	independent /ˌɪndɪˈpendənt/	unabhängig
	(to) **appeal to** /əˈpiːl tʊ/	appellieren an, bitten um
	(to) **reuse** /riːˈjuːz/	wiederverwenden
	(to) **state** /steɪt/	äußern, aussprechen
	(to) clear up /ˌklɪərˈʌp/	aufräumen
	ton /tʌn/	(die) Tonne
	(to) abolish /əˈbɒlɪʃ/	abschaffen
	carrier bag /ˈkæriə bæɡ/	(die) Tragetasche
	straw /strɔː/	(der) Strohhalm
	across the country /əˌkrɒs ðə ˈkʌntri/	im ganzen Land
	CEO (= chief executive officer) /ˌsiːiːˈəʊ, ˌtʃiːfɪɡˌzekjʊtɪvˈɒfɪsə/	(der/die) Geschäftsführer/in
	festival goer /ˈfestɪvl ˌɡəʊə/	(der/die) Festivalbesucher/in
	single-use /ˌsɪŋɡl ˈjuːs/	Einweg-
	zero waste /ˌzɪərəʊ ˈweɪst/	verpackungsfrei
	(to) cut out *(irr)* /ˌkʌtˈaʊt/	weglassen
p. 74, 12	(to) **set up** *(irr)* /ˌsetˈʌp/	aufbauen

Tossing the caber is one of the sports at the Highland Games.

The **residents** of a house or flat are the people who live in it.

We should **reduce** the amount of **waste** that we **produce**.

A **site** is an area of land.

to **reuse** = to use again

The man **has set up** a stall at the car boot sale.

Unit 4 | Part A Exploring roots

p. 79	**root** /ruːt/	(die) Wurzel	A **village** is much smaller than a town.
	village /ˈvɪlɪdʒ/	(das) Dorf	
	(to) **seek** *(irr)* /siːk/	suchen, streben nach	
	advice /ədˈvaɪs/	(der) Rat, (der) Ratschlag	
	(to) give a helping hand *(irr)* /ˌɡɪv_ə ˌhelpɪŋ ˈhænd/	helfen	
p. 80, 1	**thought** /θɔːt/	(der) Gedanke	**memory** = something that you remember
p. 80, 2	**memory** /ˈmemri/	(die) Erinnerung	
	because of /bɪˈkɒz_əv/	wegen	
	accent /ˈæksnt/	(der) Akzent	
	Korean /kəˈriːən/	(der/die) Koreaner/in; koreanisch	
	riverside /ˈrɪvəˌsaɪd/	(das) Flussufer	
	Spain /speɪn/	Spanien	
	mountain biking /ˈmaʊntɪn ˌbaɪkɪŋ/	(das) Mountainbikefahren	
p. 81, 2	(to) **grow up** *(irr)* /ˌɡrəʊˈʌp/	aufwachsen	
	(to) **take over** *(irr)* /ˌteɪkˈəʊvə/	übernehmen	
	business /ˈbɪznəs/	(das) Geschäft, (der) Handel	
	university /ˌjuːnɪˈvɜːsəti/	(die) Universität	When two people **get married**, there is usually a big party.
	(to) **get married** *(irr)* /ˌɡet ˈmærid/	heiraten	
	mixture /ˈmɪkstʃə/	(die) Mischung	
	(to) **quote** /kwəʊt/	zitieren	to **support** = to help an idea or person to be successful
	(to) **support** /səˈpɔːt/	(unter)stützen	
	as far as /əz ˈfɑːr_əz/	soweit	
	great-great-grandfather /ˌɡreɪt ˌɡreɪt ˈɡrænˌfɑːðə/	(der) Ururgroßvater	
	(to) retire /rɪˈtaɪə/	in den Ruhestand treten	
	the Science Museum /ðə ˈsaɪəns mjuːˌziːəm/	(das) Naturwissenschaftsmuseum	
	Sweden /ˈswiːdn/	Schweden	**lively** = exciting and full of life
	lively /ˈlaɪvli/	lebendig	
	West African /ˌwestˈæfrɪkən/	(der/die) Westafrikaner/in; westafrikanisch	
	Swedish /ˈswiːdɪʃ/	schwedisch	
	cuisine /kwɪˈziːn/	(die) Küche	
p. 82, 4	(to) **study** /ˈstʌdi/	studieren; lernen	to **study** = to learn
	great-grandmother /ˌɡreɪt ˈɡrænˌmʌðə/	(die) Urgroßmutter	
p. 83, 5	**south** /saʊθ/	(der) Süden; Süd-	**population** = all the people who live in an area
	population /ˌpɒpjʊˈleɪʃn/	(die) Bevölkerung	
	South Asian /ˌsaʊθˈeɪʒn/	südasiatisch	
	African /ˈæfrɪkən/	(der/die) Afrikaner/in; afrikanisch	
	Polish /ˈpəʊlɪʃ/	(das) Polnisch; polnisch	

People and Places 4	**war** /wɔː/	(der) Krieg	**former** times = times in the past
	former /ˈfɔːmə/	ehemalige(r, s); frühere(r, s)	
	colony /ˈkɒləni/	(die) Kolonie	
	East /iːst/	östlich, Ost-	
	survey /ˈsɜːveɪ/	(die) Umfrage	
	the Second World War /ðə ˌsekənd ˌwɜːld ˈwɔː/	(der) Zweite Weltkrieg	
	melting pot /ˈmeltɪŋ pɒt/	(der) Schmelztiegel	
	Bangladesh /ˌbæŋɡləˈdeʃ/	Bangladesch	
	lane /leɪn/	(die) Gasse, (die) enge Straße	
	Bengali /beŋˈɡɔːli/	(der/die) Bengale/Bengalin; bengalisch	
	is spoken /ˌɪz ˈspəʊkən/	wird gesprochen	
p. 84, 6	(to) **connect** /kəˈnekt/	verbinden	You need electricity and a machine to **print**.
	(to) **print** /prɪnt/	drucken	
	storytelling /ˈstɔːriˌtelɪŋ/	(das) Geschichtenerzählen	
p. 85, 7	(to) **join** /dʒɔɪn/	sich zu jemandem gesellen; Mitglied werden	
	(to) **tell the truth** (irr) /ˌtel ðə ˈtruːθ/	die Wahrheit sagen	
	(to) **be lucky** (irr) /ˌbiː ˈlʌki/	Glück haben	
	alive /əˈlaɪv/	lebendig, am Leben	
	(to) **keep in touch** (irr) /ˌkiːp ɪn ˈtʌtʃ/	Kontakt halten, in Verbindung bleiben	When people **emigrate**, they leave their country to live in another country.
	(to) **emigrate** /ˈemɪɡreɪt/	auswandern	
	(to) **marry** /ˈmæri/	heiraten	
	foreign /ˈfɒrɪn/	ausländisch, fremd	
	(to) **be homesick** (irr) /ˌbiː ˈhəʊmˌsɪk/	Heimweh haben	
	(to) **manage** /ˈmænɪdʒ/	zurechtkommen, es schaffen	
	while /waɪl/	(die) Weile	
	great-grandfather /ˌɡreɪt ˈɡrænˌfɑːðə/	(der) Urgroßvater	
	World War II /ˌwɜːld ˌwɔː ˈtuː/	der Zweite Weltkrieg	
	The Royal Air Force /ðə ˌrɔɪəl ˈeə fɔːs/	(die) Königliche Luftwaffe	
	air force /ˈeə fɔːs/	(die) Luftwaffe	
p. 86, 8	**dress** /dres/	(das) Kleid, (die) Kleidung	**dress**
	latest /ˈleɪtɪst/	neueste(r, s)	
	mostly /ˈməʊstli/	meistens, größtenteils	**mostly** = most of the time
	grandad (informal) /ˈɡrænˌdæd/	(der) Opa	
	still /stɪl/	nach wie vor, trotzdem	**grandpa** = **grandad** = grandfather
	grandpa (informal) /ˈɡrænˌpɑː/	(der) Opa	
	(to) **die** /daɪ/	sterben	
	cute /kjuːt/	süß, niedlich	'…, wasn't he?' oder '…, didn't he?' kannst du mit 'oder? / nicht wahr? / gell?' übersetzen.
	childhood /ˈtʃaɪldˌhʊd/	(die) Kindheit	
	heritage /ˈherɪtɪdʒ/	(das) Erbe	
p. 87, 8	**speech bubble** /ˈspiːtʃ ˌbʌbl/	(die) Sprechblase	
	at that time /æt ˈðæt ˌtaɪm/	zu jener Zeit	

	What if …? /ˌwɒt ˈɪf/	Was wäre, wenn …?
	Warsaw /ˈwɔːsɔː/	Warschau
	darling /ˈdɑːlɪŋ/	(der) Liebling, (der) Schatz
p. 87, 9	**timeline** /ˈtaɪmlaɪn/	(die) Zeitachse
	saying /ˈseɪɪŋ/	(das) Sprichwort
p. 88, 10	Turkish /ˈtɜːkɪʃ/	(das) Türkisch
p. 88, 11	**expression** /ɪkˈspreʃn/	(der) Ausdruck
p. 89, 13	**label** /ˈleɪbl/	(das) Etikett

She has a sad **expression** on her face.

Unit 4 | Part B Giving a helping hand

p. 90, 2	**herself** /həˈself/	sich; (sie) selbst
	Don't worry. /ˌdəʊnt ˈwʌri/	Mach dir keine Sorgen.
	(to) **be wrong** *(irr)* /ˌbiː ˈrɒŋ/	im Unrecht sein
p. 91, 2	**allowed** /əˈlaʊd/	erlaubt
	annoying /əˈnɔɪɪŋ/	ärgerlich
	(to) **save** /seɪv/	aufheben; sichern
	silly /ˈsɪli/	albern, dumm
	upset /ʌpˈset/	aufgebracht; aufgeregt
	I'm in! *(informal)* /ˌaɪm ˈɪn/	Ich bin dabei!
	tuition /tjuˈɪʃn/	*hier:* (die) Nachhilfe
	(to) skip /skɪp/	*hier:* ausfallen lassen
	D /diː/	*etwa:* Note 4, ausreichend
	(to) follow through /ˌfɒləʊ ˈθruː/	etwas zu Ende führen
	lame /leɪm/	lahm
p. 93, 5	**right now** /ˌraɪt ˈnaʊ/	jetzt, im Moment
	not at all /ˌnɒt ət ˈɔːl/	überhaupt nicht
	(to) **delete** /dɪˈliːt/	löschen
	guy /gaɪ/	(der) Kerl, (der) Typ
	chemistry club /ˈkemɪstri klʌb/	(die) Chemie-AG
	I'd (= I would) /aɪd, ˌaɪ ˈwʊd/	ich würde
p. 94, 6	(to) **seek advice** *(irr)* /ˌsiːk ədˈvaɪs/	Rat suchen
	(to) **judge** /dʒʌdʒ/	urteilen
	(to) **stop** /stɒp/	stoppen
	piece of advice /ˌpiːs əv ədˈvaɪs/	(der) Rat(schlag)
	right /raɪt/	(das) Recht
	official, officially /əˈfɪʃl, əˈfɪʃli/	offiziell
	(to) **suppose** /səˈpəʊz/	annehmen, vermuten
	parent /ˈpeərənt/	(das) Elternteil
	All the best! /ˌɔːl ðə ˈbest/	Alles Gute!
	Good luck! /ˌgʊd ˈlʌk/	Viel Glück!
	(to) **chat** /tʃæt/	plaudern; chatten
	unless /ənˈles/	außer wenn
	headline /ˈhedˌlaɪn/	(die) Schlagzeile; *hier:* (die) Überschrift

How about …? /ˈhaʊ ə baʊt/ Wie wäre es mit …?, Was ist mit …?
What's up? *(informal)* /ˌwɒts ˈʌp/ Was ist los?
What's wrong? *(informal)* /ˌwɒts ˈrɒŋ/ Was ist los?

to **skip** = to not do something that you normally do

right now = at the moment

How r u? /ˌhaʊ ˈɑː jʊ/ Wie geht es dir / euch?
gr8 (= great) /greɪt/ großartig
sec (= second) /sek, ˈsekənd/ (die) Sekunde

stop ≠ start

to **chat** = to talk in a friendly way

teen /tiːn/	(der) Teenager	
trained /treɪnd/	ausgebildet, geschult	
anonymous(ly) /əˈnɒnɪməs, əˈnɒnɪməsli/	anonym	
the other day /ðiˌʌðə ˈdeɪ/	neulich, vor einigen Tagen	
(to) make sure *(irr)* /ˌmeɪk ˈʃɔː/	*hier:* dafür sorgen, dass …	
(to) be left out *(irr)* /ˌbiː ˌleft ˈaʊt/	ausgeschlossen werden	
not even /ˈnɒt ˌiːvn/	nicht einmal	
p. 95, 6 — (to) **communicate** /kəˈmjuːnɪkeɪt/	kommunizieren, sprechen	Using your mobile is a good way to **communicate**.
matter /ˈmætə/	(die) Angelegenheit	
(to) **prove** *(irr)* /pruːv/	beweisen	
(to) **wish** /wɪʃ/	wünschen	
shy /ʃaɪ/	schüchtern	
(to) **tease** /tiːz/	hänseln, ärgern	When you have done something wrong, you need to **apologize**.
(to) **apologize (= apologise)** /əˈpɒlədʒaɪz/	sich entschuldigen	
helpful /ˈhelpfl/	hilfreich, nützlich	
quite a bit /ˌkwaɪt ə ˈbɪt/	ziemlich viel	
(to) keep a diary *(irr)* /ˌkiːp ə ˈdaɪəri/	Tagebuch führen	
trial phase /ˈtraɪəl feɪz/	(die) Testphase	**Screen time** is the time you spend in front of a screen.
screen time /ˈskriːn taɪm/	(die) Bildschirmzeit	
(to) joke around /ˌdʒəʊk əˈraʊnd/	herumalbern	
p. 96, 8 — school counsellor /ˌskuːl ˈkaʊnslə/	(der/die) Vertrauenslehrer/in	
p. 96, 9 — helpline /ˈhelpˌlaɪn/	*(der)* telefonische Beratungsdienst	
p. 97, 10 — (to) **deal with** *(irr)* /ˈdiːl wɪð/	sich befassen mit, umgehen mit	
dos and don'ts /ˌduːz ˌən ˈdəʊnts/	was man tun und was man nicht tun sollte	**mine** /maɪn/ meine(r, s)
word search /ˈwɜːd sɜːtʃ/	(die) Wortsuche	**yours** /jɔːz/ deine(r, s); eure(r, s); Ihre(r, s)
p. 97, 11 — **company** /ˈkʌmpni/	(die) Firma, (das) Unternehmen	**his** /hɪz/ seine(r, s)
office manager /ˈɒfɪs ˌmænɪdʒə/	(der/die) Sekretär/in	**hers** /hɜːz/ ihre(r, s)
p. 98, 12 — **hers** /hɜːz/	ihre(r, s)	**ours** /ˈaʊəz/ unsere(r, s)
ours /ˈaʊəz/	unsere(r, s)	**theirs** /ðeəz/ ihre(r, s)
neighbour /ˈneɪbə/	(der/die) Nachbar/in	
theirs /ðeəz/	ihre(r, s)	
bracket /ˈbrækɪt/	(die) Klammer	Many children are allowed to **stay up late** at the weekend or in the holidays.
p. 98, 13 — (to) **allow** /əˈlaʊ/	erlauben	
(to) **stay up (late)** /ˌsteɪ ˌʌp ˈleɪt/	lange aufbleiben	
linking part /ˈlɪŋkɪŋ pɑːt/	(das) Verbindungsteil	
linking word /ˈlɪŋkɪŋ wɜːd/	(das) Verbindungswort	
rude /ruːd/	unhöflich; primitiv	
p. 99, 15 — (to) **give advice** *(irr)* /ˌgɪv ədˈvaɪs/	Rat geben	to **give advice** = to advise
back /bæk/	(der) Rücken	
pupil /ˈpjuːpl/	(der/die) Schüler/in	
fault /fɔːlt/	(die) Schuld, (der) Fehler	

| (to) **ask for advice** /ˌɑːsk fər_əd'vaɪs/ | um Rat bitten |
| (to) panic /'pænɪk/ | in Panik geraten |

Unit 5 | Part A Inventions

p. 103	**communication** /kəˌmjuːnɪ'keɪʃn/	(die) Verständigung, (die) Kommunikation
	inventor /ɪn'ventə/	(der/die) Erfinder/in
p. 104, 1	**education** /ˌedjʊ'keɪʃn/	(die) Bildung; (die) Ausbildung, (die) Erziehung
	muscle /'mʌsl/	(der) Muskel
	power /'paʊə/	(die) Kraft
	author /'ɔːθə/	(der/die) Autor/in
	electric /ɪ'lektrɪk/	elektrisch, Elektro-
	cool /kuːl/	kühl; kalt
p. 104, 2	**toothbrush** /'tuːθbrʌʃ/	(die) Zahnbürste
	steam locomotive /'stiːm ˌləʊkəˌməʊtɪv/	(die) Dampflokomotive, (die) Dampflok
p. 105, 2	**basic** /'beɪsɪk/	grundlegend, wesentlich
	such as /'sʌtʃ_æz/	wie
	steam engine /'stiːm_ˌendʒɪn/	(die) Dampfmaschine
	(to) **pull** /pʊl/	ziehen
	passenger /'pæsɪndʒə/	(der/die) Passagier/in
	most /məʊst/	die meisten; am meisten
	engine /'endʒɪn/	(die) Maschine, (der) Motor
	American /ə'merɪkən/	(der/die) Amerikaner/in; amerikanisch
	television /'telɪˌvɪʒn/	(der) Fernseher, (das) Fernsehen
	scientist /'saɪəntɪst/	(der/die) Wissenschaftler/in
	working /'wɜːkɪŋ/	funktionierend
	(to) have a closer look *(irr)* /hæv_ə ˌkləʊsə 'lʊk/	sich etwas genauer ansehen
	named /neɪmd/	namens
	horsehair /'hɔːsˌheə/	(das) Rosshaar
	bone /bəʊn/	(der) Knochen
	high-pressure /ˌhaɪ 'preʃə/	Hochdruck-
	locomotive /ˌləʊkə'məʊtɪv/	(die) Lokomotive
	(to) patent /'peɪtnt/	sich patentieren lassen
	phone call /'fəʊn kɔːl/	(der) Telefonanruf
	long-distance /ˌlɒŋ 'dɪstəns/	Fern-
	transatlantic /ˌtrænzət'læntɪk/	transatlantisch
	(to) be credited with *(irr)* /ˌbiː 'kredɪtɪd wɪð/	zugeschrieben bekommen
p. 106, 3	railway company /'reɪlweɪ ˌkʌmpni/	(die) Eisenbahngesellschaft
p. 106, 4	passive /'pæsɪv/	(das) Passiv
	telescope /'telɪˌskəʊp/	(das) Teleskop

Education is the process or activity of teaching people.

toothbrush

was written /ˌwɒz 'rɪtn/
wurde geschrieben
was / were invented
/ˌwɒz / ˌwɜːr_ɪn'ventɪd/
wurde(n) erfunden
was made /ˌwɒz 'meɪd/
wurde gemacht
are used /ˌɑː 'juːsd/
werden benutzt
was used /ˌwɒz 'juːzd/
wurde verwendet
are pulled /ˌɑː 'pʊld/
werden gezogen
was patented
/ˌwɒz 'peɪtntɪd/
wurde patentiert
are credited with
/ˌɑː 'kredɪtɪd wɪð/
werden zugeschrieben
was presented
/ˌwɒz prɪ'zentɪd/
wurde vorgestellt
was built /ˌwɒz 'bɪlt/
wurde gebaut
was born /ˌwɒz 'bɔːn/
wurde geboren

p. 107, 5	**section** /'sekʃn/	(das) Teil, (das) Stück, (der) Abschnitt; (die) Abteilung	
	display /dɪ'spleɪ/	(die) Auslage, (die) Ausstellung	The spaceship is flying in **space**.
	space /speɪs/	(das) Weltall	
p. 108, 6	**opening times** *(pl)* /'əʊpənɪŋ taɪmz/	(die) Öffnungszeiten	
	(to) **be located** *(irr)* /ˌbi: ləʊ'keɪtɪd/	gelegen sein	
	currently /'kʌrəntli/	zurzeit, momentan	**currently** = at the moment
	wait /weɪt/	(die) Wartezeit	
	in advance /ˌɪn_əd'vɑːns/	im Voraus	
	(to) be welcome to *(irr)* /ˌbi: 'welkəm tʊ/	etwas gern (tun) können	
	picnic /'pɪknɪk/	(das) Picknick	**picnic**
	eating /'iːtɪŋ/	(das) Essen	
	the Tube /ðə 'tjuːb/	(die) (Londoner) U-Bahn	
	(to) rebuild *(irr)* /ˌriː'bɪld/	wieder aufbauen	
	(to) renovate /'renəveɪt/	renovieren	
p. 108, 7	(to) **save** /seɪv/	sparen; retten	
	practical /'præktɪkl/	praktisch	
	zip /zɪp/	(der) Reißverschluss	**zip**
	(to) **count** /kaʊnt/	zählen	
	(to) **appear** /ə'pɪə/	erscheinen, auftauchen	
	industry /'ɪndəstri/	(die) Industrie	
	construction /kən'strʌkʃn/	(der) Bau	
	(to) button /'bʌtən/	knöpfen	
	onwards /'ɒnwədz/	von … an	Sitting on a chair for a long time can be very **uncomfortable**.
p. 109, 7	**uncomfortable** /ʌn'kʌmftəbl/	unbequem	
	at all /ˌæt_'ɔːl/	überhaupt	
	simple /'sɪmpl/	einfach, simpel	
	(to) **prevent** /prɪ'vent/	verhindern, vorbeugen	
	comfortable /'kʌmftəbl/	bequem	
	tin /tɪn/	(die) Büchse, (die) Dose	
	tool /tuːl/	(das) Werkzeug	
	accidentally /ˌæksɪ'dentli/	versehentlich, zufällig	
	(to) **grow** *(irr)* /grəʊ/	wachsen	**apparently** = on the basis of what you have heard
	apparently /ə'pærəntli/	anscheinend	
	discovery /dɪ'skʌvri/	(die) Entdeckung	
	seat belt /'siːt belt/	(der) Sicherheitsgurt	
	strap /stræp/	(der) Riemen	
	leather /'leðə/	(das) Leder	
	(to) fasten /'fɑːsn/	schließen, zumachen	to **fasten** = to close
	belt /belt/	(der) Gürtel	
	seat /siːt/	(der) Sitz	
	tin opener /'tɪn_ˌəʊpnə/	(der) Dosenöffner	

(to) keep from *(irr)* /'ki:p frɒm/	*hier:* abhalten, verhindern	
(to) go bad *(irr)* /ˌgəʊ 'bæd/	verderben	
(to) come up with *(irr)* /ˌkʌm ˈʌp wɪð/	sich einfallen lassen	to **come up with** = to have an idea
inside /'ɪnˌsaɪd/	in … hinein	
tightly /'taɪtli/	fest	
(to) store /stɔ:/	lagern	
scratch /skrætʃ/	(der) Kratzer	
(to) become infected *(irr)* /bɪˌkʌm ɪnˈfektɪd/	sich infizieren	A dirty wound can **become infected**.
bacteria *(pl)* /bæk'tɪəriə/	(die) Bakterien	
antibiotic /ˌæntibaɪˈɒtɪk/	(das) Antibiotikum	
(to) cure /kjʊə/	heilen	
(Petri) dish /'pi:tri ˌdɪʃ/	(die) Petrischale	
lab /læb/	(das) Labor	at the **lab**
mould /məʊld/	(der) Schimmel	
(to) be estimated *(irr)* /ˌbi ˈestɪmeɪtəd/	geschätzt werden	
industrial /ɪn'dʌstriəl/	industriell	
(to) **adopt** /ə'dɒpt/	annehmen, übernehmen	
production /prə'dʌkʃn/	(die) Produktion	
process /'prəʊses/	(der) Prozess, (das) Verfahren	
both … and … /'bəʊθ ænd/	sowohl … als auch …	**Both** the boy **and** the girl are wearing a green jumper.
impact /'ɪmpækt/	(die) Auswirkung, (der) Einfluss	
farming /'fɑ:mɪŋ/	Ackerbau und Viehzucht	fewer = weniger *(bei zählbaren Hauptwörtern)*
modified /'mɒdɪfaɪd/	verändert, modifiziert	less = weniger *(bei nicht zählbaren Hauptwörtern)*
fewer /'fju:ə/	weniger	
(to) **rate** /reɪt/	einschätzen, bewerten	
rating /'reɪtɪŋ/	(die) Einschätzung, (die) Einstufung	**Electricity** can produce light.
electricity /ɪˌlek'trɪsəti/	(die) Elektrizität, (der) Strom	
brochure /'brəʊʃə/	(die) Broschüre	
baker /'beɪkə/	*hier: (die) Backmaschine*	
cleaning skates *(pl)* /'kli:nɪŋ ˌskeɪts/	*(die) Reinigungsskates*	
X-ray glasses *(pl)* /'eksreɪ ˌglɑ:sɪz/	*(die) Röntgenbrille*	
toilet roll /'tɔɪlət rəʊl/	(die) Toilettenpapier-Rolle	
(to) shrink *(irr)* /ʃrɪŋk/	schrumpfen	
lunchbox /'lʌntʃbɒks/	(die) Frühstücksdose	
owner /'əʊnə/	(der/die) Besitzer/in	The girl is the proud **owner** of a new blue bike.
immediate /ɪ'mi:diət/	umgehend; unmittelbar	
success /sək'ses/	(der) Erfolg	A **rich** person can spend a lot of money.
rich /rɪtʃ/	reich	
raincoat /'reɪnˌkəʊt/	(der) Regenmantel	
cereal /'sɪəriəl/	(die) Frühstücksflocken	

People and Places 5

p. 110, 8
p. 110, 9
p. 111, 10
p. 111, 11
p. 112, 12

Unit 5 | Part B Communication

p. 114, 2	**stone** /stəʊn/	(der) Stein
	development /dɪˈveləpmənt/	(die) Entwicklung
	writing /ˈraɪtɪŋ/	(die) Schrift, (das) Schreiben
	peace /piːs/	(der) Frieden
	result /rɪˈzʌlt/	(das) Ergebnis
	finding /ˈfaɪndɪŋ/	(die) Entdeckung, (das) Ergebnis
	general /ˈdʒenrəl/	allgemein
	(to) **give a presentation** *(irr)* /ˌgɪv‿ə ˌpreznˈteɪʃn/	eine Präsentation halten
	tablet /ˈtæblət/	(der) Block, (die) Platte
	technological /ˌteknəˈlɒdʒɪkl/	technologisch
	low-tech /ˌləʊˈtek/	technisch einfach
	on demand /ˌɒn dɪˈmɑːnd/	auf Anfrage
	assembly hall /əˈsembli ˌhɔːl/	(die) Aula
p. 115, 3	(to) **sign up (for)** /ˌsaɪnˈʌp/	sich anmelden
p. 116, 5	planner /ˈplænə/	(der) Kalender, (der) Planer
p. 117, 6	**network** /ˈnetˌwɜːk/	(das) Netzwerk
	method /ˈmeθəd/	(die) Methode
	(to) **research** /rɪˈsɜːtʃ/	recherchieren
	(to) **copy** /ˈkɒpi/	kopieren
	document /ˈdɒkjʊmənt/	(das) Dokument
	source /sɔːs/	(die) Quelle
	search engine /ˈsɜːtʃˌendʒɪn/	(die) Suchmaschine
	(to) be done with *(informal, irr)* /ˌbiː ˈdʌn wɪð/	fertig sein mit
p. 118, 7	**rock** /rɒk/	(der) Stein, (der) Fels
	theory /ˈθɪəri/	(die) Theorie
	function /ˈfʌŋkʃn/	(die) Aufgabe, (die) Funktion
	BC (= before Christ) /ˌbiː ˈsiː, bɪˌfɔː ˈkraɪst/	v. Chr. (= vor Christus)
	around /əˈraʊnd/	ungefähr
	AD (= Anno Domini) /ˌeɪ ˈdiː, ˌænəʊ ˈdɒmɪnaɪ/	n. Chr. (= nach Christus)
	wide /waɪd/	weit
	piece of information /ˌpiːs‿əv‿ˌɪnfəˈmeɪʃn/	(die) Information
	Egyptian /ɪˈdʒɪpʃn/	(der/die) Ägypter/in; ägyptisch
	clay /kleɪ/	(der) Lehm, (der) Ton
	printing press /ˈprɪntɪŋ pres/	(die) Druckerpresse
p. 119, 7	**rise** /raɪz/	(der) Aufstieg
	thumb /θʌm/	(der) Daumen
	once more /ˌwʌns ˈmɔː/	noch einmal

A letter is a piece of **writing**.

When you **give a presentation**, you present something to a group of people.

low-tech ≠ high-tech

A **method** is a way of doing something.

Wendungen wie 'isn't it?' oder 'aren't you?' nennt man Bestätigungsfragen (= *question tags*). Du kannst sie mit 'oder? / nicht wahr? / gell?' übersetzen und bildest sie, indem du die Verbform aus einem bejahten Aussagesatz verneinst.
You're connected to the Internet, **aren't** you?
She can speak Chinese, **can't** she?
Harry used a search engine, **didn't** he?
The friends like each other, **don't** they?
Einen verneinten Satz bejaht man: The food isn't very good, **is** it?

thumb

	(to) **message** /ˈmesɪdʒ/	eine Nachricht schicken	
	(to) **mourn** /mɔːn/	trauern	
	lost /lɒst/	verloren	
	(to) **appreciate** /əˈpriːʃiˌeɪt/	schätzen	
	uncomplicated /ʌnˈkɒmplɪˌkeɪtɪd/	unkompliziert	
p. 119, 8	**habit** /ˈhæbɪt/	(die) Gewohnheit, (die) Angewohnheit	A **call** is a conversation on the phone or a phone **call**.
	call /kɔːl/	(der) Anruf, (das) Gespräch	
p. 120, 9	**challenge** /ˈtʃæləndʒ/	*hier:* (die) Wette	
p. 120, 10	**device** /dɪˈvaɪs/	(das) Gerät, (der) Apparat	
	console /kənˈsəʊl/	(die) Konsole	
p. 121, 12	**magazine** /ˌmæɡəˈziːn/	(die) Zeitschrift	When you **download** something, you move information from the Internet to your computer.
	password /ˈpɑːsˌwɜːd/	(das) Passwort	
	(to) **download** /ˌdaʊnˈləʊd/	herunterladen	
	(to) **click on** /ˈklɪk‿ɒn/	anklicken	
	(to) **trust** /trʌst/	vertrauen	
	anybody /ˈenibɒdi/	irgendjemand; jede(r, s)	
	behaviour /bɪˈheɪvjə/	(das) Benehmen, (das) Verhalten	
	consequence /ˈkɒnsɪkwəns/	(die) Konsequenz, (die) Folge	
	(to) **treat** /triːt/	behandeln	A vet **treats** animals.
	(to) **befriend** /bɪˈfrend/	sich anfreunden mit	
	(to) **bully** /ˈbʊli/	mobben	
	respectful /rɪˈspektfl/	respektvoll	
p. 121, 13	**summary** /ˈsʌməri/	(die) Zusammenfassung	
p. 122, 14	**happy** /ˈhæpi/	zufrieden	A **structure** is the way in which parts of something are organized.
p. 122, 15	(to) **be prepared** *(irr)* /ˌbiː prɪˈpeəd/	vorbereitet sein	
p. 123, 16	**structure** /ˈstrʌktʃə/	(die) Struktur, (der) Aufbau	

Hier findest du alphabetisch sortiert alle Wörter aus dem vorliegenden Buch mit der Angabe der Seite *(p.)*, auf der das Wort das erste Mal vorkommt oder auf der es zum Lernwort gemacht wird.
Die Zahl hinter dem Komma bezeichnet die Aufgabe auf der Seite.
Lernwörter aus den vorigen Bänden sind mit „NHG 5" oder „NHG 6" markiert.
Die **fett** gedruckten Lernwörter solltest du dir merken.
(informal) bedeutet: Dieses Wort oder dieser Ausdruck ist umgangssprachlich.
Folgende Abkürzungen werden verwendet: *(pl)* = (unregelmäßige) Mehrzahlform, *(no pl)* = keine Mehrzahlform, *(irr)* = unregelmäßiges Verb, *(AE)* = amerikanisches Englisch, P&P = People and Places

A

a, an /ə/eɪ, ən/ ein(e) NHG 5

a /ə/ pro NHG 6

A /eɪ/ *etwa:* Note 1, sehr gut p. 101

abbey /ˈæbi/ Abtei(kirche) p. 78

(to) **be able to do something** *(irr)* /ˌbiˌeɪbl tə ˈduː ˌsʌmθɪŋ/ etwas tun können NHG 6

(to) **abolish** /əˈbɒlɪʃ/ abschaffen p. 73, 9

about /əˈbaʊt/ über; an NHG 5; ungefähr NHG 6

(to) **be about** *(irr)* /ˌbiˌəˈbaʊt/ gehen um; handeln von NHG 5

above /əˈbʌv/ über NHG 5; oben, oberhalb p. 60, 8

(to) **go abroad** *(irr)* /ˌgəʊˌəˈbrɔːd/ ins Ausland gehen / fahren NHG 6

absolutely /ˈæbsəluːtli/ absolut p. 8, 2

accent /ˈæksnt/ Akzent p. 80, 2

accessory /əkˈsesəri/ Accessoire p. 76

accident /ˈæksɪdnt/ Unfall p. 45, 4

by accident /ˌbaɪˌˈæksɪdnt/ zufällig; aus Versehen p. 15, 12

accidentally /ˌæksɪˈdentli/ versehentlich; zufällig p. 109, 7

according to /əˈkɔːdɪŋ ˌtuː/ nach; gemäß p. 19, 2

accordion /əˈkɔːdiən/ Akkordion p. 126

(to) **achieve** /əˈtʃiːv/ erreichen p. 40, 12

across the country /əˌkrɒs ðə ˈkʌntri/ im ganzen Land p. 73, 9

(to) **act** /ækt/ handeln; spielen NHG 6

(to) **act out** /ˌæktˌˈaʊt/ nachspielen; vorspielen NHG 5

action /ˈækʃn/ Handlung NHG 5

(to) **activate** /ˈæktɪveɪt/ aktivieren p. 8, 2

active /ˈæktɪv/ aktiv p. 33, 2

activity /ækˈtɪvəti/ Aktivität NHG 5

actor/actress /ˈæktə, ˈæktrəs/ Schauspieler/in NHG 6

actually /ˈæktʃuəli/ eigentlich; tatsächlich NHG 6

AD (= Anno Domini) /ˌeɪ ˈdiː, ˌænəʊ ˈdɒmɪnaɪ/ n. Chr. (= nach Christus) p. 118, 7

adaptation /ˌædæpˈteɪʃn/ Anpassung p. 54

(to) **add** /æd/ hinzufügen NHG 5

additional /əˈdɪʃnəl/ zusätzlich p. 129

address /əˈdres/ Adresse NHG 5

adjective /ˈædʒɪktɪv/ Adjektiv NHG 6

(to) **adopt** /əˈdɒpt/ annehmen, übernehmen P&P 5

adult /ˈædʌlt/ Erwachsene/r NHG 6

in advance /ˌɪnˌədˈvɑːns/ im Voraus p. 108, 6

adventure /ədˈventʃə/ Abenteuer NHG 6

advert (= ad) /ˈædvɜːt, æd/ Werbung; Anzeige p. 39, 9

(to) **advertise** /ˈædvətaɪz/ für etwas Werbung machen p. 63, 12

advice /ədˈvaɪs/ Rat; Ratschlag p. 79

(to) **ask for advice** /ˌɑːsk fərˌədˈvaɪs/ um Rat bitten p. 99, 15

(to) **seek advice** *(irr)* /ˌsiːkˌədˈvaɪs/ Rat suchen p. 94, 6

piece of advice /ˌpiːsˌəvˌədˈvaɪs/ Rat(schlag) p. 94, 6

(to) **advise** /ədˈvaɪz/ raten, beraten p. 46, 5

(to) **afford** /əˈfɔːd/ sich leisten p. 30

(to) **be afraid of** *(irr)* /ˌbiˌəˈfreɪdˌəv/ Angst haben vor NHG 6

African /ˈæfrɪkən/ Afrikaner/in; afrikanisch p. 83, 5

after /ˈɑːftə/ nach NHG 5

after that /ˌɑːftə ˈðæt/ danach p. 66, 2

afternoon /ˌɑːftəˈnuːn/ Nachmittag NHG 5

afterwards /ˈɑːftəwədz/ anschließend; später NHG 6

again /əˈgen/ wieder; noch einmal NHG 5

against /əˈgenst/ gegen NHG 6

age /eɪdʒ/ Alter p. 56, 2

for ages *(informal)* /fərˌˈeɪdʒɪz/ seit einer Ewigkeit p. 57, 3

(to) take ages *(informal, irr)* /ˌteɪkˌˈeɪdʒɪz/ ewig dauern p. 37, 7

... **ago** /əˈgəʊ/ vor ... NHG 6

(to) **agree** /əˈgriː/ zustimmen p. 35, 6

(to) **agree on** /əˈgriːˌɒn/ sich einigen auf p. 57, 3

air force /ˈeə fɔːs/ Luftwaffe p. 85, 7

airport /ˈeəpɔːt/ Flughafen NHG 6

alive /əˈlaɪv/ lebendig; am Leben p. 85, 7

all /ɔːl/ alle; alles; ganz; völlig NHG 5

all around /ˌɔːlˌəˈraʊnd/ überall (in) p. 39, 10

all kinds of /ˌɔːl ˈkaɪndzˌəv/ alle möglichen NHG 6

all over /ˌɔːlˌˈəʊvə/ überall NHG 6

all over the world /ˌɔːlˌəʊvə ðə ˈwɜːld/ auf der ganzen Welt NHG 6

all right /ˌɔːl ˈraɪt/ in Ordnung p. 60, 8

All the best! /ˌɔːl ðə ˈbest/ Alles Gute! p. 94, 6

all the time /ˌɔːl ðə ˈtaɪm/ die ganze Zeit NHG 6

allegedly /əˈledʒɪdli/ angeblich p. 78

(to) **be allergic to** *(irr)* /ˌbi_əˈlɜːdʒɪk
tʊ/ allergisch sein auf p. 21, 5

(to) **allow** /əˈlaʊ/ erlauben p. 98, 13

allowed /əˈlaʊd/ erlaubt p. 91, 2

(to) **be allowed (to)** *(irr)*
/ˌbi_əˈlaʊd_tə/ erlaubt sein, dürfen
NHG 6

almost /ˈɔːlməʊst/ fast; beinahe NHG 6

alone /əˈləʊn/ allein NHG 5

along /əˈlɒŋ/ entlang NHG 6

already /ɔːlˈredi/ schon; bereits NHG 5

alright /ɔːlˈraɪt/ in Ordnung p. 29

also /ˈɔːlsəʊ/ auch NHG 5

although /ɔːlˈðəʊ/ obwohl NHG 6

always /ˈɔːlweɪz/ immer NHG 5

am (= ante meridiem)
/ˌeɪˈem, ˌænti məˈrɪdiəm/ morgens,
vormittags *(nur hinter Uhrzeit
zwischen Mitternacht und 12 Uhr
mittags)* NHG 5

amazing *(informal)* /əˈmeɪzɪŋ/ toll
NHG 6

(to) **call an ambulance**
/ˌkɔːl_ən_ˈæmbjʊləns/ einen
Krankenwagen rufen p. 45, 4

ambulance /ˈæmbjʊləns/ Krankenwagen p. 163

American /əˈmerɪkən/ Amerika-
ner/in; amerikanisch p. 105, 2

amount /əˈmaʊnt/ Menge p. 136

ancient /ˈeɪnʃnt/ alt; antik NHG 6

and /ænd/ und NHG 5

and so on /ænd ˈsəʊ_ɒn/ und so
weiter NHG 6

angry /ˈæŋgri/ zornig, wütend NHG 6

animal /ˈænɪml/ Tier NHG 5

ankle /ˈæŋkl/ (Fuß)knöchel p. 46, 5

(to) announce /əˈnaʊns/ bekannt
geben p. 53

announcement /əˈnaʊnsmənt/
Mitteilung; Durchsage NHG 6

annoyed /əˈnɔɪd/ genervt NHG 6

annoying /əˈnɔɪɪŋ/ ärgerlich p. 91, 2

anonymous(ly) /əˈnɒnɪməs, .
əˈnɒnɪməsli/ anonym p. 94, 6

another /əˈnʌðə/ noch ein/e; ein
anderer/ein anderes/eine andere
NHG 5

answer /ˈɑːnsə/ Antwort NHG 5

(to) **answer** /ˈɑːnsə/ (be)antworten
NHG 5

antibiotic /ˌæntibaɪˈɒtɪk/ Antibio-
tikum p. 109, 7

any /ˈeni/ (irgend)ein(e) NHG 5;
jede(r, s); alle p. 9, 2

any more /ˌeni ˈmɔː/ noch mehr
p. 24, 8

anybody /ˈenibɒdi/ irgendjemand;
jede(r, s) p. 121, 12

anyone /ˈeniˌwʌn/ jede(r, s);
(irgend)jemand p. 67, 2

anything /ˈeniˌθɪŋ/ irgendetwas
NHG 5

anyway /ˈeniweɪ/ jedenfalls NHG 6;
sowieso p. 57, 3

anywhere /ˈeniˌweə/ überall;
irgendwo p. 56, 2

apart /əˈpɑːt/ auseinander NHG 6

apart from /əˈpɑːt frəm/ abgesehen
von p. 37, 7

(to) **apologize (= apologise)**
/əˈpɒlədʒaɪz/ sich entschuldigen
p. 95, 6

apparently /əˈpærəntli/
anscheinend p. 109, 7

(to) **appeal to** /əˈpiːl tʊ/ appellieren
an, bitten um p. 73, 9

(to) **appear** /əˈpɪə/ erscheinen,
auftauchen p. 108, 7

appendix /əˈpendɪks/ Blinddarm
p. 43, 1

apple /ˈæpl/ Apfel NHG 5

(to) apply /əˈplaɪ/ anwenden p. 8, 2

appointment /əˈpɔɪntmənt/ Termin
p. 42, 1

(to) **appreciate** /əˈpriːʃiˌeɪt/ schätzen
p. 119, 7

April /ˈeɪprəl/ April NHG 5

archery /ˈɑːtʃəri/ Bogenschießen
p. 54

area /ˈeəriə/ Gebiet; Region NHG 5

arena /əˈriːnə/ Arena; Stadion p. 77

argument /ˈɑːgjəmənt/ Argument;
Streit p. 57, 3

armour /ˈɑːmə/ Rüstung p. 66, 2

around /əˈraʊnd/ um; herum;
umher NHG 6; ungefähr p. 118,7

from (all) around the world
/frəmˌɔːl_əˌraʊnd ðə ˈwɜːld/ aus der
(ganzen) Welt p. 7

(to) **arrive** /əˈraɪv/ ankommen NHG 5

art /ɑːt/ Kunst NHG 5

piece of art /ˌpiːs_əvˈɑːt/ Kunstwerk
p. 126

article /ˈɑːtɪkl/ Artikel NHG 5

arts and crafts /ˌɑːrts_ən ˈkrɑːfts/
Basteln; Bastelarbeit p. 56, 2

as /əz/ als; wie; während NHG 5

as ... as /æz æz/ so ... wie NHG 6

as far as /əz ˈfɑːr_əz/ soweit p. 81, 2

as soon as /əzˈsuːn_əz/ so bald wie
p. 53

as well /ˌəzˈwel/ auch NHG 6

Asia /ˈeɪʒə/ Asien p. 30

(to) **ask** /ɑːsk/ fragen; bitten NHG 5

(to) **ask for advice** /ˌɑːsk fər_ədˈvaɪs/
um Rat bitten p. 99, 15

(to) **ask questions** /ˌɑːskˈkwestʃnz/
Fragen stellen NHG 5

aspect /ˈæspekt/ Aspekt; Gesichts-
punkt p. 69, 5

assembly /əˈsembli/ (Schüler)
versammlung NHG 5

assembly hall /əˈsembli ˌhɔːl/ Aula
p. 114, 2

(to) **assist** /əˈsɪst/ helfen, unterstützen p. 54

association /əˌsəʊsiˈeɪʃn/
Vereinigung p. 73, 9

at /æt/ an; in; bei; um NHG 5

at all /æt ˌ_ɔːl/ überhaupt p. 109, 7

at first /ˌæt ˈfɜːst/ zuerst NHG 6

at home /æt ˈhəʊm/ zu Hause NHG 5

at least /æt ˈliːst/ mindestens;
wenigstens NHG 6

at that time /ˌæt_ˈðæt_taɪm/ zu jener
Zeit p. 87, 8

at the back /æt ðə ˈbæk/ hinten
NHG 5

at the doctor's /ˌæt_ðə ˈdɒktəz/
beim Arzt/bei der Ärztin p. 31

at the front /ˌæt ðə ˈfrʌnt/ vorne
NHG 5

at the same time /ˌæt_ðə ˌseɪm
ˈtaɪm/ gleichzeitig; zur gleichen
Zeit p. 36, 7

athlete /ˈæθliːt/ Athlet/in p. 52

athletics *(no pl)* /æθˈletɪks/ Leichtathletik P&P 2

(to) **do athletics** *(irr)* /ˌduː_ˈæθˈletɪks/
Leichtathletik machen NHG 5

atmosphere /ˈætməsˌfɪə/
Atmosphäre p. 19, 2

(to) **attend** /əˈtend/ besuchen p. 73, 9

(to) **draw attention to** *(irr)* /ˌdrɔ_əˈtenʃn tə/ Aufmerksamkeit lenken auf p. 70, 6

(to) **pay attention (to)** *(irr)* /ˌpeɪ_əˈtenʃn tə/ aufpassen; achten auf NHG 6

attraction /əˈtrækʃn/ Attraktion NHG 6

August /ˈɔːgəst/ August NHG 5

aunt /ɑːnt/ Tante NHG 5

authentic /ɔːˈθentɪk/ authentisch p. 66, 2

author /ˈɔːθə/ Autor/in p. 104, 2

autumn /ˈɔːtəm/ Herbst NHG 6

(to) **avoid** /əˈvɔɪd/ meiden; vermeiden p. 56, 2

award ceremony /əˈwɔːd ˌserəməni/ Preisverleihung p. 53

away /əˈweɪ/ weg NHG 5

(to) **go away** *(irr)* /ˌgəʊ_əˈweɪ/ weggehen; verschwinden NHG 6

aye *(informal, Scottish)* /aɪ/ ja p. 71, 6

B

back /bæk/ zurück NHG 5; Rücken p. 99, 15

at / in the back /ˈæt/ˌɪn ðə ˈbæk/ hinten NHG 5

background /ˈbækˌgraʊnd/ Hintergrund NHG 6

bacon /ˈbeɪkən/ Schinkenspeck p. 128

bacteria *(pl)* /bækˈtɪəriə/ Bakterien p. 109, 7

bad /bæd/ schlecht; schlimm NHG 5

bag /bæg/ Tasche; Tüte NHG 5

bagpipes *(pl)* /ˈbægˌpaɪps/ Dudelsack p. 71, 6

(to) **bake** /beɪk/ backen NHG 5

baker /ˈbeɪkə/ Bäcker/in NHG 6

baker /ˈbeɪkə/ *hier:* Backmaschine p. 111, 11

balloon /bəˈluːn/ Luftballon NHG 5

banana /bəˈnɑːnə/ Banane NHG 5

bandage /ˈbændɪdʒ/ Verband p. 46, 5

(to) bandage /ˈbændɪdʒ/ bandagieren p. 77

(to) bang /bæŋ/ schlagen p. 32, 1

(to) bang one's head /bæŋ wʌnz ˈhed/ sich den Kopf anschlagen p. 45, 4

bangers and mash /ˌbæŋəz_ən ˈmæʃ/ *Würstchen mit Kartoffelbrei* P&P 1

Bangladesh /ˌbæŋgləˈdeʃ/ Bangladesch p. 30

banquet /ˈbæŋkwɪt/ Festessen p. 66, 2

barely /ˈbeəli/ kaum p. 77

bargain /ˈbɑːgɪn/ Schnäppchen p. 60, 8

basic /ˈbeɪsɪk/ grundlegend; wesentlich p. 105, 2

basil /ˈbæzl/ Basilikum p. 128

bat /bæt/ Schläger p. 39, 10; Fledermaus p. 126

(to) bat /bæt/ schlagen *(Ball)* p. 32, 1

bathroom /ˈbɑːθˌruːm/ Badezimmer NHG 5

battle /ˈbætl/ Kampf p. 67, 2

battlefield /ˈbætlˌfiːld/ Schlachtfeld p. 29

BC (= before Christ) /ˌbiː ˈsiː, bɪˌfɔː ˈkraɪst/ v. Chr. (= vor Christus) p. 118, 7

(to) **be** *(irr)* /biː/ sein NHG 5

(to) **be a shame** *(irr)* /ˌbi_ə ˈʃeɪm/ schade sein p. 24, 8

(to) **be able to do something** *(irr)* /ˌbi_ˌeɪbl tə ˈduː: ˌsʌmθɪŋ/ etwas tun können NHG 6

(to) **be about** *(irr)* /ˌbi_əˈbaʊt/ gehen um; handeln von NHG 5

(to) be about to do something *(irr)* /ˌbi_əˌbaʊt_tə ˈduː: ˌsʌmθɪŋ/ im Begriff sein, etwas zu tun p. 52

(to) **be afraid of** *(irr)* /ˌbi_əˈfreɪd_əv/ Angst haben vor NHG 6

(to) be alive *(irr)* /ˌbi_əˈlaɪv/ leben p. 102

(to) **be allergic to** *(irr)* /ˌbi_əˈlɜːdʒɪk tə/ allergisch sein auf p. 21, 5

(to) **be allowed (to)** *(irr)* /ˌbi_əˈlaʊd_tə/ erlaubt sein, dürfen NHG 6

(to) **be born** *(irr)* /ˌbi: ˈbɔːn/ geboren werden p. 40, 12

(to) be connected with *(irr)* /ˌbi: kəˈnektɪd wɪð/ in Verbindung gebracht werden p. 78

(to) be credited with *(irr)* /ˌbi: ˈkredɪtɪd wɪð/ zugeschrieben bekommen p. 105, 2

(to) **be done with** *(informal, irr)* /ˌbi: ˈdʌn wɪð/ fertig sein mit p. 117, 6

(to) **be estimated** *(irr)* /ˌbi_ˈestɪmeɪtəd/ geschätzt werden p. 109, 7

(to) **be fine with** *(irr)* /ˌbi: ˈfaɪn wɪð/ etwas in Ordnung finden p. 76

(to) **be good at doing something** *(irr)* /ˌbi: ˈgʊd_ət ˈduːɪŋ ˌsʌmθɪŋ/ gut darin sein, etwas zu tun NHG 5

(to) **be good at something** *(irr)* /ˌbi: ˈgʊd_æt ˌsʌmθɪŋ/ gut in etwas sein NHG 6

(to) be good value for money *(irr)* /ˌbi: gʊd ˌvælju: fə ˈmʌni/ sein Geld wert sein p. 19, 2

(to) **be (good/great) fun** *(irr)* /ˌbi: ˌgʊd/ˌgreɪt ˈfʌn/ (viel/großen) Spaß machen NHG 5

(to) **be homesick** *(irr)* /ˌbi: ˈhəʊmˌsɪk/ Heimweh haben p. 85, 7

(to) be in the zone *(irr)* /ˌbi_ɪn ðə ˈzəʊn/ in seinem Element sein p. 52

(to) **be interested in** *(irr)* /ˌbi_ˈɪntrəstɪd_ɪn/ interessiert sein an p. 61, 8

(to) be left out *(irr)* /ˌbi: ˌleft_ˈaʊt/ ausgeschlossen werden p. 94, 6

(to) **be located** *(irr)* /ˌbi: ləʊˈkeɪtɪd/ gelegen sein p. 108, 6

(to) be lost *(irr)* /ˌbi: ˈlɒst/ sich verirrt haben p. 126

(to) **be lucky** *(irr)* /ˌbi: ˈlʌki/ Glück haben p. 85, 7

(to) be made up of *(irr)* /ˌbi: ˌmeɪd_ˈʌp_əv/ zusammengesetzt sein aus p. 54

(to) **be missing** *(irr)* /ˌbi: ˈmɪsɪŋ/ fehlen p. 124

(to) be off *(informal, irr)* /ˌbi_ˈɒf/ *hier:* weg sein p. 52

(to) **be one's turn** *(irr)* /ˌbi: wʌnz ˈtɜːn/ an der Reihe sein NHG 5

(to) be published *(irr)* /ˌbi: ˈpʌblɪʃd/ veröffentlicht werden p. 30

(to) **be right** *(irr)* /ˌbi: ˈraɪt/ recht haben NHG 5

(to) be sick and tired of *(irr)* /ˌbi: ˈsɪk_ən ˌtaɪəd_əv/ satthaben p. 28

(to) **be stuck** *(irr)* /ˌbiː ˈstʌk/ *hier:* festhängen p. 101

(to) **be up for something** *(informal, irr)* /ˌbiˌʌp fɔː ˈsʌmθɪŋ/ Lust zu etwas haben p. 57, 3

(to) **be up to something** *(irr)* /ˌbiˌʌp tə ˈsʌmθɪŋ/ etwas vorhaben p. 57, 3

(to) **be welcome to** *(irr)* /ˌbiː ˈwelkəm tʊ/ etwas gern tun können p. 108, 6

(to) **be worth** *(irr)* /ˌbiː ˈwɜːθ/ (sich) lohnen; wert sein p. 71, 6

(to) **be wrong** *(irr)* /ˌbiː ˈrɒŋ/ im Unrecht sein p. 90, 2

(to) **be wrong (with)** *(irr)* /ˌbiː ˈrɒŋ wɪθ/ nicht in Ordnung sein (mit) p. 48, 8

beach /biːtʃ/ Strand NHG 5

beak /biːk/ Schnabel p. 127

beak-like /ˈbiːkˌlaɪk/ *schnabelähnlich* p. 127

beard /bɪəd/ Bart p. 67, 2

beautiful /ˈbjuːtəfl/ schön NHG 5

because /bɪˈkɒz/ weil; da NHG 5

because of /bɪˈkɒzˌəv/ wegen p. 80, 2

(to) **become** *(irr)* /bɪˈkʌm/ werden NHG 6

(to) become infected *(irr)* /bɪˌkʌmˌɪnˈfektɪd/ sich infizieren p. 109, 7

bed /bed/ Bett NHG 5

bedroom /ˈbedruːm/ Schlafzimmer NHG 5

bee /biː/ Biene NHG 6

beef /biːf/ Rindfleisch p. 8, 2

before /bɪˈfɔː/ bevor; zuvor, vorher; vor NHG 5

(to) **befriend** /bɪˈfrend/ sich anfreunden mit p. 121, 12

(to) **begin** *(irr)* /bɪˈɡɪn/ anfangen; beginnen NHG 5

beginning /bɪˈɡɪnɪŋ/ Anfang; Beginn NHG 6

(to) behave /bɪˈheɪv/ sich verhalten, sich benehmen p. 28

behaviour /bɪˈheɪvjə/ Benehmen; Verhalten p. 121, 12

behind /bɪˈhaɪnd/ hinter NHG 5

(to) **believe (in)** /bɪˈliːv ɪn/ glauben (an) NHG 6

bell /bel/ Glocke NHG 6

(to) **belong (to)** /bɪˈlɒŋ/ gehören (zu) P&P 2

below /bɪˈləʊ/ unten, unter NHG 6

belt /belt/ Gürtel p. 77

Bengali /benˈɡɑːli/ Bengale/ Bengalin; bengalisch P&P 4

best /best/ beste(r, s) NHG 5

All the best! /ˌɔːl ðə ˈbest/ Alles Gute! p. 94, 6

the best /ðə ˈbest/ der/die/das beste NHG 5; am besten NHG 6

(to) **like best** /ˌlaɪk ˈbest/ am liebsten mögen NHG 5

better /ˈbetə/ besser NHG 6

(to) **get better** *(irr)* /ˌɡet ˈbetə/ besser werden; gesund werden p. 37, 7

between /bɪˈtwiːn/ zwischen NHG 5

BFF (= best friends forever) *(informal)* /ˌbiː efˈef, ˌbest ˌfrendz fərˈevə/ *allerbeste Freunde/ Freundinnen* p. 8, 2

bhaji /ˈbɑːdʒi/ *indisches Gericht* p. 23, 7

bicycle bell /ˈbaɪsɪkl bel/ Fahrradklingel p. 59, 7

(to) **biff** *(informal)* /bɪf/ hauen, schlagen p. 39, 10

big /bɪɡ/ groß NHG 5

bike /baɪk/ Fahrrad NHG 6

(to) **ride a bike** *(irr)* /ˌraɪd ə ˈbaɪk/ Fahrrad fahren NHG 5

bill /bɪl/ Rechnung p. 24, 8

billion /ˈbɪljən/ Milliarde p. 147

bin /bɪn/ Abfalleimer NHG 5

bird /bɜːd/ Vogel NHG 6

bird of prey /ˌbɜːdˌəv ˈpreɪ/ Raubvogel p. 67, 2

birth /bɜːθ/ Geburt p. 54

birthday /ˈbɜːθdeɪ/ Geburtstag NHG 5

Happy birthday (to you)! /ˌhæpi ˈbɜːθdeɪ tʊ juː/ Herzlichen Glückwunsch zum Geburtstag! NHG 5

birthplace /ˈbɜːθˌpleɪs/ Geburtsort p. 149

biscuit /ˈbɪskɪt/ Keks NHG 5

bit /bɪt/ Teil; Stück p. 29

a bit /ə ˈbɪt/ ein bisschen NHG 5

quite a bit /ˌkwaɪtˌə ˈbɪt/ ziemlich viel p. 95, 6

black /blæk/ schwarz NHG 5

(to) **bleed** *(irr)* /bliːd/ bluten p. 43, 1

the blind /ðə ˈblaɪnd/ Blinde/r p. 127

blood /blʌd/ Blut NHG 6

blue /bluː/ blau NHG 5

board /bɔːd/ Tafel; Brett NHG 5

board game /ˈbɔːd ɡeɪm/ Brettspiel NHG 6

boat /bəʊt/ Boot NHG 5

body /ˈbɒdi/ Körper NHG 5

(to) **boil** /bɔɪl/ kochen *(Flüssigkeit)* p. 160

(to) **bring to the boil** *(irr)* /ˌbrɪŋ tə ðə ˈbɔɪl/ zum Kochen bringen p. 12, 7

bone /bəʊn/ Knochen p. 105, 2

book /bʊk/ Buch NHG 5

(to) **book** /bʊk/ buchen, reservieren NHG 6

bookshelf /ˈbʊkˌʃelf/ Bücherregal NHG 5

boom /buːm/ Dröhnen p. 127

boot /buːt/ Kofferraum p. 76

(to) **boot** /buːt/ einen Tritt geben p. 39, 10

bored /bɔːd/ gelangweilt NHG 6

boring /ˈbɔːrɪŋ/ langweilig NHG 5

(to) **be born** *(irr)* /ˌbiː ˈbɔːn/ geboren werden p. 40, 12

(to) **borrow** /ˈbɒrəʊ/ (aus)leihen NHG 5

both /bəʊθ/ beide p. 25, 11

both … and … /ˈbəʊθ ænd/ sowohl … als auch … P&P 5

(to) **bother** /ˈbɒðə/ stören; belästigen p. 70, 6

(to) bother /ˈbɒðə/ sich Mühe geben p. 101

bottle /ˈbɒtl/ Flasche NHG 5

(to) **bounce** /baʊns/ (auf)springen p. 39, 10

bowl /bəʊl/ Schüssel; Schale NHG 6

box /bɒks/ Kasten; Kiste NHG 5

boy /bɔɪ/ Junge NHG 5

bracket /ˈbrækɪt/ Klammer p. 98, 12

brain /breɪn/ Gehirn p. 32, 1

branch /brɑːntʃ/ Zweig; Ast p. 16, 16

bravely /breɪvli/ mutig p. 78

bread /bred/ Brot p. 15, 11

break /breɪk/ Pause NHG 5

(to) **break** *(irr)* /breɪk/ brechen; zerbrechen; kaputt machen NHG 6

breakfast /'brekfəst/ Frühstück NHG 5

out of breath /ˌaʊt_əv 'breθ/ außer Atem p. 77

breathtaking /'breθˌteɪkɪŋ/ atemberaubend p. 67, 2

bridge /brɪdʒ/ Brücke NHG 6

bright, brightly /braɪt,'braɪtli/ hell; strahlend NHG 6

brilliant /'brɪljənt/ genial, klasse NHG 5

(to) **bring** *(irr)* /brɪŋ/ mitbringen NHG 5

(to) **bring over** *(irr)* /ˌbrɪŋ_'əʊvə/ herbeibringen p. 24, 8

(to) bring to the boil *(irr)* /ˌbrɪŋ tə ðə 'bɔɪl/ zum Kochen bringen p. 12, 7

Britain /'brɪtn/ Großbritannien NHG 6

British /'brɪtɪʃ/ britisch NHG 6

broccoli /'brɒkəli/ Brokkoli p. 143

brochure /'brəʊʃə/ Broschüre p. 111, 10

broken /'brəʊkən/ gebrochen p. 42, 1; zerbrochen; kaputt p. 64, 13

brother /'brʌðə/ Bruder NHG 5

brown /braʊn/ braun NHG 5

(to) **brush one's teeth** /ˌbrʌʃ wʌnz 'tiːθ/ sich die Zähne putzen NHG 5

bubble and squeak /ˌbʌbl_ən 'skwiːk/ *Resteessen aus gebratenem Kartoffelbrei und zerstampftem Gemüse* P&P 1

buddy *(informal)* /'bʌdi/ Kumpel p. 38, 8

(to) **build** *(irr)* /bɪld/ bauen NHG 5

building /'bɪldɪŋ/ Gebäude NHG 6

(to) bully /'bʊli/ mobben p. 121, 12

burdock /'bɜːdɒk/ Große Klette p. 127

burnt /bɜːnt/ verbrannt, angebrannt p. 18, 2

(to) bury /'beri/ begraben; vergraben p. 78

business /'bɪznəs/ Geschäft; Handel p. 81, 2

busy /'bɪzi/ beschäftigt NHG 5; bewegt, ereignisreich; belebt; verkehrsreich NHG 6

but /bʌt/ aber NHG 5; außer NHG 6

(to) button /'bʌtən/ knöpfen p. 108, 7

(to) **buy** *(irr)* /baɪ/ kaufen NHG 5

(to) buzz /bʌz/ summen, brummen p. 78

by /baɪ/ von; mit NHG 5; bei, an; *hier:* (spätestens) bis NHG 6

by /baɪ/ *hier:* durch, anhand von p. 54

by *(+ Verbform mit -ing)* /baɪ/ indem NHG 6

by accident /ˌbaɪ_'æksɪdnt/ zufällig; aus Versehen p. 15, 12

by heart /ˌbaɪ 'hɑːt/ auswendig p. 14, 10

by ourselves /ˌbaɪ aʊə'selvz/ (wir) selbst p. 125

bye /baɪ/ tschüs(s) NHG 5

C

C /siː/ *etwa:* Note 3, befriedigend p. 101

cabbage /'kæbɪdʒ/ Kohl p. 9, 2

tossing the caber /ˌtɒsɪŋ ðə 'keɪbə/ Baumstammwerfen p. 71, 6

cage /keɪdʒ/ Käfig NHG 5

cake /keɪk/ Kuchen NHG 5

calculator /'kælkjʊˌleɪtə/ Taschenrechner NHG 5

calendar /'kælɪndə/ Kalender NHG 5

call /kɔːl/ Anruf; Gespräch p. 119, 8

(to) **call** /kɔːl/ anrufen NHG 6

(to) **call an ambulance** /ˌkɔːl_ən_'æmbjʊləns/ einen Krankenwagen rufen p. 45, 4

(to) **give somebody a call** *(irr)* /ˌgɪv ˌsʌmbədi_ə 'kɔːl/ jemanden anrufen p. 42, 1

(to) call in /kɔːl_'ɪn/ rufen, hereinbitten p. 42, 1

(to) be called /bi 'kɔːld/ heißen, genannt werden NHG 5

(to) **calm down** /ˌkɑːm 'daʊn/ (sich) beruhigen p. 33, 2

camera /'kæmrə/ Kamera; Fotoapparat NHG 6

camp /kæmp/ (Zelt)lager NHG 6

camping gear /'kæmpɪŋ ˌgɪə/ Campingausrüstung p. 76

camping site /'kæmpɪŋ ˌsaɪt/ Campingplatz p. 70, 6

can /kæn/ können NHG 5; Dose; Büchse p. 12, 7

can't (= cannot) /kɑːnt, 'kænɒt/ nicht können NHG 5

Canada /'kænədə/ Kanada p. 9, 2

(to) **cancel** /'kænsl/ absagen, streichen p. 57, 3

candle /'kændl/ Kerze NHG 5

cap /kæp/ Mütze NHG 6

capital /'kæpɪtl/ Hauptstadt p. 147

caption /'kæpʃn/ Bildunterschrift p. 26, 12

car /kɑː/ Auto NHG 5

car boot sale /ˌkɑː 'buːt seɪl/ *Kofferraum-Flohmarkt* p. 55

carbohydrate /ˌkɑːbəʊ'haɪdreɪt/ Kohlenhydrat p. 53

card /kɑːd/ Karte NHG 5

cardamom /'kɑːdəməm/ Kardamom p. 30

(to) **care about (doing something)** /'keər_əˌbaʊt/ sich etwas machen aus p. 32, 1

(to) **take care (of)** *(irr)* /ˌteɪk_'keər_əv/ sich kümmern um NHG 6

careful, carefully /'keəfl, 'keəfli/ vorsichtig NHG 6

Caribbean /ˌkærɪ'biən/ karibisch p. 70, 6

carnival /'kɑːnɪvl/ Volksfest, Karneval p. 72, 8

carrier bag /'kæriə bæg/ Tragetasche p. 73, 9

carrot /'kærət/ Möhre; Karotte NHG 5

(to) carry /'kæri/ tragen p. 76

case /keɪs/ Fall NHG 6

cash /kæʃ/ Geld; Bargeld p. 24, 8

cast /kɑːst/ Gips p. 42, 1

castle /'kɑːsl/ Burg; Schloss NHG 6

cat /kæt/ Katze NHG 5

(to) **catch** *(irr)* /kætʃ/ fangen NHG 5

(to) **catch a cold** *(irr)* /ˌkætʃ_ə 'kəʊld/ sich erkälten p. 42, 1

(to) catch a plane *(irr)* /ˌkætʃ_ə 'pleɪn/ ein Flugzeug nehmen p. 102

(to) catch up *(irr)* /ˌkætʃ_'ʌp/ einholen p. 77

(to) **categorize** /'kætɪgəraɪz/ kategorisieren, in Gruppen unterteilen p. 17, 17

category /'kætəgri/ Kategorie NHG 6

cathedral /kəˈθiːdrəl/ Kathedrale
p. 124

cause /kɔːz/ Grund; Ursache p. 78

(to) cause /kɔːz/ verursachen p. 127

a good cause /ə ˌɡʊd ˈkɔːz/ eine gute
Sache, ein guter Zweck p. 56, 2

cayenne pepper /ˌkeɪen ˈpepə/
Cayennepfeffer p. 13, 7

(to) **celebrate** /ˈseləˌbreɪt/ feiern
NHG 6

celebration /ˌseləˈbreɪʃn/ Feier NHG 6

cellar /ˈselə/ Keller p. 60, 8

centre /ˈsentə/ Zentrum NHG 6

shopping centre /ˈʃɒpɪŋ ˌsentə/
Einkaufszentrum NHG 5

century /ˈsentʃəri/ Jahrhundert NHG 6

CEO (= chief executive officer)
/ˌsiː_iː_ˈəʊ, ˌtʃiːf_ɪɡˌzekjʊtɪv_ˈɒfɪsə/
Geschäftsführer/in p. 73, 9

cereal /ˈsɪəriəl/ Frühstücksflocken
p. 28

certain /ˈsɜːtn/ bestimmt; gewiss
p. 35, 6

certainly /ˈsɜːtnli/ sicher; gerne
p. 22, 6

chain /tʃeɪn/ Kette NHG 6

chair /tʃeə/ Stuhl NHG 5

challenge /ˈtʃæləndʒ/ Herausfor-
derung NHG 5

challenge /ˈtʃæləndʒ/ *hier:* Wette
p. 120, 9

chance /tʃɑːns/ Möglichkeit;
Gelegenheit p. 36, 7

change /tʃeɪndʒ/ Wechselgeld NHG 5

(to) change /tʃeɪndʒ/ (sich) ändern;
verändern NHG 6

(to) **change lines** /ˌtʃeɪndʒ ˈlaɪnz/
umsteigen NHG 6

(to) **change one's mind**
/ˌtʃeɪndʒ wʌnz ˈmaɪnd/ seine
Meinung ändern NHG 6

character /ˈkærəktə/ Figur;
Charakter NHG 6

charity /ˈtʃærəti/ Wohltätigkeits-
organisation p. 56, 2

charity run /ˈtʃærəti rʌn/ Wohltätig-
keitslauf p. 56, 2

charity shop /ˈtʃærəti ʃɒp/ *Laden,
in dem gebrauchte Dinge zu
Wohltätigkeitszwecken verkauft
werden* P&P 3

(to) **chat** /tʃæt/ plaudern; chatten
p. 94, 6

cheap /tʃiːp/ billig p. 18, 2

check /tʃek/ Überprüfung;
Kontrolle p. 38, 8

(to) **check** /tʃek/ überprüfen;
kontrollieren NHG 5

(to) **check out** *(informal)*
/ˌtʃek_ˈaʊt/ sich ansehen;
ausprobieren p. 66, 2

(to) check out /ˌtʃek_ˈaʊt/ aus-
checken p. 27, 14

check-up /ˈtʃek_ʌp/ Untersuchung
p. 46, 5

(to) **cheer** /tʃɪə/ jubeln p. 53

(to) cheer somebody on /ˌtʃɪə
ˌsʌmbədi_ˈɒn/ jemanden anfeuern
p. 52

(to) cheer up /ˌtʃɪər_ˈʌp/ auf-
muntern, aufheitern p. 31

cheerful /ˈtʃɪəfl/ fröhlich, vergnügt
p. 70, 6

cheese /tʃiːz/ Käse NHG 5

chemistry club /ˈkemɪstri klʌb/
Chemie-AG p. 93, 5

cherry /ˈtʃeri/ Kirsche p. 28

chess /tʃes/ Schach p. 32, 1

chicken /ˈtʃɪkɪn/ Huhn NHG 6

(chicken) tikka masala, (chicken)
tikka /ˌtʃɪkɪn ˌtiːkə məˈsɑːlə,
ˌtʃɪkɪn ˈtiːkə/ *britisch-indisches
(Hühnchen-)Gericht* p. 11, 6

chickpea /ˈtʃɪkˌpiː/ Kichererbse p. 12, 7

child (*pl* **children**) /tʃaɪld,
ˈtʃɪldrən/ Kind NHG 5

childhood /ˈtʃaɪldˌhʊd/ Kindheit
p. 86, 8

chilli (*pl* chillies) /ˈtʃɪli, ˈtʃɪliz/ Chili;
Peperoni p. 9, 2

Chinese /ˌtʃaɪˈniːz/ Chinese /
Chinesin; chinesisch NHG 6

chips *(pl)* /tʃɪps/ Pommes frites
NHG 5

chocolate /ˈtʃɒklət/ Schokolade
NHG 5

choice /tʃɔɪs/ Auswahl; Wahl p. 19, 2

(to) choke on /ˈtʃəʊk_ɒn/ sich
verschlucken p. 27, 14

(to) **choose** *(irr)* /tʃuːz/ wählen; sich
entscheiden NHG 5

(to) **chop** /tʃɒp/ hacken p. 13, 8

chore /tʃɔː/ lästige Aufgabe;
Hausarbeit NHG 5

Christian /ˈkrɪstʃən/ Christ/in;
christlich NHG 6

Christmas /ˈkrɪsməs/ Weihnachten
NHG 6

church /tʃɜːtʃ/ Kirche NHG 6

chutney /ˈtʃʌtni/ *würzige indische
Soße* p. 63, 11

cinema /ˈsɪnəmə/ Kino NHG 5

cinnamon /ˈsɪnəmən/ Zimt p. 13, 7

city /ˈsɪti/ Stadt; Innenstadt NHG 5

city centre /ˌsɪti ˈsentə/ Innenstadt
p. 28

class /klɑːs/ Klasse; Unterrichts-
stunde NHG 5

classic /ˈklæsɪk/ klassisch p. 28

classmate /ˈklɑːsˌmeɪt/ Klassen-
kamerad/in; Mitschüler/in NHG 5

classroom /ˈklɑːsˌruːm/ Klassen-
zimmer NHG 5

clay /kleɪ/ Lehm; Ton p. 118, 7

clean /kliːn/ sauber NHG 5

(to) clean out /ˌkliːn_ˈaʊt/ ausräumen, entrümpeln p. 60, 8

(to) **clean (up)** /kliːn, ˌkliːn_ˈʌp/
sauber machen NHG 5

cleaning skates *(pl)* /ˈkliːnɪŋ
ˌskeɪts/ *Reinigungsskates* p. 111, 11

clear /klɪə/ klar; deutlich NHG 6

(to) **clear up** /ˌklɪər_ˈʌp/ aufräumen
p. 73, 9

clearly /ˈklɪəli/ klar; deutlich
NHG 6

clever /ˈklevə/ klug; schlau p. 126

(to) **click on** /ˈklɪk_ɒn/ anklicken
p. 121, 12

(to) **climb** /klaɪm/ auf etwas
(hinauf)steigen; klettern NHG 5

climbing /ˈklaɪmɪŋ/ Klettern p. 32, 1

clock /klɒk/ Uhr NHG 5

(to) **close** /kləʊz/ zumachen;
schließen NHG 5

closed /kləʊzd/ geschlossen NHG 6

closely /ˈkləʊsli/ genau p. 123, 16

(to) have a closer look *(irr)*
/hæv_ə ˌkləʊsə ˈlʊk/ sich etwas
genauer ansehen p. 105, 2

clothes *(pl)* /kləʊðz/ Kleider;
Kleidung NHG 5

clothing /ˈkləʊðɪŋ/ Kleidung p. 76

clove of garlic /ˌkləʊv_əv
ˈgɑːlɪk/ Knoblauchzehe p. 17, 17

club /klʌb/ AG; Klub NHG 5

coach /kəʊtʃ/ Trainer/in p. 45, 4

coconut /ˈkəʊkəˌnʌt/ Kokosnuss
p. 71, 6

coconut cream /ˈkəʊkəˌnʌt kriːm/
Kokosmilch P&P 1

coffee /ˈkɒfi/ Kaffee NHG 5

coffee grinder /ˈkɒfi ˌɡraɪndə/
Kaffeemühle p. 60, 8

coffee house /ˈkɒfi haʊs/ Café p. 30

coffee pot /ˈkɒfi pɒt/ Kaffeekanne
p. 60, 8

cold /kəʊld/ kalt NHG 5; Erkältung
p. 42, 1

(to) **catch a cold** (irr) /ˌkætʃ_ə
ˈkəʊld/ sich erkälten p. 42, 1

(to) **collect** /kəˈlekt/ sammeln NHG 5

collection /kəˈlekʃn/ Sammlung
NHG 6

colony /ˈkɒləni/ Kolonie P&P 4

colour /ˈkʌlə/ Farbe NHG 5

colourful /ˈkʌləfl/ farbenfroh; bunt
p. 70, 6

combat arena /ˈkɒmbæt_əˌriːnə/
Wettkampfarena p. 66, 2

combination /ˌkɒmbɪˈneɪʃn/ Kombi-
nation; Mischung NHG 6

(to) **come** (irr) /kʌm/ kommen
NHG 5

(to) come across (irr) /ˌkʌm_əˈkrɒs/
zufällig stoßen auf p. 125

(to) **come back** (irr) /ˌkʌm ˈbæk/
zurückkommen NHG 5

(to) come by (irr) /ˌkʌm ˈbaɪ/ vorbei-
kommen p. 77

(to) **come in** (irr) /ˌkʌm_ˈɪn/ herein-
kommen p. 42, 1

Come on! /ˌkʌm_ˈɒn/ Komm(t)
schon! p. 39, 10

(to) come together (irr) /ˌkʌm
təˈɡeðə/ zusammenkommen p. 54

(to) **come up with** (irr) /ˌkʌm_ˈʌp
wɪð/ sich einfallen lassen p. 109, 7

comfort food /ˈkʌmfət fuːd/ Wohl-
fühlessen p. 8, 2

comfortable /ˈkʌmftəbl/ bequem
p. 109, 7

comfy (informal) /ˈkʌmfi/ bequem
p. 100

coming soon /ˌkʌmɪŋ ˈsuːn/ in Kürze
erscheinend p. 67, 2

command /kəˈmɑːnd/ Befehl NHG 5

(to) **comment on** /ˈkɒment_ɒn/
kommentieren NHG 6

commercial /kəˈmɜːʃl/ kommerziell,
profitorientiert NHG 6

(to) **have in common** (irr) /ˌhæv_ɪn
ˈkɒmən/ gemeinsam haben NHG 6

commonly known as /ˌkɒmənli
ˈnəʊn_əz/ oft auch … genannt
p. 127

(to) **communicate** /kəˈmjuːnɪkeɪt/
kommunizieren, sprechen p. 95, 6

communication /kəˌmjuːnɪˈkeɪʃn/
Verständigung; Kommunikation
p. 103

community /kəˈmjuːnəti/ Gemein-
schaft, Gemeinde p. 40, 12

company /ˈkʌmpni/ Firma;
Unternehmen p. 97, 11

(to) **compare** /kəmˈpeə/ vergleichen
NHG 6

comparison /kəmˈpærɪsn/ Vergleich
NHG 6

(to) **compete** /kəmˈpiːt/ an einem
Wettkampf teilnehmen; kämpfen
p. 36, 7

(to) **compete in** /kəmˈpiːt_ɪn/ teilnehmen an P&P 2

competition /ˌkɒmpəˈtɪʃn/ Wettbe-
werb NHG 5

competitive /kəmˈpetətɪv/ *von
Konkurrenzdenken geprägt*
p. 33, 2

(to) **complete** /kəmˈpliːt/ vervoll-
ständigen NHG 5

complete /kəmˈpliːt/ vollständig,
komplett p. 65, 15

completely /kəmˈpliːtli/ völlig,
absolut NHG 6

complicated /ˈkɒmplɪˌkeɪtɪd/
kompliziert p. 37, 7

compromise /ˈkɒmprəmaɪz/ Kom-
promiss NHG 6

con /kɒn/ Nachteil; Kontra NHG 6

(to) **concentrate** /ˈkɒnsnˌtreɪt/ sich
konzentrieren p. 35, 6

concept /ˈkɒnsept/ Entwurf;
Konzept NHG 6

concert /ˈkɒnsət/ Konzert NHG 6

condition /kənˈdɪʃn/ Zustand p. 60, 8

conditional (clause) /kənˈdɪʃnəl klɔːz/
Konditional(satz) p. 44

conflict /ˈkɒnflɪkt/ Konflikt NHG 6

(to) **connect** /kəˈnekt/ verbinden
p. 84, 6

connection /kəˈnekʃn/ Verbindung
p. 146

(to) conquer /ˈkɒŋkə/ erobern
p. 66, 2

consequence /ˈkɒnsɪkwəns/ Konse-
quenz; Folge p. 121, 12

(to) **consist of** /kənˈsɪst_əv/ bestehen aus p. 54

console /kənˈsəʊl/ Konsole p. 76

construction /kənˈstrʌkʃn/ Bau
p. 108, 7

(to) **contact** /ˈkɒntækt/ sich in
Verbindung setzen mit NHG 6

(to) **contain** /kənˈteɪn/ ent-
halten p. 9, 2

container /kənˈteɪnə/ Behälter p. 136

content /ˈkɒntent/ Inhalt p. 67, 2

contestant /kənˈtestənt/ Wettbe-
werbsteilnehmer/in p. 71, 6

(to) **continue to do** /kənˌtɪnjuː tə
ˈduː/ weiter(hin) tun, nach wie vor
tun p. 125

(to) **control** /kənˈtrəʊl/ kontrollieren;
steuern p. 30

conversation /ˌkɒnvəˈseɪʃn/
Gespräch; Unterhaltung p. 26, 13

(to) **cook** /kʊk/ kochen NHG 5;
braten, backen NHG 6

cook /kʊk/ Koch/Köchin P&P 1

cook-along video /ˈkʊk_əˌlɒŋ ˌvɪdiəʊ/
Mitmach-Koch-Video p. 13, 7

cookbook /ˈkʊkˌbʊk/ Kochbuch p. 7

cooked /kʊkt/ gekocht p. 23, 7

cooker /ˈkʊkə/ Herd p. 17, 17

cooking /ˈkʊkɪŋ/ Kochen; Koch-
NHG 5

(to) **do the cooking** (irr)
/ˌduː ðə ˈkʊkɪŋ/ kochen NHG 5

(to) **cool** /kuːl/ kühlen p. 46, 5

cool /kuːl/ kühl; kalt p. 104, 1

cooling /ˈkuːlɪŋ/ kühlend p. 145

(to) **copy** /ˈkɒpi/ abschreiben NHG 5;
kopieren p. 117, 6

coriander /ˌkɒriˈændə/ Koriander
p. 13, 7

corner /ˈkɔːnə/ Ecke NHG 6
(to) **correct** /kəˈrekt/ korrigieren NHG 5
correct /kəˈrekt/ richtig, korrekt NHG 5
cosmetics *(pl)* /kɒzˈmetɪks/ Kosmetika p. 77
(to) **cost** *(irr)* /kɒst/ kosten NHG 5
costume /ˈkɒstjuːm/ Kostüm NHG 6
cosy /ˈkəʊzi/ gemütlich p. 19, 2
cotton /ˈkɒtn/ Baumwolle; Baumwoll- p. 125
cough /kɒf/ Husten p. 42, 1
could /kʊd/ könnte(st, n, t) NHG 5; *Vergangenheitsform von can* NHG 6
counsellor /ˈkaʊnslə/ Berater/in p. 78
(to) **count** /kaʊnt/ zählen p. 108, 7
country /ˈkʌntri/ Land NHG 6
across the country /əˌkrɒs ðə ˈkʌntri/ im ganzen Land p. 73, 9
countryside /ˈkʌntriˌsaɪd/ Land; Landschaft NHG 6
a couple of /ə ˈkʌplˌəv/ einige, ein paar NHG 6
course /kɔːs/ Kurs NHG 6
course /kɔːs/ Gang p. 28
court /kɔːt/ Platz NHG 5
cousin /ˈkʌzn/ Cousin/e NHG 5
(to) **cover** /ˈkʌvə/ bedecken NHG 6
cow /kaʊ/ Kuh NHG 6
cracker /ˈkrækə/ Kräcker p. 23, 7
arts and crafts /ˌɑːrts ˌən ˈkrɑːfts/ Basteln; Bastelarbeit p. 56, 2
(to) **crash into** /ˈkræʃ ˌɪntʊ/ zusammenstoßen mit p. 125
crazy /ˈkreɪzi/ verrückt; wahnsinnig p. 126
cream /kriːm/ Sahne p. 16, 14
(to) whip cream /ˌwɪp ˈkriːm/ Sahne schlagen p. 29
whipped cream /ˈwɪpt kriːm/ Schlagsahne p. 29
cream cheese /kriːm ˈtʃiːz/ Frischkäse p. 9, 2
(to) **create** /kriˈeɪt/ erschaffen; erzeugen NHG 5
creative /kriˈeɪtɪv/ kreativ NHG 5
(to) be credited with *(irr)* /ˌbiː ˈkredɪtɪd wɪð/ zugeschrieben bekommen p. 105, 2
cricket /ˈkrɪkɪt/ Kricket p. 32, 1

(to) **cross** /krɒs/ überqueren NHG 6
cross-country running /ˌkrɒs ˌkʌntri ˈrʌnɪŋ/ Geländelauf p. 32, 1
crowd /kraʊd/ Menschenmenge p. 56, 2
crowded /ˈkraʊdɪd/ überfüllt p. 57, 3
crumb /krʌm/ Krümel p. 12, 7
crust /krʌst/ Kruste p. 18, 2
(to) **cry** /kraɪ/ weinen; schreien NHG 6
cube /kjuːb/ Würfel p. 16, 14
cucumber /ˈkjuːˌkʌmbə/ Salatgurke p. 8, 2
cue card /ˈkjuː kɑːd/ *Stichwortkarte* NHG 6
cuisine /kwɪˈziːn/ Küche *(Kochkunst)* p. 28
culture /ˈkʌltʃə/ Kultur NHG 6
cumin /ˈkjuːmɪn/ Kreuzkümmel p. 13, 7
cup /kʌp/ Tasse NHG 5; Pokal P&P 2
cupboard /ˈkʌbəd/ Schrank p. 12, 7
(to) **cure** /kjʊə/ heilen p. 109, 7
curious /ˈkjʊəriəs/ neugierig p. 30
currently /ˈkʌrəntli/ zurzeit, momentan p. 108, 6
curried chicken /ˌkʌrid ˈtʃɪkɪn/ *Hühnchenfleisch in Curry* p. 71, 6
curry /ˈkʌri/ Curry(gericht) p. 19, 2
curry powder /ˈkʌri ˌpaʊdə/ Currypulver p. 13, 7
curtain /ˈkɜːtn/ Vorhang p. 60, 8
customer /ˈkʌstəmə/ Kunde / Kundin NHG 6
(to) **cut** *(irr)* /kʌt/ schneiden NHG 6
(to) cut off *(irr)* /ˌkʌtˌ ˈɒf/ abschneiden p. 77
(to) cut out *(irr)* /ˌkʌtˌ ˈaʊt/ weglassen p. 73, 9
(to) cut up *(irr)* /ˌkʌtˌ ˈʌp/ zerschneiden p. 29
cute /kjuːt/ süß; niedlich p. 86, 8
(to) **cycle** /ˈsaɪkl/ Rad fahren, radeln NHG 6
(to) **go cycling** *(irr)* /ˌgəʊ ˈsaɪklɪŋ/ Rad fahren gehen NHG 6

D
D /diː/ *etwa:* Note 4, ausreichend p. 91, 2
dad /dæd/ Papa; Vati NHG 5

daily /ˈdeɪli/ täglich NHG 5
dance /dɑːns/ Tanz p. 36, 7
(to) **dance** /dɑːns/ tanzen NHG 5
dancer /ˈdɑːnsə/ Tänzer/in NHG 6
dancing /ˈdɑːnsɪŋ/ Tanzen NHG 5
danger /ˈdeɪndʒə/ Gefahr NHG 6
dangerous /ˈdeɪndʒərəs/ gefährlich NHG 6
dark /dɑːk/ dunkel; Dunkelheit NHG 6
darkness /ˈdɑːknəs/ Dunkelheit NHG 6
darling /ˈdɑːlɪŋ/ Liebling; Schatz p. 52
date /deɪt/ Datum NHG 5
(to) set a date /ˌset ə ˈdeɪt/ sich verabreden p. 101
daughter /ˈdɔːtə/ Tochter NHG 5
day /deɪ/ Tag NHG 5
some day /ˈsʌmˌdeɪ/ eines Tages p. 36, 7
the other day /ðiˌ ʌðə ˈdeɪ/ neulich; vor einigen Tagen p. 94, 6
day out /ˌdeɪˌ ˈaʊt/ *Ausflugstag* NHG 6
(to) **deal with** *(irr)* /ˈdiːl wɪð/ sich befassen mit, umgehen mit p. 97, 10
dear /dɪə/ liebe/r *(Anrede)* NHG 5
dear /dɪə/ Liebes *(Anrede)* p. 29
death /deθ/ Tod p. 126
December /dɪˈsembə/ Dezember NHG 5
decent /ˈdiːsnt/ anständig p. 28
(to) **decide** /dɪˈsaɪd/ entscheiden; sich entscheiden NHG 5
(to) **decorate** /ˈdekəreɪt/ schmücken; dekorieren NHG 5
decoration /ˌdekəˈreɪʃn/ Dekoration; Schmuck NHG 6
decorative /ˈdekrətɪv/ dekorativ p. 63, 12
definitely /ˈdefnətli/ eindeutig, definitiv NHG 6
(to) **delete** /dɪˈliːt/ löschen p. 93, 5
delicious /dɪˈlɪʃəs/ köstlich, lecker NHG 6
on demand /ˌɒn dɪˈmɑːnd/ auf Anfrage p. 114, 2
dentist /ˈdentɪst/ Zahnarzt / Zahnärztin p. 42, 1

to the dentist's /ˌtʊ ðə ˈdentɪsts/ in die Zahnarztpraxis p. 163

(to) **depend on** /dɪˈpend‿ɒn/ abhängen von NHG 6

(to) **describe** /dɪˈskraɪb/ beschreiben NHG 5

description /dɪˈskrɪpʃn/ Beschreibung NHG 6

design /dɪˈzaɪn/ Entwurf; Design NHG 6

(to) **design** /dɪˈzaɪn/ entwerfen NHG 5

desk /desk/ Schreibtisch NHG 5

receptionist's desk /rɪˈsepʃnɪsts desk/ Rezeption p. 46, 5

dessert /dɪˈzɜːt/ Nachtisch p. 12, 7

(to) **destroy** /dɪˈstrɔɪ/ zerstören NHG 6

detail /ˈdiːteɪl/ Detail; Einzelheit NHG 5

detailed /ˈdiːteɪld/ genau p. 147

(to) develop /dɪˈveləp/ erarbeiten; (sich) entwickeln p. 8, 2

development /dɪˈveləpmənt/ Entwicklung p. 114, 2

device /dɪˈvaɪs/ Gerät; Apparat p. 120, 10

dialogue /ˈdaɪəˌlɒg/ Gespräch; Dialog NHG 5

diary /ˈdaɪəri/ Tagebuch NHG 6

(to) keep a diary *(irr)* /ˌkiːp‿ə ˈdaɪəri/ Tagebuch führen p. 95, 6

diary entry /ˈdaɪəriˌentri/ Tagebucheintrag NHG 6

diced /daɪst/ in Würfel geschnitten p. 143

dictionary /ˈdɪkʃənri/ Lexikon; Wörterbuch NHG 6

(to) **die** /daɪ/ sterben p. 86, 8

diet /ˈdaɪət/ Ernährung; Diät p. 14, 10

different /ˈdɪfrənt/ anders; andere(r, s); verschiedene(r, s) NHG 5

difficult /ˈdɪfɪklt/ schwierig; schwer NHG 6

Dim Sum /ˌdɪm ˈsʌm/ *traditionelles chinesisches Gericht* p. 9, 2

dining room /ˈdaɪnɪŋ ruːm/ *hier:* Speisesaal p. 66, 2

dinner /ˈdɪnə/ Abendessen NHG 5

(to) direct /daɪˈrekt/ leiten, führen p. 54

direction /daɪˈrekʃn/ Richtung p. 77

directions *(pl)* /daɪˈrekʃnz/ *hier:* Wegbeschreibungen NHG 6

(to) **give directions** *(irr)* /ˌgɪv daɪˈrekʃnz/ den Weg beschreiben NHG 6

dirty /ˈdɜːti/ dreckig; schmutzig NHG 5

disability /ˌdɪsəˈbɪləti/ Behinderung; Einschränkung p. 54

(to) **disappear** /ˌdɪsəˈpɪə/ verschwinden NHG 6

disappointed /ˌdɪsəˈpɔɪntɪd/ enttäuscht NHG 6

disappointing /ˌdɪsəˈpɔɪntɪŋ/ enttäuschend p. 18, 2

disaster /dɪˈzɑːstə/ Katastrophe p. 28

discipline /ˈdɪsəplɪn/ Disziplin p. 71, 6

(to) **discover** /dɪˈskʌvə/ entdecken NHG 6

discovery /dɪˈskʌvri/ Entdeckung p. 109, 7

discus /ˈdɪskəs/ Diskus(werfen) p. 53

(to) **discuss** /dɪˈskʌs/ besprechen; diskutieren NHG 6

discussion /dɪˈskʌʃn/ Diskussion NHG 6

disgusting /dɪsˈgʌstɪŋ/ widerlich p. 18, 2

dish *(pl* **dishes)** /dɪʃ, ˈdɪʃɪz/ Gericht; Speise p. 7

Petri dish /ˈpiːtri ˌdɪʃ/ Petrischale p. 109, 7

dishwasher /ˈdɪʃˌwɒʃə/ Spülmaschine NHG 5

(to) **dislike** /dɪsˈlaɪk/ nicht mögen p. 33, 2

(to) **display** /dɪˈspleɪ/ aushängen; zeigen NHG 5

display /dɪˈspleɪ/ Auslage, Ausstellung p. 107, 5

display /dɪˈspleɪ/ Demonstration p. 53

firework display /ˈfaɪəˌwɜːk dɪˌspleɪ/ Feuerwerk p. 67, 2

(to) **put on display** *(irr)* /ˌpʊt‿ɒn dɪˈspleɪ/ ausstellen NHG 6

distance /ˈdɪstəns/ Ferne; Entfernung p. 77

(to) **dive** /daɪv/ tauchen p. 70, 6

(to) **divide** /dɪˈvaɪd/ (auf)teilen p. 124

diving /ˈdaɪvɪŋ/ Tauchen p. 32, 1

Diwali /dɪˈwɑːli/ *hinduistisches Fest* p. 146

dizzy /ˈdɪzi/ schwindlig p. 45, 4

(to) **do** *(irr)* /duː/ tun; machen NHG 5

(to) **do athletics** *(irr)* /ˌduːˈæθˈletɪks/ Leichtathletik machen NHG 5

(to) **do gymnastics** *(irr)* /ˌduː dʒɪmˈnæstɪks/ turnen NHG 5

(to) **do research** *(irr)* /ˌduː rɪˈsɜːtʃ/ recherchieren NHG 5

(to) **do sports** *(irr)* /ˌduː ˈspɔːts/ Sport treiben NHG 6

(to) **do the cooking** *(irr)* /ˌduː ðə ˈkʊkɪŋ/ kochen NHG 5

(to) **do the shopping** *(irr)* /ˌduː ðə ˈʃɒpɪŋ/ einkaufen NHG 5

doctor /ˈdɒktə/ Arzt / Ärztin p. 31

at the doctor's /ˌæt‿ðə ˈdɒktəz/ beim Arzt / bei der Ärztin p. 31

doctor's practice /ˈdɒktəz ˌpræktɪs/ Arztpraxis p. 46, 5

(to) **see a doctor** *(irr)* /ˌsiːˈə ˈdɒktə/ einen Arzt/eine Ärztin aufsuchen p. 43, 1

document /ˈdɒkjʊmənt/ Dokument p. 117, 6

dog /dɒg/ Hund NHG 5

door /dɔː/ Tür NHG 6

dos and don'ts /ˌduːz‿ən ˈdəʊnts/ was man tun und was man nicht tun sollte p. 97, 10

double /ˈdʌbl/ doppelt, Doppel- NHG 5

down /daʊn/ hinunter; (nach) unten NHG 6

... down, ... to go /... ˌdaʊn, ... tə ˈgəʊ/ ... vorbei, es bleiben noch ... p. 53

(to) **download** /ˌdaʊnˈləʊd/ herunterladen p. 121, 12

Dr (= Doctor) /ˈdɒktə/ Dr. (= Doktor) NHG 6

draft /drɑːft/ Entwurf NHG 6

dragon /ˈdrægən/ Drache NHG 6

drama /ˈdrɑːmə/ Theater-; Schauspiel- NHG 6

dramatic /drəˈmætɪk/ dramatisch p. 43, 1

(to) **draw** *(irr)* /drɔː/ zeichnen NHG 5

(to) **draw attention to** *(irr)* /ˌdrɔːˈə ˈtenʃn tə/ Aufmerksamkeit lenken auf p. 70, 6

drawer /'drɔːə/ Schublade p. 12, 7
drawing /'drɔːɪŋ/ Zeichnung NHG 6
dream /driːm/ Traum NHG 5
dress /dres/ Kleid; Kleidung p. 86, 8
(to) **dress** /dres/ sich anziehen;
  sich kleiden p. 72, 8
dried /draɪd/ getrocknet p. 143
drink /drɪŋk/ Trinken; Getränk NHG 5
(to) **drink** /drɪŋk/ trinken NHG 5
(to) **drive** *(irr)* /draɪv/ fahren NHG 6
drone /drəʊn/ Drohne p. 124
(to) **drop** /drɒp/ fallen lassen
  p. 39,10
dry /draɪ/ trocken NHG 6
dry suit /'draɪsuːt/ Taucheranzug
  p. 38, 8
during /'djʊərɪŋ/ während NHG 6

E

each /iːtʃ/ jede(r, s) NHG 5
each and every /'iːtʃ_ən_ˌevri/
  jede(r, s) einzelne p. 39, 10
each other /ˌiːtʃ_'ʌðə/ einander
  NHG 5
ear /ɪə/ Ohr NHG 5
earlier /'ɜːliə/ vorhin, früher NHG 6
early /'ɜːli/ früh NHG 6
(to) **earn** /ɜːn/ verdienen NHG 6
earth /ɜːθ/ Erde NHG 6
easily /'iːzɪli/ leicht; mühelos p. 127
East /iːst/ östlich, Ost- P&P 4
Easter /'iːstə/ Ostern NHG 6
easy /'iːzi/ leicht; einfach NHG 5
(to) take things easy *(informal, irr)*
  /ˌteɪk θɪŋz_'iːzi/ sich keinen Stress
  machen p. 33, 2
(to) **eat** *(irr)* /iːt/ essen NHG 5
(to) **eat out** *(irr)* /ˌiːt_'aʊt/ auswärts
  essen; im Restaurant essen p. 7
eating /'iːtɪŋ/ Essen p. 108, 6
eating habit /'iːtɪŋ ˌhæbɪt/ Essgewohnheit p. 30
(to) **echo** /'ekəʊ/ (wider)hallen p. 127
(to) **edit** /'edɪt/ bearbeiten NHG 5
education /ˌedjʊ'keɪʃn/ Bildung;
  Ausbildung; Erziehung p. 104, 1
educational /ˌedjʊ'keɪʃnəl/ lehrreich
  p. 76
effect /ɪ'fekt/ Wirkung p. 145
egg /eg/ Ei NHG 5
Egypt /'iːdʒɪpt/ Ägypten p. 6

Egyptian /ɪ'dʒɪpʃn/ Ägypter/in;
  ägyptisch p. 118, 7
not ... either /ˌnɒt_'aɪðə/ auch nicht
  p. 24, 8
either ... or ... /ˌaɪðə 'ɔː/ entweder ...
  oder ... NHG 6
elastic /ɪ'læstɪk/ elastisch; flexibel
  p. 46, 5
elbow pad /'elbəʊ ˌpæd/ Ellenbogen-
  schützer p. 39, 10
electric /ɪ'lektrɪk/ elektrisch;
  Elektro- p. 104, 1
electrical /ɪ'lektrɪkl/ elektrisch p. 139
electricity /ɪˌlek'trɪsəti/ Elektrizität;
  Strom p. 110, 9
else /els/ anders; sonst NHG 5
emergency /ɪ'mɜːdʒnsi/ Notfall
  p. 45, 4
emergency services *(pl)* /ɪ'mɜːdʒnsi
  ˌsɜːvɪsɪz/ Notdienst, Rettungs-
  dienst p. 45, 4
(to) **emigrate** /'emɪgreɪt/ aus-
  wandern p. 85, 7
(to) **empty** /'empti/ ausleeren;
  ausräumen NHG 5
end /end/ Ende; Schluss NHG 5
(to) **end** /end/ enden; beenden
  NHG 6
in the end /ˌɪn ði_'end/ am Ende,
  schließlich NHG 6
ending /'endɪŋ/ Ende; Schluss NHG 6
endless /'endləs/ endlos p. 63, 12
enemy /'enəmi/ Feind/in p. 126
energy /'enədʒi/ Energie; Kraft p. 130
engine /'endʒɪn/ Maschine; Motor
  p. 105, 2
engineer /ˌendʒɪ'nɪə/ Ingenieur / in
  NHG 6
mechanical engineering
  /mɪˌkænɪkl_endʒɪ'nɪərɪŋ/ Maschi-
  nenbau *(Studienfach)* p. 124
English /'ɪŋglɪʃ/ Englisch; englisch
  NHG 5
English-speaking
  /'ɪŋglɪʃ ˌspiːkɪŋ/ englischsprachig
  p. 25, 10
(to) **enjoy** /ɪn'dʒɔɪ/ genießen
  NHG 5
Enjoy! /ɪn'dʒɔɪ/ Guten Appetit!
  p. 17, 17
enough /ɪ'nʌf/ genug NHG 5

(to) **enter** /'entə/ eingeben;
  betreten NHG 6
entertainment /ˌentə'teɪnmənt/
  Unterhaltung NHG 6
entrance /'entrəns/ Eingang;
  Eintritt NHG 6
entry /'entri/ Eintritt NHG 6;
  Eintrag p. 66, 2
entry /'entri/ Zutritt p. 125
diary entry /'daɪəri ˌentri/ Tagebucheintrag NHG 6
environment /ɪn'vaɪrənmənt/
  Umwelt; Umgebung NHG 6
equipment /ɪ'kwɪpmənt/ Ausrüs-
  tung; Ausstattung NHG 5
eraser /ɪ'reɪzə/ Radiergummi NHG 5
(to) **escape** /ɪ'skeɪp/ fliehen;
  entkommen NHG 5
especially /ɪ'speʃli/ besonders; vor
  allem NHG 5
(to) be estimated *(irr)*
  /ˌbi_'estɪmeɪtəd/ geschätzt werden
  p. 109, 7
Europe /'jʊərəp/ Europa NHG 6
(to) **evaporate** /ɪ'væpəreɪt/ ver-
  dampfen, verdunsten p. 139
even /'iːvn/ selbst; sogar NHG 5
evening /'iːvnɪŋ/ Abend NHG 5
event /ɪ'vent/ Ereignis; Veranstal-
  tung NHG 5
ever /'evə/ jemals NHG 6
ever since /ˌevə 'sɪns/ seitdem p. 101
every /'evri/ jede(r, s) NHG 5
each and every /'iːtʃ_ən_ˌevri/
  jede(r, s) einzelne p. 39, 10
everybody /'evriˌbɒdi/ alle; jeder
  NHG 5
everyday /'evriˌdeɪ/ alltäglich,
  Alltags- NHG 6
everyone /'evriwʌn/ alle; jeder
  NHG 5
everything /'evriθɪŋ/ alles NHG 5
everywhere /'evriweə/ überall
  NHG 5
exactly /ɪg'zækli/ genau NHG 6
exam /ɪg'zæm/ Prüfung p. 100
(to) **examine** /ɪg'zæmɪn/ untersuchen p. 46, 5
example /ɪg'zɑːmpl/ Beispiel NHG 5
for example /fər_ɪg'zɑːmpl/ zum
  Beispiel NHG 5

excellent /ˈeksələnt/ ausgezeichnet NHG 5

except /ɪkˈsept/ außer NHG 6

exchange student /ɪksˈtʃeɪndʒ ˌstjuːdnt/ Austauschschüler/in p. 49, 10

excited /ɪkˈsaɪtɪd/ aufgeregt NHG 6

exciting /ɪkˈsaɪtɪŋ/ aufregend NHG 5

Excuse me! /ɪkˈskjuːz ˌmi/ Entschuldigung! NHG 5

exercise /ˈeksəsaɪz/ Übung NHG 6

exercise /ˈeksəsaɪz/ Bewegung p. 124

(to) exercise /ˈeksəsaɪz/ trainieren p. 36, 7

exercise book /ˈeksəsaɪz ˌbʊk/ Heft NHG 5

exhausted /ɪgˈzɔːstɪd/ erschöpft p. 36, 7

exhausting /ɪgˈzɔːstɪŋ/ anstrengend p. 34, 4

exhibition /ˌeksɪˈbɪʃn/ Ausstellung NHG 6

(to) **exist** /ɪgˈzɪst/ existieren NHG 6

(to) exit /ˈeksɪt/ verlassen p. 127

(to) **expect** /ɪkˈspekt/ erwarten NHG 6

expensive /ɪkˈspensɪv/ teuer NHG 6

experience /ɪkˈspɪəriəns/ Erfahrung NHG 5

experiment /ɪkˈsperɪmənt/ Experiment; Versuch NHG 5

expert /ˈekspɜːt/ Experte/Expertin NHG 6

(to) **explain** /ɪkˈspleɪn/ erklären NHG 5

(to) **explore** /ɪkˈsplɔː/ erforschen; untersuchen NHG 6

(to) **express** /ɪkˈspres/ ausdrücken NHG 6

expression /ɪkˈspreʃn/ Ausdruck p. 88, 11

(to) go extinct (irr) /ˌgəʊ ɪkˈstɪŋkt/ aussterben p. 126

extra /ˈekstrə/ zusätzlich NHG 5

extremely /ɪkˈstriːmli/ äußerst, höchst; außerordentlich p. 22, 6

eye /aɪ/ Auge NHG 5

(to) keep an eye on (irr) /ˌkiːp ən ˈaɪ ɒn/ im Auge behalten p. 126

eyeball /ˈaɪbɔːl/ Augapfel p. 125

eyesight /ˈaɪsaɪt/ Sehvermögen p. 54

F

face /feɪs/ Gesicht NHG 5

fact /fækt/ Tatsache; Fakt NHG 5

fact file /ˈfækt faɪl/ Steckbrief NHG 5

fake /feɪk/ gefälscht, falsch p. 15, 11

(to) **fall** (irr) /fɔːl/ fallen p. 43, 1

(to) **fall off** (irr) /ˌfɔːl ˈɒf/ (herunter) fallen p. 51, 16

false /fɔːls/ falsch NHG 5

family /ˈfæmli/ Familie NHG 5

famous /ˈfeɪməs/ berühmt NHG 5

fancy /ˈfænsi/ nobel p. 28

fantastic /fænˈtæstɪk/ fantastisch; super NHG 5

far /fɑː/ weit NHG 5

far /fɑː/ hier: weit weg p. 102

farm /fɑːm/ Bauernhof NHG 6

farming /ˈfɑːmɪŋ/ Ackerbau und Viehzucht P&P 5

fashion /ˈfæʃn/ Mode NHG 6

fast /fɑːst/ schnell NHG 5

(to) fasten /ˈfɑːsn/ schließen; zumachen p. 109, 7

hook-and-loop fastener /ˌhʊk ən ˈluːp ˌfɑːsnə/ Klettverschluss p. 127

father /ˈfɑːðə/ Vater NHG 5

fault /fɔːlt/ Schuld; Fehler p. 99, 15

favourite /ˈfeɪvrət/ Liebling; Lieblings- NHG 5

February /ˈfebruəri/ Februar NHG 5

fee /fiː/ Gebühr; Geld p. 56, 2

registration fee /ˌredʒɪˈstreɪʃn fiː/ Anmeldegebühr p. 56, 2

(to) **feed** (irr) /fiːd/ füttern NHG 6

feedback /ˈfiːdbæk/ Feedback; Rückmeldung NHG 5

(to) **feel** (irr) /fiːl/ (sich) fühlen NHG 6

feeling /ˈfiːlɪŋ/ Gefühl NHG 6

felt-tip /ˈfelt tɪp/ Filzstift NHG 5

festival /ˈfestɪvl/ Fest; Festival NHG 6

festival goer /ˈfestɪvl ˌgəʊə/ Festivalbesucher/in p. 73, 9

fever /ˈfiːvə/ Fieber p. 42, 1

a few /ə ˈfjuː/ einige; wenige NHG 6

fewer /ˈfjuːə/ weniger P&P 5

field /fiːld/ Feld NHG 5

playing field /ˈpleɪɪŋ ˌfiːld/ Sportplatz p. 45, 4

field trip /ˈfiːld trɪp/ Exkursion p. 124

FIFA /ˈfiːfə/ FIFA (internationaler Fußballverband) p. 54

fight /faɪt/ Kampf; Streit p. 66, 2

(to) **fight** (irr) /faɪt/ bekämpfen; ankämpfen gegen NHG 6

(to) **fill** /fɪl/ füllen NHG 6

(to) **fill in** /ˌfɪl ˈɪn/ eintragen, ausfüllen NHG 5

filled /fɪld/ gefüllt p. 23, 7

(to) **film** /fɪlm/ drehen, filmen NHG 6

final /ˈfaɪnl/ letzte(r, s); endgültig NHG 5

finally /ˈfaɪnli/ schließlich; endlich p. 57, 3

find /faɪnd/ Fund p. 56, 2

(to) **find** (irr) /faɪnd/ finden NHG 5

(to) **find out** (irr) /ˌfaɪnd ˈaʊt/ herausfinden NHG 5

finding /ˈfaɪndɪŋ/ Entdeckung; Ergebnis p. 114, 2

fine /faɪn/ in Ordnung, gut NHG 5

(to) be fine with (irr) /ˌbiː ˈfaɪn wɪð/ etwas in Ordnung finden p. 76

(to) **finish** /ˈfɪnɪʃ/ beenden; enden; fertigstellen NHG 6; aufessen p. 8, 2

finished /ˈfɪnɪʃt/ fertig p. 29

finishing line /ˈfɪnɪʃɪŋ ˌlaɪn/ Ziellinie p. 52

fire /ˈfaɪə/ Feuer NHG 6

firefighter /ˈfaɪəˌfaɪtə/ Feuerwehrmann/-frau NHG 6

firework display /ˈfaɪəˌwɜːk dɪˌspleɪ/ Feuerwerk p. 67, 2

fireworks (pl) /ˈfaɪəˌwɜːks/ Feuerwerk NHG 6

first /fɜːst/ erste(r, s); zuerst NHG 5

at first /ˌæt ˈfɜːst/ zuerst NHG 6

fish (pl fish or fishes) /fɪʃ, fɪʃ, ˈfɪʃɪz/ Fisch NHG 5

fish and chips /ˌfɪʃ ən ˈtʃɪps/ Fisch mit Pommes P&P 1

fisherman (pl fishermen) /ˈfɪʃəmən/ Fischer; Angler p. 8, 2

(to) **fit** /fɪt/ passen NHG 5

(to) **keep fit** (irr) /ˌkiːp ˈfɪt/ fit bleiben, (sich) fit halten p. 31

flag /flæg/ Fahne; Flagge p. 52

flat /flæt/ Wohnung NHG 6

flatbread /ˈflætbred/ Fladen p. 8, 2

flea market /ˈfliː ˌmɑːkɪt/ Flohmarkt p. 57, 3

flexible /ˈfleksəbl/ biegsam,
gelenkig p. 36, 7
(to) **flip** /flɪp/ wenden p. 29
floor /flɔː/ Fußboden NHG 5
flour /ˈflaʊə/ Mehl p. 23, 7
flow chart /ˈfləʊ tʃɑːt/ Flussdia-
gramm p. 32, 1
flower /ˈflaʊə/ Blume NHG 6
flowerpot /ˈflaʊəˌpɒt/ Blumentopf
p. 60, 8
(to) **fly** *(irr)* /flaɪ/ fliegen NHG 6
(to) **fly by** *(irr)* /ˌflaɪ ˈbaɪ/ vorbei-
sausen p. 77
(to) **focus on** /ˈfəʊkəs_ɒn/ sich
konzentrieren auf NHG 5
folder /ˈfəʊldə/ Mappe; Ordner
NHG 5
(to) **follow** /ˈfɒləʊ/ folgen; verfolgen
NHG 6
(to) follow through /ˌfɒləʊ ˈθruː/
etwas zu Ende führen p. 91, 2
following /ˈfɒləʊɪŋ/ folgende(r, s)
NHG 6
food /fuːd/ Essen NHG 5
foot *(pl feet)* /fʊt, fiːt/ Fuß NHG 5
football /ˈfʊtˌbɔːl/ Fußball NHG 5
football 5-a-side /ˌfʊtbɔːl ˌfaɪv_ə
ˈsaɪd/ 5er-Fußball p. 54
for /fɔː/ für NHG 5
for *(+ Zeitraum)* /fɔː/ … lang NHG 6
for /fɔː/ denn p. 78
for a while /fər_ə ˈwaɪl/ eine Weile
p. 36, 7
for ages *(informal)* /fər_ˈeɪdʒɪz/ seit
einer Ewigkeit p. 57, 3
for example /fər_ɪgˈzɑːmpl/ zum
Beispiel NHG 5
for free /fə ˈfriː/ gratis NHG 6
for some time /fə ˌsʌm ˈtaɪm/ eine
Zeitlang p. 37, 7
for the first time /fə ðə ˈfɜːst_taɪm/
zum ersten Mal NHG 6
(to) **force** /fɔːs/ zwingen; erzwingen
p. 76
foreign /ˈfɒrɪn/ ausländisch; fremd
p. 85, 7
forest /ˈfɒrɪst/ Wald NHG 6
forever /fərˈevə/ ewig, für immer
p. 56, 2
(to) **forget** *(irr)* /fəˈget/ vergessen
NHG 5

fork /fɔːk/ Gabel NHG 5
form /fɔːm/ Klasse NHG 5
former /ˈfɔːmə/ ehemalige(r, s);
frühere(r, s) P&P 4
foxhunting *(no pl)* /ˈfɒks ˌhʌntɪŋ/
Fuchsjagd p. 14, 10
France /frɑːns/ Frankreich NHG 5
free /friː/ frei; kostenlos NHG 6
for free /fə ˈfriː/ gratis NHG 6
free time /friː ˈtaɪm/ Freizeit NHG 5
French /frentʃ/ Französisch NHG 5
French /frentʃ/ Franzose/Französin;
französisch p. 29
fresh /freʃ/ frisch; neu NHG 6
Friday /ˈfraɪdeɪ/ Freitag NHG 5
(on) Fridays /ˈfraɪdeɪz/ freitags NHG 5
fridge /frɪdʒ/ Kühlschrank p. 12, 7
fried /fraɪd/ gebraten p. 9, 2
fried egg /ˌfraɪd ˈeg/ Spiegelei p. 52
friend /frend/ Freund/in NHG 5
friendly /ˈfrendli/ freundlich NHG 6
(to) **make friends (with)** *(irr)*
/ˌmeɪk ˈfrendz/ sich anfreunden
(mit) NHG 6
friendship /ˈfrenʃɪp/ Freundschaft
NHG 6
from /frɒm/ von; aus NHG 5
from (all) around the world
/frəm_ˌɔːl_ə,raʊnd ðə ˈwɜːld/ aus der
(ganzen) Welt p. 7
from all over the world
/frəm_ˌɔːl_ˌəʊvə ðə ˈwɜːld/ aus der
ganzen Welt NHG 5
at / in the front /ˌæt/ˌɪn ðə ˈfrʌnt/
vorne NHG 5
in front of /ˌɪn ˈfrʌnt_əv/ vor NHG 5
fruit /fruːt/ Frucht; Obst NHG 5
frustrated /frʌˈstreɪtɪd/ frustriert
NHG 6
full /fʊl/ voll, vollständig NHG 6;
satt p. 8, 2
full of /ˈfʊl_əv/ voller p. 76
fun /fʌn/ Spaß NHG 5; lustig;
witzig NHG 6
(to) **be (good/great) fun** *(irr)* /ˌbiː
ˌgʊd/ˌgreɪt ˈfʌn/ (viel/großen) Spaß
machen NHG 5
(to) **have (a lot of) fun** *(irr)* /ˌhæv_ə
ˌlɒt_əv_ˈfʌn/ (viel) Spaß haben NHG 6
function /ˈfʌŋkʃn/ Aufgabe;
Funktion p. 118, 7

funny /ˈfʌni/ lustig; komisch NHG 5
furniture /ˈfɜːnɪtʃə/ Möbel(stück)
NHG 5
future /ˈfjuːtʃə/ Zukunft NHG 6

G

g (= gram) /græm/ Gramm p. 160
gallery walk /ˈgæləri wɔːk/ *Gruppen-
diskussion in Stationsarbeit*
p. 41, 13
(to) **gallop** /ˈgæləp/ galoppieren p. 77
game /geɪm/ Spiel NHG 5
board game /ˈbɔːd geɪm/ Brettspiel
NHG 6
(to) **game** /geɪm/ spielen p. 76
gap /gæp/ Lücke NHG 5
garden /ˈgɑːdn/ Garten NHG 5
garlic /ˈgɑːlɪk/ Knoblauch p. 9, 2
clove of garlic /ˌkləʊv_əv ˈgɑːlɪk/
Knoblauchzehe p. 17, 17
gate /geɪt/ Tor NHG 6
general /ˈdʒenrəl/ allgemein p. 114, 2
in general /ɪn ˈdʒenrəl/ im Allgemeinen P&P 1
geography /dʒiˈɒgrəfi/ Erdkunde
NHG 5
German /ˈdʒɜːmən/ Deutsch;
deutsch NHG 5
Germany /ˈdʒɜːməni/ Deutschland
NHG 5
gerund /ˈdʒerənd/ Gerundium p. 34
(to) **get** *(irr)* /get/ bekommen; holen;
kaufen NHG 5; kommen; gelangen;
werden NHG 6; bringen p. 24, 8
(to) **get** *(irr)* /get/ *hier:* gehen p. 77;
verstehen p. 101
(to) **get along** *(irr)* /ˌget_əˈlɒŋ/ sich
verstehen NHG 6
(to) **get away** *(irr)* /ˌget_əˈweɪ/ weg-
kommen, flüchten p. 102
(to) **get better** *(irr)* /ˌget ˈbetə/
besser werden; gesund werden
p. 37, 7
(to) **get dressed** *(irr)* /ˌget_ˈdrest/
sich anziehen p. 76
(to) **get killed** *(irr)* /ˌget ˈkɪld/ umge-
bracht werden p. 76
(to) **get lost** *(irr)* /ˌget ˈlɒst/ verloren
gehen, sich verirren p. 124
(to) **get married** *(irr)* /ˌget ˈmærid/
heiraten p. 81, 2

(to) **get rid of** *(irr)* /ˌget ˈrɪd_əv/ loswerden p. 61, 8

(to) **get stuck** *(irr)* /ˌget ˈstʌk/ festsitzen p. 102

(to) **get together** *(irr)* /ˌget_tə'geðə/ zusammenkommen NHG 5

(to) **get up** *(irr)* /ˌget_ˈʌp/ aufstehen NHG 6

(to) **get well** *(irr)* /ˌget ˈwel/ gesund werden p. 49, 12

Get well soon! /ˌget ˌwel ˈsuːn/ Gute Besserung! p. 48, 7

ghost /gəʊst/ Geist; Gespenst NHG 6

giant /ˈdʒaɪənt/ riesig p. 77

ginger /ˈdʒɪndʒə/ Ingwer p. 23, 7

girl /gɜːl/ Mädchen NHG 5

(to) **give** *(irr)* /gɪv/ geben NHG 5; angeben, mitteilen NHG 6

(to) **give a helping hand** *(irr)* /ˌgɪv_ə ˌhelpɪŋ ˈhænd/ helfen p. 79

(to) **give a presentation** *(irr)* /ˌgɪv_ə ˌpreznˈteɪʃn/ eine Präsentation halten p. 114, 2

(to) **give a reason** *(irr)* /ˌgɪv_ə ˈriːzn/ einen Grund nennen p. 56, 2

(to) **give a talk** *(irr)* /ˌgɪv_ə ˈtɔːk/ einen Vortrag halten p. 39, 9

(to) **give a try** *(irr)* /ˌgɪv_ə ˈtraɪ/ ausprobieren p. 100

(to) **give advice** *(irr)* /ˌgɪv_ədˈvaɪs/ Rat geben p. 99, 15

(to) **give directions** *(irr)* /ˌgɪv daɪˈrekʃnz/ den Weg beschreiben NHG 6

(to) **give off** *(irr)* /ˌgɪv_ˈɒf/ abgeben p. 127

(to) **give somebody a call** *(irr)* /ˌgɪv ˌsʌmbədi_ə ˈkɔːl/ jemanden anrufen p. 42, 1

glad /glæd/ glücklich, froh p. 24, 8

glass /glɑːs/ Glas NHG 6

VR **glasses** *(pl)* /ˌviː_ˈɑː ˌglɑːsɪz/ VR-Brille p. 125

X-ray **glasses** *(pl)* /ˈeksreɪ ˌglɑːsɪz/ *Röntgenbrille* p. 111, 11

glue /gluː/ Klebstoff NHG 5

(to) **go** *(irr)* /gəʊ/ gehen; fahren NHG 5

(to) **go abroad** *(irr)* /ˌgəʊ_əˈbrɔːd/ ins Ausland gehen / fahren NHG 6

(to) **go away** *(irr)* /ˌgəʊ_əˈweɪ/ weggehen; verschwinden NHG 6

(to) go bad *(irr)* /ˌgəʊ ˈbæd/ verderben p. 109, 7

(to) **go cycling** *(irr)* /ˌgəʊ ˈsaɪklɪŋ/ Rad fahren gehen NHG 6

(to) go extinct *(irr)* /ˌgəʊ_ɪkˈstɪŋkt/ aussterben p. 126

(to) go for the top *(irr)* /ˌgəʊ fə ðə ˈtɒp/ sich um Höchstleistungen bemühen p. 52

(to) **go hiking** *(irr)* /ˌgəʊ ˈhaɪkɪŋ/ wandern gehen NHG 6

(to) go off *(irr)* /ˌgəʊ_ˈɒf/ weggehen p. 77

(to) **go on** *(irr)* /ˌgəʊ_ˈɒn/ passieren; weitergehen, weiterreden p. 26, 12

(to) **go out** *(irr)* /ˌgəʊ_ˈaʊt/ (hinaus) gehen; ausgehen NHG 6

(to) **go riding** *(irr)* /ˌgəʊ ˈraɪdɪŋ/ reiten gehen NHG 6

(to) **go shopping** *(irr)* /ˌgəʊ ˈʃɒpɪŋ/ einkaufen gehen NHG 6

(to) **go swimming** *(irr)* /ˌgəʊ ˈswɪmɪŋ/ schwimmen gehen NHG 6

(to) **go with** *(irr)* /ˌgəʊ ˈwɪθ/ gehören zu; passen zu NHG 6

in one go /ˌɪn wʌn ˈgəʊ/ auf einmal p. 136

goal /gəʊl/ Tor NHG 5

goalkeeper /ˈgəʊlˌkiːpə/ Tormann/ Torfrau p. 54

(to) be going to *(irr)* /ˌbi ˈgəʊɪŋ tʊ/ werden NHG 6

gone /gɒn/ weg NHG 6

good /gʊd/ gut NHG 5

(to) **be good at something** *(irr)* /ˌbi ˈgʊd_æt ˌsʌmθɪŋ/ gut in etwas sein NHG 6

I'm good, thanks. /aɪm ˈgʊd ˌθæŋks/ Es geht mir gut, danke. NHG 5

a good cause /ə ˌgʊd ˈkɔːz/ eine gute Sache, ein guter Zweck p. 56, 2

Good luck! /ˌgʊd ˈlʌk/ Viel Glück! p. 94, 6

Good morning! /ˌgʊd ˈmɔːnɪŋ/ Guten Morgen! NHG 5

goodbye /ˌgʊdˈbaɪ/ auf Wiedersehen NHG 5

goods *(pl)* /gʊdz/ Waren p. 30

gotta (= have got to) *(informal)* /ˈgɒtə/ müssen p. 102

government /ˈgʌvənmənt/ Regierung p. 73, 9

GP (= General Practitioner) /ˌdʒiː ˈpiː, ˌdʒenrəl prækˈtɪʃnə/ Hausarzt / Hausärztin p. 46, 5

(to) **grab** /græb/ sich schnappen; greifen p. 39, 10

g (= gram) /græm/ Gramm p. 160

grammar /ˈgræmə/ Grammatik p. 10

grandad *(informal)* /ˈgrænˌdæd/ Opa p. 86, 8

grandchild (*pl* grandchildren) /ˈgrænˌtʃaɪld, ˈgrænˌtʃɪldrən/ Enkelkind p. 89, 13

grandfather /ˈgrænˌfɑːðə/ Großvater NHG 5

grandma *(informal)* /ˈgrænˌmɑː/ Oma p. 6

grandmother /ˈgrænˌmʌðə/ Großmutter NHG 5

grandpa *(informal)* /ˈgrænˌpɑː/ Opa p. 86, 8

grandparents *(pl)* /ˈgrænˌpeərənts/ Großeltern NHG 6

grape /greɪp/ (Wein)traube NHG 6

grass /grɑːs/ Gras NHG 6

gravy /ˈgreɪvi/ (Braten)soße p. 8, 2

great /greɪt/ groß; großartig NHG 5

Great Britain /ˌgreɪt ˈbrɪtn/ Großbritannien P&P 1

great-grandchild (*pl* great-grandchildren) /ˌgreɪt ˈgrænˌtʃaɪld, ˌgreɪt ˈgrænˌtʃɪldrən/ Urenkelkind p. 89, 13

great-grandfather /ˌgreɪt ˈgrænˌfɑːðə/ Urgroßvater p. 85, 7

great-grandmother /ˌgreɪt ˈgrænˌmʌðə/ Urgroßmutter p. 82, 4

great-great-grandfather /ˌgreɪt ˌgreɪt ˈgrænˌfɑːðə/ Ururgroßvater p. 81, 2

great-uncle /ˈgreɪt_ˌʌŋkl/ Großonkel p. 89, 13

greatly /ˈgreɪtli/ sehr p. 78

Greece /griːs/ Griechenland p. 8, 2

Greek /griːk/ Grieche / Griechin; griechisch p. 18, 1

green /griːn/ grün NHG 5; umweltfreundlich, ökologisch p. 55

greetings *(pl)* /ˈgriːtɪŋz/ Grüße p. 8, 2

grey /greɪ/ grau NHG 5

(to) grieve /griːv/ traurig sein, trauern p. 102

grilled /grɪld/ gegrillt p. 8, 2

ground /graʊnd/ Boden NHG 6

group /gruːp/ Gruppe NHG 5

(to) **grow** *(irr)* /grəʊ/ anbauen NHG 6; wachsen p. 109, 7

(to) **grow up** *(irr)* ˌgrəʊ_ˈʌp/ erwachsen sein, erwachsen werden NHG 6; aufwachsen p. 81, 2

gruel /ˈgruːəl/ Haferschleim; Grütze p. 76

(to) **guess** /ges/ (er)raten NHG 5

guest /gest/ Gast NHG 5

guide /gaɪd/ Führer/in p. 54; Führer *(Buch)* p. 56, 2

guided /ˈgaɪdɪd/ geführt p. 124

guitar /gɪˈtaː/ Gitarre NHG 5

guy /gaɪ/ Kerl; Typ p. 76

(you) guys *(pl, informal)* /gaɪz/ Leute *(umgangssprachl.)* NHG 6

gym (= gymnasium) /dʒɪm, dʒɪmˈneɪziəm/ Turnhalle NHG 5

gymnastics *(pl)* /dʒɪmˈnæstɪks/ Turnen p. 162

(to) **do gymnastics** *(irr)* /ˌduː dʒɪmˈnæstɪks/ turnen NHG 5

H

habit /ˈhæbɪt/ Gewohnheit, Angewohnheit p. 119, 8

eating habit /ˈiːtɪŋ ˌhæbɪt/ Essgewohnheit p. 30

hair /heə/ Haar; Haare NHG 5

hairdresser /ˈheəˌdresə/ Friseur/in NHG 6

half /haːf/ halb NHG 5

half *(pl halves)* /haːf, haːvz/ Hälfte NHG 6

hall /hɔːl/ Halle p. 125

ham /hæm/ Schinken p. 128

(to) **hammer** /ˈhæmə/ hämmern p. 126

(to) **hand** /hænd/ übergeben p. 53

(to) give a helping hand *(irr)* /ˌgɪv_ə ˌhelpɪŋ ˈhænd/ helfen p. 79

on the one hand, ... /ˌɒn ðə ˈwʌn hænd/ einerseits ... p. 69, 5

on the other hand, ... /ˌɒn ðiˈʌðə hænd/ andererseits ... p. 69, 5

(to) **hand in** /ˌhænd_ˈɪn/ einreichen; abgeben NHG 6

(to) **handle** /ˈhændl/ bewältigen, umgehen mit p. 24, 8

(to) **hang on** *(irr)* /ˌhæŋ_ˈɒn/ sich festhalten p. 77

(to) **hang out** *(informal, irr)* /ˌhæŋ_ˈaʊt/ rumhängen; Zeit mit jemandem verbringen p. 49, 12

(to) **hang (up)** *(irr)* /ˌhæŋ_ˈʌp/ hängen, aufhängen NHG 6

(to) **happen** /ˈhæpən/ geschehen; passieren NHG 5

happy /ˈhæpi/ glücklich NHG 5; zufrieden p. 122, 15

Happy birthday (to you)! /ˌhæpi ˈbɜːθdeɪ tʊ juː/ Herzlichen Glückwunsch zum Geburtstag! NHG 5

hard /haːd/ hart, schwierig NHG 6; fest; kräftig p. 45, 4

hardly /ˈhaːdli/ kaum p. 127

(to) **hate** /heɪt/ hassen; nicht ausstehen können NHG 5

(to) **have** *(irr)* /hæv/ haben; essen; trinken NHG 5

(to) have a closer look *(irr)* /ˌhæv_ə ˌkləʊsə ˈlʊk/ sich etwas genauer ansehen p. 105, 2

(to) **have a look at** *(irr)* /ˌhæv_ə ˈlʊk_ət/ sich ansehen NHG 6

(to) **have (a lot of) fun** *(irr)* /ˌhæv_ə ˌlɒt_əv_ˈfʌn/ (viel) Spaß haben NHG 6

(to) **have got** *(irr)* /ˌhæv ˈgɒt/ haben NHG 5

(to) **have in common** *(irr)* /ˌhæv_ɪn ˈkɒmən/ gemeinsam haben NHG 6

(to) **have to** *(irr)* /ˈhæv tə/ müssen NHG 5

he /hiː/ er NHG 5

head /hed/ Kopf NHG 6

(to) head /hed/ köpfen p. 39, 10

(to) bang one's head /ˌbæŋ wʌnz ˈhed/ sich den Kopf anschlagen p. 45, 4

headache /ˈhedeɪk/ Kopfschmerzen p. 42, 1

heading /ˈhedɪŋ/ Überschrift; Titel NHG 6

headline /ˈhedˌlaɪn/ Schlagzeile; *hier:* Überschrift p. 94, 6

headteacher /ˌhedˈtiːtʃə/ Schulleiter/in; Rektor/in p. 53

health /helθ/ Gesundheit p. 31

healthy /ˈhelθi/ gesund NHG 6

(to) **hear** *(irr)* /hɪə/ hören NHG 5

heart /haːt/ Herz NHG 6

by heart /ˌbaɪ ˈhaːt/ auswendig p. 14, 10

(to) **heat** /hiːt/ erhitzen p. 13, 8

heavy /ˈhevi/ schwer NHG 5

hedgehog /ˈhedʒˌhɒg/ Igel NHG 6

height /haɪt/ Höhe NHG 6

heir to the throne /ˌeə tʊ ðə ˈθrəʊn/ Thronfolger/in p. 78

hello /həˈləʊ/ hallo NHG 5

helmet /ˈhelmɪt/ Helm p. 39, 10

help /help/ Hilfe NHG 5

(to) **help** /help/ helfen NHG 5

(to) **help out** /ˌhelp_ˈaʊt/ aushelfen p. 49, 10

helpful /ˈhelpfl/ hilfreich; nützlich p. 95, 6

(to) give a helping hand *(irr)* /ˌgɪv_ə ˌhelpɪŋ ˈhænd/ helfen p. 79

helpline /ˈhelpˌlaɪn/ *telefonischer Beratungsdienst* p. 96, 9

her /hɜː/ ihr/ihre; sie NHG 5

herb /hɜːb/ (Gewürz)kraut p. 12, 7

here /hɪə/ hier; hierher NHG 5

Here you are! /ˌhɪə juˈaː/ Hier, bitte! NHG 5

heritage /ˈherɪtɪdʒ/ Erbe p. 86, 8

hers /hɜːz/ ihre(r, s) p. 98, 12

herself /həˈself/ sich; (sie) selbst p. 90, 2

(to) **hide** *(irr)* /haɪd/ (sich) verstecken NHG 6

high /haɪ/ hoch NHG 5

high jump /ˈhaɪ dʒʌmp/ Hochsprung p. 53

high-pressure /ˌhaɪ ˈpreʃə/ Hochdruck- p. 105, 2

high-speed train /ˌhaɪspiːd ˈtreɪn/ Hochgeschwindigkeitszug p. 127

highlight /ˈhaɪˌlaɪt/ Höhepunkt p. 67, 2

(to) take a hike *(AE, informal, irr)* /ˌteɪk_ə ˈhaɪk/ abhauen p. 102

(to) **go hiking** *(irr)* /ˌgəʊ ˈhaɪkɪŋ/ wandern gehen NHG 6

hill /hɪl/ Hügel NHG 6

him /hɪm/ ihm, ihn NHG 5

himself /hɪmˈself/ selbst; sich (selbst) NHG 6

Hinduism /ˈhɪnduˌɪzm/ Hinduismus NHG 6

(to) **hire** /ˈhaɪə/ mieten NHG 6

his /hɪz/ sein; seine(r, s) NHG 5

historical /hɪˈstɒrɪkl/ geschichtlich; historisch p. 78

history /ˈhɪstri/ Geschichte NHG 5

(to) **hit** *(irr)* /hɪt/ schlagen NHG 5

(to) hit *(irr)* /hɪt/ treffen; stoßen gegen p. 127

(to) **hold** *(irr)* /həʊld/ (fest)halten NHG 5

hole /həʊl/ Loch NHG 5

Holi /ˈhəʊli/ *hinduistisches Fest der Farben* p. 146

holiday /ˈhɒlɪdeɪ/ Feiertag NHG 6

holiday(s) /ˈhɒlɪdeɪ(z)/ Ferien; Urlaub NHG 5

home /həʊm/ nach Hause; zu Hause; daheim NHG 5; Zuhause; Haus NHG 6

at home /æt ˈhəʊm/ zu Hause NHG 5

home town /ˈhəʊm ˌtaʊn/ Heimatstadt NHG 5

home-made /ˌhəʊmˈmeɪd/ hausgemacht, selbst gemacht p. 22, 6

(to) **be homesick** *(irr)* /biː ˈhəʊmˌsɪk/ Heimweh haben p. 85, 7

homework /ˈhəʊmwɜːk/ Hausaufgaben NHG 5

honest /ˈɒnɪst/ ehrlich NHG 6

honey /ˈhʌni/ Honig p. 137

hook /hʊk/ Haken p. 127

hook-and-loop fastener /ˌhʊk_ən ˈluːp ˌfɑːsnə/ *Klettverschluss* p. 127

(to) **hope** /həʊp/ hoffen NHG 5

hopefully /ˈhəʊpfli/ hoffentlich p. 42,1

horrible /ˈhɒrəbl/ schrecklich; gemein NHG 6

horse /hɔːs/ Pferd NHG 6

(to) **ride a horse** *(irr)* /ˌraɪd_ə ˈhɔːs/ reiten NHG 5

horse riding /ˈhɔːs ˌraɪdɪŋ/ Reiten p. 76

horsehair /ˈhɔːsˌheə/ Rosshaar p. 105, 2

hospital /ˈhɒspɪtl/ Krankenhaus NHG 6

(to) host /həʊst/ ausrichten p. 54

hot /hɒt/ heiß NHG 6; scharf p. 9, 2

hour /ˈaʊə/ Stunde NHG 5

house /haʊs/ Haus NHG 5

how /haʊ/ wie NHG 5

How about ...? /ˈhaʊ_əˌbaʊt/ Wie wäre es mit / Was ist mit ...? p. 90,1

How are you? /ˌhaʊ_ˈɑː jʊ/ Wie geht es dir / euch / Ihnen? NHG 5

How much is it? /ˌhaʊ mʌtʃˈˌɪz_ɪt/ Wie viel kostet es? NHG 5

how to /ˈhaʊ tʊ/ wie man p. 29

however /haʊˈevə/ aber; wie auch immer p. 78

huge /hjuːdʒ/ riesig NHG 6

hundred /ˈhʌndrəd/ Hundert NHG 6

hungry /ˈhʌŋgri/ hungrig NHG 5

treasure hunting /ˈtreʒə ˌhʌntɪŋ/ Schatzsuchen p. 57, 3

hurdle /ˈhɜːdl/ Hürde(nlauf) p. 52

(to) **hurry (up)** /ˌhʌri_ˈʌp/ sich beeilen NHG 5

in a hurry /ˌɪn_ə ˈhʌri/ in Eile p. 52

(to) **hurt** *(irr)* /hɜːt/ wehtun; schmerzen; verletzen p. 42, 1

husband /ˈhʌzbənd/ Ehemann NHG 5

hysterical /hɪˈsterɪkl/ hysterisch p. 125

I

I /aɪ/ ich NHG 5

I don't know. /ˌaɪ ˌdəʊnt ˈnəʊ/ Ich weiß es nicht. NHG 5

I don't like ... /ˌaɪ ˈdəʊnt laɪk/ Ich mag ... nicht. NHG 5

I'd (= I would) /aɪd, ˈaɪ wʊd/ ich würde p. 93, 5

I'd love to ... /aɪd ˈlʌv tə/ Ich würde sehr gern ... NHG 5

ice /aɪs/ Eis NHG 6

ice cream /ˈaɪs ˌkriːm/ Eis NHG 5

ice hockey /ˈaɪs ˌhɒki/ Eishockey p. 129

(to) **ice-skate** /ˈaɪsˌskeɪt/ Schlittschuh laufen NHG 5

ICT (= Information and Communication Technology) /ˌaɪˌsiːˈtiː, ˌɪnfəˈmeɪʃn_ən kəˌmjuːnɪˈkeɪʃn tekˌnɒlədʒi/ Informatik *(Schulfach)* NHG 5

idea /aɪˈdɪə/ Idee; Vorstellung NHG 5

if /ɪf/ wenn; falls; ob NHG 5

What if ...? /ˌwɒt_ˈɪf/ Was wäre, wenn ...? p. 87, 8

ill /ɪl/ krank NHG 6

illness /ˈɪlnəs/ Krankheit p. 49, 11

image /ˈɪmɪdʒ/ Bild p. 101

(to) **imagine** /ɪˈmædʒɪn/ sich etwas vorstellen NHG 5

immediate /ɪˈmiːdiət/ umgehend; unmittelbar p. 112, 12

immediately /ɪˈmiːdiətli/ sofort p. 53

immigrant /ˈɪmɪgrənt/ Einwanderer/in; Immigrant/in p. 70, 6

impact /ˈɪmpækt/ Auswirkung; Einfluss P&P 5

important /ɪmˈpɔːtnt/ wichtig NHG 5

the most important ones /ðə ˌməʊst_ɪmˈpɔːtnt wʌnz/ die wichtigsten p. 41, 13

impossible /ɪmˈpɒsəbl/ unmöglich NHG 6

impression /ɪmˈpreʃn/ Eindruck p. 100

impressive /ɪmˈpresɪv/ beeindruckend p. 70, 6

(to) **improve** /ɪmˈpruːv/ verbessern; besser werden NHG 6

in /ɪn/ in; auf NHG 5

I'm in! *(informal)* /ˌaɪmˈˌɪn/ Ich bin dabei! p. 91, 2

in a hurry /ˌɪn_ə ˈhʌri/ in Eile p. 52

in advance /ˌɪn_ədˈvɑːns/ im Voraus p. 108, 6

in front of /ˌɪn ˈfrʌnt_əv/ vor NHG 5

in general /ˌɪn ˈdʒenrəl/ im Allgemeinen P&P 1

in my opinion /ɪn ˈmaɪ_əˌpɪnjən/ meiner Meinung nach NHG 6

in one go /ˌɪn wʌn ˈgəʊ/ auf einmal p. 130

in order to /ˌɪn_ˈɔːdə tʊ/ um zu p. 33, 2

in the back /ˌɪn ðə ˈbæk/ hinten NHG 5

in the end /ˌɪn ðiˈˌend/ am Ende, schließlich NHG 6

in the front /ˌɪn ðə ˈfrʌnt/ vorne NHG 5

(to) **include** /ɪnˈkluːd/ beinhalten; einbeziehen NHG 6

including /ɪnˈkluːdɪŋ/ einschließlich p. 54

increasingly /ɪnˈkriːsɪŋli/ zunehmend p. 30

independent /ˌɪndɪˈpendənt/ unab-
hängig p. 73, 9

India /ˈɪndiə/ Indien p. 11, 6

Indian /ˈɪndiən/ Inder/in; indisch
P&P 1

individual /ˌɪndɪˈvɪdʒuəl/ individuell;
einzeln P&P 2

indoor /ˈɪndɔː/ Hallen- p. 36, 7

indoors /ˌɪnˈdɔːz/ drinnen, im Haus
p. 32, 1

industrial /ɪnˈdʌstriəl/ industriell
P&P 5

industry /ˈɪndəstri/ Industrie p. 108, 7

(to) become infected (irr)
/bɪˌkʌm_ɪnˈfektɪd/ sich infizieren
p. 109, 7

infection /ɪnˈfekʃn/ Infektion p. 43, 1

influence /ˈɪnfluəns/ Einfluss p. 66, 2

(to) inform /ɪnˈfɔːm/ informieren
NHG 6

informal /ɪnˈfɔːml/ informell p. 28

information (no pl) /ˌɪnfəˈmeɪʃn/
Informationen NHG 5

piece of information
/ˌpiːs_əv_ˌɪnfəˈmeɪʃn/ Information
p. 118, 7

ingredient /ɪnˈɡriːdiənt/ Zutat
p. 13, 7

injury /ˈɪndʒəri/ Verletzung p. 46, 5

inside /ˈɪnˌsaɪd/ innerhalb NHG 5;
innen; drinnen; hinein NHG 6

inside /ˈɪnˌsaɪd/ in ... hinein p. 109, 7

inspiration /ˌɪnspəˈreɪʃn/ Inspiration;
Idee p. 57, 3

(to) inspire /ɪnˈspaɪə/ inspirieren
p. 127

inspired /ɪnˈspaɪəd/ inspiriert p. 127

instruction /ɪnˈstrʌkʃn/ Anweisung;
Instruktion NHG 6

interest /ˈɪntrəst/ Interesse p. 78

interested /ˈɪntrəstɪd/ interessiert
NHG 6

(to) be interested in (irr)
/ˌbi_ˈɪntrəstɪd_ɪn/ interessiert sein
an p. 61, 8

interesting /ˈɪntrəstɪŋ/ interessant
NHG 5

(to) interrupt /ˌɪntəˈrʌpt/ unterbrechen p. 101

(to) interview /ˈɪntəˌvjuː/ inter-
viewen, befragen NHG 5

into /ˈɪntuː/ in NHG 5

(to) introduce /ˌɪntrəˈdjuːs/ ein-
führen; vorstellen NHG 5

introduction /ˌɪntrəˈdʌkʃn/ Ein-
leitung NHG 5

(to) invent /ɪnˈvent/ erfinden NHG 6

invented /ɪnˈventɪd/ erfunden
p. 15, 12

invention /ɪnˈvenʃn/ Erfindung NHG 6

inventor /ɪnˈventə/ Erfinder/in p. 103

invitation /ˌɪnvɪˈteɪʃn/ Einladung
NHG 5

(to) invite /ɪnˈvaɪt/ einladen NHG 5

Ireland /ˈaɪələnd/ Irland NHG 6

island /ˈaɪlənd/ Insel p. 78

issue /ˈɪʃuː/ Frage; Thema p. 31

it /ɪt/ es NHG 5

it's (= it is) /ɪts, ˈɪt_ɪz/ hier: es
kostet NHG 5

Italian /ɪˈtæljən/ Italiener/in;
italienisch p. 18, 1

Italy /ˈɪtəli/ Italien NHG 5

item /ˈaɪtəm/ Gegenstand p. 55

its /ɪts/ sein(e), ihr(e) (sächlich)
NHG 5

itself /ɪtˈself/ selbst, sich selbst
p. 70, 6

J

jacket /ˈdʒækɪt/ Jacke NHG 6

(to) jangle /ˈdʒæŋɡl/ klirren,
klimpern p. 77

January /ˈdʒænjuəri/ Januar NHG 5

Japanese /ˌdʒæpəˈniːz/ Japaner/in;
japanisch p. 127

jar /dʒɑː/ (Glas)gefäß p. 12, 7

javelin /ˈdʒævlɪn/ Speerwerfen
p. 52

jewellery (no pl) /ˈdʒuːəlri/
Schmuck NHG 6

Jewish /ˈdʒuːɪʃ/ jüdisch NHG 6

(to) jingle /ˈdʒɪŋɡl/ klingeln,
bimmeln p. 77

job /dʒɒb/ Aufgabe; Beruf NHG 6

(to) join /dʒɔɪn/ mitmachen (bei)
NHG 5; sich zu jemandem
gesellen; Mitglied werden p. 85, 7

(to) join in /ˌdʒɔɪn_ˈɪn/ sich beteili-
gen an; mitmachen bei NHG 6

(to) joke around /ˌdʒəʊk_əˈraʊnd/
herumalbern p. 95, 6

journey /ˈdʒɜːni/ Reise; Fahrt NHG 6

(to) judge /dʒʌdʒ/ urteilen;
beurteilen p. 94, 6

juice /dʒuːs/ Saft NHG 5

juicy /ˈdʒuːsi/ saftig p. 19, 2

July /dʒʊˈlaɪ/ Juli NHG 5

(to) jump /dʒʌmp/ springen NHG 5

jump /dʒʌmp/ Sprung p. 52

June /dʒuːn/ Juni NHG 5

just /dʒʌst/ nur; bloß NHG 5;
einfach; wirklich; gerade NHG 6

K

(to) keep (irr) /kiːp/ halten;
behalten; aufbewahren NHG 5

(to) keep a diary (irr) /ˌkiːp_ə ˈdaɪəri/
Tagebuch führen p. 95, 6

(to) keep an eye on (irr)
/ˌkiːp_ən_ˈaɪ_ɒn/ im Auge behalten
p. 126

(to) keep doing something (irr)
/ˌkiːp ˈduːɪŋ sʌmθɪŋ/ etwas weiter
tun p. 33, 2

(to) keep fit (irr) /ˌkiːp ˈfɪt/ fit
bleiben, (sich) fit halten p. 31

(to) keep from (irr) /ˈkiːp frɒm/ hier:
abhalten, verhindern p. 109, 7

(to) keep in touch (irr) /ˌkiːp_ɪn
ˈtʌtʃ/ Kontakt halten; in Verbindung bleiben p. 85, 7

(to) keep up (irr) /ˌkiːp_ˈʌp/ hier:
hochlegen p. 46, 5

kg (= kilogram) /ˈkɪləˌɡræm/ Kilo-
gramm NHG 6

(to) kick /kɪk/ treten NHG 5

kid /kɪd/ Kind NHG 5

(to) kill /kɪl/ töten p. 14, 10

(to) get killed (irr) /ˌɡet ˈkɪld/ umge-
bracht werden p. 76

kind /kaɪnd/ Art; Sorte NHG 5

kindly /ˈkaɪndli/ freundlich p. 78

all kinds of /ˌɔːl ˈkaɪndz_əv/ alle
möglichen NHG 6

king /kɪŋ/ König NHG 6

kingdom /ˈkɪŋdəm/ Königreich p. 78

kingfisher /ˈkɪŋˌfɪʃə/ Eisvogel p. 127

kitchen /ˈkɪtʃən/ Küche NHG 5

kitchen sink /ˌkɪtʃən ˈsɪŋk/ Spüle
p. 29

km (= kilometre) /ˈkɪləˌmiːtə/ Kilometer p. 56, 2

km/h (= kilometres per hour) /ˌkeɪ_em_ˈeɪtʃ/ Kilometer pro Stunde p. 127

knee /niː/ Knie NHG 6

knee pad /ˈniː ˌpæd/ Knieschützer p. 39, 10

knife *(pl* **knives)** /naɪf, naɪvz/ Messer NHG 5

knight /naɪt/ Ritter p. 15, 11

(to) **knock** /nɒk/ klopfen NHG 6

(to) knock over /ˌnɒk_ˈəʊvə/ umstoßen p. 52

(to) **know** *(irr)* /nəʊ/ wissen; kennen NHG 5

I don't know. /ˌaɪ ˌdəʊnt ˈnəʊ/ Ich weiß es nicht. NHG 5

Korean /kəˈriːən/ Koreaner/in; koreanisch p. 80, 2

korma /ˈkɔːmə/ *indisches Gericht* p. 19, 2

L

lab /læb/ Labor p. 109, 7

label /ˈleɪbl/ Etikett p. 89, 13

(to) **label** /ˈleɪbl/ beschriften NHG 5

lad *(informal, Scottish)* /læd/ Junge p. 71, 6

lady /ˈleɪdi/ Frau; Dame p. 25, 11

Lahmacun /ˌlaməˈdʒuːn/ *traditionelles türkisches Gericht* p. 8, 2

lake /leɪk/ See NHG 5

lamb /læm/ Lamm p. 8, 2

lame /leɪm/ lahm p. 91, 2

lamp /læmp/ Lampe p. 60, 8

(to) **land** /lænd/ landen p. 71, 6

lane /leɪn/ Gasse; enge Straße P&P 4

language /ˈlæŋgwɪdʒ/ Sprache NHG 5

lantern /ˈlæntən/ Laterne NHG 6

large /lɑːdʒ/ groß NHG 6

lass *(informal, Scottish)* /læs/ Mädchen p. 71, 6

lassi /ˈlæsi/ *Joghurtgetränk* p. 23, 7

(to) **last** /lɑːst/ (an)dauern NHG 6

last /lɑːst/ letzte(r, s) NHG 5

last /lɑːst/ als Letzte(r, s) p. 53

late /leɪt/ (zu) spät NHG 5

(to) **stay up (late)** /ˌsteɪ_ˌʌp ˈleɪt/ lange aufbleiben p. 98, 13

later /ˈleɪtə/ später NHG 5

latest /ˈleɪtɪst/ neueste(r, s) p. 86, 8

(to) **laugh** /lɑːf/ lachen NHG 6

lazy /ˈleɪzi/ faul NHG 6

lead /liːd/ Leine NHG 6

leader /ˈliːdə/ Leiter/in NHG 6

leaf *(pl* **leaves)** /liːf, liːvz/ Blatt NHG 6

leaflet /ˈliːflət/ Prospekt; Broschüre p. 41, 13

(to) **learn** *(irr)* /lɜːn/ lernen NHG 6

least /liːst/ am wenigsten p. 67, 2

leather /ˈleðə/ Leder p. 28

(to) **leave** *(irr)* /liːv/ weggehen NHG 5; verlassen, abfahren; (übrig) lassen; zurücklassen; hinterlassen NHG 6

(to) leave behind *(irr)* /ˌliːv bɪˈhaɪnd/ zurücklassen p. 102

Lebanese /ˌlebəˈniːz/ Libanese / Libanesin; libanesisch p. 18, 1

Lebanon /ˈlebənən/ der Libanon p. 8, 2

left /left/ links, nach links NHG 6; übrig p. 12, 7

on the left /ˌɒn ðə ˈleft/ links, auf der linken Seite NHG 5

(to) be left out *(irr)* /ˌbiː ˌleft_ˈaʊt/ ausgeschlossen werden p. 94, 6

(to) have something left *(irr)* /ˌhæv sʌmθɪŋ ˈleft/ etwas übrig haben p. 57, 3

leg /leg/ Bein NHG 6

legend /ˈledʒnd/ Legende p. 78

lemon /ˈlemən/ Zitrone NHG 5

lemonade /ˌleməˈneɪd/ Limonade p. 23, 7

less /les/ weniger NHG 6

lesson /ˈlesn/ Stunde; Unterricht NHG 5

(to) **let** *(irr)* /let/ lassen NHG 5

(to) let in *(irr)* /ˌlet_ˈɪn/ hereinlassen p. 28

let's (= let us) /lets, ˈlet_əs/ lass(t) uns NHG 5

letter /ˈletə/ Buchstabe NHG 5; Brief NHG 6

level /ˈlevl/ Stufe; Level NHG 5

library /ˈlaɪbrəri/ Bücherei NHG 5

(to) lick /lɪk/ (ab)lecken p. 29

life *(pl* **lives)** /laɪf, laɪvz/ Leben NHG 5

lifestyle /ˈlaɪfstaɪl/ Lebensstil p. 31

(to) **lift** /lɪft/ (hoch)heben p. 71, 6

light /laɪt/ Licht NHG 5

(to) **light** *(irr)* /laɪt/ anzünden NHG 6

like /laɪk/ wie; mögen NHG 5

I would like ... (= I'd like ...) /aɪ ˌwʊd ˈlaɪk, aɪd ˈlaɪk/ Ich würde gern ... / Ich hätte gern ... NHG 5

(to) **like best** /ˌlaɪk ˈbest/ am liebsten mögen NHG 5

(to) **like doing something** /laɪk ˈduːɪŋ ˌsʌmθɪŋ/ etwas gern tun NHG 6

like that /ˌlaɪk ˈðæt/ so p. 39, 10

limited /ˈlɪmɪtɪd/ begrenzt p. 136

line /laɪn/ Linie; Zeile NHG 5

linking part /ˈlɪŋkɪŋ pɑːt/ Verbindungsteil p. 98, 13

linking word /ˈlɪŋkɪŋ wɜːd/ Verbindungswort p. 98, 13

The Lion King /ðə ˈlaɪən ˌkɪŋ/ *Musical: Der König der Löwen* p. 56, 2

list /lɪst/ Liste NHG 5

(to) **list** /lɪst/ auflisten NHG 5

(to) **listen (to)** /ˈlɪsn/ zuhören, anhören NHG 5

listening /ˈlɪsnɪŋ/ Hören p. 11, 6

literally /ˈlɪtrəli/ buchstäblich, wirklich p. 67, 2

literature /ˈlɪtrətʃə/ Literatur p. 100

little /ˈlɪtl/ klein NHG 5

little /ˈlɪtl/ wenig p. 54

a little /ə ˈlɪtl/ ein bisschen NHG 6

(to) **live** /lɪv/ leben; wohnen NHG 5

lively /ˈlaɪvli/ lebendig p. 81, 2

living /ˈlɪvɪŋ/ Lebensstil p. 31

living /ˈlɪvɪŋ/ lebend p. 76

living room /ˈlɪvɪŋ ˌruːm/ Wohnzimmer NHG 5

'll (= will) /l, wɪl/ werden NHG 6

(to) **load** /ləʊd/ laden NHG 5

load /ləʊd/ Ladung p. 29

loads of /ˈləʊdz_əv/ jede Menge p. 76

(to) **locate** /ləʊˈkeɪt/ lokalisieren, orten p. 54

locomotive /ˌləʊkəˈməʊtɪv/ Lokomotive p. 105, 2

log /lɒg/ Baumstamm p. 71, 6

logical thinking /ˌlɒdʒɪkl ˈθɪŋkɪŋ/ logisches Denken p. 33, 2

lonely /ˈləʊnli/ einsam NHG 6

long /lɒŋ/ lang NHG 5

long jump /ˈlɒŋ dʒʌmp/ Weitsprung p. 52

long-distance /ˌlɒŋ ˈdɪstəns/ Fern-
p. 105, 2

loo /luː/ Klo, WC p. 124

look /lʊk/ Aussehen; Look p. 72, 8

(to) **look** /lʊk/ aussehen NHG 5

(to) **have a look at** *(irr)*
/ˌhæv_ə ˈlʊk_ət/ sich ansehen NHG 6

(to) have a closer look *(irr)*
/hæv_ə ˌkləʊsə ˈlʊk/ sich etwas
genauer ansehen p. 105, 2

(to) **look after** /ˌlʊk_ˈɑːftə/ sich
kümmern um; aufpassen auf
NHG 5

(to) **look (at)** /ˈlʊk_ət/ (an)sehen,
(an)schauen NHG 5

(to) **look for** /ˈlʊk fə/ suchen nach
NHG 5

(to) **look forward to** /ˌlʊk
ˈfɔːwəd_tʊ/ sich freuen auf NHG 6

(to) look out for /ˌlʊk_ˈaʊt fə/ *hier:*
sich kümmern um p. 40, 12

(to) **look up** /ˌlʊk_ˈʌp/ hoch-
schauen; nachschlagen p. 35, 6

-looking /ˈlʊkɪŋ/ aussehend p. 28

(to) **lose** *(irr)* /luːz/ verlieren p. 32, 1

loser /ˈluːzə/ Verlierer/in p. 33, 2

lost /lɒst/ verloren p. 119, 7

(to) get lost *(irr)* /ˌget ˈlɒst/ verloren
gehen, sich verirren p. 124

a lot /ə ˈlɒt/ viel, sehr NHG 5

thanks a lot /ˌθæŋks_ə ˈlɒt/ vielen
Dank NHG 5

a lot (of) /ə ˈlɒt/ viel(e), jede
Menge NHG 5

lots of /ˈlɒts_əv/ viel(e) NHG 5

loud /laʊd/ laut NHG 5

love /lʌv/ viele Grüße; alles Liebe
(in Briefen) NHG 6

(to) **love** /lʌv/ lieben, sehr
mögen NHG 5

(to) **love doing something**
/lʌv ˈduːɪŋ ˌsʌmθɪŋ/ etwas sehr
gern tun NHG 5

lovely /ˈlʌvli/ schön p. 29

lover /ˈlʌvə/ Liebhaber/in p. 70, 6

low-tech /ˌləʊ ˈtek/ technisch
einfach p. 114, 2

lower /ˈləʊə/ niedriger p. 54

loyal /ˈlɔɪəl/ treu; loyal p. 78

Good luck! /ˌgʊd ˈlʌk/ Viel Glück!
p. 94, 6

(good) luck /lʌk/ Glück NHG 6

luckily /ˈlʌkɪli/ glücklicherweise p. 53

lunch /lʌntʃ/ Mittagessen NHG 5

lunch break /ˈlʌntʃ breɪk/ Mittags-
pause p. 53

lunchbox /ˈlʌntʃbɒks/ Frühstücks-
dose p. 111, 11

lychee /ˈlaɪtʃi/ Litschi p. 137

M

machine /məˈʃiːn/ Maschine;
Apparat NHG 6

made /meɪd/ hergestellt, gemacht
p. 23, 7

is made /ˌɪz ˈmeɪd/ wird gemacht
P&P 1

magazine /ˌmægəˈziːn/ Zeitschrift
p. 121, 12

main /meɪn/ Haupt- NHG 5

main (course) /ˈmeɪn kɔːs/ Hauptgericht p. 17, 17

main entrance /ˌmeɪn_ˈentrəns/
Haupteingang p. 125

mainly /ˈmeɪnli/ hauptsächlich P&P 3

(to) **make** *(irr)* /meɪk/ machen NHG 5

(to) **make friends (with)** *(irr)*
/ˌmeɪk ˈfrendz/ sich anfreunden
(mit) NHG 6

(to) make money *(irr)* /ˌmeɪk ˈmʌni/
Geld verdienen p. 165

(to) **make notes** *(irr)* /ˌmeɪk ˈnəʊts/
sich Notizen machen NHG 5

(to) **make somebody do
something** *(irr)* /meɪk ˌsʌmbədi ˈduː:
ˌsʌmθɪŋ/ jemanden dazu bringen,
etwas zu tun p. 37, 7

(to) **make sure** *(irr)* /ˌmeɪk ˈʃɔː/
darauf achten, dass ... NHG 6

(to) make sure *(irr)* /ˌmeɪk ˈʃɔː/ *hier:*
dafür sorgen, dass ... p. 94, 6; sich
versichern; achten auf p. 124

(to) **make up** *(irr)* /ˌmeɪk_ˈʌp/
erfinden, sich ausdenken NHG 6

man *(pl* **men)** /mæn, men/ Mann
NHG 5

(to) **manage** /ˈmænɪdʒ/ zurecht-
kommen, es schaffen p. 85, 7

many /ˈmeni/ viele NHG 5

map /mæp/ Karte NHG 5

March /mɑːtʃ/ März NHG 5

mark /mɑːk/ Note; Zensur NHG 6

(to) **mark** /mɑːk/ markieren,
kennzeichnen p. 50, 14

market /ˈmɑːkɪt/ Markt NHG 5

(to) **be married** *(irr)* /ˌbiː ˈmærɪd/
verheiratet sein NHG 6

(to) **get married** *(irr)* /ˌget ˈmærɪd/
heiraten p. 81, 2

(to) **marry** /ˈmæri/ heiraten p. 85, 7

martial arts *(pl)* /ˌmɑːʃl_ˈɑːts/
Kampfsport p. 32, 1

masala /məˈsaːlə/ *Gewürzmischung*
P&P 1

mashed potatoes *(pl)* /ˌmæʃt
pəˈteɪtəʊz/ Kartoffelbrei p. 8, 2

match /mætʃ/ Spiel NHG 5

(to) **match** /mætʃ/ passen zu NHG 6

(to) **match (with/to)** /mætʃ/ zuord-
nen NHG 5

maths *(informal)* /mæθ/ Mathe
(Schulfach) NHG 5

matter /ˈmætə/ Angelegenheit
p. 95, 6

What's the matter? /ˌwɒts_ðə
ˈmætə/ Was ist los? p. 42, 1

May /meɪ/ Mai NHG 5

may /meɪ/ können; dürfen NHG 6

maybe /ˈmeɪbi/ vielleicht NHG 5

me, to me /miː/ mir; mich; ich
NHG 5

meal /miːl/ Mahlzeit; Essen NHG 5

(to) **mean** *(irr)* /miːn/ meinen;
bedeuten NHG 6

meaning /ˈmiːnɪŋ/ Bedeutung p. 46, 5

meanwhile /ˈmiːnˌwaɪl/ inzwischen;
unterdessen p. 77

meat /miːt/ Fleisch p. 9, 2

mechanic /mɪˈkænɪk/ Mechani-
ker/in NHG 6

mechanical engineering
/mɪˌkænɪkl_endʒɪˈnɪərɪŋ/ Maschi-
nenbau *(Studienfach)* p. 124

the media /ðə ˈmiːdiə/ die Medien
p. 14, 9

mediation /ˌmiːdiˈeɪʃn/ Sprachmittlung; Mediation p. 15, 12

medical /ˈmedɪkl/ medizinisch
p. 51, 16

medicine /ˈmedsn/ Medizin;
Medikamente p. 43, 1

medieval /ˌmediˈiːvl/ mittelalterlich
p. 76

medium /'mi:diəm/ mittel(groß)
p. 17, 17

(to) **meet** *(irr)* /mi:t/ treffen; sich
treffen NHG 5; kennenlernen NHG 6

Nice to meet you. /ˌnaɪs tə ˈmi:t jə/
Schön, dich / euch / Sie zu
treffen. NHG 5

meeting /'mi:tɪŋ/ Versammlung;
Treffen NHG 6

meeting point /'mi:tɪŋ pɔɪnt/ Treff-
punkt p. 125

melting pot /'meltɪŋ pɒt/ Schmelz-
tiegel P&P 4

member /'membə/ Mitglied NHG 5

memory /'memri/ Erinnerung p. 80, 2

mental /'mentl/ geistig, mental
p. 36, 7

(to) **mention** /'menʃn/ erwähnen
p. 57, 3

menu /'menju:/ Speisekarte; Menü
NHG 5

mess /mes/ Unordnung p. 29

message /'mesɪdʒ/ Nachricht;
Botschaft NHG 5

(to) message /'mesɪdʒ/ eine
Nachricht schicken p. 119, 7

method /'meθəd/ Methode p. 117, 6

metre /'mi:tə/ Meter NHG 6

middle /'mɪdl/ Mitte NHG 5

the Middle Ages *(pl)* /ðə
ˌmɪdl ˈeɪdʒɪz/ Mittelalter p. 77

might /maɪt/ könnte(st, n, t) NHG 6

mile /maɪl/ Meile NHG 6

milk /mɪlk/ Milch NHG 5

milkshake /'mɪlkˌʃeɪk/ Milchshake
p. 52

mill /mɪl/ Mühle p. 125

(to) mime /maɪm/ mimen, pantomi-
misch darstellen p. 49, 11

minced meat /ˌmɪnst ˈmi:t/ Hack-
fleisch p. 8, 2

mind /maɪnd/ Geist; Verstand p. 36, 7

(to) **change one's mind**
/ˌtʃeɪndʒ wʌnz ˈmaɪnd/ seine
Meinung ändern NHG 6

mine /maɪn/ meine(r, s) p. 18, 2

mineral water /'mɪnrəl ˌwɔ:tə/
Mineralwasser p. 23, 7

mischief /'mɪstʃɪf/ Unfug p. 76

(to) **miss** /mɪs/ vermissen;
verpassen NHG 5

missing /'mɪsɪŋ/ fehlend NHG 5

(to) be missing *(irr)* /ˌbi: ˈmɪsɪŋ/
fehlen p. 124

mistake /mɪˈsteɪk/ Fehler p. 13, 7

mix /mɪks/ Mischung P&P 1

(to) **mix** /mɪks/ sich (ver)mischen
NHG 6

(to) mix in /ˌmɪks ˈɪn/ untermischen
p. 17, 17

mixed /mɪkst/ gemischt p. 23, 7

mixture /'mɪkstʃə/ Mischung p. 81, 2

mobile (phone) /'məʊbaɪl/ Handy
NHG 6

modal verb /'məʊdl vɜ:b/ Modalverb
p. 47, 6

model /'mɒdl/ Modell NHG 6

modified /'mɒdɪfaɪd/ verändert,
modifiziert p. 54

Monday /'mʌndeɪ/ Montag NHG 5

(on) Mondays /'mʌndeɪz/ montags
NHG 5

money /'mʌni/ Geld NHG 5

pocket money /'pɒkɪt ˌmʌni/
Taschengeld p. 57, 3

(to) be good value for money *(irr)*
/ˌbi: gʊd ˌvælju: fə ˈmʌni/ sein Geld
wert sein p. 19, 2

(to) make money *(irr)* /ˌmeɪk ˈmʌni/
Geld verdienen p. 165

month /mʌnθ/ Monat NHG 5

mood /mu:d/ Laune; Stimmung
NHG 6

moon /mu:n/ Mond NHG 5

more /mɔ:/ mehr; weitere NHG 5

morning /'mɔ:nɪŋ/ Morgen NHG 5

Morocco /məˈrɒkəʊ/ Marokko p. 13, 7

mosque /mɒsk/ Moschee NHG 6

most /məʊst/ die meisten;
am meisten p. 105, 2

most of the time /ˌməʊst əv ðə
ˌtaɪm/ meistens p. 37, 7

mostly /'məʊstli/ meistens,
größtenteils p. 86, 8

mother /'mʌðə/ Mutter NHG 5

motorbike /'məʊtəˌbaɪk/ Motorrad
p. 28

mould /məʊld/ Schimmel p. 109, 7

mountain /'maʊntɪn/ Berg NHG 5

mountain biking /'maʊntɪn ˌbaɪkɪŋ/
Mountainbikefahren p. 80, 2

(to) mourn /mɔ:n/ trauern p. 119, 7

move /mu:v/ Bewegung NHG 5

(to) **move** /mu:v/ umziehen NHG 6;
(sich) bewegen p. 36, 7

on the move /ˌɒn ðə ˈmu:v/ unterwegs p. 102

(to) move out /ˌmu:v ˈaʊt/ ausszie-
hen p. 139

(to) **move something** /'mu:v
ˌsʌmθɪŋ/ etwas wegräumen, etwas
woanders hinstellen NHG 6

moving /'mu:vɪŋ/ beweglich NHG 6

Mr /'mɪstə/ Herr *(Anrede)* NHG 5

Mrs /'mɪsɪz/ Frau *(Anrede)* NHG 5

Ms /mɪz/ Fr. (= Frau) *(Anrede)* p. 53

much /mʌtʃ/ viel NHG 5; sehr p. 60, 8

mud /mʌd/ Schlamm p. 72, 8

muddy /'mʌdi/ matschig;
schlammig p. 70, 6

multicultural /ˌmʌltiˈkʌltʃərəl/
multikulturell p. 70, 6

mum /mʌm/ Mama; Mutti NHG 5

muscle /'mʌsl/ Muskel p. 104, 1

muscular /'mʌskjʊlə/ muskulös
p. 32, 1

mushroom /'mʌʃru:m/ Pilz p. 9, 2

music /'mju:zɪk/ Musik NHG 5

musician /mjʊˈzɪʃn/ Musiker/in
NHG 6

Muslim /'mʊzləm/ Muslim/in;
muslimisch NHG 6

must /mʌst/ müssen NHG 6

mustn't (= must not) /'mʌsnt,
mʌst ˈnɒt/ nicht dürfen NHG 6

my /maɪ/ mein(e) NHG 5

myself /maɪˈself/ mir/mich/ich
(selbst) p. 36, 7

myth /mɪθ/ Mythos p. 67, 2

mythical /'mɪθɪkl/ sagenumwoben
p. 78

N

naan bread /'nɑ:n bred/ *indisches
Fladenbrot* p. 19, 2

(to) **name** /neɪm/ (be)nennen
NHG 5

named /neɪmd/ namens p. 105, 2

national park /ˌnæʃnl ˈpɑ:k/
Nationalpark NHG 6

nature /'neɪtʃə/ Natur NHG 5

near /nɪə/ nahe, in der Nähe von
NHG 5

nearby /ˌnɪəˈbaɪ/ in der Nähe (gelegen) p. 18, 2

nearly /ˈnɪəli/ fast; beinahe p. 12, 7

necessary /ˈnesəsri/ notwendig, erforderlich NHG 5

(to) **need** /niːd/ brauchen NHG 5

(to) **need to** /ˈniːd ˌtʊ/ müssen NHG 5

No need to worry. /nəʊ ˈniːd ˌtə ˌwʌri/ Wir müssen uns keine Sorgen machen. p. 12, 7

negative /ˈnegətɪv/ negativ NHG 6

neighbour /ˈneɪbə/ Nachbar/in p. 98, 12

neighbourhood /ˈneɪbəˌhʊd/ Viertel; Nachbarschaft NHG 5

neither /ˈnaɪðə, ˈniːðə/ auch nicht p. 57, 3

nervous /ˈnɜːvəs/ nervös NHG 5

net /net/ Netz NHG 5

network /ˈnetˌwɜːk/ Netzwerk p. 117, 6

never /ˈnevə/ nie, niemals NHG 5

nevertheless /ˌnevəðəˈles/ trotzdem, dennoch p. 30

new /njuː/ neu NHG 5

New Year /ˌnjuː ˈjɪə/ Neujahr NHG 6

news *(no pl)* /njuːz/ Neuigkeit; Nachrichten p. 46, 5

newspaper /ˈnjuːzˌpeɪpə/ Zeitung NHG 6

next /nekst/ nächste(r, s) NHG 5; dann, als Nächstes NHG 6

next to /ˈnekstˌtə/ neben NHG 5

nice /naɪs/ schön; nett NHG 5

Nice to meet you. /ˌnaɪs tə ˈmiːt jə/ Schön, dich / euch / Sie zu treffen. NHG 5

night /naɪt/ Nacht; Abend NHG 6

no /nəʊ/ kein(e); nein NHG 5

no longer /ˌnəʊ ˈlɒŋgə/ nicht mehr p. 73, 9

no one /ˈnəʊ wʌn/ keiner NHG 6

nobody /ˈnəʊbədi/ niemand; keiner p. 57, 3

noise /nɔɪz/ Geräusch; Lärm NHG 6

noodle /ˈnuːdl/ Nudel p. 11, 6

normally /ˈnɔːmli/ normalerweise P&P 2

north /nɔːθ/ Norden; Nord- p. 19, 2

North Africa /ˌnɔːθ ˈæfrɪkə/ Nordafrika p. 9, 2

northern /ˈnɔːðən/ nördlich, Nord- NHG 6

nose /nəʊz/ Nase NHG 5

not /nɒt/ nicht NHG 5

not ... either /ˌnɒtˈˌaɪðə/ auch nicht p. 24, 8

not any /ˌnɒtˈeni/ kein(e) NHG 5

not anymore /ˌnɒtˌeni ˈmɔː/ nicht mehr NHG 6

not anyone /ˌnɒtˈeniwʌn/ niemand p. 70, 6

not anything /ˌnɒtˈeniˌθɪŋ/ nichts NHG 6

not anywhere /ˌnɒtˈeniˌweə/ nirgendwo NHG 6

not at all /ˌnɒtˌətˈˌɔːl/ überhaupt nicht p. 93, 5

not even /ˈnɒtˌiːvn/ nicht einmal p. 94, 6

not yet /nɒt ˈjet/ noch nicht NHG 6

note /nəʊt/ Nachricht; Notiz NHG 5

(to) **note** /nəʊt/ beachten, zur Kenntnis nehmen NHG 6

notepad /ˈnəʊtˌpæd/ Notizblock NHG 5

(to) **make notes** *(irr)* /ˌmeɪk ˈnəʊts/ sich Notizen machen NHG 5

nothing /ˈnʌθɪŋ/ nichts NHG 6

(to) **notice** /ˈnəʊtɪs/ bemerken; wahrnehmen NHG 6

noticeboard /ˈnəʊtɪsˌbɔːd/ Schwarzes Brett NHG 5

noun /naʊn/ Hauptwort; Substantiv; Nomen NHG 5

November /nəʊˈvembə/ November NHG 5

now /naʊ/ jetzt NHG 5

nowhere /ˈnəʊweə/ nirgends; nirgendwo p. 53

number /ˈnʌmbə/ Zahl; Nummer; Anzahl NHG 5

phone number /ˈfəʊn ˌnʌmbə/ Telefonnummer NHG 5

nurse /nɜːs/ Krankenschwester; Krankenpfleger NHG 6

O

o'clock /əˈklɒk/ Uhr *(bei Nennung einer Uhrzeit)* NHG 5

object /ˈɒbdʒekt/ Gegenstand NHG 6

obviously /ˈɒbviəsli/ offensichtlich p. 77

occasion /əˈkeɪʒn/ Gelegenheit; Anlass p. 21, 5

October /ɒkˈtəʊbə/ Oktober NHG 5

octopus /ˈɒktəpəs/ Tintenfisch p. 8, 2

odd /ɒd/ merkwürdig, seltsam p. 63, 12

odd one out /ˌɒd wʌnˈˌaʊt/ *Wort, das nicht zu den anderen passt* p. 16, 15

of /əv/ von; aus NHG 5

Of course! /əv ˈkɔːs/ Natürlich! NHG 5

off /ɒf/ von; hinunter, herunter NHG 6

offer /ˈɒfə/ Angebot p. 128

(to) **offer** /ˈɒfə/ anbieten NHG 6

office /ˈɒfɪs/ Büro NHG 5

office manager /ˈɒfɪs ˌmænɪdʒə/ Sekretär/in p. 97, 11

official, officially /əˈfɪʃl, əˈfɪʃli/ offiziell p. 94, 6

often /ˈɒfn/ oft; häufig NHG 5

oh dear *(informal)* /əʊ ˈdɪə/ oje p. 43, 1

oil /ɔɪl/ Öl p. 17, 17

old /əʊld/ alt NHG 5

the Olympic Games *(pl)* /ðiˌəˌlɪmpɪk ˈgeɪmz/ Olympische Spiele p. 54

the Olympics *(pl)* /ðiˌəˈlɪmpɪks/ Olympische Spiele p. 54

OMG! (= Oh my God!) /ˌəʊˌem ˈdʒiː/ Oh mein Gott! p. 26, 12

on /ɒn/ auf; an; in NHG 5

on /ɒn/ *hier:* über p. 124

on demand /ˌɒn dɪˈmɑːnd/ auf Anfrage p. 114, 2

on one's own /ˌɒn ˌwʌnzˈˌəʊn/ allein NHG 5

on the left /ˌɒn ðə ˈleft/ links, auf der linken Seite NHG 5

on the move /ˌɒn ðə ˈmuːv/ unterwegs p. 102

on the one hand, ... /ˌɒn ðə ˈwʌn hænd/ einerseits ... p. 69, 5

on the other hand, ... /ˌɒn ðiˈʌðə hænd/ andererseits ... p. 69, 5

on the right /ˌɒn ðə ˈraɪt/ rechts, auf der rechten Seite NHG 5

on time /ˌɒn ˈtaɪm/ pünktlich NHG 5

once /wʌns/ einmal p. 58, 5

once /wʌns/ früher p. 146

once again /ˌwʌns_əˈgen/ abermals p. 53

once more /ˌwʌns ˈmɔː/ noch einmal p. 119, 7

once upon a time /ˌwʌns_əˌpɒn_ə ˈtaɪm/ es war einmal p. 78

one /wʌn/ ein(e); eins NHG 5; eine(r, s) p. 64, 13

another one /əˈnʌðə wʌn/ noch ein/e; ein anderer / ein anderes / eine andere p. 64, 13

one-minute /ˌwʌnˈmɪnɪt/ einminütig p. 39, 9

onion /ˈʌnjən/ Zwiebel p. 8, 2

only /ˈəʊnli/ nur, bloß; erst; einzige(r, s) NHG 5

onto /ˈɒntə/ auf, in NHG 6

onwards /ˈɒnwədz/ von ... an p. 108, 7

(to) open /ˈəʊpən/ öffnen; aufmachen NHG 5; sich öffnen, aufgehen; eröffnen NHG 6

open /ˈəʊpən/ offen; geöffnet NHG 5

open-air /ˌəʊpənˈeə/ im Freien p. 70, 6

tin opener /ˈtɪnˌəʊpnə/ Dosen-öffner p. 109, 7

opening times (pl) /ˈəʊpənɪŋ taɪmz/ Öffnungszeiten NHG 6

operator /ˈɒpəˌreɪtə/ Telefonist/in p. 45, 4

opinion /əˈpɪnjən/ Meinung; Ansicht NHG 6

in my opinion /ɪn ˈmaɪ_əˌpɪnjən/ meiner Meinung nach NHG 6

opponent /əˈpəʊnənt/ Gegner/in p. 52

opposite /ˈɒpəzɪt/ Gegenteil NHG 5

option /ˈɒpʃn/ Wahlmöglichkeit p. 9, 2

or /ɔː/ oder NHG 5

orange /ˈɒrɪndʒ/ Orange; Apfelsine; orange NHG 5

order /ˈɔːdə/ Reihenfolge; Ordnung NHG 6

order /ˈɔːdə/ Bestellung p. 22, 6; Befehl p. 125

in order to /ɪnˈɔːdə tʊ/ um zu p. 33, 2

(to) take an order (irr) /ˌteɪk_ən_ˈɔːdə/ eine Bestellung aufnehmen p. 22, 6

(to) order (in) /ˈɔːdə, ˌɔːdərˈɪn/ bestellen p. 8, 2

(to) organize (= organise) /ˈɔːgənaɪz/ organisieren NHG 6

organizer /ˈɔːgəˌnaɪzə/ Organisa-tor/in p. 70, 6

original, originally /əˈrɪdʒnəl, əˈrɪdʒnəli/ ursprünglich p. 6

other /ˈʌðə/ andere(r, s) NHG 5

the other day /ðiˌʌðə ˈdeɪ/ neulich; vor einigen Tagen p. 94, 6

otherwise /ˈʌðəˌwaɪz/ sonst, im Übrigen p. 33, 2

our /aʊə/ unser(e) NHG 5

ours /ˈaʊəz/ unsere(r, s) p. 98, 12

ourselves /aʊəˈselvz/ uns; wir selbst p. 36, 7

by ourselves /ˌbaɪ aʊəˈselvz/ (wir) selbst p. 125

out /aʊt/ heraus, hinaus; aus NHG 5; draußen NHG 6

out and about /ˌaʊt_ən_əˈbaʊt/ unterwegs p. 63, 12

out of /ˈaʊt_əv/ aus NHG 6

out of breath /ˌaʊt_əv ˈbreθ/ außer Atem p. 77

outdoor /ˌaʊtˈdɔː/ Outdoor-, im Freien p. 33, 2

outdoors /ˌaʊtˈdɔːz/ draußen; im Freien p. 32, 1

outside /ˌaʊtˈsaɪd/ außen; (nach) draußen NHG 5

oven /ˈʌvn/ Ofen P&P 1

over /ˈəʊvə/ über, hinüber; vorbei NHG 5

over there /ˌəʊvə ˈðeə/ dort (drüben) NHG 5

all over the world /ˌɔːlˌəʊvə ðə ˈwɜːld/ auf der ganzen Welt NHG 6

overcooked /ˌəʊvəˈkʊkt/ verkocht p. 19, 2

ow (= ouch) (informal) /aʊ, aʊtʃ/ aua, autsch p. 42, 1

own /əʊn/ eigene(r, s) NHG 5

(to) own /əʊn/ besitzen p. 63, 12

on one's own /ˌɒn ˌwʌnzˈəʊn/ allein NHG 5

owner /ˈəʊnə/ Besitzer/in p. 112, 12

P

p. (= page) /peɪdʒ/ Seite p. 8, 1

p (= penny, pl pence) /piː, ˈpeni, pens/ Penny (britische Währung) NHG 5

(to) pack /pæk/ packen NHG 5

packaging /ˈpækɪdʒɪŋ/ Verpackung p. 73, 9

packed /pækt/ voll p. 129

packet /ˈpækɪt/ Packung NHG 5

page /peɪdʒ/ Seite NHG 5

pain /peɪn/ Schmerz p. 102

in pain /ˌɪn ˈpeɪn/ unter/mit Schmerzen p. 49, 10

painful /ˈpeɪnfl/ schmerzhaft p. 43, 1

painkiller /ˈpeɪnˌkɪlə/ Schmerzmittel p. 77

(to) paint /peɪnt/ (an)malen NHG 5

painting /ˈpeɪntɪŋ/ Bild; Gemälde NHG 5

pair /peə/ Paar NHG 6

(a pair of) trousers /əˌpeər_əv ˈtraʊzəz/ Hose NHG 5

palace /ˈpæləs/ Palast NHG 6

palak paneer /ˌpɑːlək pəˈnɪə/ indisches Gericht p. 23, 7

pan /pæn/ Pfanne p. 29

pancake /ˈpænˌkeɪk/ Pfannkuchen P&P 1

(to) panic /ˈpænɪk/ in Panik geraten p. 77

paper /ˈpeɪpə/ Papier NHG 6

paper /ˈpeɪpə/ hier: Klausur p. 101

paprika /ˈpæprɪkə/ Paprikapulver p. 13, 7

paragraph /ˈpærəˌgrɑːf/ Absatz; Abschnitt NHG 6

Paralympic /ˌpærəˈlɪmpɪk/ paralym-pisch p. 54

the Paralympic Games (pl) /ðə ˌpærəlɪmpɪkˈgeɪmz/ Paralympische Spiele p. 54

the Paralympics (pl) /ðə ˌpærəˈlɪmpɪks/ Olympische Spiele für Menschen mit Behinderungen p. 54

parent /ˈpeərənt/ Elternteil p. 94, 6

parents (pl) /ˈpeərənts/ Eltern NHG 5

(to) park /pɑːk/ parken p. 76

parliament /ˈpɑːləmənt/ Parlament NHG 6

part /pɑːt/ Teil NHG 5; Rolle p. 65, 15

particularly /pəˈtɪkjʊləli/ besonders;
vor allem p. 62, 10

(to) **pass** /pɑːs/ geben, herüber-
reichen NHG 5

passenger /ˈpæsɪndʒə/
Passagier/in p. 105, 2

passive /ˈpæsɪv/ Passiv p. 106

password /ˈpɑːsˌwɜːd/ Passwort
p. 121, 12

past /pɑːst/ nach; Vergangenheit
NHG 5; vorbei; vorüber NHG 6

past progressive /ˌpɑːst prəʊˈgresɪv/
Verlaufsform der Vergangenheit
p. 68

pasta /ˈpæstə/ Nudeln p. 12, 7

pastry /ˈpeɪstri/ Brandteig;
Blätterteig p. 23, 7

(to) **pat** /pæt/ einen Klaps geben
p. 39, 10

(to) **patent** /ˈpeɪtnt/ sich paten-
tieren lassen p. 105, 2

path /pɑːθ/ Weg; Pfad NHG 6

(to) **pay** *(irr)* /peɪ/ (be)zahlen NHG 5

(to) **pay attention (to)** *(irr)*
/ˌpeɪ əˈtenʃn tʊ/ aufpassen; achten
auf NHG 6

payment /ˈpeɪmənt/ Bezahlung NHG 6

PE (= Physical Education) /ˌpiːˈiː,
ˌfɪzɪkl_edjʊˈkeɪʃn/ Sport *(Schulfach)*
NHG 5

pea /piː/ Erbse p. 12, 7

peace /piːs/ Frieden p. 114, 2

peaceful /ˈpiːsfl/ friedlich;
friedfertig p. 67, 2

peanut butter /ˈpiːnʌt ˌbʌtə/ Erd-
nussbutter p. 52

peel /piːl/ Schale p. 29

(to) **peel** /piːl/ schälen p. 29

pen /pen/ Stift NHG 5

pencil /ˈpensl/ Bleistift NHG 5

pencil case /ˈpensl ˌkeɪs/ Feder-
mäppchen NHG 5

pencil sharpener /ˈpensl ˌʃɑːpnə/
Bleistiftspitzer NHG 5

people /ˈpiːpl/ Leute; Menschen
NHG 5

pepper /ˈpepə/ Paprika; Pfeffer p. 9, 2

per /pɜː/ pro NHG 5

perfect /ˈpɜːfɪkt/ perfekt NHG 5

(to) **perform** /pəˈfɔːm/ aufführen;
durchführen NHG 6

performance /pəˈfɔːməns/ Auffüh-
rung; Leistung NHG 6

perhaps /pəˈhæps/ vielleicht p. 54

permission /pəˈmɪʃn/ Erlaubnis;
Genehmigung NHG 6

personal /ˈpɜːsnəl/ persönlich NHG 5

pet /pet/ Haustier NHG 5

(Petri) dish /ˈpiːtri ˌdɪʃ/ Petrischale
p. 109, 7

phew *(informal)* /fjuː/ puh p. 46, 5

phone /fəʊn/ Telefon NHG 5

phone call /ˈfəʊn kɔːl/ Telefonanruf
p. 105, 2

phone number /ˈfəʊn ˌnʌmbə/
Telefonnummer NHG 5

photo /ˈfəʊtəʊ/ Foto NHG 5

(to) **take a photo** *(irr)* /ˌteɪk ə
ˈfəʊtəʊ/ ein Foto machen NHG 5

photograph /ˈfəʊtəˌgrɑːf/ Fotogra-
fie; Foto NHG 6

photographer /fəˈtɒgrəfə/ Foto-
graf/in NHG 6

phrase /freɪz/ Satz; Ausdruck NHG 5

phrase book /ˈfreɪz bʊk/ *Sammlung
von Redewendungen* p. 25, 10

physical /ˈfɪzɪkl/ körperlich p. 35, 6

piano /piˈænəʊ/ Klavier NHG 5

(to) **pick** /pɪk/ pflücken; sammeln
p. 125

(to) **pick up** /ˌpɪk_ˈʌp/ aufheben;
abholen NHG 5

pickpocket /ˈpɪkˌpɒkɪt/ Taschen-
dieb/in p. 69 5

picnic /ˈpɪknɪk/ Picknick p. 108, 6

picture /ˈpɪktʃə/ Bild NHG 5

(to) **take a picture** *(irr)* /ˌteɪk_ə
ˈpɪktʃə/ ein Foto machen NHG 5

pie /paɪ/ Pastete; Kuchen p. 28

piece /piːs/ Stück; Teil NHG 6

piece of advice /ˌpiːs_əv_ədˈvaɪs/
Rat(schlag) p. 94, 6

piece of art /ˌpiːs_əv_ˈɑːt/ Kunstwerk
p. 126

piece of information
/ˌpiːs_əv_ˌɪnfəˈmeɪʃn/ Information
p. 118, 7

pile /paɪl/ Stapel; Haufen p. 101

pinch (*pl* pinches) /pɪntʃ, ˈpɪntʃɪz/
Prise p. 16, 14

place /pleɪs/ Ort; Platz; Haus,
Zuhause NHG 5

(to) **place** /pleɪs/ platzieren; stellen
NHG 5

(to) **take place** *(irr)* /ˌteɪk ˈpleɪs/
stattfinden NHG 6

(to) **plan** /plæn/ planen NHG 5

plane /pleɪn/ Flugzeug NHG 6

(to) catch a plane *(irr)* /ˌkætʃ_ə
ˈpleɪn/ ein Flugzeug nehmen p. 102

planner /ˈplænə/ Kalender; Planer
p. 116, 5

plant /plɑːnt/ Pflanze NHG 6

plaster /ˈplɑːstə/ Gips; Pflaster
p. 43, 1

plastic /ˈplæstɪk/ Plastik NHG 6

plate /pleɪt/ Teller NHG 5

platform /ˈplætˌfɔːm/ Bahnsteig;
Plattform NHG 6

play /pleɪ/ Spiel; (Theater)stück
NHG 6

(to) **play** /pleɪ/ spielen NHG 5

player /ˈpleɪə/ Spieler/in NHG 5

playground /ˈpleɪˌgraʊnd/ Spiel-
platz NHG 5

playing /ˈpleɪɪŋ/ Spielen NHG 5

playing field /ˈpleɪɪŋ ˌfiːld/ Sportplatz p. 45, 4

please /pliːz/ bitte NHG 5

pleased /pliːzd/ erfreut; zufrieden
p. 53

pm (= post meridiem) /ˌpiːˈem,
ˌpəʊst məˈrɪdiəm/ nachmittags;
abends *(nur hinter Uhrzeit
zwischen 12 Uhr mittags und
Mitternacht)* NHG 5

pocket /ˈpɒkɪt/ (Hosen)tasche p. 69, 5

pocket money /ˈpɒkɪt ˌmʌni/
Taschengeld p. 57, 3

poem /ˈpəʊɪm/ Gedicht NHG 5

poet /ˈpəʊɪt/ Dichter/in p. 39, 10

point /pɔɪnt/ Punkt NHG 5

(to) **point (at/to)** /pɔɪnt/ deuten
(auf); zeigen (auf) NHG 5

Poland /ˈpəʊlənd/ Polen NHG 5

police /pəˈliːs/ Polizei p. 125

police officer /pəˈliːs_ˌɒfɪsə/
Polizeibeamter / Polizeibeamtin
NHG 6

Polish /ˈpəʊlɪʃ/ Polnisch; polnisch
p. 83, 5

polite /pəˈlaɪt/ höflich NHG 6

poor /pɔː/ arm NHG 6

poppadom /ˈpɒpədəm/ *dünnes indisches Brot* p. 23, 7
popular /ˈpɒpjələ/ beliebt NHG 6
population /ˌpɒpjʊˈleɪʃn/ Bevölkerung p. 83, 5
pork /pɔːk/ Schweinefleisch p. 8, 2
porridge /ˈpɒrɪdʒ/ Haferbrei p. 52
positive /ˈpɒzətɪv/ positiv NHG 6
possibility /ˌpɒsəˈbɪləti/ Möglichkeit NHG 6
possible /ˈpɒsəbl/ möglich p. 46, 5
(to) post /pəʊst/ posten; bekannt geben NHG 6
post office /ˈpəʊstˌɒfɪs/ Postamt p. 89, 13
postcard /ˈpəʊstˌkɑːd/ Postkarte; Ansichtskarte NHG 5
pot /pɒt/ Topf p. 12, 7
potato (pl potatoes) /pəˈteɪtəʊ, pəˈteɪtəʊz/ Kartoffel p. 8, 2
pound (= £) /paʊnd/ Pfund *(britische Währung)* NHG 5
Poutine /puːˈtiːn/ *traditionelles kanadisches Gericht* p. 9, 2
powder /ˈpaʊdə/ Pulver p. 30
power /ˈpaʊə/ Kraft p. 104, 1
practical /ˈpræktɪkl/ praktisch p. 108, 7
practice /ˈpræktɪs/ Übung; Training NHG 6; Praxis p. 42, 1
doctor's practice /ˈdɒktəz ˌpræktɪs/ Arztpraxis p. 46, 5
(to) practise /ˈpræktɪs/ üben; trainieren NHG 5
prayer /preə/ Gebet NHG 6
pre-owned by /priːˈəʊnd baɪ/ vormals Eigentum von p. 63, 12
(to) prefer /prɪˈfɜː/ vorziehen; bevorzugen p. 32, 1
(to) prepare /prɪˈpeə/ vorbereiten NHG 5; zubereiten p. 12, 7
(to) prepare for /prɪˈpeə fɔː/ sich vorbereiten auf p. 68, 3
(to) be prepared *(irr)* /ˌbi: prɪˈpeəd/ vorbereitet sein p. 122, 15
present /ˈpreznt/ Geschenk NHG 5; Gegenwart NHG 6
present perfect /ˌpreznt ˈpɜːfɪkt/ Perfekt p. 10
present progressive /ˌpreznt prəʊˈgresɪv/ *Verlaufsform der Gegenwart* p. 22, 6

(to) present (to) /prɪˈzent/ präsentieren, vorstellen NHG 5
presentation /ˌprezn̩ˈteɪʃn/ Präsentation; Vortrag NHG 5
(to) give a presentation *(irr)* /ˌgɪv ə ˌprezn̩ˈteɪʃn/ eine Präsentation halten p. 114, 2
pressure /ˈpreʃə/ Druck p. 73, 9
pretty /ˈprɪti/ ziemlich NHG 5
(to) prevent /prɪˈvent/ verhindern, vorbeugen p. 109, 7
price /praɪs/ Preis *(Kosten)* P&P 3
price tag /ˈpraɪs tæg/ Preisschild p. 60, 8
(to) print /prɪnt/ drucken p. 84, 6
printing press /ˈprɪntɪŋ pres/ Druckerpresse p. 118, 7
prize /praɪz/ Preis; Gewinn p. 35, 6
pro /prəʊ/ Vorteil; Pro NHG 6
probably /ˈprɒbəbli/ wahrscheinlich NHG 6
No problem. /ˌnəʊ ˈprɒbləm/ *hier:* Keine Ursache. p. 46, 5
process /ˈprəʊses/ Prozess; Verfahren P&P 5
(to) produce /prəˈdjuːs/ herstellen NHG 6; produzieren p. 73, 9
product /ˈprɒdʌkt/ Produkt p. 147
production /prəˈdʌkʃn/ Produktion P&P 5
profile /ˈprəʊfaɪl/ Profil; Porträt p. 33, 2
programme /ˈprəʊgræm/ Programm NHG 6
project /ˈprɒdʒekt/ Projekt NHG 6
(to) promise /ˈprɒmɪs/ versprechen p. 46, 5
(to) pronounce /prəˈnaʊns/ aussprechen NHG 6
prop /prɒp/ Requisite p. 27, 14
prop word /ˈprɒp wɜːd/ Stützwort p. 64, 13
properly /ˈprɒpəli/ richtig p. 47, 6
(to) protect /prəˈtekt/ beschützen NHG 6
proud(ly) /praʊd, ˈpraʊdli/ stolz NHG 6
(to) prove *(irr)* /pruːv/ beweisen p. 94, 6
pub /pʌb/ Kneipe p. 19, 2
public /ˈpʌblɪk/ öffentlich NHG 6

the public /ðə ˈpʌblɪk/ die Öffentlichkeit NHG 6
(to) publish /ˈpʌblɪʃ/ veröffentlichen; herausgeben NHG 6
(to) be published *(irr)* /ˌbi: ˈpʌblɪʃd/ veröffentlicht werden p. 30
pudding /ˈpʊdɪŋ/ Nachspeise P&P 1
(to) pull /pʊl/ ziehen p. 105, 2
pumpkin /ˈpʌmpkɪn/ Kürbis NHG 6
pupil /ˈpjuːpl/ Schüler/in p. 99, 15
purple /ˈpɜːpl/ violett; lila NHG 5
(to) push /pʊʃ/ schieben; stoßen NHG 6
(to) put *(irr)* /pʊt/ setzen; stellen; legen NHG 5
(to) put aside *(irr)* /ˌpʊt əˈsaɪd/ beiseitelegen p. 16, 14
(to) put down *(irr)* /ˌpʊt ˈdaʊn/ ablegen p. 29; eintragen p. 52
(to) put in *(irr)* /ˌpʊt ˈɪn/ hineintun, hinzufügen p. 12, 7
(to) put on *(irr)* /ˌpʊt ˈɒn/ anlegen; auftragen p. 46, 5; anziehen *(Kleidung)* p. 68, 3
(to) put on display *(irr)* /ˌpʊt ɒn dɪˈspleɪ/ ausstellen NHG 6
(to) put together *(irr)* /ˌpʊt təˈgeðə/ zusammenstellen; zusammensetzen NHG 6
(to) put up *(irr)* /ˌpʊt ˈʌp/ aufhängen; aufstellen NHG 6
puzzle /ˈpʌzl/ Rätsel p. 33, 2

Q

quality /ˈkwɒləti/ Qualität p. 18, 2
quantifier /ˈkwɒntɪˌfaɪə/ *hier:* Mengenangabe p. 16, 13
quarter /ˈkwɔːtə/ Viertel NHG 5
queen /kwiːn/ Königin NHG 6
question /ˈkwestʃn/ Frage NHG 5
queue /kjuː/ Schlange; Reihe p. 100
quick /kwɪk/ schnell, kurz p. 12, 7
quickly /ˈkwɪkli/ schnell NHG 6
quiet /ˈkwaɪət/ leise; ruhig NHG 5
quite /kwaɪt/ ziemlich NHG 6
quite a bit /ˌkwaɪt ə ˈbɪt/ ziemlich viel p. 95, 6
quotation /kwəʊˈteɪʃn/ Zitat p. 148
(to) quote /kwəʊt/ zitieren p. 81, 2

R

rabbit /ˈræbɪt/ Kaninchen NHG 5
race /reɪs/ Rennen P&P 2
(to) race /reɪs/ rennen p. 53
railway company /ˈreɪlweɪ ˌkʌmpni/ Eisenbahngesellschaft p. 106, 3
rain /reɪn/ Regen NHG 6
(to) **rain** /reɪn/ regnen NHG 5
raincoat /ˈreɪnˌkəʊt/ Regenmantel p. 112, 12
rainy /ˈreɪni/ regnerisch NHG 5
(to) raise /reɪz/ aufziehen, großziehen p. 78
(to) rank /ræŋk/ einstufen; anordnen p. 19, 2
(to) **rate** /reɪt/ einschätzen; bewerten p. 110, 8
rather /ˈrɑːðə/ eher, lieber NHG 6
rather than /ˈrɑːðə ðæn/ anstatt NHG 6
rating /ˈreɪtɪŋ/ Einschätzung; Einstufung p. 110, 8
raw /rɔː/ roh p. 21, 5
RE (= Religious Education) /ˌɑːrˈiː, reˌlɪdʒəsˌedjʊˈkeɪʃn/ Religion *(Schulfach)* NHG 5
(to) **reach** /riːtʃ/ erreichen p. 33, 2
(to) **react (to)** /riˈækt/ reagieren (auf) NHG 6
reaction /riˈækʃn/ Reaktion NHG 6
(to) **read (irr)** /riːd/ lesen NHG 5
(to) **read along (irr)** /ˌriːd əˈlɒŋ/ mitlesen NHG 5
(to) **read out (irr)** /ˌriːd ˈaʊt/ (laut) vorlesen p. 47, 5
reading /ˈriːdɪŋ/ Lesen NHG 5; Lesung p. 43, 1
ready /ˈredi/ fertig, bereit NHG 5
real /rɪəl/ wirklich; echt NHG 6
(to) **realize (= realise)** /ˈrɪəlaɪz/ sich bewusst sein, erkennen NHG 6
really /ˈrɪəli/ wirklich NHG 5
reason /ˈriːzn/ Grund NHG 6
for no reason /fə ˌnəʊ ˈriːzn/ ohne Grund, grundlos p. 14, 10
(to) give a reason *(irr)* /ˌɡɪv ə ˈriːzn/ einen Grund nennen p. 56, 2
(to) **rebuild (irr)** /ˌriːˈbɪld/ wieder aufbauen p. 108, 6
(to) **receive** /rɪˈsiːv/ erhalten; empfangen p. 127

receptionist /rɪˈsepʃnɪst/ Empfangsdame/Empfangschef p. 42, 1
receptionist's desk /rɪˈsepʃnɪsts desk/ Rezeption p. 46, 5
recipe /ˈresəpi/ Rezept p. 12, 7
(to) recognize (= recognise) /ˈrekəgnaɪz/ erkennen p. 78
(to) **recommend** /ˌrekəˈmend/ empfehlen NHG 6
recommendation /ˌrekəmenˈdeɪʃn/ Empfehlung p. 22, 6
record /ˈrekɔːd/ Rekord p. 53
(to) **record** /riˈkɔːd/ aufnehmen NHG 5
recording /rɪˈkɔːdɪŋ/ Aufnahme NHG 5
red /red/ rot NHG 5
(to) **reduce** /rɪˈdjuːs/ reduzieren p. 73, 9
(to) **refer to** /rɪˈfɜː tu/ hinweisen auf, gelten für P&P 1
(to) **register** /ˈredʒɪstə/ registrieren, anmelden p. 76
registration /ˌredʒɪˈstreɪʃn/ *Überprüfung der Anwesenheit* NHG 5
registration fee /ˌredʒɪˈstreɪʃn fiː/ Anmeldegebühr p. 56, 2
regular /ˈreɡjʊlə/ üblich, normal NHG 6
regularly /ˈreɡjʊləli/ regelmäßig p. 36, 7
relative /ˈrelətɪv/ Verwandte/r NHG 6
relative clause /ˌrelətɪv ˈklɔːz/ Relativsatz p. 58
relative pronoun /ˌrelətɪv ˈprəʊnaʊn/ Relativpronomen p. 58, 5
(to) **relax** /rɪˈlæks/ entspannen NHG 5
relaxed /rɪˈlækst/ entspannt NHG 6
relaxing /rɪˈlæksɪŋ/ entspannend p. 35, 6
relay /ˈriːleɪ/ Staffellauf p. 53
religious /rəˈlɪdʒəs/ religiöse(r, s) NHG 6
remarkable /rɪˈmɑːkəbl/ bemerkenswert; erstaunlich p. 53
(to) **remember** /rɪˈmembə/ sich erinnern an NHG 5
(to) **remove** /rɪˈmuːv/ entfernen NHG 6
(to) renovate /ˈrenəveɪt/ renovieren p. 108, 6
(to) **repair** /rɪˈpeə/ reparieren NHG 6

(to) **repeat** /rɪˈpiːt/ wiederholen NHG 5
(to) **reply** /rɪˈplaɪ/ antworten; erwidern NHG 6
(to) **report** /rɪˈpɔːt/ sich melden NHG 6
(to) report /rɪˈpɔːt/ berichten; melden p. 30
reported speech /ˌrɪ pɔːtɪd ˈspiːtʃ/ indirekte Rede p. 92
(to) **research** /rɪˈsɜːtʃ/ recherchieren p. 117, 6
(to) **do research (irr)** /ˌduː rɪˈsɜːtʃ/ recherchieren NHG 5
reservation /ˌrezəˈveɪʃn/ Reservierung p. 22, 6
resident /ˈrezɪdnt/ Bewohner/in p. 72, 8
respect /rɪˈspekt/ Respekt NHG 6
(to) **respect** /rɪˈspekt/ respektieren NHG 6
respectful /rɪˈspektfl/ respektvoll p. 121, 12
(to) **rest** /rest/ ausruhen p. 46, 5
result /rɪˈzʌlt/ Ergebnis p. 114, 2
(to) retire /rɪˈtaɪə/ in den Ruhestand treten p. 81, 2
(to) **return** /rɪˈtɜːn/ zurückgeben NHG 6
(to) **reuse** /riːˈjuːz/ wiederverwenden p. 73, 9
review /rɪˈvjuː/ Kritik; Rezension p. 18, 2
(to) **rewrite (irr)** /ˌriːˈraɪt/ überarbeiten, umschreiben p. 22, 6
rhyming word /ˈraɪmɪŋ wɜːd/ Reimwort p. 39, 10
rice /raɪs/ Reis NHG 5
rich /rɪtʃ/ reich p. 112, 12
(to) **get rid of (irr)** /ˌget ˈrɪd əv/ loswerden p. 61, 8
riddle /ˈrɪdl/ Rätsel p. 33, 2
(to) **ride (irr)** /raɪd/ fahren; reiten NHG 5
(to) **ride a bike (irr)** /ˌraɪd ə ˈbaɪk/ Fahrrad fahren NHG 5
(to) **ride a horse (irr)** /ˌraɪd ə ˈhɔːs/ reiten NHG 5
riding /ˈraɪdɪŋ/ Reiten p. 32, 1
(to) **go riding (irr)** /ˌgəʊ ˈraɪdɪŋ/ reiten gehen NHG 6

right /raɪt/ richtig NHG 5; rechts, nach rechts; genau; direkt NHG 6; Recht p. 94, 6

(to) **be right** *(irr)* /ˌbiː ˈraɪt/ recht haben NHG 5

on the right /ˌɒn ðə ˈraɪt/ rechts, auf der rechten Seite NHG 5

right now /ˌraɪt ˈnaʊ/ jetzt; im Moment p. 93, 5

rightful /ˈraɪtfl/ rechtmäßig p. 78

ripple /ˈrɪpl/ leichte Welle p. 127

rise /raɪz/ Aufstieg p. 119, 7

river /ˈrɪvə/ Fluss NHG 6

riverside /ˈrɪvəˌsaɪd/ Flussufer p. 80, 2

road /rəʊd/ Straße NHG 5

roast /rəʊst/ Braten; gebraten, geröstet p. 8, 2

robot /ˈrəʊbɒt/ Roboter p. 125

rock /rɒk/ Stein; Fels p. 118, 7

role /rəʊl/ Rolle NHG 6

role play /ˈrəʊl pleɪ/ Rollenspiel NHG 6

(to) **roll** /rəʊl/ rollen p. 39, 10

rolled /rəʊld/ gerollt p. 8, 2

Roman /ˈrəʊmən/ Römer/in; römisch NHG 6

Rome /rəʊm/ Rom p. 54

room /ruːm/ Platz; Raum; Zimmer NHG 5

waiting room /ˈweɪtɪŋ ˌruːm/ Wartezimmer p. 46, 5

root /ruːt/ Wurzel p. 79

round /raʊnd/ rund NHG 5; (um …) herum NHG 6

rowing /ˈrəʊɪŋ/ Rudern p. 32, 1

royal /ˈrɔɪəl/ königlich NHG 6

The Royal Air Force /ðə ˌrɔɪəl ˈeə fɔːs/ Königliche Luftwaffe p. 85, 7

rubbish /ˈrʌbɪʃ/ Müll NHG 5

rude /ruːd/ unhöflich; primitiv p. 98, 13

ruin /ˈruːɪn/ Ruine p. 78

rule /ruːl/ Regel NHG 5

(to) **rule** /ruːl/ herrschen, regieren NHG 6

ruler /ˈruːlə/ Lineal NHG 5

run /rʌn/ Lauf p. 56, 2

(to) **run** *(irr)* /rʌn/ laufen; rennen NHG 6; leiten, betreiben P&P 3

runner /ˈrʌnə/ Läufer/in NHG 6

running /ˈrʌnɪŋ/ laufend . 163

running race /ˈrʌnɪŋ reɪs/ Wettrennen p. 54

cross-country running /ˌkrɒs ˌkʌntri ˈrʌnɪŋ/ Geländelauf p. 32, 1

rural /ˈrʊərəl/ ländlich p. 142

(to) **rush** /rʌʃ/ eilen p. 78

S

sad /sæd/ traurig NHG 6

safe /seɪf/ sicher; ungefährlich NHG 6

safety /ˈseɪfti/ Sicherheit NHG 6

salad /ˈsæləd/ Salat p. 8, 2

salmon /ˈsæmən/ Lachs p. 22, 6

salt /sɔːlt/ Salz NHG 5

the same /ðə ˈseɪm/ der/die/das Gleiche; derselbe/dieselbe/dasselbe NHG 5

at the same time /æt ðə ˌseɪm ˈtaɪm/ gleichzeitig; zur gleichen Zeit p. 36, 7

samosa /səˈməʊsə/ *indische gefüllte Teigtasche* p. 23, 7

Saturday /ˈsætədeɪ/ Samstag NHG 5

(on) Saturdays /ˈsætədeɪz/ samstags NHG 5

sauce /sɔːs/ Soße p. 9, 2

sausage /ˈsɒsɪdʒ/ Wurst; Würstchen P&P 1

(to) **save** /seɪv/ aufheben; sichern p. 91, 2; sparen; retten p. 108, 7

savoury /ˈseɪvəri/ pikant; salzig p. 8, 2

(to) **say** *(irr)* /seɪ/ sagen NHG 5

saying /ˈseɪɪŋ/ Sprichwort p. 87, 9

(to) **scan** /skæn/ absuchen, überfliegen p. 33, 2

scared /skeəd/ verängstigt, ängstlich NHG 6

(to) be scared (of) /ˌbiː ˈskeəd əv/ Angst haben (vor) NHG 5

scary /ˈskeəri/ Furcht erregend NHG 6

scene /siːn/ Szene NHG 5

school /skuːl/ Schule NHG 5

school counsellor /ˌskuːl ˈkaʊnslə/ Vertrauenslehrer/in p. 96, 8

school grounds *(pl)* /ˈskuːl ˌɡraʊndz/ Schulgelände NHG 6

schoolbag /ˈskuːlˌbæɡ/ Schultasche NHG 5

science /ˈsaɪəns/ Naturwissenschaft NHG 5

the Science Museum /ðə ˈsaɪəns mjuːˌziːəm/ Naturwissenschaftsmuseum p. 81, 2

scientist /ˈsaɪəntɪst/ Wissenschaftler/in p. 105, 2

(a pair of) scissors /ˈsɪzəz/ Schere NHG 5

score /skɔː/ Punktestand p. 76

Scotland /ˈskɒtlənd/ Schottland NHG 5

scratch /skrætʃ/ Kratzer p. 109, 7

(to) **scream** /skriːm/ schreien p. 32, 1

screen /skriːn/ Bildschirm NHG 6

screen time /ˈskriːn taɪm/ Bildschirmzeit p. 95, 6

script /skrɪpt/ Drehbuch; Skript NHG 6

search /sɜːtʃ/ Suche NHG 5

(to) **search** /sɜːtʃ/ suchen NHG 5

search engine /ˈsɜːtʃ ˌendʒɪn/ Suchmaschine p. 117, 6

(to) **search the Internet** /ˌsɜːtʃ ði ˈɪntənet/ im Internet suchen NHG 5

seaside /ˈsiːˌsaɪd/ (Meeres)küste; Meer NHG 6

season /ˈsiːzn/ Saison p. 14, 10

seat /siːt/ Sitz p. 109, 7

(to) **take a seat** *(irr)* /ˌteɪk ə ˈsiːt/ sich setzen p. 22, 6

seat belt /ˈsiːt belt/ Sicherheitsgurt p. 109, 7

second /ˈsekənd/ Sekunde; zweite(r, s) NHG 5

the Second World War /ðə ˌsekənd ˌwɜːld ˈwɔː/ Zweiter Weltkrieg P&P 4

second-hand /ˌsekənd ˈhænd/ gebraucht p. 55

secret /ˈsiːkrət/ geheim p. 126

section /ˈsekʃn/ Teil, Stück, Abschnitt; Abteilung p. 107, 5

(to) **see** *(irr)* /siː/ sehen NHG 5; empfangen, drannehmen p. 42, 1

(to) **see a doctor** *(irr)* /ˌsiː ə ˈdɒktə/ einen Arzt/eine Ärztin aufsuchen p. 43, 1

See you (soon)! /ˌsi: ju: ˈsu:n/
Bis bald! NHG 6

seed /si:d/ Samen p. 127

(to) **seek** *(irr)* /si:k/ suchen, streben
nach p. 79

(to) **seek advice** *(irr)* /ˌsi:k‿ədˈvaɪs/
Rat suchen p. 94, 6

(to) **seem** /si:m/ scheinen p. 36, 7

selection /sɪˈlekʃn/ Auswahl p. 9, 2

self-esteem /ˌself‿ɪˈsti:m/ Selbst-
wertgefühl p. 36, 7

(to) **sell** *(irr)* /sel/ verkaufen p. 57, 3

seller /ˈselə/ Verkäufer/in p. 60, 8

(to) **send** *(irr)* /send/ schicken NHG 5

sentence /ˈsentəns/ Satz NHG 5

September /sepˈtembə/ September
NHG 5

series /ˈsɪəri:z/ Folge; Serie p. 35, 6

serious /ˈsɪəriəs/ ernst p. 70, 6

(to) **serve** /sɜ:v/ servieren;
reichen für p. 9, 2

session /ˈseʃn/ Stunde; Session
NHG 5

set /set/ *hier:* Einstellung p. 113, 15

(to) set a date /ˌset‿ə ˈdeɪt/ sich
verabreden p. 101

(to) **set the table** /ˌset ðə ˈteɪbl/ den
Tisch decken NHG 5

(to) **set up** *(irr)* /ˌset‿ˈʌp/ aufbauen
p. 74, 12

several /ˈsevrəl/ einige; verschiedene p. 62, 10

Shakshuka /ʃəkˈʃu:kə/ *traditionelles
israelisches und nordafrikani-
sches Gericht* p. 9, 2

shall /ʃæl/ sollen; werden p. 13, 7

(to) **be a shame** *(irr)* /ˌbi‿ə ˈʃeɪm/
schade sein p. 24, 8

(to) **share** /ʃeə/ teilen NHG 5

she /ʃi:/ sie NHG 5

sheet /ʃi:t/ Blatt; Bogen NHG 6

shelf *(pl shelves)* /ʃelf, ʃelvz/ Regal
NHG 5

(to) shine *(irr)* /ʃaɪn/ scheinen p. 52

ship /ʃɪp/ Schiff p. 102

shirt /ʃɜ:t/ Hemd NHG 5

shoe /ʃu:/ Schuh NHG 6

(to) **shoot** *(irr)* /ʃu:t/ schießen p. 39, 10

shop /ʃɒp/ Geschäft; Laden NHG 5

shop assistant /ˈʃɒp‿əˌsɪstnt/
Verkäufer/in NHG 6

shopkeeper /ˈʃɒpˌki:pə/ Laden-
inhaber/in p. 165

shopping /ˈʃɒpɪŋ/ Einkaufen;
Einkaufs- NHG 5

(to) **do the shopping** *(irr)*
/ˌdu: ðə ˈʃɒpɪŋ/ einkaufen NHG 5

(to) **go shopping** *(irr)* /ˌgəʊ ˈʃɒpɪŋ/
einkaufen gehen NHG 6

shopping centre /ˈʃɒpɪŋ ˌsentə/
Einkaufszentrum NHG 5

short /ʃɔ:t/ kurz NHG 5

should /ʃʊd/ sollte(st, n, t) NHG 6

shoulder /ˈʃəʊldə/ Schulter p. 42, 1

(to) shout /ʃaʊt/ rufen; schreien
p. 77

(to) **shout at somebody** /ˈʃaʊt‿ət
ˌsʌmbədi/ jemanden anschreien
NHG 6

(to) **show** *(irr)* /ʃəʊ/ zeigen NHG 5

(to) show somebody around *(irr)*
/ˌʃəʊ ˌsʌmbədi‿əˈraʊnd/ jemanden
herumführen p. 124

(to) show to the table *(irr)* /ˌʃəʊ tə
ðə ˈteɪbl/ zum Tisch führen p. 22, 6

(to) **shrink** *(irr)* /ʃrɪŋk/ schrumpfen
p. 111, 11

shy /ʃaɪ/ schüchtern p. 95, 6

sick /sɪk/ krank NHG 6

(to) be sick and tired of *(irr)* /ˌbi:
ˈsɪk‿ən ˌtaɪəd‿əv/ satthaben p. 28

side /saɪd/ Seite NHG 6

side (dish) /ˈsaɪd‿dɪʃ/ Beilage P&P 1

on the side /ˌɒn ðə ˈsaɪd/ als
Beilage p. 22, 6

sight /saɪt/ Sehenswürdigkeit NHG 5

sighted /ˈsaɪtɪd/ sehend p. 54

sign /saɪn/ Zeichen; Schild NHG 6

(to) **sign** /saɪn/ unterschreiben
p. 46, 5

(to) **sign up (for)** /ˌsaɪn‿ˈʌp/ sich
anmelden p. 115, 3

silly /ˈsɪli/ albern; dumm p. 91, 2

similar /ˈsɪmɪlə/ ähnlich NHG 6

simple /ˈsɪmpl/ einfach; simpel
p. 109, 7

simple past /ˌsɪmpl ˈpɑ:st/ *einfache
Vergangenheit* p. 82

simply /ˈsɪmpli/ einfach NHG 6

since /sɪns/ seit NHG 6

since /sɪns/ da; weil p. 52

(to) **sing** *(irr)* /sɪŋ/ singen NHG 5

(to) **sing along** *(irr)* /ˌsɪŋ‿əˈlɒŋ/ mit-
singen NHG 5

singer /ˈsɪŋə/ Sänger/in NHG 6

singing /ˈsɪŋɪŋ/ singend p. 59, 7

single /ˈsɪŋgl/ einzelne(r, s) NHG 6

single-use /ˌsɪŋgl ˈju:s/ Einweg-
p. 73, 9

kitchen sink /ˌkɪtʃən ˈsɪŋk/ Spüle
p. 29

sir/Sir /sɜ:/ Sir; Herr *(Anrede vor
Vornamen)* p. 22, 6

sister /ˈsɪstə/ Schwester NHG 5

(to) **sit** *(irr)* /sɪt/ sitzen p. 33, 2

(to) **sit down** *(irr)* /ˌsɪt‿ˈdaʊn/ sich
hinsetzen NHG 5

site /saɪt/ Stelle; Platz p. 73, 9

size /saɪz/ Größe NHG 5

skateboarding /ˈskeɪtbɔ:dɪŋ/ Skate-
boardfahren NHG 5

cleaning skates *(pl)* /ˈkli:nɪŋ ˌskeɪts/
Reinigungsskates p. 111, 11

sketch *(pl sketches)* /sketʃ, ˈsketʃɪz/
Skizze p. 72, 8

skewer /ˈskju:ə/ Spieß p. 23, 7

skill /skɪl/ Fähigkeit; Geschick p. 33, 2

skill /skɪl/ Fertigkeit; Kompetenz
p. 9, 2

(to) **skim** /skɪm/ überfliegen p. 18, 2

(to) **skip** /skɪp/ *hier:* ausfallen
lassen p. 91, 2

skirt /skɜ:t/ Rock NHG 5

slave /sleɪv/ Sklave/Sklavin p. 125

sleep /sli:p/ Schlaf p. 36, 7

(to) **sleep** *(irr)* /sli:p/ schlafen NHG 5

(to) sleep in *(irr)* /ˌsli:p‿ˈɪn/ aus-
schlafen p. 129

(to) **slice** /slaɪs/ in Scheiben
schneiden p. 13, 8

slide /slaɪd/ Folie p. 41, 13

slide show /ˈslaɪd ʃəʊ/ Bildschirm-
präsentation p. 41, 13

slow, slowly /sləʊ, ˈsləʊli/ langsam
NHG 6

small /smɔ:l/ klein NHG 5

smart /smɑ:t/ schlau, clever NHG 6

(to) **smile** /smaɪl/ lächeln NHG 6

so /səʊ/ also; deshalb; daher NHG 5

so far /ˌsəʊ fɑ:/ bisher NHG 6

so that /ˌsəʊ ðæt/ damit NHG 6

soap /səʊp/ Seife p. 77

soccer *(AE)* /ˈsɒkə/ Fußball p. 39, 10

social media /ˌsəʊʃl ˈmiːdiə/ soziale
Medien p. 97, 10

sock /sɒk/ Socke P&P 2

soft /sɒft/ weich p. 9, 2

solution /səˈluːʃn/ Lösung NHG 6

(to) **solve** /sɒlv/ lösen NHG 6

some /sʌm/ einige, ein paar; etwas
NHG 5

some day /ˈsʌmˌdeɪ/ eines Tages
p. 36, 7

somebody /ˈsʌmbədi/ jemand;
irgendwer NHG 6

someone /ˈsʌmwʌn/ jemand;
irgendwer NHG 5

something /ˈsʌmθɪŋ/ etwas NHG 5

sometimes /ˈsʌmtaɪmz/ manchmal
NHG 5

somewhere /ˈsʌmweə/ irgendwo
NHG 6

son /sʌn/ Sohn NHG 5

song /sɒŋ/ Lied NHG 5

soon /suːn/ bald p. 43, 1

See you (soon)! /ˌsiː juː ˈsuːn/ Bis
bald! NHG 6

coming soon /ˌkʌmɪŋ ˈsuːn/ in Kürze
erscheinend p. 67, 2

sore throat /ˌsɔː ˈθrəʊt/ Halsschmerzen p. 42, 1

sorry /ˈsɒri/ es tut mir leid,
Entschuldigung NHG 5

sort /sɔːt/ Sorte; Art NHG 6

(to) **sort** /sɔːt/ sortieren NHG 5

(to) **sound** /saʊnd/ klingen, sich
anhören NHG 5

sound /saʊnd/ Geräusch; Klang NHG 6

sound wave /ˈsaʊnd weɪv/ Schall-
welle p. 127

soup /suːp/ Suppe p. 20, 3

sour /ˈsaʊə/ sauer p. 137

source /sɔːs/ Quelle p. 117, 6

south /saʊθ/ Süden; Süd- p. 83, 5

South Asian /ˌsaʊθˈeɪʒn/ südasia-
tisch p. 30

South India /ˌsaʊθ ˈɪndiə/ Südindien
p. 30

south-west /ˌsaʊθˈwest/ Südwest-
p. 70, 6

soy /sɔɪ/ Soja p. 140

space /speɪs/ Raum; Platz NHG 6;
Weltall p. 107, 5

Spain /speɪn/ Spanien p. 80, 2

(to) **speak (irr)** /spiːk/ sprechen;
reden NHG 5

This is … speaking. /ðɪs ɪz …
ˈspiːkɪŋ/ Hier spricht … p. 42, 1

special /ˈspeʃl/ besondere(r, s);
besonders NHG 5

speciality /ˌspeʃiˈæləti/ Spezialität
p. 8, 2

species (pl species) /ˈspiːʃiːz/ Art;
Spezies NHG 6

spectacle /ˈspektəkl/ Spektakel
p. 71, 6

spectacular /spekˈtækjələ/ atemberaubend; spektakulär p. 67, 2

speech bubble /ˈspiːtʃ ˌbʌbl/
Sprechblase p. 87, 8

speedy /ˈspiːdi/ schnell p. 63, 12

(to) **spell (irr)** /spel/ buchstabieren
NHG 5

spelling /ˈspelɪŋ/ Buchstabieren;
Rechtschreibung NHG 6

(to) **spend (irr)** /spend/ verbringen
(Zeit); ausgeben *(Geld)* NHG 6

spice /spaɪs/ Gewürz p. 12, 7

spicy /ˈspaɪsi/ würzig; scharf p. 8, 2

spider /ˈspaɪdə/ Spinne p. 26, 12

(to) **spin (irr)** /spɪn/ drehen, einen
Drall geben p. 39, 10; spinnen p. 77

spinach /ˈspɪnɪdʒ/ Spinat p. 23, 7

Spinning Jenny /ˌspɪnɪŋ ˈdʒeni/ *Fein-
spinnmaschine* p. 125

spinning wheel /ˈspɪnɪŋ ˌwiːl/ Spinnrad p. 76

spirit /ˈspɪrɪt/ Geist; Stimmung p. 52

spoken /ˈspəʊkən/ gesprochen p. 30

spoon /spuːn/ Löffel NHG 5

sport /spɔːt/ Sport; Sportart NHG 5

sports day /ˈspɔːts deɪ/ *Sportfest*
P&P 2

sportsperson /ˈspɔːts ˌpɜːsn/ Sport-
ler/Sportlerin p. 162

sporty /ˈspɔːti/ sportlich p. 37, 7

spot on *(informal)* /ˌspɒt ˈɒn/ genau
richtig, goldrichtig p. 52

sprained /spreɪnd/ verstaucht p. 46, 5

spring /sprɪŋ/ Frühling NHG 6

spring roll /ˈsprɪŋ rəʊl/ Frühlings-
rolle p. 9, 2

stack /stæk/ Stapel p. 29

stage /steɪdʒ/ Bühne NHG 6

stair /steə/ Stufe NHG 6

stairs (pl) /steəz/ Treppe NHG 6

stall /stɔːl/ Stand p. 56, 2

(to) **stand (irr)** /stænd/ stehen NHG 6

(to) **stand for (irr)** /ˈstænd fɔː/
stehen für NHG 6

star /stɑː/ Stern NHG 5

(to) **stare at** /ˈsteər ət/ anstarren
p. 28

start /stɑːt/ Anfang; Beginn NHG 5

(to) **start** /stɑːt/ anfangen;
beginnen NHG 5

starter /ˈstɑːtə/ Vorspeise p. 17, 17

(to) **starve** /stɑːv/ verhungern p. 12, 7

(to) **state** /steɪt/ äußern, aussprechen p. 73, 9

statement /ˈsteɪtmənt/ Äußerung,
Aussage NHG 5

station /ˈsteɪʃn/ U-Bahn-Station;
Bahnhof NHG 5

station /ˈsteɪʃn/ *hier:* Station p. 125

(to) **stay** /steɪ/ bleiben; wohnen
NHG 5

(to) **stay away from** /ˌsteɪ əˈweɪ
frɒm/ meiden; sich fernhalten
von p. 18, 2

(to) stay off /ˌsteɪ ˈɒf/ wegbleiben,
sich fernhalten p. 54

(to) **stay up (late)** /ˌsteɪ ˌʌp ˈleɪt/
lange aufbleiben p. 98, 13

(to) **steal (irr)** /stiːl/ stehlen p. 69, 5

steam engine /ˈstiːm ˌendʒɪn/
Dampfmaschine p. 105, 7

steam locomotive /ˈstiːm
ˌləʊkəˌməʊtɪv/ Dampflokomotive;
Dampflok p. 104, 2

steam machine /ˈstiːm məˈʃiːn/
Dampfmaschine p. 126

steel drum /ˌstiːl ˈdrʌm/ *Steeldrum*
p. 70, 6

step /step/ Stufe; Schritt NHG 5

(to) **step** /step/ treten; steigen
NHG 6

(to) step back in time /ˌstep ˌbæk ˌɪn
ˈtaɪm/ sich in die Vergangenheit
zurückversetzen p. 66, 2

stick /stɪk/ Stock p. 127

(to) **stick (irr)** /stɪk/ festhängen p. 76

(to) **stick to (irr)** /ˈstɪk tʊ/ kleben;
hier: sich halten an p. 127

still /stɪl/ (immer) noch NHG 5; nach
wie vor, trotzdem p. 86, 8

still /stɪl/ still; bewegungslos p. 33, 2

(to) **stir in** /ˌstɜːrˈɪn/ einrühren; unterrühren p. 13, 8

vegetable stock /ˈvedʒtəbl stɒk/ Gemüsebrühe p. 13, 7

stomach /ˈstʌmək/ Magen; Bauch p. 43, 1

stomach ache *(no pl)* /ˈstʌməkˌeɪk/ Bauchschmerzen p. 43, 1

stone /stəʊn/ Stein p. 114, 2

(to) **stop** /stɒp/ stehen bleiben; anhalten NHG 5; aufhören NHG 6; stoppen p. 94, 6

(to) **store** /stɔː/ lagern p. 109, 7

story /ˈstɔːri/ Geschichte, Erzählung NHG 5

storytelling /ˈstɔːriˌtelɪŋ/ Geschichtenerzählen p. 84, 6

straight on /ˌstreɪtˈɒn/ geradeaus NHG 6

strange /streɪndʒ/ sonderbar; merkwürdig NHG 6

strap /stræp/ Riemen p. 109, 7

strategy /ˈstrætədʒi/ Strategie p. 35, 6

straw /strɔː/ Strohhalm p. 73, 9

strawberry /ˈstrɔːbri/ Erdbeere p. 16, 14

streamer /ˈstriːmə/ Wimpel; Fähnchen p. 52

street /striːt/ Straße NHG 5

strength /streŋθ/ Kraft; Stärke p. 32, 1

stress /stres/ Betonung NHG 6

(to) **stress** /stres/ stressen p. 36, 7

stressed /strest/ gestresst p. 36, 7

strict /strɪkt/ streng NHG 6

string /strɪŋ/ Schnur; Kordel NHG 6

strong /strɒŋ/ stark p. 32, 1

structure /ˈstrʌktʃə/ Struktur; Aufbau p. 123, 16

student /ˈstjuːdnt/ Schüler/in NHG 5; Student/in p. 66, 2

(to) **study** /ˈstʌdi/ studieren; lernen p. 82, 4

stuff *(informal)* /stʌf/ Zeug NHG 6

stuffed /stʌft/ ausgestopft p. 126

(to) **stumble** /ˈstʌmbl/ stolpern p. 77

stupid /ˈstjuːpɪd/ dumm, blöd NHG 6

(to) stutter /ˈstʌtə/ stottern p. 78

style /staɪl/ Stil NHG 6

(to) **style** /staɪl/ frisieren p. 68, 3

subject /ˈsʌbdʒɪkt/ Schulfach NHG 5; Thema; Betreff *(in Emails)* NHG 6

(to) **succeed** /səkˈsiːd/ Erfolg haben p. 78

success /səkˈses/ Erfolg p. 112, 12

successful /səkˈsesfl/ erfolgreich p. 36, 7

such /sʌtʃ/ so; solch p. 71, 6

such as /ˈsʌtʃˌæz/ wie p. 105, 2

suddenly /ˈsʌdnli/ plötzlich NHG 6

(to) **suffer** /ˈsʌfə/ leiden p. 78

sugar /ˈʃʊɡə/ Zucker NHG 6

(to) **suggest** /səˈdʒest/ vorschlagen NHG 6

suggestion /səˈdʒestʃn/ Vorschlag NHG 6

summary /ˈsʌməri/ Zusammenfassung p. 121, 13

summer /ˈsʌmə/ Sommer NHG 5

sun /sʌn/ Sonne NHG 5

Sunday /ˈsʌndeɪ/ Sonntag NHG 5

(on) Sundays /ˈsʌndeɪz/ sonntags NHG 5

sunny /ˈsʌni/ sonnig NHG 5

sunrise /ˈsʌnˌraɪz/ Sonnenaufgang p. 28

sunshine /ˈsʌnˌʃaɪn/ Sonnenschein NHG 5

superlative /suˈpɜːlətɪv/ Superlativ p. 20, 3

(to) **support** /səˈpɔːt/ stützen, unterstützen p. 81, 2

(to) **suppose** /səˈpəʊz/ annehmen, vermuten p. 94, 6

sure /ʃɔː/ sicher NHG 5

(to) **make sure** *(irr)* /ˌmeɪk ˈʃɔː/ darauf achten, dass … NHG 6

surprise /səˈpraɪz/ Überraschung p. 29

surprised /səˈpraɪzd/ überrascht; erstaunt NHG 6

surprising /səˈpraɪzɪŋ/ überraschend NHG 6

survey /ˈsɜːveɪ/ Umfrage P&P 4

(to) **sweat** /swet/ schwitzen p. 52

Sweden /ˈswiːdn/ Schweden p. 81, 2

Swedish /ˈswiːdɪʃ/ schwedisch p. 81, 2

sweet /swiːt/ süß NHG 5; Süßigkeit NHG 6

sweetcorn /ˈswiːtˌkɔːn/ Mais p. 23, 7

(to) **swim** *(irr)* /swɪm/ schwimmen NHG 5

swimming /ˈswɪmɪŋ/ Schwimmen NHG 5

(to) **go swimming** *(irr)* /ˌɡəʊ ˈswɪmɪŋ/ schwimmen gehen NHG 6

swimming pool /ˈswɪmɪŋ puːl/ Schwimmbad NHG 5

(to) **switch off** /ˌswɪtʃˈɒf/ ausschalten p. 41, 13

(to) **switch on** /ˌswɪtʃˈɒn/ einschalten NHG 5

swollen /ˈswəʊlən/ geschwollen p. 42, 1

sword /sɔːd/ Schwert p. 76

syllable /ˈsɪləbl/ Silbe p. 20, 4

synchronized swimming /ˌsɪŋkrənaɪzd ˈswɪmɪŋ/ Synchronschwimmen p. 32, 1

T

table /ˈteɪbl/ Tisch NHG 5; Tabelle NHG 6

(to) **set the table** /ˌset ðə ˈteɪbl/ den Tisch decken NHG 5

table tennis /ˈteɪbl ˌtenɪs/ Tischtennis NHG 5

tablespoon /ˈteɪblˌspuːn/ Esslöffel p. 17, 17

tablet /ˈtæblət/ Block; Platte p. 114, 2

tactic /ˈtæktɪk/ Taktik p. 35, 6

(to) **take** *(irr)* /teɪk/ nehmen; bringen; benötigen; brauchen NHG 5; dauern NHG 6

(to) take a hike *(AE, informal, irr)* /ˌteɪk ə ˈhaɪk/ abhauen p. 102

(to) **take a photo** *(irr)* /ˌteɪk ə ˈfəʊtəʊ/ ein Foto machen NHG 5

(to) **take a picture** *(irr)* /ˌteɪk ə ˈpɪktʃə/ ein Foto machen NHG 5

(to) **take a seat** *(irr)* /ˌteɪk ə ˈsiːt/ sich setzen p. 22, 6

(to) **take a turn** *(irr)* /ˌteɪk ə ˈtɜːn/ *hier:* es auch einmal versuchen p. 78

(to) take ages *(informal, irr)* /ˌteɪk ˈeɪdʒɪz/ ewig dauern p. 37, 7

(to) **take an order** *(irr)* /ˌteɪk ənˈɔːdə/ eine Bestellung aufnehmen p. 22, 6 (to) **take an X-ray** *(irr)* /ˌteɪk‿ən ˈeksreɪ/ eine Röntgenaufnahme machen p. 42, 1

(to) **take away** *(irr)* /ˌteɪk‿əˈweɪ/ wegnehmen; mitnehmen NHG 6

(to) **take care (of)** *(irr)* /ˌteɪk‿ˈkeər‿əv/ sich kümmern um NHG 6

(to) take in *(irr)* /ˌteɪk‿ˈɪn/ aufnehmen p. 78

(to) **take notes (on)** *(irr)* /ˌteɪk ˈnəʊts/ sich Notizen machen (zu) NHG 5

(to) **take out** *(irr)* /ˌteɪk‿ˈaʊt/ hinausbringen NHG 5; herausnehmen p. 43, 1

(to) **take over** *(irr)* /ˌteɪk‿ˈəʊvə/ übernehmen p. 81, 2

(to) **take part in** *(irr)* /ˌteɪk ˈpɑːt‿ɪn/ teilnehmen an NHG 6

(to) **take place** *(irr)* /ˌteɪk ˈpleɪs/ stattfinden NHG 6

(to) take things easy *(informal, irr)* /ˌteɪk θɪŋz‿ˈiːzi/ sich keinen Stress machen p. 33, 2

(to) **take turns** *(irr)* /ˌteɪk ˈtɜːnz/ sich abwechseln NHG 6

(to) **take up time** *(irr)* /ˌteɪk‿ʌp ˈtaɪm/ Zeit beanspruchen p. 133

takeaway /ˈteɪkəˌweɪ/ Essen zum Mitnehmen; Imbissbude p. 18, 1

talented /ˈtæləntɪd/ **talentiert** p. 125

talk /tɔːk/ Gespräch; Vortrag p. 39, 9

(to) **give a talk** *(irr)* /ˌɡɪv‿ə ˈtɔːk/ einen Vortrag halten p. 39, 9

(to) **talk about** /ˈtɔːk‿əˌbaʊt/ sprechen über NHG 5

(to) **talk (to)** /tɔːk/ sprechen (mit); reden (mit) NHG 5

tall /tɔːl/ groß NHG 6

target task /ˈtɑːɡɪt ˌtɑːsk/ Zielaufgabe p. 17, 17

task /tɑːsk/ Aufgabe NHG 5

taste /teɪst/ Geschmack p. 60, 8

(to) **taste** /teɪst/ schmecken NHG 6

tasty /ˈteɪsti/ lecker p. 19, 2

tea /tiː/ Tee NHG 5

(to) **teach** *(irr)* /tiːtʃ/ unterrichten NHG 5

teacher /ˈtiːtʃə/ Lehrer/in NHG 5

(to) **tease** /tiːz/ hänseln, ärgern p. 95, 6

teaspoon /ˈtiːˌspuːn/ Teelöffel p. 13, 7

technique /tekˈniːk/ Technik p. 52

technological /ˌteknəˈlɒdʒɪkl/ technologisch p. 114, 2

technology /tekˈnɒlədʒi/ Technologie; Technik NHG 6

teddy bear /ˈtedi beə/ Teddybär p. 69, 5

teen /tiːn/ Teenager p. 94, 6

(to) **brush one's teeth** /ˌbrʌʃ wʌnz ˈtiːθ/ sich die Zähne putzen NHG 5

telephone /ˈtelɪˌfəʊn/ Telefon NHG 6

telescope /ˈtelɪˌskəʊp/ Teleskop p. 106, 4

television /ˈtelɪˌvɪʒn/ Fernseher; Fernsehen p. 105, 2

(to) **tell** *(irr)* /tel/ erzählen NHG 5

(to) **tell the truth** *(irr)* /ˌtel ðə ˈtruːθ/ die Wahrheit sagen p. 85, 7

temp (= temperature) /ˈtemprɪtʃə/ Temperatur p. 113, 15

tender /ˈtendə/ zart p. 140

tent /tent/ Zelt p. 70, 6

term /tɜːm/ Trimester; Begriff NHG 5

terrible /ˈterəbl/ schrecklich NHG 5

(to) **text** /tekst/ eine Textnachricht schreiben NHG 5

text (message) /ˈtekst ˌmesɪdʒ/ Textnachricht NHG 5

Textiles Gallery /ˈtekstaɪlz ˌɡæləri/ *Bereich im Museum, in dem es um Stoffe geht* p. 125

Thai /taɪ/ Thailänder/in; thailändisch p. 18, 1

than /ðæn/ als *(bei Vergleich)* NHG 6

thank you /ˈθæŋk ju/ danke NHG 5

thanks /θæŋks/ danke NHG 5

thanks a lot /ˌθæŋks‿ə ˈlɒt/ vielen Dank NHG 5

that /ðæt/ das; der/die/das (dort); dass NHG 5; so NHG 6

that's (= that is) /ðæts, ˈðæt‿ɪz/ *hier:* das kostet NHG 5

the /ðə/ der/die/das NHG 5

theatre /ˈθɪətə/ Theater NHG 6

their /ðeə/ ihr(e) NHG 5

theirs /ðeəz/ ihre(r, s) p. 98, 12

them /ðem/ sie; ihnen NHG 5

theme /θiːm/ Thema NHG 6

themselves /ðəmˈselvz/ sich; selbst p. 126

then /ðen/ dann NHG 5

theory /ˈθɪəri/ Theorie p. 118, 7

there /ðeə/ dort; dahin NHG 5

there are /ðeər‿ˈɑː/ dort sind; es gibt NHG 5

there's (= there is) /ðeəz, ðeər‿ˈɪz/ dort ist, es gibt NHG 5

these *(pl of this)* /ðiːz/ diese; das NHG 5

they /ðeɪ/ sie NHG 5

thin /θɪn/ dünn p. 8, 2

thing /θɪŋ/ Ding; Gegenstand NHG 5

(to) take things easy *(informal, irr)* /ˌteɪk θɪŋz‿ˈiːzi/ sich keinen Stress machen p. 33, 2

(to) **think** *(irr)* /θɪŋk/ denken; glauben NHG 5

(to) **think about** *(irr)* /ˈθɪŋk‿əˌbaʊt/ denken an, nachdenken über NHG 5

(to) **think of** *(irr)* /ˈθɪŋk‿əv/ denken an, sich ausdenken NHG 5

logical thinking /ˌlɒdʒɪkl ˈθɪŋkɪŋ/ logisches Denken p. 33, 2

third /θɜːd/ dritte(r, s) NHG 5

this /ðɪs/ diese(r, s) NHG 5

This is … speaking. /ðɪs‿ɪz … ˈspiːkɪŋ/ Hier spricht … p. 42, 1

this way /ˈðɪs weɪ/ hier entlang p. 22, 6

those *(pl of that)* /ðəʊz/ diese, jene NHG 5

though *(nachgestellt)* /ðəʊ/ jedoch p. 28

thought /θɔːt/ Gedanke p. 80, 1

thought bubble /ˈθɔːt ˌbʌbl/ Gedankenblase p. 26, 12

thousand /ˈθaʊznd/ tausend NHG 6

sore throat /ˌsɔː ˈθrəʊt/ Halsschmerzen p. 42, 1

throne /θrəʊn/ Thron p. 78

heir to the throne /ˌeə tʊ ðə ˈθrəʊn/ Thronfolger/in p. 78

through /θruː/ durch NHG 6

throughout /θruːˈaʊt/ während P&P 2

throw /θrəʊ/ Wurf p. 53

(to) **throw** *(irr)* /θrəʊ/ werfen NHG 5

(to) **throw away** *(irr)* /ˌθrəʊ_ə'weɪ/ wegwerfen NHG 6

throwing /'θrəʊɪŋ/ Weitwurf p. 53

thumb /θʌm/ Daumen p. 119, 7

Thursday /'θɜːzdeɪ/ Donnerstag NHG 5

(on) Thursdays /'θɜːzdeɪz/ donnerstags NHG 5

tidy /'taɪdi/ ordentlich; aufgeräumt NHG 5

(to) **tidy (up)** /'taɪdi, ˌtaɪdi_'ʌp/ aufräumen NHG 5

tie /taɪ/ Krawatte NHG 5

tightly /'taɪtli/ fest p. 109, 7

till /tɪl/ bis NHG 5

time /taɪm/ Zeit; Mal NHG 5

all the time /ˌɔːl ðə 'taɪm/ die ganze Zeit NHG 6

at that time /æt_'ðæt_taɪm/ zu jener Zeit p. 87, 8

at the same time /ˌæt_ðə ˌseɪm 'taɪm/ gleichzeitig; zur gleichen Zeit p. 36, 7

for some time /fə ˌsʌm 'taɪm/ eine Zeitlang p. 37, 7

for the first time /fə ðə 'fɜːst_taɪm/ zum ersten Mal NHG 6

most of the time /'məʊst_əv ðə ˌtaɪm/ meistens p. 37, 7

on time /ˌɒn 'taɪm/ pünktlich NHG 5

What time is it?, What's the time (please)? /wɒt_'taɪm_ɪz_ɪt, ˌwɒts ðə 'taɪm pliːz/ Wie spät ist es (bitte)? NHG 5

(to) **step back in time** /ˌstep_ˌbæk_ɪn 'taɪm/ sich in die Vergangenheit zurückversetzen p. 66, 2

(to) **take up time** *(irr)* /ˌteɪk_ʌp 'taɪm/ Zeit beanspruchen p. 133

time management /'taɪm_ˌmænɪdʒmənt/ Zeitmanagement p. 168

time travelling /'taɪm ˌtrævlɪŋ/ Zeitreisen p. 126

timeline /'taɪmlaɪn/ Zeitachse p. 87, 9

timetable /'taɪmteɪbl/ Stundenplan NHG 5; Fahrplan NHG 6

tin /tɪn/ Büchse; Dose p. 109, 7

tin opener /'tɪn_ˌəʊpnə/ Dosenöffner p. 109, 7

tip /tɪp/ Tipp NHG 6

tired /'taɪəd/ müde NHG 6

(to) be sick and tired of *(irr)* /ˌbiː 'sɪk_ən ˌtaɪəd_əv/ satthaben p. 28

title /'taɪtl/ Titel; Überschrift NHG 6

to /tʊ/ (um) zu; in; nach; zu; an; bis; vor NHG 5

toad in the hole /ˌtəʊd_ɪn ðə 'həʊl/ *Bratwürste in einem Yorkshire Pudding* P&P 1

today /tə'deɪ/ heute NHG 5; heutzutage NHG 6

toe /təʊ/ Zeh NHG 5

together /tə'geðə/ zusammen NHG 5

toilet /'tɔɪlət/ Toilette NHG 5

toilet roll /'tɔɪlət rəʊl/ Toilettenpapier-Rolle p. 111, 11

Tokyo /'təʊkiəʊ/ Tokio p. 54

tomato *(pl tomatoes)* /tə'mɑːtəʊ, tə'mɑːtəʊz/ Tomate NHG 5

tomb /tuːm/ Grab; Gruft p. 78

tomorrow /tə'mɒrəʊ/ morgen NHG 5

ton /tʌn/ Tonne p. 73, 9

tonight /tə'naɪt/ heute Abend p. 28

too /tuː/ auch; zu NHG 5

tool /tuːl/ Werkzeug p. 109, 7

tooth *(pl teeth)* /tuːθ, tiːθ/ Zahn p. 42, 1

toothache *(no pl)* /'tuːθeɪk/ Zahnschmerzen p. 42, 1

toothbrush /'tuːθbrʌʃ/ Zahnbürste p. 104, 2

top /tɒp/ beste(r, s) NHG 5; oberes Ende; Spitze NHG 6

(to) go for the top *(irr)* /ˌgəʊ fə ðə 'tɒp/ sich um Höchstleistungen bemühen p. 52

topic /'tɒpɪk/ Thema NHG 5

topping /'tɒpɪŋ/ Belag p. 9, 2

tor /tɔː/ Felsturm p. 78

torch /tɔːtʃ/ Taschenlampe NHG 6

torture /'tɔːtʃə/ Folter p. 126

(to) toss /tɒs/ werfen p. 71, 6

tossing the caber /ˌtɒsɪŋ ðə 'keɪbə/ Baumstammwerfen p. 71, 6

(to) **touch** /tʌtʃ/ berühren NHG 5

(to) **keep in touch** *(irr)* /ˌkiːp_ɪn 'tʌtʃ/ Kontakt halten; in Verbindung bleiben p. 85, 7

tournament /'tʊənəmənt/ Turnier p. 35, 6

towards /tə'wɔːdz/ in Richtung, zu; gegenüber NHG 6

tower /'taʊə/ Turm NHG 6

town /taʊn/ Stadt NHG 5

toy /tɔɪ/ Spielzeug NHG 5

track /træk/ *hier:* Bahn p. 53

trade /treɪd/ Handel p. 30

(to) trade /treɪd/ Geschäfte machen; handeln p. 30

trader /'treɪdə/ Händler/in p. 30

traditional /trə'dɪʃnəl/ traditionell NHG 6

train /treɪn/ Zug NHG 5

(to) **train** /treɪn/ trainieren p. 33, 2

high-speed train /ˌhaɪspiːd 'treɪn/ Hochgeschwindigkeitszug p. 127

trained /treɪnd/ ausgebildet, geschult p. 94, 6

trainer /'treɪnə/ Trainer/in p. 67, 2

transatlantic /ˌtrænzət'læntɪk/ transatlantisch p. 105, 2

(to) **translate** /træns'leɪt/ übersetzen p. 15, 11

transport /'trænspɔːt/ Transport; Verkehrsmittel NHG 6

(to) **transport** /træns'pɔːt/ transportieren p. 130

travel /'trævl/ Reise NHG 6

(to) **travel** /'trævl/ reisen; fahren NHG 5

travelling /'trævlɪŋ/ Reisen NHG 6

treasure /'treʒə/ Schatz P&P 3

treasure hunting /'treʒə ˌhʌntɪŋ/ Schatzsuchen p. 57, 3

(to) **treat** /triːt/ behandeln p. 121, 12

tree /triː/ Baum NHG 5

trial phase /'traɪəl feɪz/ Testphase p. 95, 6

trick /trɪk/ Trick; Kunststück NHG 5

trip /trɪp/ Ausflug; Fahrt NHG 6

(to) **trip** /trɪp/ stolpern p. 43, 1

triple jump /'trɪpl dʒʌmp/ Dreisprung p. 53

trophy /'trəʊfi/ Trophäe p. 53

trouble /'trʌbl/ Ärger; Schwierigkeiten NHG 6

(a pair of) trousers /ə ˌpeər_əv 'traʊzəz/ Hose NHG 5

truck /trʌk/ Lastwagen p. 102

true /truː/ wahr NHG 5

truly /ˈtruːli/ wirklich, wahrhaftig
p. 78

(to) **trust** /trʌst/ vertrauen p. 121, 12

(to) **tell the truth** *(irr)* /ˌtel ðə ˈtruːθ/
die Wahrheit sagen p. 85, 7

(to) **try** /traɪ/ (aus)probieren;
versuchen NHG 5

give a try *(irr)* /ˌɡɪv‿ə ˈtraɪ/ ausprobieren p. 100

(to) **try on** /ˌtraɪ‿ˈɒn/ anprobieren
p. 60, 8

(to) **try out** /ˌtraɪ‿ˈaʊt/ ausprobieren p. 17, 17

the Tube /ðə ˈtjuːb/ (Londoner)
U-Bahn p. 108, 6

Tuesday /ˈtjuːzdeɪ/ Dienstag NHG 5

(on) Tuesdays /ˈtjuːzdeɪz/ diens-
tags NHG 5

tug-of-war /ˌtʌɡ‿əv ˈwɔː/ Tauziehen
p. 32, 1

tuition /tjuˈɪʃn/ *hier:* Nachhilfe
p. 91, 2

tunic /ˈtjuːnɪk/ Tunika p. 76

Turkey /ˈtɜːki/ die Türkei p. 88, 10

Turkish /ˈtɜːkɪʃ/ türkisch p. 8, 2;
Türkisch p. 88, 10

turmeric /ˈtɜːmərɪk/ Kurkuma p. 30

(to) **turn** /tɜːn/ abbiegen NHG 6

(to) **be one's turn** *(irr)* /ˌbiː wʌnz
ˈtɜːn/ an der Reihe sein NHG 5

(to) take a turn *(irr)* /ˌteɪk‿ə ˈtɜːn/
es auch einmal versuchen p. 78

(to) turn around /ˌtɜːn‿əˈraʊnd/ sich
umdrehen p. 77

(to) **turn off** /ˌtɜːn‿ˈɒf/ ausschalten
p. 39, 10

(to) **turn over** /ˌtɜːn‿ˈəʊvə/ (sich)
umdrehen p. 71, 6

(to) turn to /ˈtɜːn tʊ/ (sich) wenden
an p. 127

(to) **take turns** *(irr)* /ˌteɪk ˈtɜːnz/ sich
abwechseln NHG 6

TV (= television) /ˌtiː ˈviː, ˈtelɪˌvɪʒn/
Fernsehen; Fernseher NHG 6

(to) **watch TV** /ˌwɒtʃ tiː ˈviː/ Fernsehen gucken NHG 5

twice /twaɪs/ zweimal p. 36, 7

twin /twɪn/ Zwilling; Zwillings-
NHG 5

type /taɪp/ Art NHG 6

typical /ˈtɪpɪkl/ typisch NHG 5

U

ugly /ˈʌɡli/ hässlich NHG 6

the UK (= United Kingdom)
/ðə ˌjuː ˈkeɪ, juːˌnaɪtɪd ˈkɪŋdəm/
Vereinigtes Königreich NHG 6

UltraCane /ˈʌltrəˌkeɪn/ *elektronische
Orientierungshilfe für Sehbehin-
derte* p. 127

umbrella /ʌmˈbrelə/ Regenschirm
p. 126

uncle /ˈʌŋkl/ Onkel NHG 5

uncomfortable /ʌnˈkʌmftəbl/
unbequem p. 109, 7

uncomplicated /ʌnˈkɒmplɪˌkeɪtɪd/
unkompliziert p. 119, 7

under /ˈʌndə/ unter NHG 5

underground /ˈʌndəˌɡraʊnd/
U-Bahn NHG 6

(to) **understand** *(irr)* /ˌʌndəˈstænd/
verstehen NHG 5

unfortunately /ʌnˈfɔːtʃnətli/
unglücklicherweise NHG 6

unique /juˈniːk/ einzigartig p. 56, 2

unit /ˈjuːnɪt/ Kapitel p. 41, 13

university /ˌjuːnɪˈvɜːsəti/ Universität
p. 81, 2

unless /ənˈles/ außer wenn p. 94, 6

unreliable /ˌʌnrɪˈlaɪəbl/ unzuver-
lässig p. 145

(to) unscramble /ʌnˈskræmbl/ ord-
nen, in die richtige Reihenfolge
bringen p. 50, 13

until /ənˈtɪl/ bis NHG 6

unusual /ʌnˈjuːʒuəl/ ungewöhnlich
NHG 5

up /ʌp/ nach oben; hinauf; oben
NHG 5

What's up? *(informal)* /ˌwɒts‿ˈʌp/
Was ist los? p. 90, 2

(to) be up for something *(informal,
irr)* /ˌbiː‿ʌp fɔː ˈsʌmθɪŋ/ Lust zu
etwas haben p. 57, 3

(to) be up to something *(irr)*
/ˌbiː‿ʌp tə ˈsʌmθɪŋ/ etwas vorhaben
p. 57, 3

upper /ˈʌpə/ obere(r, s) p. 71, 6

upset /ʌpˈset/ aufgebracht;
aufgeregt p. 91, 2

upstairs /ˌʌpˈsteəz/ (nach) oben
p. 100

us /ʌs/ uns NHG 5

**the USA (= United States of
America)** /ðə ˌjuːˌes‿ˈeɪ, juːˌnaɪtɪd
ˌsteɪts‿əv‿əˈmerɪkə/ USA; Vereinigte
Staaten von Amerika NHG 6

use /juːs/ Verwendung; Einsatz
p. 73, 9

(to) **use** /juːz/ benutzen NHG 5

used to + *infinitive* /ˈjuːst‿tuː/ früher + *Vergangenheitsform* NHG 6

useful /ˈjuːsfl/ nützlich NHG 5

user /ˈjuːzə/ Benutzer/in p. 127

usual /ˈjuːʒuəl/ gewöhnlich, üblich
p. 29

usually /ˈjuːʒuəli/ gewöhnlich;
normalerweise NHG 5

V

(to) **vacuum** /ˈvækjuəm/ staub-
saugen NHG 5

(to) be good value for money *(irr)*
/ˌbiː ɡʊd ˌvæljuː fə ˈmʌni/ sein Geld
wert sein p. 19, 2

vegan /ˈviːɡən/ Veganer/in;
vegan p. 9, 2

vegetable /ˈvedʒtəbl/ Gemüse p. 8, 2

vegetable stock /ˈvedʒtəbl stɒk/
Gemüsebrühe p. 13, 7

vegetarian /ˌvedʒəˈteəriən/
Vegetarier/in; vegetarisch p. 8, 2

veggie *(informal)* /ˈvedʒi/ Gemüse
p. 12, 7

Velcro® /ˈvelkrəʊ/ *Klettverschluss*
p. 127

verse /vɜːs/ Strophe; Vers NHG 6

version /ˈvɜːʃn/ Version, Fassung
NHG 5

very /ˈveri/ sehr NHG 5

very much /ˌveri ˈmʌtʃ/ sehr NHG 6

the very first /ðə ˌveri ˈfɜːst/
der/die/das allererste p. 101

vet /vet/ Tierarzt/-ärztin NHG 6

victory /ˈvɪktri/ Sieg NHG 6

Vietnamese /viˌetnəˈmiːz/
Vietnamese/Vietnamesin;
vietnamesisch p. 18, 1

view /vjuː/ (Aus)sicht NHG 6

Viking /ˈvaɪkɪŋ/ Wikinger/in;
Wikinger- p. 66, 1

village /ˈvɪlɪdʒ/ Dorf p. 79

vindaloo /ˌvɪndəˈluː/ *indisches
Gericht* p. 19, 2

visit /ˈvɪzɪt/ Besuch NHG 5

(to) **visit** /ˈvɪzɪt/ besuchen NHG 6

visitor /ˈvɪzɪtə/ Besucher/in NHG 6

voice /vɔɪs/ Stimme NHG 6

volunteer /ˌvɒlənˈtɪə/ ehrenamt-
liche/r Mitarbeiter/in P&P 3

voyager ˈvɔɪɪdʒə/ Reisende/r p. 66, 2

VR glasses *(pl)* /ˌviˈɑː ˌglɑːsɪz/
VR-Brille p. 125

W

wait /weɪt/ Wartezeit p. 108, 6

(to) **wait** /weɪt/ (er)warten NHG 5

waiter/waitress /ˈweɪtə, ˈweɪtrəs/
Kellner/in p. 22, 6

waiting room /ˈweɪtɪŋ ˌruːm/ Wartezimmer p. 46, 5

(to) **wake up** *(irr)* /ˌweɪk ˈʌp/ auf-
wachen NHG 6

(to) wake up *(irr)* /ˌweɪk ˈʌp/ auf-
wecken p. 76

walk /wɔːk/ Spaziergang NHG 5

(to) **walk** /wɔːk/ gehen NHG 5

(to) walk around /ˌwɔːk əˈraʊnd/
herumlaufen p. 125

walking stick /ˈwɔːkɪŋ stɪk/ Spazier-
stock; Krückstock p. 127

wall /wɔːl/ Wand NHG 6

(to) wander around
/ˌwɒndər əˈraʊnd/ umherstreifen
p. 125

(to) wander off /ˌwɒndər ˈɒf/
weggehen, weglaufen p. 125

(to) **want (to)** /wɒnt/ wollen NHG 5

war /wɔː/ Krieg P&P 4

World War II /ˌwɜːld ˌwɔː ˈtuː/ Zweiter
Weltkrieg p. 85, 7

(to) **warn** /wɔːn/ warnen p. 22, 6

warrior /ˈwɒriə/ Krieger/in p. 66, 2

Warsaw /ˈwɔːsɔː/ Warschau p. 87, 8

(to) **wash** /wɒʃ/ waschen; sich
waschen NHG 5

waste /weɪst/ Abfall p. 73, 9

(to) **waste** /weɪst/ verschwenden
p. 24, 8

watch /wɒtʃ/ (Armband)uhr NHG 6

(to) **watch** /wɒtʃ/ beobachten;
ansehen NHG 5

(to) **watch TV** /ˌwɒtʃ tiː ˈviː/ Fernsehen gucken NHG 5

water /ˈwɔːtə/ Wasser NHG 5

water polo /ˈwɔːtə ˌpəʊləʊ/ Wasser-
ball *(Sportart)* p. 32, 1

way /weɪ/ Weg; Art NHG 5

this way /ˈðɪs weɪ/ hier entlang
p. 22, 6

we /wiː/ wir NHG 5

(to) **wear** *(irr)* /weə/ tragen
(Kleidung) NHG 5

weather /ˈweðə/ Wetter NHG 5

web page /ˈweb peɪdʒ/ Webseite;
Internetseite p. 11, 6

Wednesday /ˈwenzdeɪ/ Mittwoch
NHG 5

(on) Wednesdays /ˈwenzdeɪz/
mittwochs NHG 5

week /wiːk/ Woche NHG 5

weekend /ˌwiːkˈend/ Wochenende
NHG 5

weight /weɪt/ Gewicht p. 130

weight training /ˈweɪt ˌtreɪnɪŋ/ Kraft-
training p. 32, 1

welcome (to) /ˈwelkəm tʊ/ willkom-
men (in) NHG 5

(to) be welcome to *(irr)* /ˌbiː ˈwelkəm
tʊ/ etwas gern (tun) können
p.108,6

You're welcome. /jɔː ˈwelkəm/ Gern
geschehen.; Keine Ursache.
p. 65, 15

well /wel/ nun NHG 5; gut NHG 6

well done /ˌwel ˈdʌn/ gut gemacht
NHG 6

well-known /ˌwelˈnəʊn/ bekannt;
berühmt P&P 2

(to) **get well** *(irr)* /ˌget ˈwel/ gesund
werden p. 49, 12

West African /ˌwest ˈæfrɪkən/ West-
afrikaner/in; westafrikanisch
p. 81, 2

Western /ˈwestən/ West-, westlich
p. 30

wet /wet/ nass NHG 6

what /wɒt/ was; welche(r, s) NHG 5

What ... would you like?
/ˌwɒt ... wəd jə ˈlaɪk/ Was für ein /
eine ... hättest du / hättet ihr /
hätten Sie gern? NHG 5

What about ...? /ˌwɒt əˌbaʊt ˈ.../ Was
ist / Wie wäre es mit ...? NHG 5

What if ...? /ˌwɒt ˈɪf/ Was wäre,
wenn ...? p. 87, 8

**What time is it?/ What's the time
(please)?** /wɒt ˈtaɪm ɪz ɪt,
ˌwɒts ðə ˈtaɪm pliːz/ Wie spät ist es
(bitte)? NHG 5

What's on? *(informal)*
/ˌwɒts ˈɒn/ Was ist los? NHG 6

What's the matter? /ˌwɒts ðə
ˈmætə/ Was ist los? p. 42, 1

What's up? *(informal)*
/ˌwɒts ˈʌp/ Was ist los? p. 90, 2

What's wrong? *(informal)*
/ˌwɒts ˈrɒŋ/ Was ist los? p. 90, 2

whatever /wɒtˈevə/ was (auch
immer) NHG 6

wheel /wiːl/ Rad NHG 6

wheelchair /ˈwiːltʃeə/ Rollstuhl
p. 36, 7

when /wen/ wann; wenn; als NHG 5

whenever /wenˈevə/ wann auch
immer p. 63, 12

where /weə/ wo; wohin NHG 5

which /wɪtʃ/ welche(r, s); was NHG 5

while /waɪl/ während NHG 6;
Weile p. 85, 7

for a while /fər ə ˈwaɪl/ eine Weile
p. 36, 7

(to) whip cream /ˌwɪp ˈkriːm/ Sahne
schlagen p. 29

whipped cream /ˌwɪpt kriːm/
Schlagsahne p. 29

white /waɪt/ weiß NHG 5

who /huː/ wer; der/die/das NHG 5

whole /həʊl/ ganz, gesamt NHG 6

whose /huːz/ wessen NHG 5

why /waɪ/ warum NHG 5

wide /waɪd/ weit p. 118, 7

wife *(pl wives)* /waɪf, waɪvz/ Ehe-
frau NHG 5

WiFi /ˈwaɪ faɪ/ WLAN p. 113, 15

wildlife /ˈwaɪldˌlaɪf/ Tier- und Pflan-
zenwelt; Flora und Fauna NHG 6

will /wɪl/ werden NHG 6

(to) **win** *(irr)* /wɪn/ gewinnen p. 32, 1

window /ˈwɪndəʊ/ Fenster NHG 5

winner /ˈwɪnə/ Gewinner/in p. 53

(to) **wish** /wɪʃ/ wünschen p. 95, 6

with /wɪð/ mit; bei NHG 5

without /wɪðˈaʊt/ ohne NHG 5

wizard /ˈwɪzəd/ Zauberer p. 78

woman *(pl women)* /ˈwʊmən,
ˈwɪmɪn/ Frau NHG 5

won't /wəʊnt/ nicht werden NHG 6

wonder /ˈwʌndə/ Wunder p. 43, 1

(to) **wonder** /ˈwʌndə/ sich fragen NHG 6

wonderful /ˈwʌndəfl/ wunderbar, wundervoll NHG 6

wood /wʊd/ Holz NHG 6

wooden /ˈwʊdn/ Holz-, hölzern p. 76

woollen /ˈwʊlən/ aus Wolle p. 76

word /wɜːd/ Wort NHG 5

word search /ˈwɜːd sɜːtʃ/ Wortsuche p. 97, 10

word web /ˈwɜːd web/ Wortnetz NHG 5

wordbank /ˈwɜːdbæŋk/ *Wortsammlung* NHG 5

work /wɜːk/ Arbeit; Werk NHG 5

(to) **work** /wɜːk/ arbeiten NHG 5; funktionieren NHG 6

(to) work out /ˌwɜːk ˈaʊt/ ausarbeiten p. 100; *hier:* aufgehen p. 101

workbook /ˈwɜːkbʊk/ Arbeitsheft p. 8, 1

working /ˈwɜːkɪŋ/ funktionierend p. 105, 2

workout /ˈwɜːkaʊt/ Training p. 36, 7

worksheet /ˈwɜːkʃiːt/ Arbeitsblatt p. 14, 9

world /wɜːld/ Welt NHG 5

all over the world /ˌɔːl ˌəʊvə ðə ˈwɜːld/ auf der ganzen Welt NHG 6

from (all) around the world /frəm ˌɔːl əˌraʊnd ðə ˈwɜːld/ aus der (ganzen) Welt p. 7

from all over the world /frəm ˌɔːl ˌəʊvə ðə ˈwɜːld/ aus der ganzen Welt NHG 5

World War II /ˌwɜːld ˌwɔː ˈtuː/ Zweiter Weltkrieg p. 85, 7

world-famous /ˌwɜːld ˈfeɪməs/ weltberühmt p. 70, 6

worried /ˈwʌrid/ beunruhigt; besorgt NHG 6

worry /ˈwʌri/ Sorge p. 78

(to) **worry** /ˈwʌri/ sich Sorgen machen NHG 5

Don't worry. /ˌdəʊnt ˈwʌri/ Mach dir keine Sorgen. p. 90, 2

No need to worry. /nəʊ ˈniːd tə ˌwʌri/ Wir müssen uns keine Sorgen machen. p. 12, 7

worse /wɜːs/ schlechter, schlimmer NHG 6

the worst /ðə ˈwɜːst/ der/die/das schlechteste/schlimmste; am schlechtesten/schlimmsten NHG 6

would /wʊd/ würde(st, n, t) NHG 5

I would like … (= I'd like …) /aɪ ˌwʊd ˈlaɪk, aɪd ˈlaɪk/ Ich würde gern … / Ich hätte gern … NHG 5

Would you like …? /ˌwʊd ju ˈlaɪk/ Hättest du / Hättet ihr / Hätten Sie gern …? NHG 5

wound /wuːnd/ Wunde p. 43, 1

wrist /rɪst/ Handgelenk p. 42, 1

(to) **write** *(irr)* /raɪt/ schreiben NHG 5

(to) **write down** *(irr)* /ˌraɪt ˈdaʊn/ aufschreiben NHG 5

writing /ˈraɪtɪŋ/ Schrift; Schreiben p. 114, 2

written /ˈrɪtn/ schriftlich NHG 6

wrong /rɒŋ/ falsch NHG 6

(to) **be wrong** *(irr)* /ˌbiː ˈrɒŋ/ im Unrecht sein p. 90, 2

(to) **be wrong (with)** *(irr)* /ˌbiː ˈrɒŋ wɪθ/ nicht in Ordnung sein (mit) p. 48, 8

What's wrong? *(informal)* /ˌwɒts ˈrɒŋ/ Was ist los? p. 90, 2

X

X-ray /ˈeksreɪ/ Röntgenbild p. 46, 5

(to) **take an X-ray** *(irr)* /ˌteɪk ən ˈeksreɪ/ eine Röntgenaufnahme machen p. 42, 1

X-ray glasses *(pl)* /ˈeksreɪ ˌglɑːsɪz/ *Röntgenbrille* p. 111, 11

Y

year /jɪə/ Jahr NHG 5; Schuljahr; Klasse NHG 6

yellow /ˈjeləʊ/ gelb NHG 5

yes /jes/ ja NHG 5

yesterday /ˈjestədeɪ/ gestern NHG 6

yet /jet/ schon; noch p. 46, 5

Yorkshire pudding /ˌjɔːkʃə ˈpʊdɪŋ/ *britische gebackene Beilage* p. 8, 2

you /juː/ du; dich; dir; man; ihr; euch; Sie; Ihnen NHG 5

young /jʌŋ/ jung NHG 6

your /jɔː/ dein(e); euer/eure; Ihr(e) NHG 5

yours /jɔːz/ deine(r, s); eure(r, s); Ihre(r, s) NHG 6

yours sincerely /ˌjɔːz sɪnˈsɪəli/ mit freundlichen Grüßen *(am Ende eines formellen Briefes)* NHG 6

yourself /jɔːˈself/ dir, dich; sich NHG 5

youth club /ˈjuːθ ˌklʌb/ Jugendklub NHG 6

yummy *(informal)* /ˈjʌmi/ lecker p. 13, 7

Z

zero waste /ˌzɪərəʊ ˈweɪst/ verpackungsfrei p. 73, 9

zip /zɪp/ Reißverschluss p. 108, 7

(to) be in the zone *(irr)* /ˌbiː ɪn ðə ˈzəʊn/ in seinem Element sein p. 52

Names

First names

Agata *(f.)* /əˈgɑːtə/
Alex *(m., f.)* /ˈæliks/
Alexander *(m.)*
　/ˌælɪgˈzɑːndə/
Amira *(f.)* /əˈmiːrə/
Andy *(m., f.)* /ˈændi/
Anna *(f.)* /ˈænə/
Arthur *(m.)* /ˈɑːθə/
Ava *(f.)* /ˈeɪvə/
Becky *(f.)* /ˈbeki/
Ben, Benjamin *(m.)*
　/ben, ˈbendʒəmɪn/
Billie *(m., f.)* /ˈbɪli/
Bob *(m., f.)* /bɒb/
Cathy *(f.)* /ˈkæθi/
Charles *(m.)* /tʃɑːlz/
Chloe *(f.)* /ˈkləʊi/
Chris *(m., f.)* /krɪs/
Claire *(f.)* /kleə/
Dan, Daniel *(m.)*
　/dæn, ˈdænjəl/
Delia *(f.)* /ˈdiːliə/
Demir *(m.)* /deˈmɪə/
Ector *(m.)* /ˈektə/
Edward *(m.)* /ˈedwəd/
Edyta *(f.)* /əˈdiːtə/
Ellie *(f.)* /ˈeli/
Emily *(f.)* /ˈeməli/
Emma *(f.)* /ˈemə/
Eric *(m.)* /ˈerɪk/
Erika *(f.)* /ˈerɪkə/
Faisal *(m.)* /ˈfaɪsl/
Filip *(m.)* /ˈfɪlɪp/
Fiona *(f.)* /fiˈəʊnə/
Gemma *(f.)* /ˈdʒemə/
George *(m.)* /dʒɔːdʒ/
Harry *(m., f.)* /ˈhæri/
Harvey *(m.)* /ˈhɑːvi/
Isabel *(f.)* /ˈɪzəbel/
Jack *(m.)* /dʒæk/
Jacob *(m.)* /ˈdʒeɪkəb/
Jada *(f.)* /ˈdʒeɪdə/
James *(m.)* /dʒeɪmz/
Jamie *(m.)* /ˈdʒeɪmi/
Jan *(m., f.)* /dʒæn, jæn, jɑːn/
Janina *(f.)* /dʒəˈniːnə/
Jason *(m.)* /ˈdʒeɪsn/

Jemima *(f.)* /dʒɪˈmaɪmə/
Jenna *(f.)* /ˈdʒenə/
Jill *(f.)* /dʒɪl/
Joe *(m., f.)* /dʒəʊ/
John *(m.)* /dʒɒn/
Josh *(m.)* /dʒɒʃ/
Joshua *(m.)* /ˈdʒɒʃjuə/
Juan *(m.)* /wɑːn/
Karim *(m.)* /kəˈriːm/
Katie *(f.)* /ˈkeɪti/
Kay *(m., f.)* /keɪ/
Kristin *(f.)* /krɪˈstiːn/
Laura *(f.)* /ˈlɔːrə/
Leon *(m.)* /ˈliːən/
Leona *(f.)* /liˈəʊnə/
Levi *(m.)* /ˈliːvaɪ/
Lily *(f.)* /ˈlɪli/
Linda *(f.)* /ˈlɪndə/
Logie *(m.)* /ˈləʊgi/
Louise *(f.)* /luˈiːz/
Lucy *(f.)* /ˈluːsi/
Makena *(f.)* /məˈkiːnə/
Marc *(m.)* /mɑːk/
Margo *(f.)* /ˈmɑːgəʊ/
Marianne *(f.)* /ˌmæriˈæn/
Martin *(m.)* /ˈmɑːtɪn/
Matilda *(f.)* /məˈtɪldə/
Matt *(m.)* /mæt/
Matthew *(m.)* /ˈmæθjuː/
Merlin *(m.)* /ˈmɜːlɪn/
Mia *(f.)* /ˈmiːə/
Michael *(m.)* /ˈmaɪkl/
Michelle *(f.)* /miːˈʃel/
Mira *(f.)* /ˈmaɪrə/
Murat *(m.)* /ˈmurət/
Nils *(m.)* /nɪlz/
Noah *(m.)* /ˈnəʊə/
Oliver *(m.)* /ˈɒlɪvə/
Olivia *(f.)* /əˈlɪviə/
Ollie *(m.)* /ˈɒli/
Paolo *(m.)* /pəˈəʊləʊ/
Paul *(m.)* /pɔːl/
Pavel *(m.)* /ˈpɑːvl/
Peter *(m.)* /ˈpiːtə/
Phil *(m.)* /fɪl/
Radek *(m.)* /ˈrɑːdek/
Raymond *(m.)* /ˈreɪmənd/
Richard *(m.)* /ˈrɪtʃəd/
Robert *(m.)* /ˈrɒbət/

Ryan *(m.)* /ˈraɪən/
Sally *(f.)* /ˈsæli/
Sam *(m., f.)* /sæm/
Sami *(m.)* /ˈsæmi/
Sarah *(f.)* /ˈseərə/
Sebastian *(m.)* /səˈbæstiən/
Sheree *(f.)* /ʃəˈriː/
Sophie *(f.)* /ˈsəʊfi/
Stephen *(m.)* /ˈstiːvn/
Steven *(m.)* /ˈstiːvn/
Suzy *(f.)* /ˈsuːzi/
Tarek *(m.)* /ˈtærɪk/
Thomas *(m.)* /ˈtɒməs/
Tim *(m.)* /tɪm/
Toby *(m.)* /ˈtəʊbi/
Tom *(m.)* /tɒm/
Tony *(m., f.)* /ˈtəʊni/
Uther *(m.)* /ˈjuːθə/
William *(m.)* /ˈwɪljəm/
Zara *(f.)* /ˈzɑːrə/

Families

Addis /ˈædɪs/
Adil /əˈdiːl/
Baird /beəd/
Barlow /ˈbɑːləʊ/
Bell /bel/
Bohlin /ˈbɔːlɪn/
Carter /ˈkɑːtə/
Cooper /ˈkuːpə/
Dill /dɪl/
Dunkerley /ˈdʌŋkəli/
Durand /ˈdʌrənd/
Eilish /ˈaɪlɪʃ/
Fisher /ˈfɪʃə/
Fleming /ˈflemɪŋ/
Graham /ˈgreɪəm/
Hamilton /ˈhæmltən/
Hawk /hɔːk/
Hawking /ˈhɔːkɪŋ/
Henderson /ˈhendəsən/
Hill /hɪl/
Kellog /ˈkelɒg/
Kershaw /ˈkɜːʃɔː/
Kogan /ˈkəʊgən/
Macintosh /ˈmækɪntɒʃ/
Miller /ˈmɪlə/
Murpledale /ˈmɜːpldeɪl/

Norris /ˈnɒrɪs/
Patel /pəˈtel/
Peters /ˈpiːtəz/
Reed /riːd/
Rogers /ˈrɒdʒəz/
Rosen /ˈrəʊzn/
Spratt /spræt/
Stephenson /ˈstiːvnsən/
Strauss /straʊs/
Thomas /ˈtɒməs/
Tomlinson /ˈtɒmlɪnsən/
Trevithick /ˈtrevɪθɪk/
Watson /ˈwɒtsn/
Watt /wɒt/
Weston /ˈwestən/
Williams /ˈwɪljəmz/
Zephaniah /ˌzefəˈnaɪə/

Other names

Adventuring Andy
　/ədˌventʃərɪŋ ˈændi/
American football
　/əˌmerɪkən ˈfʊtˌbɔːl/
Arundel Castle
　/ˈærəndl kɑːsl/
Ayaz London /ˌaɪəzˈlʌndən/
bangers and mash
　/ˌbæŋəz_ən ˈmæʃ/
Barbican /ˈbɑːbɪkən/
Barley Hall /ˌbɑːli ˈhɔːl/
bhaji /ˈbɑːdʒi/
The Black Horse
　/ðə ˌblæk ˈhɔːs/
bubble and squeak
　/ˌbʌbl_ən ˈskwiːk/
burdock /ˈbɜːdɒk/
Cancer Research UK
　/ˌkænsə rɪˌsɜːtʃ ˌjuː ˈkeɪ/
(chicken) tikka (masala),
　(chicken) tikka
　/ˌtʃɪkɪn ˌtiːkə məˈsɑːlə,
　ˌtʃɪkɪn ˈtiːkə/
Dim Sum /ˌdɪm ˈsʌm/
Diwali /dɪˈwɑːli/
Double /ˈdʌbl/
East India Company
　/ˌiːstˌɪndiə ˈkʌmpni/
Excalibur /ekˈskælɪbə/

Farmhouse /ˈfɑːmˌhaʊs/
Feastival /ˈfiːstɪvl/
FIFA /ˈfiːfə/
Foodlover /ˈfuːdˌlʌvə/
Glastonbury Abbey /ˌglæstənbəri ˈæbi/
Glastonbury Tor /ˌglæstənbəri ˈtɔː/
Gujarati /ˌgʊdʒəˈrɑːti/
The Highland Games /ðə ˈhaɪlənd geɪmz/
Hindi /ˈhɪndi/
hippo roller /ˈhɪpəʊ ˌrəʊlə/
Holi /ˈhəʊli/
Holland Park /ˌhɒlənd ˈpɑːk/
Hyde Park /ˌhaɪd ˈpɑːk/
Isabel3589 /ˌɪzəbel ˌθriː faɪv ˌeɪt ˈnaɪn/
Jorvik /ˈjɔː vɪk/
kari /ˈkɑːri/
kebab /kɪˈbæb/
The King's Head /ðə ˌkɪŋz ˈhed/
kingfisher /ˈkɪŋˌfɪʃə/
korma /ˈkɔːmə/
Kung Pao /ˌkʊŋ ˈpɑːəʊ/
Lahmacun /ˌlɑːməˈdʒuːn/
lassi /ˈlæsi/
The London Eye /ðə ˌlʌndən ˈaɪ/
Lonelygirl /ˈləʊnliˌgɜːl/
Lyceum Theatre /laɪˌsiːəm ˈθɪətə/
Manchester Cathedral /ˌmæntʃɪstə kəˈθiːdrəl/
Margherita /ˌmɑːgəˈriːtə/
masala /məˈsɑːlə/
Mastederontomtom /ˌmæstədrənˈtɒmtɒm/
naan /nɑːn/
Nazi /ˈnɑːtsi/
Notting Hill /ˌnɒtɪŋ ˈhɪl/
Notting Hill Carnival /ˌnɒtɪŋ hɪl ˈkɑːnɪvl/
The Olympic Games (pl) /ði əˌlɪmpɪk ˈgeɪmz/
The Olympics (pl) /ði əˈlɪmpɪks/
one-pot pasta /ˌwʌnˌpɒt ˈpæstə/
Oxfam /ˈɒksfæm/

The Palace of India /ðə ˈpæləs ˌəv ˈɪndiə/
palak paneer /ˌpɑːlək pəˈnɪə/
The Paralympic Games (pl) /ðə ˌpærəlɪmpɪk ˈgeɪmz/
The Paralympics (pl) /ðə ˌpærəˈlɪmpɪks/
parkour /pɑːˈkʊə/
Pizza Extra /ˌpiːtsəˈekstrə/
poppadom /ˈpɒpədəm/
Portobello Market /ˌpɔːtəˌbeləʊ ˈmɑːkɪt/
Portobello Road /ˌpɔːtəˌbeləʊ ˈrəʊd/
Poutine /puːˈtiːn/
Preppy Rappy /ˌprepi ˈræpi/
Punjabi /pʌnˈdʒɑːbi/
The Royal Air Force /ðə ˌrɔɪəlˈeə fɔːs/
RSPCA (= Royal Society for the Prevention of Cruelty to Animals) /ˌɑːr es piː siːˈeɪ, ˌrɔɪəl səˌsaɪəti fə ðə prɪˌvenʃn əv ˌkruːəlti təˈænɪmlz/
samosa /səˈməʊsə/
Science and Industry Museum /ˌsaɪəns ˌən ˈɪndəstri mjuːˌziːəm/
The Science Museum /ðə ˈsaɪəns mjuːˌziːəm/
Shakshuka /ʃəkˈʃuːkə/
sitting volleyball /ˌsɪtɪŋ ˈvɒlibɔːl/
Skatepark Project /ˈskeɪtpɑːk ˌprɒdʒekt/
spaghetti bolognese /spəˌgeti ˌbɒləˈneɪz/
Spinning Jenny /ˌspɪnɪŋ ˈdʒeni/
St James /sənt ˈdʒeɪmz/
Sunnyday /ˈsʌniˌdeɪ/
Supreme /səˈpriːm/
Sushi Blue /ˌsuːʃi ˈbluː/
The Taj Mahal /ðə ˌtɑːdʒ məˈhɑːl/
Tamil /ˈtæməl/
Textiles Gallery /ˈtekstaɪlz ˌgæləri/

Tiramisu /ˌtɪrəmiˈsuː/
toad in the hole /ˌtəʊd ˌɪn ðə ˈhəʊl/
Tokyo /ˈtəʊkiəʊ/
Trouble /ˈtrʌbl/
UltraCane /ˈʌltrəˌkeɪn/
Urdu /ˈʊədu:/
Uther Pendragon /ˌjuːθə penˈdrægən/
Vegetariana /ˌvedʒəteəriˈɑːnə/
Velcro® /ˈvelkrəʊ/
Viking Lodge /ˈvaɪkɪŋ lɒdʒ/
vindaloo /ˌvɪndəˈluː/
Wonton /ˌwɒnˈtɒn/
Yorkshire pudding /ˌjɔːkʃə ˈpʊdɪŋ/

Geographical Names

Asia /ˈeɪʒə/
Avalon /ˈævəlɒn/
Bangladesh /ˌbæŋgləˈdeʃ/
Battersea /ˈbætəsi/
Bayswater /ˈbeɪzˌwɔːtə/
Berlin /bɜːˈlɪn/
Birmingham /ˈbɜːmɪŋəm/
Braemar /ˌbreɪˈmɑː/
Brick Lane /ˈbrɪk leɪn/
Brighton /ˈbraɪtn/
Bristol /ˈbrɪstl/
Britain /ˈbrɪtn/
Brixton /ˈbrɪkstən/
Canada /ˈkænədə/
China /ˈtʃaɪnə/
Chinatown /ˈtʃaɪnəˌtaʊn/
the Cotswolds /ðə ˈkɒtswəʊldz/
Edinburgh /ˈedɪnbərə/
Egypt /ˈiːdʒɪpt/
Elephant & Castle /ˌelɪfənt ˌən ˈkɑːsl/
England /ˈɪŋglənd/
Exeter /ˈeksɪtə/
Exhibition Road /ˌeksɪˈbɪʃn rəʊd/
Finsbury Park /ˈfɪnzbəri pɑːk/
Germany /ˈdʒɜːməni/
Ghana /ˈgɑːnə/
Glastonbury /ˈglæstənbəri/

Golders Green /ˌgəʊldəz ˈgriːn/
Great Britain /ˌgreɪt ˈbrɪtn/
Greece /griːs/
Hammersmith /ˈhæməsmɪθ/
Highland /ˈhaɪlənd/
Hong Kong /ˌhɒŋ ˈkɒŋ/
India /ˈɪndiə/
Isle of Wight /ˌaɪl əv ˈwaɪt/
Israel /ˈɪzreɪl/
Istanbul /ˌɪstænˈbʊl/
Italy /ˈɪtəli/
Japan /dʒəˈpæn/
Korea /kəˈrɪə/
Lebanon /ˈlebənən/
Leeds /liːdz/
Liverpool /ˈlɪvəpuːl/
London /ˈlʌndən/
Los Angeles /lɒsˈændʒəliːz/
Manchester /ˈmæntʃɪstə/
Mars /mɑːz/
Merton /ˈmɜːtn/
Morocco /məˈrɒkəʊ/
New Delhi /ˌnjuː ˈdeli/
North Africa /ˌnɔːθˈæfrɪkə/
Pakistan /ˌpɑːkɪˈstɑːn/
Poland /ˈpəʊlənd/
Rome /rəʊm/
Scotland /ˈskɒtlənd/
South India /ˌsaʊθˈɪndiə/
South Kensington /ˌsaʊθ ˈkenzɪŋtən/
Southall /ˈsaʊθɔːl/
Spain /speɪn/
Stoke-on-Trent /ˌstəʊk ɒn ˈtrent/
Sweden /ˈswiːdn/
Trinidad /ˈtrɪnɪdæd/
Turkey /ˈtɜːki/
the UK (= United Kingdom) /ðə ˌjuː ˈkeɪ, juːˌnaɪtɪd ˈkɪŋdəm/
the USA (= United States of America) /ðə ˌjuː esˈeɪ, juːˌnaɪtɪd ˌsteɪts əv əˈmerɪkə/
Wales /weɪlz/
Warsaw /ˈwɔːsɔː/
York /jɔːk/

Numbers

0	oh, zero, nil /əʊ, ˈzɪərəʊ, nɪl/	1st	first /fɜːst/
1	one /wʌn/	2nd	second /ˈsekənd/
2	two /tuː/	3rd	third /θɜːd/
3	three /θriː/	4th	fourth /fɔːθ/
4	four /fɔː/	5th	fifth /fɪfθ/
5	five /faɪv/	6th	sixth /sɪksθ/
6	six /sɪks/	7th	seventh /sevnθ/
7	seven /sevn/	8th	eighth /eɪtθ/
8	eight /eɪt/	9th	ninth /naɪnθ/
9	nine /naɪn/	10th	tenth /tenθ/
10	ten /ten/	11th	eleventh /ɪˈlevnθ/
11	eleven /ɪˈlevn/	12th	twelfth /twelfθ/
12	twelve /twelv/	13th	thirteenth /ˌθɜːˈtiːnθ/
13	thirteen /ˌθɜːˈtiːn/	19th	nineteenth /ˌnaɪnˈtiːnθ/
14	fourteen /ˌfɔːˈtiːn/	20th	twentieth /ˈtwentiəθ/
15	fifteen /ˌfɪfˈtiːn/		
16	sixteen /ˌsɪksˈtiːn/	21st	twenty-first /ˌtwentiˈfɜːst/
17	seventeen /ˌsevnˈtiːn/	22nd	twenty-second /ˌtwentiˈsekənd/
18	eighteen /ˌeɪˈtiːn/	23rd	twenty-third /ˌtwentiˈθɜːd/
19	nineteen /ˌnaɪnˈtiːn/		
20	twenty /ˈtwenti/	30th	thirtieth /ˈθɜːtiəθ/
		40th	fortieth /ˈfɔːtiəθ/
21	twenty-one /ˌtwentiˈwʌn/	50th	fiftieth /ˈfɪftiəθ/
30	thirty /ˈθɜːti/	60th	sixtieth /ˈsɪkstiəθ/
33	thirty-three /ˌθɜːtiˈθriː/	70th	seventieth /ˈsevntiəθ/
40	forty /ˈfɔːti/	80th	eightieth /ˈeɪtiəθ/
45	forty-five /ˌfɔːtiˈfaɪv/	90th	ninetieth /ˈnaɪntiəθ/
50	fifty /ˈfɪfti/	100th	hundredth /ˈhʌndrədθ/
56	fifty-six /ˌfɪftiˈsɪks/		
60	sixty /ˈsɪksti/		
67	sixty-seven /ˌsɪkstiˈsevn/		
70	seventy /ˈsevnti/		
78	seventy-eight /ˌsevntiˈeɪt/		
80	eighty /ˈeɪti/		
89	eighty-nine /ˌeɪtiˈnaɪn/		
90	ninety /ˈnaɪnti/		

Daten schreibst du im britischen
Englisch so:
1 August, 2 January, 5 November
oder so: 1st / 1st August,
2nd / 2nd January, 5th / 5th November

100	a/one hundred /ə/wʌn ˈhʌndrəd/
101	one hundred and one /wʌn ˌhʌndrəd_ən ˈwʌn/
200	two hundred /tuː ˈhʌndrəd/
1,000	one thousand /ə/wʌn ˈθaʊznd/
2,000	two thousand /tuː ˈθaʊznd/

Jahreszahlen sprichst du so aus:
1939 nineteen thirty-nine
1951 nineteen fifty-one
2010 two thousand and ten

Bei Zahlen mit vier oder mehr Ziffern
werden, falls erforderlich, im
Englischen Kommata verwendet,
keine Punkte!

$\frac{1}{2}$	a / one half	/ə/wʌn ˈhaːf/
$\frac{1}{3}$	a / one third	/ə/wʌn ˈθɜːd/
$\frac{1}{4}$	a / one quarter	/ə/wʌn ˈkwɔːtə/
$\frac{1}{8}$	a / one eighth	/ə/wʌn_ˈeɪtθ/
$\frac{3}{4}$	three quarters	/θriː ˈkwɔːtəz/

Irregular verbs

infinitive	simple past	past participle	German
(to) be /biː/	was/were /wɒz/wɜː/	been /biːn/	sein
(to) become /bɪˈkʌm/	became /bɪˈkeɪm/	become /bɪˈkʌm/	werden
(to) begin /bɪˈgɪn/	began /bɪˈgæn/	begun /bɪˈgʌn/	anfangen; beginnen
(to) bleed /bliːd/	bled /bled/	bled /bled/	bluten
(to) break /breɪk/	broke /brəʊk/	broken /ˈbrəʊkən/	(zer)brechen; kaputt machen
(to) bring /brɪŋ/	brought /brɔːt/	brought /brɔːt/	mitbringen
(to) build /bɪld/	built /bɪlt/	built /bɪlt/	bauen
(to) buy /baɪ/	bought /bɔːt/	bought /bɔːt/	kaufen
(to) catch /kætʃ/	caught /kɔːt/	caught /kɔːt/	fangen
(to) choose /tʃuːz/	chose /tʃəʊz/	chosen /ˈtʃəʊzn/	wählen; sich entscheiden
(to) come /kʌm/	came /keɪm/	come /kʌm/	kommen
(to) cost /kɒst/	cost /kɒst/	cost /kɒst/	kosten
(to) cut /kʌt/	cut /kʌt/	cut /kʌt/	schneiden
(to) deal with /ˈdiːl wɪð/	dealt with /ˈdelt wɪð/	dealt with /ˈdelt wɪð/	sich befassen mit, umgehen mit
(to) do /duː/	did /dɪd/	done /dʌn/	machen; tun
(to) draw /drɔː/	drew /druː/	drawn /drɔːn/	zeichnen
(to) drink /drɪŋk/	drank /dræŋk/	drunk /drʌŋk/	trinken
(to) drive /draɪv/	drove /drəʊv/	driven /ˈdrɪvn/	fahren
(to) eat /iːt/	ate /et/eɪt/	eaten /ˈiːtn/	essen
(to) fall /fɔːl/	fell /fel/	fallen /ˈfɔːlən/	fallen
(to) feed /fiːd/	fed /fed/	fed /fed/	füttern
(to) feel /fiːl/	felt /felt/	felt /felt/	(sich) fühlen
(to) fight /faɪt/	fought /fɔːt/	fought /fɔːt/	bekämpfen; ankämpfen gegen
(to) find /faɪnd/	found /faʊnd/	found /faʊnd/	finden
(to) fly /flaɪ/	flew /fluː/	flown /fləʊn/	fliegen
(to) forget /fəˈget/	forgot /fəˈgɒt/	forgotten /fəˈgɒtən/	vergessen
(to) get /get/	got /gɒt/	got /gɒt/	bekommen; holen; kaufen; kommen, gelangen; werden; bringen
(to) give /gɪv/	gave /geɪv/	given /ˈgɪvn/	geben; angeben, mitteilen
(to) go /gəʊ/	went /went/	gone /gɒn/	gehen; fahren
(to) grow /grəʊ/	grew /gruː/	grown /grəʊn/	wachsen; anbauen
(to) hang (up) /ˌhæŋ ˈʌp/	hung (up) /ˌhʌŋ ˈʌp/	hung (up) /ˌhʌŋ ˈʌp/	hängen, aufhängen
(to) have /hæv/	had /hæd/	had /hæd/	haben; essen; trinken
(to) hear /hɪə/	heard /hɜːd/	heard /hɜːd/	hören
(to) hide /haɪd/	hid /hɪd/	hidden /ˈhɪdn/	(sich) verstecken
(to) hit /hɪt/	hit /hɪt/	hit /hɪt/	schlagen; stoßen gegen; treffen
(to) hold /həʊld/	held /held/	held /held/	(fest)halten
(to) hurt /hɜːt/	hurt /hɜːt/	hurt /hɜːt/	wehtun, schmerzen; verletzen

Irregular verbs

infinitive	simple past	past participle	German
(to) keep /kiːp/	kept /kept/	kept /kept/	aufbewahren; (be)halten
(to) know /nəʊ/	knew /njuː/	known /nəʊn/	wissen; kennen
(to) learn /lɜːn/	learnt/learned /lɜːnt/lɜːnd/	learnt/learned /lɜːnt/lɜːnd/	lernen
(to) leave /liːv/	left /left/	left /left/	weggehen; verlassen, abfahren; (übrig) lassen; zurücklassen; hinterlassen
(to) let /let/	let /let/	let /let/	lassen
(to) light /laɪt/	lit /lɪt/	lit /lɪt/	anzünden
(to) lose /luːz/	lost /lɒst/	lost /lɒst/	verlieren
(to) make /meɪk/	made /meɪd/	made /meɪd/	machen
(to) mean /miːn/	meant /ment/	meant /ment/	meinen; bedeuten
(to) meet /miːt/	met /met/	met /met/	(sich) treffen; kennenlernen
(to) pay /peɪ/	paid /peɪd/	paid /peɪd/	(be)zahlen
(to) prove /pruːv/	proved /pruːvd/	proved/proven /pruːvd/ˈpruːvn/	beweisen
(to) put /pʊt/	put /pʊt/	put /pʊt/	setzen; stellen; legen
(to) read /riːd/	read /red/	read /red/	lesen
(to) rebuild /ˌriːˈbɪld/	rebuilt /ˌriːˈbɪlt/	rebuilt /ˌriːˈbɪlt/	wieder aufbauen
(to) rewrite /ˌriːˈraɪt/	rewrote /ˌriːˈrəʊt/	rewritten /ˌriːˈrɪtn/	überarbeiten, umschreiben
(to) ride /raɪd/	rode /rəʊd/	ridden /ˈrɪdn/	fahren; reiten
(to) run /rʌn/	ran /ræn/	run /rʌn/	laufen; rennen; leiten, betreiben
(to) say /seɪ/	said /sed/	said /sed/	sagen
(to) see /siː/	saw /sɔː/	seen /siːn/	sehen; empfangen, drannehmen
(to) seek /siːk/	sought /sɔːt/	sought /sɔːt/	suchen, streben nach
(to) sell /sel/	sold /səʊld/	sold /səʊld/	verkaufen
(to) send /send/	sent /sent/	sent /sent/	schicken
(to) shine /ʃaɪn/	shone /ʃɒn/	shone /ʃɒn/	scheinen
(to) shoot /ʃuːt/	shot /ʃɒt/	shot /ʃɒt/	schießen
(to) show /ʃəʊ/	showed /ʃəʊd/	shown /ʃəʊn/	zeigen
(to) shrink /ʃrɪŋk/	shrank/shrunk /ʃræŋk/ʃrʌŋk/	shrunk/shrunken /ʃrʌŋk/ˈʃrʌŋkən/	schrumpfen
(to) sing /sɪŋ/	sang /sæŋ/	sung /sʌŋ/	singen
(to) sit /sɪt/	sat /sæt/	sat /sæt/	sitzen
(to) sit down /ˌsɪtˈdaʊn/	sat down /ˌsætˈdaʊn/	sat down /ˌsætˈdaʊn/	sich hinsetzen
(to) sleep /sliːp/	slept /slept/	slept /slept/	schlafen
(to) speak /spiːk/	spoke /spəʊk/	spoken /ˈspəʊkən/	reden; sprechen
(to) spell /spel/	spelt/spelled /spelt/speld/	spelt/spelled /spelt/speld/	buchstabieren
(to) spend /spend/	spent /spent/	spent /spent/	ausgeben (Geld); verbringen (Zeit)
(to) spin /spɪn/	spun/span /spʌn/spæn/	spun /spʌn/	spinnen; drehen

Irregular verbs

infinitive	simple past	past participle	German
(to) stand /stænd/	stood /stʊd/	stood /stʊd/	stehen
(to) steal /stiːl/	stole /stəʊl/	stolen /ˈstəʊlən/	stehlen
(to) stick /stɪk/	stuck /stʌk/	stuck /stʌk/	festhängen
(to) swim /swɪm/	swam /swæm/	swum /swʌm/	schwimmen
(to) take /teɪk/	took /tʊk/	taken /ˈteɪkən/	nehmen; bringen; benötigen; brauchen; dauern
(to) teach /tiːtʃ/	taught /tɔːt/	taught /tɔːt/	unterrichten
(to) tell /tel/	told /təʊld/	told /təʊld/	erzählen
(to) think /θɪŋk/	thought /θɔːt/	thought /θɔːt/	denken; glauben
(to) throw /θrəʊ/	threw /θruː/	thrown /θrəʊn/	werfen
(to) understand /ˌʌndəˈstænd/	understood /ˌʌndəˈstʊd/	understood /ˌʌndəˈstʊd/	verstehen
(to) wake up /ˌweɪk ˈʌp/	woke up /ˌwəʊk ˈʌp/	woken up /ˌwəʊkən ˈʌp/	aufwachen; aufwecken
(to) wear /weə/	wore /wɔː/	worn /wɔːn/	tragen *(Kleidung)*
(to) win /wɪn/	won /wʌn/	won /wʌn/	gewinnen
(to) write /raɪt/	wrote /rəʊt/	written /ˈrɪtn/	schreiben

Tipp:

Einige Verben bilden das **simple past** und das **past participle** nach einem ähnlichen Muster. Wenn du sie dir in Gruppen sortierst, kannst du dir die Formen vielleicht besser merken.
Findest du weitere Beispiele für diese Gruppen oder andere Gruppen?

bring	brought	brought	mitbringen
buy	bought	bought	kaufen
catch	c**au**ght	c**au**ght	fangen
fight	fought	fought	bekämpfen
think	thought	thought	denken; glauben
sing	sang	sung	singen
swim	swam	swum	schwimmen
draw	drew	dr**aw**n	zeichnen
fly	flew	flown	fliegen
grow	grew	grown	wachsen
know	knew	known	kennen; wissen
throw	threw	thrown	werfen
cost	cost	cost	kosten
cut	cut	cut	schneiden
hit	hit	hit	schlagen
let	let	let	lassen
put	put	put	legen, setzen, stellen

Seite Lern- phasen	Inhalte	Kompetenzen	Sprachliche Mittel

7 | Unit 1 – Food (Kompetenzschwerpunkt: Schreiben)

PART A – Delicious dishes

Seite Lern-phasen	Inhalte	Kompetenzen	Sprachliche Mittel
8 Activate	Über verschiedene (Lieblings-) Gerichte lesen und sprechen	**Reading:** *text messages* und *blog posts* lesen **Speaking:** über Lieblingsgerichte sprechen, Fragen stellen	**Wortschatz** *food, likes and dislikes*
10 Practise	Strukturen bewusst machen und festigen	**Writing:** über etwas schreiben, das noch andauert bzw. Auswirkungen auf die Gegenwart hat	**Strukturen** *present perfect* **Wortschatz** *food*
11 Develop	Essen in der Schulkantine Eine Mahlzeit zubereiten	**Listening:** einem Gespräch folgen **Reading:** einen Dialog lesen, einen Limerick verstehen **Viewing:** einen Videoclip verstehen **Mediation:** einen Podcast sprachmitteln	**Wortschatz** *food, ingredients, recipe*
16 Practise	Strukturen festigen, Vorbereitung auf die Target task	**Writing:** ein *word web* zum Thema *cooking* erstellen	**Strukturen** *quantifiers*
17 Apply	Target task Our international cookbook	**Writing:** ein Rezept aufschreiben	**Wortschatz** *food, quantities*

PART B – At a restaurant

Seite Lern-phasen	Inhalte	Kompetenzen	Sprachliche Mittel
18 Activate	Restaurants in der eigenen Umgebung Verschiedene Restaurants in Großbritannien	**Speaking:** über Restaurants in der eigenen Umgebung sprechen, Bewertungskriterien für Restaurants finden **Reading:** Restaurantkritiken lesen	**Wortschatz** *food, eating out*
20 Practise	Strukturen bewusst machen und festigen	**Writing:** Vergleiche anstellen	**Strukturen** *comparison of adjectives*
21 Develop	Einen Restaurantbesuch planen Im Restaurant ein Gericht aussuchen und bestellen	**Listening:** einen Dialog verstehen **Speaking:** über ein Bild sprechen, eine Szene beschreiben **Reading:** einer Speisekarte Informationen entnehmen **Writing:** eine Textnachricht schreiben, eine Restaurantkritik verfassen **Viewing:** einen Videoclip verstehen	**Wortschatz** *at a restaurant*
26 Practise	Strukturen festigen, Vorbereitung auf die Target task	**Writing:** verschiedene Restaurantszenen beschreiben und weiterführen	**Wortschatz** *at a restaurant* **Strukturen** *present progressive*
27 Apply	Target task Our restaurant role play Check out Selbsteinschätzung	**Speaking:** ein Rollenspiel vorbereiten und präsentieren	**Wortschatz** *at the restaurant*
28 Story	Jamie and Lucy: Delicious disaster	**Reading:** ein Kapitel der Fortsetzungsgeschichte lesen	
30 Challenge	Curious about curry?	**Reading:** einen Artikel über Herkunft, Geschichte und Bedeutung des Curry lesen	

Ausführliches Inhaltsverzeichnis

Seite Lernphasen	Inhalte	Kompetenzen	Sprachliche Mittel
31	**Unit 2 – Healthy living (Kompetenzschwerpunkt: Sprechen)**		
	PART A – Keeping fit		
32 Activate	Über verschiedene Sportarten sprechen	**Reading:** einen Entscheidungsbaum verstehen, kurze Statements lesen **Writing:** Empfehlungen aussprechen	**Wortschatz** *sports, keeping fit*
34 Practise	Strukturen bewusst machen und festigen	**Writing:** über Aktivitäten schreiben	**Strukturen** *gerund* **Wortschatz** *sports*
35 Develop	Etwas über Schach erfahren Darüber lesen und sprechen, was zum eigenen Wohlbefinden beiträgt	**Listening:** ein Interview verstehen **Reading:** verschiedene Posts über Sportarten und Aktivitäten lesen, Gedichte lesen **Speaking:** mit einem Partner darüber sprechen, wann und warum man sich wohlfühlt **Writing:** ein Gedicht schreiben **Mediation:** ein Video sprachmitteln	**Wortschatz** *keeping fit*
40 Practise	Strukturen festigen, Vorbereitung auf die Target task	**Listening:** verstehen, was eine Skateboarderin über ihren Sport sagt	**Strukturen** *gerund* **Wortschatz** *keeping fit, sports*
41 Apply	Target task Tips for a healthy lifestyle	**Writing:** Tipps für einen gesunden Lebensstil sammeln und vorstellen	**Wortschatz** *keeping fit, sports*
	PART B – At the doctor's		
42 Activate	Über verschiedene Krankheiten und Unfälle lesen	**Reading:** kurze Dialoge lesen **Writing:** Wortmaterial sammeln **Speaking:** einen Dialog mit einem Partner vorlesen	**Wortschatz** *body, health*
44 Practise	Strukturen bewusst machen und festigen	**Writing:** Wenn-Dann-Sätze schreiben	**Strukturen** *conditional I*
45 Develop	Tarek nach einem Unfall auf dem Hockeyfeld ins Krankenhaus begleiten	**Reading:** Dialoge lesen, eine Textnachricht verstehen **Listening:** einem Notruf folgen **Writing:** ein eigenes Meme erstellen **Speaking:** jemandem Ratschläge für schnelle Genesung erteilen **Mediation:** bei einem Arztbesuch sprachmitteln	**Wortschatz** *body, health, at the doctor's*
50 Practise	Strukturen festigen, Vorbereitung auf die Target task	**Writing:** Fragen und Antworten formulieren	**Strukturen** *questions* **Wortschatz** *body, health, at the doctor's*
51 Apply	Target task A medical problem Check out Selbsteinschätzung	**Speaking:** eine Szene beim Arzt entwickeln und als Rollenspiel präsentieren	**Wortschatz** *body, health, at the doctor's*
52 Story	Jamie and Lucy: Sports day	**Reading:** ein Kapitel der Fortsetzungsgeschichte lesen	
54 Challenge	Paralympics	**Reading:** eine Magazinseite über die Paralympischen Spiele lesen	

Seite Lern- phasen	Inhalte	Kompetenzen	Sprachliche Mittel
55	**Unit 3 – What's on? (Kompetenzschwerpunkt: Lesen)**		
	PART A – At the car boot sale		
56 Activate	Über verschiedene Freizeitangebote lesen	**Speaking:** darüber sprechen, was man am Wochenende gern macht **Reading:** einen Flyer verstehen	**Wortschatz** *What's on?*
58 Practise	Strukturen bewusst machen und festigen	**Writing:** Personen und Gegenstände näher beschreiben	**Strukturen** *relative clauses*
59 Develop	Etwas über *car boot sales* erfahren Kaufen und Verkaufen	**Listening:** einen Dialog verstehen, Bilder zuordnen **Reading:** einem Dialog folgen **Viewing:** einen Videoclip verstehen **Speaking:** nach Preisen fragen und Auskunft erteilen **Writing:** die Geschichte eines Gegenstandes schreiben **Mediation:** bei einem Verkaufsgespräch vermitteln	**Wortschatz** *buying and selling*
64 Practise	Strukturen festigen, Vorbereitung auf die Target task	**Writing:** Verkaufsdialoge	**Strukturen** *prop word „one"* **Wortschatz** *buying and selling*
65 Apply	Target task Secondhand-Shopping	**Speaking:** eine Flohmarktszene entwickeln und als Rollenspiel präsentieren	**Wortschatz** *buying and selling*
	PART B – Festivals		
66 Activate	Das *Jorvik Viking Festival* kennenlernen	**Reading:** einem Poster Informationen entnehmen, einen Blogeintrag lesen **Speaking:** über ein Festival sprechen	**Wortschatz** *What's on?, events*
68 Practise	Strukturen bewusst machen und festigen	**Writing:** über Vergangenes schreiben **Speaking:** Fragen über Vergangenes stellen und beantworten	**Strukturen** *past progressive* **Wortschatz** *What's on?*
69 Develop	Mehr über das *Jorvik Viking Festival* erfahren Weitere Großveranstaltungen im Vereinigten Königreich kennenlernen	**Listening:** Statements zum *Jorvik Viking Festival* verstehen **Reading:** Blogeinträge verstehen und Notizen machen **Speaking:** Fragen über verschiedene Veranstaltungen stellen und beantworten **Viewing:** einer Slideshow folgen **Mediation:** einen Zeitungsartikel sprachmitteln	**Wortschatz** *What's on?, festivals*
74 Practise	Strukturen festigen, Vorbereitung auf die Target task	**Writing:** Situationen beschreiben	**Strukturen** *past progressive*
75 Apply	Target task A blog post Check out Selbsteinschätzung	**Writing:** einen Blogeintrag über ein Festival oder eine Veranstaltung schreiben	**Wortschatz** *What's on?, events*
76 Story	Jamie and Lucy: Medieval mischief	**Reading:** ein Kapitel der Fortsetzungsgeschichte lesen	
78 Challenge	Glastonbury and the legend of King Arthur	**Reading:** einen Sachtext über Glastonbury und den sagenhaften *King Arthur* lesen	

Seite Lern-phasen	Inhalte	Kompetenzen	Sprachliche Mittel
79	**Unit 4 – You are not alone (Kompetenzschwerpunkt: Hören)**		
	PART A – Exploring roots		
80 Activate	Heimat und Herkunft	**Speaking:** über den Ort, an dem man lebt, sprechen **Reading:** Posts von Menschen, die in London leben, lesen	**Wortschatz** *family history, home*
82 Practise	Strukturen bewusst machen und festigen	**Writing:** über die Vergangenheit schreiben	**Strukturen** *simple past*
83 Develop	Vier Stadtteile in London näher kennen lernen	**Listening:** verstehen, was Menschen über Stadtteile in London erzählen **Reading:** einer Webseite Informationen entnehmen **Speaking:** zu Bildern spekulieren, über den Begriff *„home"* diskutieren **Writing:** Notizen erstellen, einen Brief schreiben, einen Tagebucheintrag erstellen **Mediation:** Informationen von einer Webseite sprachmitteln	**Wortschatz** *home, family history*
88 Practise	Strukturen festigen, Vorbereitung auf die Target task	**Writing:** Fragen zur Vergangenheit formulieren	**Strukturen** *simple past* **Wortschatz** *home, family* **Aussprache** */s/ und /z/*
89 Apply	Target task A life story	**Writing:** über die Lebensgeschichte einer Person schreiben	**Wortschatz** *family history*
	PART B – Giving a helping hand		
90 Activate	Gefühle	**Speaking:** darüber sprechen, wie man sich fühlt **Reading:** verschiedene Dialoge verstehen und Bildern zuordnen	**Wortschatz** *feelings*
92 Practise	Strukturen bewusst machen und festigen	**Writing:** wiedergeben, was andere mitteilen, über Gefühle schreiben **Listening:** kurze Statements verstehen	**Strukturen** *reported speech* **Wortschatz** *feelings*
93 Develop	Sorgen und Nöte von Teenagern Hilfe im Internet	**Reading:** Problemschilderungen und Ratschläge verstehen **Listening:** einem Telefongespräch folgen **Writing:** Probleme anderer in eigenen Worten wiedergeben **Mediation:** einem Austauschschüler helfen	**Strukturen** *reported speech* **Wortschatz** *feelings, seeking and giving advice*
98 Practise	Strukturen festigen, Vorbereitung auf die Target task	**Writing:** Adjektive, Adverbien und Konjunktionen verwenden	**Strukturen** *possessive determiners, linking words*
99 Apply	Target task Giving a helping hand Check out Selbsteinschätzung	**Speaking:** eine Szene entwickeln und als Rollenspiel präsentieren	**Wortschatz** *describing people, good style*
100 Story	Jamie and Lucy: Wrong impressions	**Reading:** ein Kapitel der Fortsetzungsgeschichte lesen	
102 Challenge	On the Move Again	**Reading:** ein Gedicht lesen	

Seite Lern- phasen	Inhalte	Kompetenzen	Sprachliche Mittel
103	**Unit 5 – Everyday science (Kompetenzschwerpunkt: Sprachmittlung)**		
	PART A – Inventions		
104 Activate	Über Erfindungen sprechen und lesen	**Speaking:** darüber sprechen, auf welche Alltagsgegenstände man nicht verzichten könnte **Reading:** über britische Erfindungen lesen	**Wortschatz** *inventions*
106 Practise	Strukturen bewusst machen und festigen	**Writing:** über Erfindungen schreiben	**Strukturen** *passive* **Wortschatz** *inventions*
107 Develop	Etwas über das London Science Museum erfahren Erfindungen und ihre Entstehungsgeschichten	**Listening:** einem Dialog Informationen entnehmen **Reading:** Informationstexte zu verschiedenen Erfindungen lesen **Mediation:** einen Flyer sprachmitteln	**Strukturen** *passive* **Wortschatz** *inventions*
112 Practise	Strukturen festigen, Vorbereitung auf die Target task	**Writing:** Erfindungen beschreiben	**Strukturen** *passive* **Aussprache** *Betonungen*
113 Apply	Target task Ideas for a new invention	**Speaking:** eine Idee für eine neue Erfindung präsentieren	**Wortschatz** *inventions, presenting something*
	PART B – Communication		
114 Activate	eine Projektwoche zum Thema Kommunikation	**Speaking:** über verschiedene Kommunikationswege sprechen **Reading:** Beschreibungen verschiedener Workshops verstehen	**Strukturen** *going to-future* **Wortschatz** *communication*
116 Practise	Strukturen bewusst machen und festigen	**Writing:** über die absehbare Zukunft schreiben	**Strukturen** *going to-future*
117 Develop	Recherche zum Thema Kommunikation in Vergangenheit und Zukunft	**Listening:** ein Gespräch verstehen **Reading:** kurze Sachtexte verstehen **Speking:** ein Interview zum Thema Kommunikation durchführen **Mediation:** Informationen aus einer Broschüre sprachmitteln **Viewing:** einer Präsentation folgen	**Wortschatz** *communication, giving feedback*
122 Practise	Strukturen festigen, Vorbereitung auf die Target task	**Writing:** schriftlich Feedback zu einer Präsentation geben	**Wortschatz** *giving feedback*
123 Apply	Target task A three-minute talk Check out Selbsteinschätzung	**Speaking:** einen *three-minute talk* halten	**Wortschatz** *presenting something*
124 Story	Jamie and Lucy: A field trip	**Reading:** ein Kapitel der Fortsetzungsgeschichte lesen	
127 Challenge	Inventions inspired by nature	**Reading:** kurze Sachtexte über von der Natur inspirierte Erfindungen lesen	
128	**Get together**		

Seite	Inhalt
146	**Projects**
146	Project 1: A country profile: India
148	Project 2: Music
150	**Skills**
150	Wortschatzarbeit
151	Hören
152	Mit anderen sprechen
153	Schreiben
154	Lesen
155	Sprachmittlung
156	Videoclips verstehen
157	Im Internet recherchieren
158	Präsentationen halten
159	Eine Szene vorspielen
160	**Wordbanks**
160	Eating and eating out
162	Keeping fit
163	Health
164	What's on? / Buying and selling
165	Events / Expressing opinions
166	Family history / Talking about pictures
167	Feelings / Seeking and giving advice
168	Inventions / Presenting something
169	Communication / Going online
170	**Classroom phrases**
172	**Grammar**
172	Das Perfekt: Aussagen *(revision)*
173	Das Perfekt: Fragen *(revision)*
174	Mengenangaben *(revision)*
175	Die Steigerung von Adjektiven *(revision)*
176	Die Verlaufsform der Gegenwart *(revision)*
177	Das Gerundium
178	Bedingungssätze 1
179	Modalverben *(revision)*
180	Relativsätze
181	Die Stützwörter *one* und *ones*
182	Die Verlaufsform der Vergangenheit: Aussagen
183	Die Verlaufsform der Vergangenheit: Fragen
184	Die einfache Vergangenheit: Aussagen *(revision)*
185	Die einfache Vergangenheit: Fragen *(revision)*
186	Indirekte Rede 1
187	Das Passiv
188	Das Futur mit *going to*: Aussagen *(revision)*
189	Das Futur mit *going to*: Fragen *(revision)*
190	**Words**
190	Erläuterung und richtige Aussprache
192	Bekannte Wörter
193	Wortlisten nach Units
219	*Dictionary*
252	*Names, Numbers*
255	*Irregular verbs*
264	**Bild- und Textquellen**

Bildquellen

|Alamy Stock Photo, Abingdon/Oxfordshire: agefotostock 71.2; Allsorts Stock Photo 108.1; Alternative Occasions 67.5; Ammentorp Photography 80.1; Art Directors & TRIP 92.3; Baker, Darren 80.2; Baldesare, Paul 79.1; Ballard, Laura Clay 62.5; Barton, William 83.2; BasPhoto 103.1; Cavan Images 67.3; Chilvers, Clive 70.2; Classic Picture Library 109.1; Dack, Simon 155.1; Daemmrich, Bob 54.1, 54.2, 54.3; Dale, Veryan 79.4; David R. Frazier Photolibrary, Inc. 59.1; Doering, Olaf 119.8; Doyle, Paul 71.1; E.J.Westmacott 55.2; Farrell, Wayne 70.1; Fernandez, Antonio Guillem 79.3; Gilbert, Jeff 55.3; Gustafsson, Jeppe 63.1; Hoare, Jeremy 83.4; Hrda, Lucia 72.5; Huang, I-Wei 59.2; Image Source 92.1; Imagebroker 65.1; imageBROKER 65.2; Janine Wiedel Photolibrary 79.2; John Freeman 111.1; Karki, Hari 19.3; Liasi, Theodore 38.1; Lloyd 78.1; Lordprice Collection 108.2; Lyons, David 72.3; MacDonald, Dennis 35.2; MBI 31.2; Muller, Cora 59.5; Noir, Nathaniel 19.1; PA Images 66.1, 67.2, 67.6; Pearson, David 73.1; Perepelytsia, Oleksandr 62.2; Pound, Philip 72.1; PURPLE MARBLES YORK 1 66.2; Reinholds, Aigars 62.1; Richardson, Jason 72.4; Rivera M, Carlos J 18.1; robertharding 30.4; Roger Cracknell 01/classic 72.2; Saxena, Ashok 83.1; Scantlebury, Brian 8.4; Spitzbart, Wolfgang 75.2; Tack, Jochen 75.1; Torontonian 15.2; True Images 119.1; Vorobiev, Mikhail 62.4; Walmsley, Alan 67.1, 67.4; WENN Rights Ltd 83.3; Whitefoot, Tracey 78.2; Yarvin World Journeys 62.6; YAY Media AS 59.8. |Alamy Stock Photo (RMB), Abingdon/Oxfordshire: anther Media GmbH 62.3; Art Directors & TRIP 7.3; Camandona, Fabio 31.1; Finizio, Roberto 149.1; MacDonald, Dennis 35.1; Picture Partners 127.5; Studioshots 169.2; World History Archive 106.1; © Mike Booth 104.10. |Amortegui, Miguel, Brighton: 15.1, 25.1, 38.2, 48.6, 62.7, 96.1, 110.2. |Arrandale, Denise, Neumünster: 49.1. |Courtesy of Kopernik, kopernik.info: 130.1, 133.1, 136.1. |Fast, Lisa, Hannover: 13.1, 59.4, 120.1, 166.1. |fotolia.com, New York: davidevison 146.1; denis_vermenko 7.5; ExQuisine 20.1; fergregory 78.3; Gennadiy Poznyakov 148.2; Gorilla 34.2; RRF 104.7; Shaiith 20.2; Steiner, C. 20.4; Stocksnapper 127.2. |Getty Images, München: AFP 66.3; Stringer 40.1; Wheeler, Nik 55.1. |Getty Images (RF), München: fstop123 92.2; Mcbride, Joe 39.1. |Hardy, Helen, Braunschweig: 120.3. |Interfoto, München: Delimont, Danita/Merrill, John & Lisa 36.1. |iStockphoto.com, Calgary: aggiebilly Titel; Arnese, Claudio 59.3; Circle Creative Studio 81.1; coffeekai 31.3; Daisy-Daisy 31.4; dejankrsmanovic 65.3; djedzura 63.2; Elizaquibel, Jorge 81.2; Fudio 9.1; HAYKIRDI 33.1; Iaroshenko, Maryna 9.2; kissesfromholland 104.8; Korkiat 9.3; mgstudyo 92.4; Okea 112.1; perrygerenday 63.3; Philary 18.2; Ridofranz 31.5; serikbaib 59.9; SolStock 7.1; undefined undefined 103.3; visual7 147.1; Wirestock 168.2; Yobro10 36.2; © travellinglight 14.1, 30.3. |mauritius images GmbH, Mittenwald: Westend61 /Fischinger, Mareen 7.4. |Nordzieke, Paula: 89.1. |OKAPIA KG - Michael Grzimek & Co., Frankfurt/M.: BIOS/Labat, Jean-Michel 118.2; Groß 127.4; imagebroker/Robiller, Franz Christoph 127.3; Vock, Karl Gottfried 127.1. |PantherMedia GmbH (panthermedia.net), München: Popov, Andriy 49.2, 49.3; Schmid, Christophe 154.1. |Picture-Alliance GmbH, Frankfurt a.m.: Bildagentur-online 8.1; Schönherr, Maximilian 104.9; ZB/Thieme, Wolfgang 110.1. |Science Museum Group © The Board of Trustees of the Science Museum: Boer War rations, gravy soup. 1965-239/6/2/5Science Museum Group Collection Online. Accessed September 20, 2023. https , Lizenz Creative Commons Zero 109.2. |Shutterstock.com, New York: Agarianna76 139.1, 142.1, 145.1; AJR_photo 33.3; auremar 169.1; chrisdorney 84.1; DenPhotos 103.4; Es sarawuth 103.2; Esin, Deniz 8.6; Gingell, Ben 36.3; gkrphoto 19.2; Kumar Barui, Tutun 59.7; Monkey Business Images 7.2; muzsy 34.1; Rehorst, Bernd 59.6; yackers1 8.3. |stock.adobe.com, Dublin: Alvaro 8.2; Aphotostudio 148.3; asife 37.1; cougarsan 48.5; denisgorelkin 119.2, 119.3, 119.4, 119.7; guteksk7 120.2; Iakov Kalinin 82.1; mdurson 33.2; nikolaydonetsk 8.5; peregrinus 48.3; Richardt, Dagmar 118.1; Schwier, Christian 168.1; sebastian 119.6; sergojpg 148.1; sinhyu 109.3; somegirl 30.1; SpicyTruffel 119.5; Sughra 48.1, 48.2; UJac 20.3; valvectors 48.4; victoria p. 30.2. |Todd, Gary, Henan: Anyang-Museum 118.3. |Visuelle Lebensfreude - Bodem + Sötebier GbR, Hannover: 11.1, 11.2, 11.3, 11.4, 11.5, 104.1, 104.2, 104.3, 104.4, 104.5, 104.6.

Textquellen

14 „Vegan Steven" Benjamin Zephaniah, „The little book of vegan poems – Explicit vegan lyrics", AK Press, Edinburgh, 2002.

39 „Choose your sports", Martin Dejnicki, Toronto, Canada. 25.7.2022: https://wordswan.com/author/martin-dejnicki/sports-poems

39 „Skateboarding", Margo L. Dill, St. Louis, Missouri, USA. 26.7.2022: https://www.scrapbook.com/poems/cat/38.html

39 „What Can You Do With a Football?", James Carter, „Journey to The Centre Of My Brain", London, Macmillan Children's Books, 2012.

114 „On the Move Again", „On the Move: Poems About Migration" by Michael Rosen with drawings by Quentin Blake, Walker Books Ltd., London, 2020.

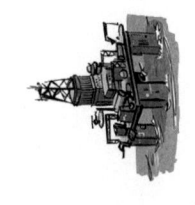

Shetland Islands

North Sea

Orkney Islands

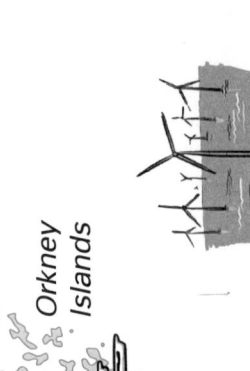

Aberdeen

Balmoral

▲ Ben Nevis
1344 m

Scotland

Hadrian's Wall

Edinburgh

Tweed

Newcastle

Glasgow

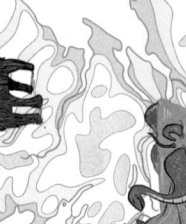

Lewis

Outer Hebrides

Skye

Atlantic Ocean